For Jack -
Happy Bir~
always my love
Dad
4/9/92
& Belinda !

The Best of
PLIMPTON

The Best of
PLIMPTON

George Plimpton

A MORGAN ENTREKIN BOOK
THE ATLANTIC MONTHLY PRESS
NEW YORK
·

Most of the material in this book originally appeared in such magazines as *Sports Illustrated, Esquire, Harper's, Smart, New York,* and *Audubon* and, on occasion, somewhat edited for this volume, as sections from the longer works.

Published simultaneously in Canada
Printed in the United States of America

FIRST EDITION

Library of Congress Cataloging-in-Publication Data

Plimpton, George.
The best of Plimpton / George Plimpton.
ISBN 0-87113-391-1
1. Plimpton, George—Anecdotes. 2. Journalism—United States—
Anecdotes. I. Title.
PN4857.P56   1990   818'.5403—dc20   90-42037

Design by Laura Hough

The Atlantic Monthly Press
19 Union Square West
New York, NY 10003

FIRST PRINTING

For Sarah Dudley

Contents

PARTICIPATIONS

PERSONAGES

CODA

PARTICIPATIONS

This collection begins with descriptions of the various con-frontations I have experienced in the practice of participatory journalism. It seems appropriate to start the book this way. Almost everyone aware of this aspect of my curious literary career wants to know, Well, what was it really like? What was it like with the Boston Bruins? Or in the ring with Archie Moore? Even readers of my books still want to know—as if their curiosity could never be quite satisfied.

I suspect this same curiosity got me going in the first place—curiosity about people endowed with the extraordinary skills that brought them to the top of their professions, whether athletic or artistic. Not only that, but in childhood through adolescence, as with most daydreaming kids, it wasn't so much curiosity as a surety that I would make it to some such pinnacle myself. When I went to concerts at Carnegie Hall at the age of eleven, I would imagine that I had composed the music we were about to hear, everyone on hand for the world premiere, and the conductor would bring his baton down and the strains of my work, entitled *Beethoven's Fifth*, composed the month before, would fill the hall.

Then, of course, the reality sets in. It is not going to happen. One learns this finishing in fifth place in the high school hun-dred-yard dash. Or being picked last for the softball game, playing the game deep in right field under the shade of an oak tree. One doesn't make the school choir. So one drifts back into the utopian world of the daydream where all things are possible and indeed happen.

When I began writing professionally, I happened to read Paul Gallico's book *Farewell to Sport*. A crack sportswriter for the *Daily News* in the thirties, the so-called Golden Age of Sport (Ruth, Grange, Dempsey, Tilden, Bobby Jones, et al.), he decided to quit that particular beat to write novels (*The Poseidon Adventure,* among others). In *Farewell to Sport* there is a famous chapter (at least to sportswriters) in which Gallico describes his self-appointed reporting assignments to find out firsthand about athletic skills at their very best—catching Herb Pennock's curveball; playing tennis with Vinnie Richards and golf with Bobby Jones; sparring with Jack Dempsey and getting knocked down ("The ring and the audience outside were making a complete clockwise revolution, came to a stop, and then went back again counterclockwise"), but also managing to get up and learn that "there is no sweeter sound than the bell that calls a halt to the hostilities." There were other self-indulgences. He experienced the Indianapolis Speedway crammed in a racing car with Cliff Bergere. He went down the Olympic ski run at Garmisch, Italy, quite a feat because he had only been on skis once in his life. Oddly, the most fear Gallico ever experienced traveling at high speed was in a locomotive cab on the straight stretch between Fort Wayne, Indiana, and Chicago—"The thrill of pelting through a small town, all out and wide open, including the crossing of some thirty or forty frogs and switches, all of which must be set right. But that wasn't sport. That was just plain excitement."

I read this with envy—what a lucky writer Gallico was to have experienced all this. Then I began to wonder if it wouldn't be possible to undertake the same kind of research myself and expand it somewhat—to find out not only about athletic skills at their best, but also something about the society of athletes, to join a team as a kind of "amateur professional." I had an enormous advantage, of course, writing for *Sports Illustrated,* whose editors agreed that the exercise was interesting and who were helpful in setting up the confrontations.

It was appropriate that the first of the stints involved baseball. When I was a youngster I was convinced that the highest achievement one could hope for in life was to play baseball in the major leagues. My idea of the perfect death was to be beamed by a heavily bearded pitcher late in my career. In my particular case I wanted to pitch. My hero was the New York Giants' ace pitcher of the time, Carl Hubbell, tall, gawky, and master of the screwball. He had thrown so many of them—a kind of reverse curve—that his arm was literally deformed. You could see it when he walked out to the mound, the palm turned slightly outward. When I was eleven (the same year my works were being premiered at Carnegie Hall) I walked around with my arm turned out in the hope I'd be mistaken for a screwball pitcher. My father made me stop it. He said it looked as if I had tumbled out a window and my parents didn't have enough money to have the broken arm set properly.

The real game I played in was a postseason affair in Yankee Stadium between teams from the National and American leagues headed respectively by Willie Mays and Mickey Mantle. Mays had left New York with the Giants the season before. His wondrous play had been sorely missed in New York and about twenty thousand turned out to see the game. My involvement occurred in a pregame affair—the idea being that I was to pitch to both lineups, the team that scored the most runs dividing a thousand-dollar prize put up by *Sports Illustrated.*

5

One of the recurring truths about my type of participatory journalism is that the results have very little to do with what happens in daydreams. I had an awful time in Yankee Stadium. Ernest Hemingway said of my stint that it was "the dark side of the moon of Walter Mitty."

Nonetheless, there were compensations. If briefly, I had actually been thrust into one of the most sacrosanct of worlds. The editors of *Sports Illustrated* were pleased enough with my account to continue helping me arrange further adventures on the "dark side of the moon of Walter Mitty." Whatever the humiliations, if one remained the observer, what one experienced and learned could be set down later. There were things to be said.

Baseball

It was, in the vernacular, a pretty fair country ball club. At first base was Mickey Vernon, twice winner of the American League batting championship and a very stylish and graceful fielder besides. He fits the general prescription for a first baseman—namely, that he should be long, lean, and left-handed. At second was Chicago's Nelson Fox—his round Kewpie-doll face distorted by the big wad of Favorite tobacco he stuffs in his left cheek. He chewed licorice before he reached the big leagues, but his manager got him to change to plugs because the licorice made him sick. His partner at second base was shortstop Billy Martin, the fiery ex-Yankee. He has a deceptively pleasant face, with melancholy brown eyes in it, and a long nose that got him into the early fights when his schoolmates ribbed him about it. It is a mobile face that has often worked hard and furiously an inch or so away from an umpire's. The Great Agitator, the press sometimes calls him, but he's more popularly known as the Kid. He was one of the few players who took a personal interest in my struggle that afternoon—sensing, I think, the loneliness and the awkwardness of being new and raw in a situation that in my case I could hardly hope to cope with skillfully. A spirited cockiness was his own defense. Riding into New York that first time, coming up on the long train ride from the St. Petersburg training camp, a reporter found him reading a magazine as the train moved into the Penn Station tunnel. Pretty excited about seeing New York for the first time? "Nah," said Martin, not yet then twenty, "I saw it in the movies." It may have been a mask, this spirit, to hide the insecurity endured in a childhood of misery and poverty in the California town where he was raised, but it had made him, despite limitations as a ballplayer, a competitor whose drive picked up a whole team. He had such an excess of that competitive confidence that there seemed enough to pass around to his teammates—like pep pills. He tried to give me some of it. He kept up a steady chatter of encouragement while I was working—at least for a while—and I was grateful for it.

Down the line from Martin at third was Boston's Frank Malzone, silent while I toiled away, but the best man in the league at his position—sharp-featured, wiry, and fast. Durocher once appraised him: "The guy's got a fault? Dandruff, maybe." He's a wonderful defensive player who as the pitch is thrown leans in toward the batter in a pigeon-toed crouch. He has slightly bowed legs, and big feet, and when he poises on his toes to get a jump on the ball he looks like a flippered skin diver about to plunge off a rock. Behind him, out in left field, was Bob Cerv, who that year had a brilliant season for the Athletics despite a fractured jaw which, being tightly wired for much of the season, limited his talk to the tight-lipped variety—whatever his mood— and required him to take sustenance—vegetable soups, orange juices, and such—through a tube stuck in a gap providentially left by a missing tooth in the side of his mouth. He'd lost weight that summer. He usually eats coloches, big Bohemian meatballs, and at his usual playing weight he's powerfully heavy—a grim competitor with a hard, determined countenance marked by a nose flattened in a boyhood injury.

Playing over in right field was Harvey Kuenn, twice winner of the American League batting championship. A serious, unflamboyant professional, he keeps his baseball cap pulled down low over his eyes, so first you see the multifaceted Gothic D for Detroit embroidered on the front of the cap, then, under the brim, the lower part of his face, severe, deeply burned, and, like Fox, with a plug of tobacco tucked in the cheek. In center field was Mickey Mantle. Of all of them standing there, Mantle's was the power you sensed—seeing it in the heavy shoulders and arms sloping from a neck as thick as a water main. His large boyish face has gone heavy; he turns his head slowly, his eyes pale and impassive, so that there is something in his manner of the cat family: imperturbable, arch, and yet because the boyishness is still there he wears a faint expression of suspicious stubbornness, of petulance. The face of the final member of the team, my battery mate, the Yankees' Elston Howard, wore a puzzled frown because the reporters had been busy with him earlier—his exploits in left field during the World Series, particularly one fine tumbling catch in the fifth game, made him copy as the World Series hero—and I don't believe anyone had had the chance to tell him why he was to put on his catching tools half an hour before the scheduled game. The infield players gathered around the mound.

At this point the recorded music which had been drifting in from center field stopped abruptly, in mid-chorus of "Tea for Two," then a stentorian cough came over the public-address system and we heard as follows: *"Your attention, please.* (pause) *George . . . P . . . P . . . P,"* then another pause, the announcer apparently working over a name scribbled on a pad, *"Prufrock,"* and then repeated with immeasurable confidence that boomed through the stadium, "GEORGE PRUFROCK *of Sports Illustrated will now pitch against the* ENTIRE *National League team, and the* ENTIRE *American League team . . . that team which collects the most hits to be awarded a prize of one thousand dollars by Sports Illustrated."*

"You let 'em hit, kid," said Billy Martin. He handed me the ball. "And right at us, *pul-lease,* on the ground and in big quick hops."

A few of the players laughed and someone said, "That's right, kid—you're out here to do the work; we're along for the ride," and around the circle they smiled again, trying to impart confidence, and as we stood together—waiting for something to happen to release us—I felt a sudden kinship with them. It was an entirely unexpected emotion, since I was so obviously an outsider, but it came: that warm sense of camaraderie one gets, if briefly, as a team member, or in a platoon, or just sitting around a café with friends, never mentioned but there nonetheless, almost tangible, and it was very strong before abruptly it was dissipated. Someone said, "O.K., let's go," and the huddle broke up.

When they headed for their positions, leaving me standing alone, it was like being unveiled—and one sensed the slow massive attention of the spectators—by then almost twenty thousand of them—wheel and concentrate, and almost physically I felt the weight of it. My palms were slick with sweat. I walked around the pitcher's mound to find the resin bag. There wasn't one there. I kept looking out at my infielders, trying to recapture the confidence I'd felt fleetingly in their company; they seemed very far away; they were busy scooping up grounders Vernon was lobbing to them from first base. When Malzone at third wound up and threw the ball, it was close enough to sigh past in a trajectory so flat that the ball never rose above eye level on its way into Vernon's glove. Out beyond the base paths, the outfielders had reached their positions. They were so far away I didn't feel we were identified with the same project. The spaces between them were vast. Everything seemed very peaceful and quiet out there. Deep back in the bleachers I could see a man, sitting up there alone, removing his coat to enjoy the afternoon sun.

I finally faced the plate. Howard was there waiting, his big dust-gray mitt up for the warm-up pitches. I threw him a couple. Then I wasn't so conscious of the crowd. Mostly you hear your own voice—chattering away, keeping you company in the loneliness, cajoling and threatening if things begin to go badly, heavy in praise at times, much of everything being said half aloud, the lips moving, because although you know you're being watched, no one can hear you, and the sound of your voice is truly a steady influence—the one familiar verity in those strange circumstances. I recall the first sentence I spoke to myself was "O.K., bo, you're goin' to be O.K. Nothin' at all to worry about, nothin', nothin'," and at that moment, like a crack lawyer springing to rebut, the public-address system announced the arrival at the plate of the National League's lead-off batter—Richie Ashburn.

He stepped into the batter's box wearing the bright candy-red pin-striped uniform of the Phillies. A left-handed batter, he punches at the ball, slapping it for a multitude of singles. The outfielders deploy for him like softball players. He chokes so far up on the bat that as he waited I could see his fingers flexing two or three inches up on the bat handle. He presented a surprisingly small target—as indeed all the batters seemed smaller than expected. Half-consciously I expected them to rear high over the plate, threatening, portraits of power . . . but in fact their physical presence at the plate was not as overpowering as *recognizing* them—to look in and see under the batter's helmet a face that, jarringly familiar even from the pitcher's mound, one had only associated previously with bubble-gum cards, news-print, and the photographs of the sports sections.

Behind the plate Howard had settled in his crouch, his big mitt up for the target. Concentrating on it, barely aware then of Ashburn, I toed the rubber with my spikes and with an almost physical jolt of will, I swung into a slow windup. Under the pressure of the moment I half expected to exhibit a pitching form as spastic as the cartwheeling fall of a man from a high tree. But conditioned reflexes took over, and I was surprised at the ease with which I got the pitch off. I was not prepared, however, for what then happened: that, rather than speeding for the bulk of Howard's catcher's mitt, the ball, flung with abandon and propelled by a violent mixture of panic and pent-up anxiety let loose, headed straight for Ashburn's head. Down he went, flat on his back, the bat flung away, and an explosion of sound—a sharp gasp from the crowd—sailed out of the stands as I hurried off the mound calling out, "Sorry! Sorry!"

I ran halfway to the plate. The ball had shot by Ashburn, hit the edge of Howard's glove, and skidded off toward the stands. Ashburn picked himself up easily, collected his bat, and looked out at me calmly, his face imperturbable. He is one of the few players who don't lace their speech with cussing; his demeanor was gentle, but I could think of nothing to say to him. So I shrugged—an inadvertent gesture that under the circumstances could only have indicated to Ashburn, and to Howard, standing peering at me through the bars of his mask, that I had no control whatsoever over my pitches. I did not look to see how the gesture was interpreted. I busied myself fielding a ball, a new one someone had rolled out from the first-base dugout. Then I wheeled for the mound to try again.

I threw three more pitches to Ashburn, finding myself growing in confidence as I pitched. I threw him another ball, then a pitch that he chopped foul. On the next delivery he punched under the ball and lifted a high fly between third and home. Howard threw off his mask with a violence that rolled it almost to the backstop, and with shinguards clattering he went after the ball, got under it, and stomped around with his face upturned like a Piute praying for rain until finally the ball came down and he smothered it in his big glove.

It took a few seconds, while the ball was being thrown around the infield, before there was any sense of accomplishment—it coming haltingly because, after all, one had expected devastation, not a harmless foul ball glinting in the sun, and finally it did come and I lurched happily in a tight circle around the pitcher's mound, digging and scraping at the dirt with my spikes, pretending preoccupation, and if there'd been a resin bag I'd have picked it up and fussed briefly with it. What had seemed an inhospitable place, a steep uneven hill of dirt on which one moved gingerly and awkwardly, suddenly became something of a natural habitat—all around everything was familiar, neat, and orderly. But just as I began to admire the unmarked base paths, the bases unoccupied, with the fielders relaxed in their positions, a player with an established reputation for creating disorder in the pitcher's domain trotted up out of the National League dugout—San Francisco's Willie Mays.

I didn't see him at first. But from the stands a mounting roar of welcome greeted him. He'd been sorely missed in New York that summer, and the majority of the twenty thousand were there in the hope of seeing him perform the miracles of play that would leave them breathless and cheering and yet a little guilty, too, to think that his ability, once practically a landmark in the city, was now on display elsewhere.

He gets set quickly at the plate, hopping eagerly into the batter's box, where he nervously jiggles and tamps his feet in the dust, twisting on his rear foot to get it solidly placed, staring down at the plate in concentration—to sense when his legs feel set—and when they do, he reaches out and taps the plate, twice, three times, with the bat before he sweeps it back over his right shoulder and cocks it. Then for the first time he looks out at the pitcher.

Most batters tuck their chins down and glower out at the pitcher from under the brims of their batting helmets—which makes them look properly sinister and threatening. Mays, on the other hand, who has a pleasant face to start with, looks out at the pitcher with a full, honest regard, his chin out, his eyes wide as if slightly myopic, and he seems to inspect the pitcher as if he were a harmless but puzzling object recently deposited on the pitcher's mound by the groundkeeper. Furthermore, when Mays's face is set in determination, his eyebrows arch up, so that under the batter's helmet his expression is a lingering look of astonishment, as if his manager had just finished addressing him at length in Turkish. But the deception is mild; you see the coiled power of his stance as he waits.

I threw Mays three pitches. The motion felt easy and the first two pitches were low and didn't miss by much. With the third pitch, though, I was aware that the ball, almost as it left my hand, was heading accurately for the plate and that Mays, flexing his bat back to increase the purchase of his swing, was going to go for it. As his bat came through into the pitch, I could sense the explosive power generated and I flinched involuntarily—not sure that my hands, hung low and relaxed at the completion of the follow-through, didn't start up instinctively if futilely for protection. But from this flurry of power the ball rose straight, a foul ball like Ashburn's, I thought at first, but then I saw the ball carrying out over the infield. I had a glimpse of it high above me, small but astonishingly bright in the sunlight, directly above it seemed, and remembering that a pitcher leaves the fielding plays to his infielders, I ran head down toward first base to vacate the mound for them.

I misjudged the ball badly. Actually, it came down back of the shortstop's position. Billy Martin was there to catch it and as I walked back to the mound, he threw the ball to Malzone, and the ball began to go from infielder to infielder—in that fine ritual of speeding the ball around the "horn" that gives the pitcher a moment to peek modestly out from under his cap and savor what he's just done. It was fine. It was truly all I could do to keep from grinning.

Actually, the pitcher is happiest with his arm idle. He prefers to dawdle in the present, knowing that as soon as he gets on the mound and starts his windup he delivers himself to the uncertainty of the future. The ritual of throwing the ball around the infield allows the pitcher to postpone the future; it allows him to fuss around on his hill of dirt like a gawky hen; he can pick up and drop the resin bag; he's given a moment or so in which to preen himself on his accomplishments. It is the fine moment of his profession. It was certainly the fine moment of my afternoon. When Mays hit that towering fly and it was evident it was going to be caught, I stood absorbing that October instant so that it would be forever available for recall—now blurred, of course, and fragmentary like the nickelodeon films of the Dempsey-Firpo fight you see in the amusement parks, but still sufficient to put one back there on the mound: seeing again, and feeling the sudden terror of Mays uncoiling his bat, but then watching in surprise the ball rise clean and harmless, Billy Martin circling under it, hooded and efficient with his sunglasses down, catching it then and removing it from his glove to peer at it as if he'd never seen a baseball before, then firing it down to Malzone, who also looked at it, across then to Vernon for his inspection, and during this you felt coming on a maniac grin of achievement that you had to control, knowing that pitchers don't grin after getting a man out, and so you solemnly stomped around the mound, tidying it up, watching with sidelong glances the ball whip from infielder to infielder, the great blue-shadowed humming tiers of the Stadium out of focus beyond, until finally you remember Nelson Fox, the big orange-size plug pushing out the side of his face, trotting into the mound, looking at the ball in his hand, jiggling it, inflicting it with magic, then popping it in the air at you and saying, "Come on, kid, easy, easy, easy."

That is all of that day that I really care to remember. Perhaps a bit more: that when I got the ball from Fox it felt familiar to the hand, a weapon suddenly adaptable, an instrument perfectly suited to my design. Of course, I should have known better. Polishing the ball, the glove slung on the wrist, I turned on the mound and saw Frank Robinson, the great Cincinnati slugger, standing in the batter's box, and I knew then that the pitcher's pleasure is a fragmentary thing, that the dugouts, like sausage machines, eject an unending succession of hitters to destroy any momentary complacency a pitcher may feel during an afternoon of work.

Regardless, as I looked in at Robinson—Howard behind him adjusting his mask—I thought, Well, why not, I've done pretty well so far—now's the time to unleash the curveball, the hook. And perhaps if the hook works, I'll chance the change-of-pace and maybe even the knuckler. Swallowing hard, nervous again after the heady triumph of retiring the first two batters, I worked my fingers around the seams until I had the ball held properly for the curve. Robinson, the victim, was standing easily in the batter's box; Howard had settled into his position, his glove raised as a target. I knew I should tell my catcher that a curve was coming up; but I didn't see how I could tell Howard without tipping off Robinson. My catcher would have to fend for himself as best he could, I thought, and I pumped my arm twice and swung into the windup.

In baseball parlance they speak of a pitch "getting away" from the pitcher. As I came through the delivery of my curve, I failed to snap my wrist sufficiently and my hook got away from me in majestic style—sailing far over both Robinson's and Howard's head to the wire screen behind home plate. If it had hit a foot or so higher, the ball would have caught the netting of the foul screen and run up it to the press boxes. It was such an extraordinarily wild pitch that I felt I had to make some comment; so once again I hurried off the mound calling out, "Sorry! Sorry!" Howard and Robinson gazed out at me, both startled, I think, perhaps even awed by the strange trajectory of my pitch, which was wild enough to suggest that I had suddenly decided to throw the ball to someone in the stands.

It took me a few pitches to steady down after the attempted hook. Finally I threw a pitch Robinson found to his liking. He is a thin, long-boned player who hangs his head over the plate to watch the pitch coming in. He has wonderful wrists, strong and supple, and in St. Louis he once sprained his wrists while checking his swing—which would indicate both his power and his speed of reaction. He brought his hands around on the sixth pitch I threw him (a friend in the stands acting as statistician was keeping track) and it was over the plate and chest high. Often a pitcher has a premonition as soon as the ball leaves his hand that the batter is going to feast on it. He sees the bat flex back and instinctively he knows that the batter's timing is right, that the ball's not going to do anything to escape the sweep of the bat coming through, and as it *does* he hears the sharp disheartening *whack* of ash against the ball and the drive lines out past his ears. In Robinson's case, the ball soared between Mantle and Cerv in deep left-center field, dropped between them and rolled for the Babe Ruth memorial out by the flagpole. By the time the ball was back in the infield, Robinson was standing on second.

The public address system announced "two points for the National League" and Robinson, his job done, trotted in from second base.

Actually, it didn't feel too disheartening, that double, because Robinson didn't stay on base to remind you of it. If he'd been leading off second, swaying his body, poised for flight, and you had to work off the stretch, peering around and worrying about him, you would have had the evidence of your inadequacy as a pitcher right there nagging at you. Perhaps the one, if very slight, compensation for the pitcher who has a home run hit off him is that it leaves the bases uncluttered of the opposition and in the pristine state the pitcher prefers. His dismay may be intense watching the ball fly out of the park, but at least it is temporary: the batter circles the bases and is back in the obscurity of the dugout within seconds.

So I didn't have to worry about a man jiggling up and down the base paths. But there was something else bothering me as I watched Ernie Banks, the home run king of the National League, step out of the on-deck circle and head for the plate. Of the six pitches I'd thrown to Robinson one or two had seemed to me to catch the strike zone. He hadn't gone for them, and there was no umpire to contradict his choice.

I hadn't arranged for an umpire for the simple reason that I didn't trust my control. I'd had a recurrent presentiment of losing control of my pitches and having an umpire award an unending succession of bases on ball. Such nightmarish things did, after all, happen even in the major leagues. Not long ago, Ray Scarborough, a pitcher on the Washington Senators, after giving up seven runs in the first inning of his first appearance in the majors, which was against the Yankees, started against the Red Sox soon after and walked the first seven men he faced. Bucky Harris was his patient manager at the time, and when the seventh batter tossed aside his bat and started trotting down to first, he walked out to Scarborough and reached for the ball. "Son," he is supposed to have said mildly, "I think maybe we've had our workout for the day, don't you?"

Under the peculiar setup of my pitching stint, if there'd been rigid rulings on balls and strikes, I might easily have eclipsed Scarborough's feat, and found myself, as a result, standing uneasily in the magazine office downtown after the game trying to explain what I'd done for the $1,000—namely, that I'd enjoyed the opportunity of walking every man I'd faced—which (not throwing to the pitchers) would have been a total of sixteen.

So I made no arrangements about umpires.

I didn't consider, however, the possibility that the batters—and quite properly since money was at stake—would get finicky about the pitches and wait for one they felt they could get a "holt" of—as they say.

However, as I stood on the mound watching Banks set himself at the plate, I wasn't overly worried. After all, I'd thrown thirteen pitches to three batters, which indicated the control was reasonable, and not bad pitching—considering who was throwing them—even if one of them had nearly beaned a batter, another was probably the tallest curve ever thrown in Yankee Stadium, and the last one Robinson had smacked for a stand-up double.

I had a grand opportunity to study Banks. Or, rather, Banks was up at the plate for such a long time that for days afterwards a slight and regretted tug at the memory would unveil him clear in my mind's eye: a right-handed batter, slender, standing very quietly back in the farthest recesses of the batter's box with none of the nervous fidgeting of a Mays or a Ted Williams, his bat steady and cocked up vertically behind his right ear, rarely leveled out in a practice swing as he waited with his eyes peering out calmly from beneath the Cubs' outsized and peaked cap. His whole attitude was of such detachment that I found it unnerving to pitch to him. Once in a while he'd step out of the batter's box and, resting his bat against his knees, he'd slowly pour dust from one palm to the other before settling back in with an attitude of faint disdain, as if in his opinion the pitcher's stature was that of a minor functionary whose sole duty was to serve up a fat pitch.

As it happened, a fat pitch was certainly what Banks wanted. He won a Most Valuable Player award for his performance that year, crediting his success to his ability to lay off the bad pitches. An excellent habit, obviously, and he had no intention of breaking it as he stood in against me. I threw him a total of twenty-three pitches. Sometimes he would lean over and watch the ball right into Howard's glove, then look up with a small encouraging smile, as if to indicate that it was *close*—that if the pitch had been a shade nearer the center of the plate, why, he would have whipped his bat around. Occasionally he would foul a pitch off into the stands, and from the first-base dugout someone would roll a new ball out to the mound; I'd pick it up, stalk back onto the mound, gaze mournfully at Banks, concentrate then on the bulk of Howard's catcher's mitt, crank up, and let fly. As I worked away, my control began to vanish under the pressure. My sense of well-being, not bothered by Robinson's double, began to deteriorate; I started to talk to myself loudly; the mound, the pitching rubber, previously so familiar, quickly became alien ground that I stumbled over and couldn't get the feel of with my spikes; the baseball itself seemed noticeably heavier, the seams awry; the whole process of throwing a baseball with accuracy became an absurdly hard task, and as I pitched Banks seemed to recede into the distance, along with Howard, until the two of them looked like figures viewed through the wrong end of a telescope.

What does a pitcher do when things begin to collapse around him? Almost surely he looks for assistance, someone to trot in to the mound and minimize his difficulties, to bolster him up with encouragement. If the situation indicates that his skill has leaked away under the pressure, he expects his manager to come out and replace him. Bob Turley, the great Yankee speed pitcher, once described a jam he'd manufactured for himself in the 1955 World Series—the first Series game he ever played in. He loaded the bases in the first inning and had Roy Campanella to face. Fidgeting, trying to pull himself together by breathing in great gulps of air, Turley turned and looked hopefully out at the bullpen. Nothing was going on. He peered into the dugout. His manager, Casey Stengel, was sitting with his legs crossed, leaning forward and looking up at the box where the Yankee owners were sitting. Turley had one quick image of working in Washington the next season—then the ultimate penalty for ineptitude. But then Yogi Berra came waddling out toward him from the plate, and Turley felt better. At last, he thought, I'm going to be all right because here comes Yogi to give me some advice. "Boy," Turley reported Berra as saying when he reached the mound, "boy, you're in one *hell*uva jam."

The gravity of my situation with Ernie Banks was compounded by not having anyone I could turn to. Even such cold words of comfort as Berra offered Turley would have been welcome; but Elston Howard, my catcher, cared so little for the business at hand—having a full game to catch later on—that often if my pitches were out of the strike zone, or in the dust, he'd let them skip by without budging for them and the balls would thud ignominiously against the backstop. I don't think he was at all clear why he was engaged in this pre-game malarkey. Occasionally he would rise from his position behind the plate, turn to the dugout, and shrug his shoulders in a massive pantomime of bewilderment. Once I heard him shout to someone in the dugout, "Hey, gettin' bushed out here"—referring to himself.

A quick, embarrassed look around my infield was no help. Their faces were averted: Mickey Vernon was looking solemnly into his first baseman's glove; the others were either preoccupied with their shoetops or scratching with their spikes in the dirt of the base paths. In the outfield I caught one awful glimpse of Mickey Mantle—turned toward one of the other outfielders and patting his mouth in an ostentatious yawn to show his boredom.

I turned hurriedly from that spectacle, rushed up on the mound, and began spraying pitches in at Banks as if by sheer volume I'd get one where he'd swing away. Occasionally the fouls would lift lazily into the stands and out of the corner of my eye I'd glimpse the people in that section rise, their arms outstretched, and the ball would fall in, engulfed like a pebble tossed into a field of wheat.

I asked my statistician, Bob Silvers, after the game what the spectators' reaction had been during the time of my troubles with Banks, and he said they took it very calmly—more calmly certainly than the febrile activity on the mound suggested I was taking it. He jotted down the following conversation between two men sitting in the sun in their shirt sleeves, one of them wearing a straw hat.

"Hey, who's that guy?"

"What guy?"

"Guy pitching."

"Donno. Some guy called Prufrock."

"Which?"

"Prufrock!"

"Who the hell's Prufrock?"

"Beats me."

Each sentence was followed by a long pause, while the beer was sipped from the big paper cups, the mind just barely ticking over in that splendid October sun.

Finally, on pitch number twenty-three, Banks lifted a high fly ball out to Mickey Mantle in right-center field, who was not so busy yawning that he didn't see the ball arch out toward him, and standing on the mound I saw he was going to catch it, and I gave a big shuddering sigh of relief to think that no longer did I have to look in to see Banks standing there with those red-striped blue socks high on his legs, his small head leaning over the plate, the thin smile . . . and when he came up after the game and we joked about it I told him that one of the lasting impressions of that afternoon would be the relief I felt watching him trudge back to the dugout, trailing his bat along behind him as if it had become heavy during that long stay of his at the plate.

Ernie Banks was followed in the batter's box by Frank Thomas, then playing for the Pittsburgh Pirates. He was the only batter I faced who loomed over the plate. Despite a large, homely, friendly face over which his blue plastic helmet perched like a paper birthday hat, Thomas's size made him look dangerous; he had an upright batting stance, which made him easier to pitch to than Banks, but the bat looked small and limber in his hands, and when he swung and missed one of my first pitches to him I imagined I heard the bat sing in the air like a willow switch. For the first time the batter's box seemed close up, and I could understand why many pitchers manipulate the follow-through of their pitching motion, which brings them in toward the plate by as much as six feet, so that the glove can be flicked up to protect the head in the event of a hard shot toward the mound. You never can tell. In 1947 Schoolboy Rowe threw in a pitch toward Stan Musial and back came the top half of a bat cracked directly in two, whirring at him with the speed and directness of a boomerang, and struck him a brutal blow on the elbow of his upflung arm. Even batters worry about crippling a pitcher over that distance. A hard-hit line drive, after all, will cover those sixty feet, six inches in one-fifth of a second. Babe Ruth had nightmares of such a thing, and there's a body of thought that believes his fear of smacking down a pitcher was why he changed his batting style (he was originally a line drive hitter in the early days with Baltimore) and started swinging from the heels of his pipestem legs to get loft and distance.

According to my statistician in the stands, it was the seventh pitch that Thomas whacked in a long high arc, very much like that of a Ruthian home run, deep into the upper deck in left field. The ball looped in at the downward end of its trajectory, and above the swelling roar of the crowd I could hear it smack against the slats of an empty seat. The upper deck was deserted and it was a long time before a scampering boy, leaping the empty rows like a chamois, found the ball and held it aloft, triumphant, the white of it just barely visible at that great distance.

The ball was hit well over four hundred feet, and after the roar that had accompanied its flight had died down you could hear the crowd continue buzzing.

My own reaction, as I stood on the mound, was not one of shame, or outrage. Perhaps it should have been, particularly following my difficulties with Banks, but actually my reaction was one of wonderment at the power necessary to propel a ball out of a major league park. I could hardly believe a ball could be hit so far.

In actual fact I felt a certain sense of pride in that home run. Every time I return to Yankee Stadium I automatically look up into the section where the ball hit, it was section 34, remembering then that I felt no sense of stupidity but in fact enjoyed a strong feeling of identification with Thomas's feat—as if I was his partner rather than opposing him, and that between us we'd connived to arrange what had happened. It was as if I'd wheeled to watch the ball climb that long way for the upper deck and called out "Look, look what I've helped engineer!"

Gil Hodges was the next batter. I remember a number of things about his lengthy tenure at the plate, right from the beginning as he stepped into the batter's box, hitching up his baseball pants, reaching out then and rubbing up the fat part of his bat as he set himself, picking again at those pants as if about to wade into a shallow pond. He has outsized hands that you notice when he stands in at the plate. They span over twelve inches, and Peewee Reese, his captain, used to say of him, in connection with those big hands, that he only used a glove for fielding at first base because it was fashionable. They call him Moon, and I remember how he looked, the rather beefy pleasant face under the blue helmet, and the blue piping of the Dodger uniform, and I remember the line drive single he hit, how easy and calculated his swing, and how sharp that hit of his was going out . . . but mainly I remember something else.

It was while Hodges was at the plate that the inner voice, which had been mumbling inaudibly at first, and calmly, began to get out of control. On the pitcher's mound one was conscious not of the hum of the crowd or even, closer at hand, the encouragement of the infielders. What you remembered was this voice chattering away within the head, offering comfort, encouragement, advice. I was acutely aware of this separation of mind and body: the mind seemed situated in a sort of observation booth high above the physical self, which, clumsy and ill-equipped in these unnatural surroundings, took on the aspect of an untrustworthy machine—a complicated crane-like bipedal mechanism sporting two jointed appendages, one of which with a rusty creak of rarely used parts was supposed to hurl a horsehide spheroid sixty feet, six inches with accuracy. That was the function of the physical plant, and high above, peering down like a skeptical foreman, the mental self offered a steady commentary which reflected how well the machine was doing.

There is nothing remarkable about this dichotomous condition. Tommy Byrne was a tall, stooped figure who toiled for the Yankees in the early fifties. Sometimes you could hear him all over the park, not so much talking to himself as offering a general running commentary to anyone within earshot:

his infielders, the batter, the crowd. Often, if a batter listened carefully, he'd hear Byrne say, "Gonna throw you a hook, mistah," and sometimes he'd get one and sometimes he wouldn't. The ballplayers had a fine name for Byrne. "The Broadcaster" they called him, and Casey Stengel, whose own famous brand of talk invariably seems an extension of the subconscious, was so genuinely fond of him that he kept him around much longer than his ability called for. There are others: Ed Plank, the great procrastinator, a fidgeter who took so long staring in at the plate that a batter's eyes would water waiting for the pitch to come down, who before beginning his motion would further dismay the batter by discussing him audibly: *Easy man. No hit. One down, two to go. Nobody hits.* More recently Jim Brosnan, the bespectacled relief pitcher who refers to the inner voice as Silent Screaming in his valuable chronicle *The Long Season,* occasionally erupts vocally: *Ils ne passeront pas,* he is said to have mumbled at a startled batter.

My own voice stuck to English. It had no form; it just chatted away from limbo as normally as it could under the circumstances. During the first moments on the pitcher's mound, as Richie Ashburn set himself at the plate, it occupied itself with the general urging to "calm down and take it easy"— but you felt the hypocrisy nonetheless . . . the hysteria lurking close at the edge of the voice, like a hyena beyond the firelight, and the mouth was very dry.

After the astonishing success with Richie Ashburn and Willie Mays, their high flies both caught in the infield, the voice became almost uncontrollable with delight. In its pleasure at the machine under observation it cried out to it "How t'*go* bébé!" and "Boy, you *kid!*" and also there bounced around within my head such strange effusive exclamations as "Gol-*ding* it!" and "Gee-*zus!*" and when the grin tried to spread across the face it was in reaction to this close harmony between body and spirit.

So successful was the machine during its early operation that for a while the inner voice took scant notice that quickly thereafter the machine's performance began to suffer. After the debacle of the curve thrown Frank Robinson, high over his head and almost up the screen behind home plate, and the subsequent line-drive double, the inner voice still remained chipper and confident—booming phrases back and forth within the skull as hearty as late-afternoon conversation in the locker room of a golf club. "You doin' just *fine,* heah? Just fine," it would say—for mysterious reasons of its own with a Southern inflection. It wasn't until Ernie Banks's extended presence at the plate that the voice's tone became somewhat more shrill and panicky. Still, it remained under control. It offered advice: "Y'all *pushing* the ball, bo," it would say. "Don't push the ball like that, all stiff-like . . . easy *does* it, bo," and then quite often during the windup it would say: "O.K. now Mistah Banks, y'all gonna swing at this pitch, you heah? O.K.? Now heah she comes, please m'boy, *swing* at it, SWING AT IT. . . . Oh chrissake, hey, what's wrong with y'all, Mistah Banks, can't y'all *see?*" this last in a high whine as Elston Howard would retrieve the ball from the dust where he'd blocked it and whip it back.

It was during Banks's tenure that the inner voice refused to stay contained within the head. The lips began to move and my mumbled voice became increasingly audible on that lonely hill, mooning and squeaking like the fluttery breath of a tuckered hound.

"Lookit that thing go on *out* theah!" it gasped when Banks had finally gone, and Frank Thomas's long home run started for the depths of the upper deck. *"Lawd Almighty!"*

The voice still wasn't strained with gloom, however, or even edgy following that tremendous blow; it was assessing the situation, and while there was awe in its tone and breathlessness, along with that strange Southern-cracker inflection, it was a sturdy voice, and it would have been hard to guess that within four minutes or so that same voice would crack utterly under the strain.

What caused it to crack was a string of seven balls I threw to Gil Hodges before he hit three fouls in a row and then his single, none of these first pitches close enough to the plate to get him to so much as twitch the bat off his shoulder. At first the voice offered its usual counsel not to push the ball and to take things easy; presently it got exasperated—"Hey, come on now, bear *down*, Ah say"—like a short-tempered farmer training a pup to come to heel; then finally, as the control continued to flag, the panic surged in not by degrees but coming quickly, like a prowler's bulk suddenly filling a doorway, and it came in and throttled the voice so that all that came out was a thin high squeak.

And then this curious thing happened. *It turned traitor.* The voice went defeatist on me. It escaped and ran off, washing its hands of the whole miserable business. But it didn't desert me completely. Much worse, it capered around out there on the periphery—jeering and catcalling. "You fat fool!" it would call out, not concerned that the object of its raillery was splinter-thin, and, with the sweat pouring off, getting thinner, "You po' fat *fool . . .* y'think y'all pretty fat and *smart* standing out theah pitching, hey?

Well, lemme tell yo' sumpin. Y'all can't pitch yo' way out of a paper bag, that's what. Jes' try. Jes' le's see yo' *try* putting the ball ovah the plate."

So I would try—and when the ball missed the strike zone under Hodges's watchful eye, the voice would cackle gleefully: "Y'all see that? Oh *my!* Y'all see that ball roll in the dust? Ladies an' gen'men, d'yall ob*serve* that ball drop down theah in the dirt. Haw! Haw! Haw!" it would roar gustily in my head. "Haw! Haw! Haw!"

My statistician has some further notes on those two men sitting in front of him. One of them had put a white handkerchief around his neck to protect it from the sun, and they sat relaxed, slowly rocking the beer around in the big paper cups, and they said as follows:

"Feel that sun, hey? Injun summer."

"Mmmm."

"Hey, you know something? I never heard of no guy called Prufrock. You sure that guy pitching's called Prufrock?"

"That's the way it come over the P.A. system—Prufrock."

"There's a guy around the league what they call Marv *Blay*lock, or there *was*—and then there's Ike Delock of the Red Sox, a pitcher, y'know, but, man, that fellow out there don't look like no ol' Ike, know whatta mean?"

They sipped at their beer, and presently, the one with the handkerchief around his neck leaned forward and squinted out at the field.

"Hey, you know something?"

"No, what?"

"I'll tell you one thing about that guy pitching out there. He's the *palest* pitcher I ever saw. Lookit that face of his—shining out there like a six-hundred-watt bulb. You ever see anything like that?"

"Yeh, how 'bout that . . ."

"Hey, you know something else?"

"No, what?"

"Tell me this. Who's he talking at? He's talking like a house afire out there. You know what I think . . . I think the sun's affected him, or something."

"You got a point, y'know. Lookit that strange herky-jerky pitchin' motion of his. He looks pretty shook up."

It was true. The physical disintegration had started in while Hodges was at the plate and it progressed quickly. For twenty minutes I had been burning every pitch in, feeling that if I let up and tried to guide the ball across the plate the control would vanish utterly. I hadn't bothered to pace myself, and by the time Hodges stood in at the plate I was exhausted. I felt the numbness of it seep through the system like a sea mist. Acutely conscious of the physical self, I fancied I could *see* that engine straining and laboring—the heart crashing and thundering in the rib cage like an overworked pump, the lungs billowing in and out as they whistled heavy warm gouts of air up the long shaft of the throat, and below, the stomach churning and ambulating and wondering why breakfast hadn't been sent down to it that day, or lunch, for that matter, and peeved about it, and then this whole oscillating edifice would tip and sway in the delivery of a pitch, the muscles convoluting and squeaking, off the pitch would go, and then as everything came to a shuddering and wheezing pause at the end of the follow-through, down the long thin corridors and shaftways between the taut tendons would drift that jeering inner voice of mine: "You nut! You fat fool nut! Y'all missed the plate AGAIN!!"

When I finally got the ball over and Hodges lined out his hit, I felt like lying down. My interest in the proceedings was strongly affected by that oncoming dizziness—with its high ringing sound like the mooning hum of a tiny bug caught deep back in the confines of the ear, and while the ball was being fired in by Mickey Mantle in center, I was bent over, puffing hard, and trying to clear my head of its sounds and mists. I could feel the October sun pressing on my neck. When I looked up, Stan Lopata, the Phillies catcher, was settling himself in the batter's box. He has a pronounced crouch at the plate as he awaits the pitch, hunched over as if he'd been seized by a sudden stomach cramp. Naturally, his stance diminishes his strike zone considerably, despite the fact that he's a big man, and I looked down at him in dismay. In fact, my voice, still jeering from the sidelines, produced a perky comment about Lopata which made me smile in spite of myself. "Mah God!" it said. "Lookit what y'all got yo'self into *now . . .*"

I threw him fifteen pitches. My mouth was ajar with fatigue, and I was swept by the numbing despair that must grip English bowlers who often have to work on the same pair of batsmen for two or three hours, often more. Lopata and I were a sturdy pair, joined together by the umbilical cord of my wildness—and also by his propensity for hitting fouls. He hit six of them, lashing out like a cobra from his coil, and the ball would flee in big hops down past the coaching boxes or loft into the stands.

I threw Lopata four quick balls, wide of the plate. At this point, Elston Howard, my long-suffering catcher, took a sudden, almost proprietary interest in the proceedings. I think that crouching there in the dust behind home plate he'd counted on his fingers and realized that if we could get Lopata out,

24

there was only one more batter to go, and then he'd be able to walk slowly for the shadows of the dugout, thinking of the slight electric hum of the water cooler and how that stream of cool water would feel against the roof of his mouth, and how he'd flop down on the bench and stick his legs straight out and feel the kinks fade away from them. Previously, his reluctance to enter the spirit of things was such that he could barely persuade himself to lift his glove for a target. Now he began to rise from his crouch after every pitch and fire the ball back with increasing speed—steaming it back trying to snap me out of my wildness. He threw the ball with an accuracy that mocked my control, harder than I was pitching it to him, and finally at such velocity into my weakly padded glove that I suffered a deep bone bruise which discolored my left hand for over a week. "Come on, kid, *lay* it in," I heard him call out once, making a fist of his right hand and pumping it at me as if by sheer determination he could will my pitches into the strike zone. Then he'd crouch down and look gloomily off into the stands, often into his team's dugout, thinking about the water and perhaps to check if relief might be forthcoming, and finally he'd get set and plant his feet in position, and just as you began to swing into the windup he'd pop up the big dusty circumference of his glove fast, as if he was pulling up a target in a shooting gallery. You'd stare at that glove, the eyes watering, concentrating on it so that it seemed to fill the entire field of your vision. But the pitch always seemed to tail off, missing by an inch, perhaps a foot—a moan escaping you as it did—and then you had to face the agony of Howard's return slapping hard enough in the glove to force a sharp intake of breath.

Suddenly the inner voice burst loudly upon my senses. It had been saying nothing of importance—just the usual raillery, still calling me a "fat fool" and an "aggressive nut," but from a distance, hardly distinguishable at times from the high whine of dizziness humming in my ears. But then my hand drifted up and touched my brow, finding it was as wet and cold as the belly of a trout. It was a disclosure which sent the voice spinning off in a cracker-Cassandra's wail of doom. "Mah God!" it cried out, "y'all gonna *faint* out heah. Lawd *Almah*ty! Y'gonna *faint!*"

I'd just caught the ball from Howard, grimacing as it whacked into the glove, and as I felt the lurch of nausea and that piercing disclosure echo in the brain I dropped the ball from fingers which began bumping gently against each other in a disembodied fashion which suggested that they too had joined the voice in revolt. I stared at the fingers, fascinated. When I bent for the ball, the head cleared slightly, and the fingers came back under control. But

I knew then that it was only a matter of time, and not too much of it, before that prescient wail would be proved accurate—and into my mind reeled a terrifying hallucination: the brown canvas of the stretcher I'd seen pegged to the wall in the corridor near the dugout, hands reaching briskly for it, while outside I suddenly seemed suspended far above the field in the high clear air where the Stadium pigeons worked the quick currents on dihedral wings, and far below I could see the physical husk of me, deserted now by both mind and eye, stiff-limbed, yet spastic, reeling around the mound trying to pull itself together for that last awful pitch. The crowd was standing now, leaning forward. "You mean to say that guy's Al Schacht? . . . the clown prince of baseball, *that* guy . . . well, I don't know what *he* thinks is funny, but I mean that's just terrible, just *hor*rible what's going on out there . . ." They chatted among themselves, the stretcher-bearers waiting in the runway, smoking cigarettes, and as we watched the grotesque figure shiver into its final windup, the right arm moving as stiffly as an old maid throwing her knitting bag at something scuttling in a dark corner, the ball fell from its feeble grip, hopping slowly down off the mound like an infant rabbit let loose, and after it, plunging forward as if to recapture it, the body lurched and began to collapse to the ground in sections—the head twisting in the dust, then the shoulders, and the knees touching so that, in the jackknifed position of a man looking under a bed for a collar button, the posterior alone remained aloft for one defiant cataleptic instant before it swayed far to one side and toppled in the dust *thump*. We watched the stretcher-bearers flip their cigarettes and start up the steps of the dugouts where the ballplayers stood and rocked back and forth like trolley passengers in their glee, whooping and hollering and giggling at the demise of the impostor: "Man, d'ja see that big tall cat fall *down* out there—hooo-eeee!"

I had one frightening glimpse of my Armageddon, vivid as a lightning flash, and then, waiting, on the mound, the cold sweat standing out in beads that formed as soon as I brushed a finger through them, I tried to persuade myself that you don't collapse out on the pitcher's mound in front of twenty thousand people. It isn't done and therefore it couldn't happen. Casey Stengel tells a story of a rookie shortstop who fainted in his debut when the first batted ball hopped out toward him; but that was a question of nerves—if you were to believe the story—not of exhaustion.

But I knew, as I stood there in that momentary calm of self-appraisal, that the energy was draining from me like meal from a punctured burlap sack, and that presently I would stumble and go down like the figure in the vision.

It was an inexorable fact. Of course, I could have walked off the field. But calling off the whole thing—just stopping—seemed too complicated. What would happen then? There was no one to finish the job. The American League couldn't bat, therefore. What would Mickey Mantle say? How would the $1,000 be divided? Anything seemed infinitely more complicated than staying. So I became absolutely resigned to continuing, even if it meant falling in a heap, as limp and pale on the mound as a massive rosin bag, while downtown in the magazine offices the editors were told over the phone by someone growling through the thick mesh of a chewed cigar that one of their writers had passed out on the pitcher's mound and the groundkeepers wanted to know what to do about it.

There remained one small hope: if I could last through Lopata and Bill Mazeroski of the Pittsburgh Pirates, the last batter in the National League lineup, I might get a chance while the teams changed sides to puff a bit in the cool of the dugout, to put a wet towel around the back of the neck, and perhaps find a second wind to get through Fox and Mantle and Kuenn and the others in the American League batting order. It was a forlorn hope, and not one to look forward to with eagerness; as soon as I started throwing to Lopata again, the weight of the twenty previous minutes of hard throwing— by then I'd thrown a few pitches short of seventy—pressed down hard like a stifling tropic heat . . . the field seemed as limitless under that blazing sun as a desert, spreading out forever on all sides, unreal, and the players stiff and distant as obelisks in a surrealist landscape. The whine in my ears increased, the nausea fulminating, the knees rubbery, so shaky that the desert's fixity was disturbed and the ground itself then began to undulate softly and thickly, like a bog, and there were times when the motion became violent and the pitcher's mound hunched up under me so that I teetered on its summit, on the cone of a vast anthill whose slopes beat with that insect hum; at times its physical aspect would be inverted, and I would find myself at the bottom of a murky hollow—the air heavy and clammy—and I would twist and convolute and hurl up the long sides of that bowl a baseball as heavy and malleable as a ripe mango—throwing it up toward Lopata, perched on that distant rim as implacable as a squatting Sphinx.

I don't remember Lopata grounding out, but he did, finally, hitting a big, hopping ground ball toward the shortstop position where—according to my statistician—Billy Martin first gave a little startled jump as if in surprise to hear the *whack* of the ball being hit, then moved for it on legs that seemed "stiff from disuse," as my statistician friend put it (after all, he'd been standing in his position for some time), and promptly fumbled it. I don't remember that at all.

I don't remember Bill Mazeroski either. I only know I pitched to him that afternoon because my statistician wrote in his notes *Mazeroski at plate . . . takes:* and then four downward strokes in a row with his pencil to indicate the batter stood with his bat on his shoulder and watched either four or one thousand one hundred and eleven balls go by.

With Mazeroski at the plate, Ralph Houk—the tough, confident, chaw-chewing Yankee coach the ballplayers call "Major" for his rank in the Rangers during the war, and who is now Casey Stengel's replacement as the Yankee manager—suddenly appeared. I was first aware of him when I sensed a movement on the first-base foul line and turned to see him coming toward me. I glowered at him. Whatever his reputation, as he came out over the base line I looked upon him as an intruder. He came on, a slow nonchalant amble, looking off into the outfield, then down in front of his feet, never at me, and there was no apparent purpose in mind—just a man strolling across the infield—and then he came within the dirt circumference of the pitcher's mound, climbing stiff-legged up toward me, and he put his hand out for the ball.

Perhaps he thought that I'd be relieved to see him. I don't think he expected the belligerency that blazed in that pale face. He shifted the chaw to speak—and I could see a grin working at his mouth. He told me later that he'd relieved many pitchers in his time (he once managed the Denver team in the American Association) but that he'd never seen anyone like that—it was like . . . well . . . and with a headshake he'd left the sentence unfinished, as if it all beggared description.

"Needle-lily-eh?"

"What!" I cried at him.

"Need a little help, hey?"

I stared furiously at him.

"Kid, you look a little tired out," he said patiently. "Don't you want some help?" He kept his hand out for the ball.

"No, no, no," I said. My voice came out in a croak. "Gotta finish. Lemme pitch just a li'l more." But Houk didn't turn for the dugout; he smiled, very broadly this time, and kept his hand out.

Like many pitchers, I wasn't taking kindly to being removed—despite being as weak as a convalescent. It's curious that no matter how brutally the opposition is treating him, a pitcher will often turn mulish when the manager reaches the mound. In extreme cases a pitcher will react to the indignity of being relieved by throwing the ball away in a rage. Pitching in Philadelphia, Walter Beck of the Dodgers turned away from his manager, and rather than give up the ball he wound up and hit the Lifebuoy sign with it, which in the old Baker Field was a very long toss from the pitcher's mound indeed. Early Wynn of the Chicago White Sox chose to throw the ball *at* his manager, and threw it into the stomach of Al Lopez, stepping out to relieve him, with such accuracy and dispatch that legend has it that Lopez stumbled back into the dugout murmuring that his star pitcher had shown with his speed and control that he was not in need of relief.

Houk had no such trouble with me. I said "No, no" a few more times, but finally I took a step forward, dropped the ball in his hand, and stumbled off the mound.

I walked slowly toward the first-base dugout. Most of the players in the dugout were standing up, watching me come in, and many of them were grinning. Just as I reached the base line, behind me Ralph Houk threw a single pitch to Mazeroski, which in a sort of final irony, he hit high and lazy to Bob Cerv in left field. Since my back was to the diamond I didn't see the ball caught, but when it was, the players in the field ran for the dugout, streaming by me without a word and clambering down the steps, most of them headed for the water cooler. I was bewildered by that rush of movement past me; I didn't know what was going on until Billy Martin fell into slow step beside me. "Man," he said, smiling broadly, "it's O.K. . . . it's over," and I said weakly, "Sure," and went with him into the dugout, where I turned and sagged down on the bench. The *Sports Illustrated* photographer assigned the story leaned into the dugout and took a picture at that moment: in it you see Whitey Ford, the Yankee pitcher, grinning and looking at the figure seated next to him visibly in some stage of shock—the mouth ajar, the eyes staring, the body itself slack and disjointed as if a loosely stuffed bag had been tossed on the bench. Some months later, an elderly English colonel caught a glimpse of that photograph and said the face reminded him of the stunned look of a bagpipe player who had survived the British thrust at Passchendaele in '17. Someone else, with less reference to draw from but plenty of imagination, said no, the face belonged to a man who sees his wife lean out of the sofa during cocktails and inexplicably garrote the family cat with a length of cord. Whichever, I wore a look of bleak horror, and I remember Ford and Martin, who came over and squeezed in beside me, laughing as I sat between them.

"Know something?" said Ford. "We've been making book here in the dugout as to when you'd keel over."

"No kidding," I said weakly.

"Yup. He was sure sweating out there, wasn't he, Billy? Leaking out of him like it was sawdust." He leaned across me, waiting for verification and Martin's comment. He was already grinning in anticipation.

"Sawdust? That was *blood,* man. First time," said Martin, "I ever thought I'd be running in for a mound conference to find out what was going on was a *funeral service,*" and he and Ford leaned off the bench and bellowed with laughter that turned heads down the length of the dugout. They wanted to know what Martin had said, and so he said it again, and from down the line they were all looking and grinning. They called up the questions: "Hey, kid, what'ja think of it, hey? How'd ja like it out there? Pretty rough, hey?"— their joshing friendly, but you could tell they were pleased their profession had treated me as roughly as it had.

"Really sumpin'," I said.

"What'd he say?" someone called out.

"Really *sump*in' out there," I repeated.

I didn't see anyone in the locker room. I took off the baseball outfit slowly and sat for a long time in the cubicle looking down at my bare toes, working them up and down, and thinking of nothing, trying to keep the mind blank because when you thought back to what had been going on just minutes before, the excitement began to jitter through you again. Finally I hopped up and went into the shower and stood under a nozzle that malfunctioned and worked in spiteful gusts. The soap in the metal dishes was an astonishing pink color. The water was cool. The trainer told me later he hadn't expected anyone to be in the showers so early; after all, he wanted to know, how many pitchers were driven to the showers before the game had even started? But the cool water was pleasant. Under it, luxuriating, I remembered Bruce Pearson, the barely articulate catcher from Mark Harris's great baseball novel *Bang the Drum Slowly*—which our generation thought good enough to make Ring Lardner and the epistolary device of his *You Know Me, Al* cork up and take a backseat when it came to baseball fiction—and I thought of Pearson speculating idly with his teammates about the best moments of baseball . . . how even hitting a foul ball was part of it, to look up and see how high you drove it, and how the best part of all perhaps was coming in stinking from the sun and ripping off the suit and getting under the shower and thinking about eating. I thought about it because for the first time that day I was suddenly hungry. Roy Campanella once said that you had to have an awful lot of little boy in you to play baseball for a living. So it was, when you recalled it, that the simple, basic sensations came to mind—like being hungry when it was all over, and the sluice of shower water on your arms, and before that, on the field, the warmth of the sun, and the smell of leather, the neat's-foot sweating out of the glove's pocket in the heat, and the cool of the grass and the dirt when the shade fell across it late in the afternoon, and the sharp cork sounds of the bats against each other, and the rich smell of grass torn by spikes—all these condiments to the purpose, to be sure, which was the game itself, and winning . . . but still such a part of baseball with the other sounds, and what else you saw, and felt, that finally the actual event itself was eclipsed: the game and its feats and the score became the dry statistics, and what you remembered were the same pressures that once kept you and the others out in the long summer evenings until the fireflies were out and the street lights shining dimly through the pale silver underside of leaves, and you groped at the edge of the honeysuckle and threw up that last one high fly for someone to catch and hoped they would see it against that deep sky—and the fact that your team in the brighter hours of the afternoon had lost twenty-four to six and your sister had made eight errors in right field wasn't important. The disasters didn't amount to much. Standing under the shower, I found myself thinking not of the trembling misery of the last minutes on the mound but those two high flies that Ashburn and Mays hit, how they worked up into that clear sky, and how you knew they were harmless and would be caught. You could be a bona fide pitcher like Hal Kelleher of the Phillies and suffer the indignity of allowing twelve runs in one inning—which he did back in 1938—and in desolation punt your glove around the clubhouse while the trainer stood in a corner pretending to fold towels . . . and yet that startling statistic was not what Kelleher would remember about baseball. What he *would* remember made you envy him, and all the others that came before and after who were good at it, and you wondered how they could accept quitting when their legs went. Of course, there were a few who didn't feel so strongly. In 1918, a rookie named Harry Heitman walked in for his major league debut with the Brooklyn Dodgers, gave up in succession a single, a triple, and a single . . . was taken out, went to the clubhouse, showered, left the ballpark for a recruiting station, and enlisted in the United States Navy. To hell with it, he said.

But when I dressed in my street clothes it was with regret that I stuffed

31

the baseball outfit back into the carry-all. I found myself looking around the locker room carefully so that I could remember it, not to write about it as much as to convince myself that I had been there. I noticed the red boxes still on the table, filled with baseballs the players had been autographing earlier, and I went over and looked down at them. I had an irresistible urge to sign one of them—perhaps just a scribbled initial. I started looking for a pen. I felt the whole afternoon was slipping away and had to be commemorated, even if by this sad sort of *graffiti*—scratching a name so that there would be evidence, no matter how insignificant, to prove that day. It seemed very important. But the door of the locker room swung open. Some players came in, and I never got the thing done.

After the baseball stint, the *Sports Illustrated* editors suggested, why not boxing? I wrote a polite letter to the light-heavyweight champion of the world, Archie Moore, known in the fight game as "the Mongoose." I did this despite some disagreeable facts about him in the record books—namely that he had knocked out more opponents than anyone else in the history of the ring (eventually 146 souls), starting off with a man named Piano-Mover Jones. Why was I going into the ring against someone who had beaten a man with such an awesome name as Piano-Mover Jones? The answer is that very early on one commits oneself. One tells the editor, yes, of course I'll jump out of an airplane, climb K-2, fight the light-heavyweight champion or whatever, and having said that to the editor one has to live up to one's promise. Then the matter becomes public. At a cocktail party, talking to a pretty young woman, very suave, one says, yes, I'm getting ready to fight so-and-so, the champion; her eyes widen. I trained. I quit smoking. I ran around the Central Park reservoir. I sparred in a squash court at the Yale Club. Inexorably, as if on a moving stairway, I was borne along to the day of commitment.

Boxing

The fight, or exhibition, or what people later called "that time when you . . ." took place in Stillman's Gym, which was a famous and rickety boxers' establishment on Eighth Avenue just down from Columbus Circle. A dark stairway led up into a gloomy vaultlike room, rather like the hold of an old galleon. One heard the sound before one's eyes acclimatized: the *slap-slap* of the ropes being skipped, the thud of leather into the big heavy bags that squeaked from their chains as they swung, the rattle of the speed bags, the muffled sounds of gym shoes on the canvas of the rings (there were two rings), the snuffle of the fighters breathing out through their noses, and, every three minutes, the sharp clang of the ring bell. The atmosphere was of a fetid jungle twilight. When Gene Tunney trained at Stillman's, he wanted to open the windows, which were so caked that it was hard to pick out where they were in the wall. "Let's clear this place out with some fresh air," he had said, and everybody there had looked at him, astonished. Johnny Dundee, the featherweight champion at the time, made an oft-quoted remark: "Fresh air? Why, that stuff is likely to kill us!"

The proprietor was Lou Stillman himself. His real name was Lou Ingber, but he had managed Stillman's so long—it was originally opened by a pair of philanthropist millionaires as a charity mission to bring in kids off the street—that he found himself named for the gym that he made famous. His attitude about his place was as follows: "The way these guys like it, the filthier it is, the better. Maybe it makes them feel more at home." He announced this in what Budd Schulberg had once described as a "garbage-disposal voice." He sat up on a high stool under the automatic timer that set off the ring bell.

I remember him for leaning forward off the stool and delivering himself

34

of a succession of tiny spits—oh, the size of BB shots—and though there were signs nailed up everywhere that read NO RUBBISH OR SPITTING ON THE FLOOR, UNDER PENALTY OF THE LAW, Stillman himself expectorated at almost every breath. Perhaps he felt that he was exonerated by the infinitesimal size of his offerings.

I had gone in there to ask him if we could take over the premises for an hour or so; I told him about Archie Moore and what we hoped to do. *Sports Illustrated* would pay him a small sum for the inconvenience. He did not seem especially surprised. An eyebrow might have been raised. It turned out that he condoned almost anything that would break the dreary tedium of the workouts—the never-ending three-minute doomsday clang of the ring bell, the mind-stupefying slamming of the punching-bag equipment. In the grim steerage-hold atmosphere much more hanky-panky and joking went on, perhaps as a sort of therapy, than one might have expected. For years the fall guy for practical jokes had been a huge scar-faced black fighter known as Battling Norfolk, employed by Stillman as a rubdown man, who became such a target for a hotfoot, or a bucket of water on the nape of the neck, that as he moved around the gym he *revolved,* turning to make sure no one was coming up on him from behind. They never let up on him. When he answered the phone, an explosive charge would go off; a skeleton was set up in the little cubicle in the back reaches of the gym where he gave his rubdowns, and when he saw it there, glistening in the dull light, he gave a scream and was said to have fainted, crashing up against the wood partition.

Perhaps Stillman saw me as another in the line of Battling Norfolks. He agreed to turn over his premises, though he told me what a businesslike establishment he was running there, and what a considerable inconvenience it was going to be to stop operations for the hour or so of the exhibition. Couldn't *Sports Illustrated* come up with more scratch? I said that I would see what I could do. I told him that, frankly, it was the least of my worries.

As the day of the fight approached, I began to get notes in the mail. I don't know who sent them. Most of them were signed with fighters' names— aphorisms, properly terse, and almost all somewhat violent in tone. I suspected Peter Gimbel, my sparring partner, but he would not fess up.

One of them read, "If you get belted and see three fighters through a haze, go after the one in the middle. That's what ruined me—going after the other two guys."—MAX BAER.

Another, on the back of a postcard that had a cat sitting next to a vase of roses on the front, announced succinctly, "Go on in there, he can't hurt us."—LEO P. FLYNN, FIGHT MANAGER.

Another had the curious words Eddie Simms murmured when Art Donovan, the referee, went over to his corner to see how clearheaded he was after being poleaxed by Joe Louis in their Cleveland fight: "Come on, let's take a walk on the roof. I want some fresh air."

Joe Louis's famous remark about Billy Conn turned up one morning: "He can run, but he can't hide." So did James Braddock's description of what it was like to be hit by a Joe Louis jab: ". . . like someone jammed an electric bulb in your face and busted it."

One of the lengthier messages was a parody of a type of column Jimmy Cannon occasionally wrote for the New York *Journal-American* in which he utilized the second person for immediacy and dramatic effect. "Your name is Joe Louis," a column might start. "You are in the twilight of your career . . ." The one I received read as follows: "Your name is George Plimpton. You have had an appointment with Archie Moore. Your head is now a concert hall where Chinese music will never stop playing."

Occasionally someone of a more practical mind than the mysterious message-sender would call up with a positive word of advice. One of the stranger suggestions was that I avail myself of the services of a spellcaster named Evil Eye Finkel. He possessed what he called the "Slobodka Stare," which he boasted was what had finally finished off Adolf Hitler.

"Think of that," I said.

"Evil Eye's got a manager," I was told. "Name of Mumbles Sober. The pair of them can be hired for fifty dollars to five hundred dollars depending— so it says in the brochure—on the 'wealth of the employer and the difficulty of the job.' "

I wondered aloud what the price difference would be between saving my skin in the ring against Archie Moore and what it had cost to preserve the Western democracies from Fascism.

"I don't know," I was told. "You'll have to ask Mumbles."

As it was, I picked corner men who were literary rather than evil-eyed, or even pugilistic—composed of the sort of friends one might have as ushers at a wedding (or perhaps, more appropriately, as someone pointed out, as bearers at a funeral) rather than at a boxing showdown in a gymnasium. They were Peter Matthiessen, the novelist and explorer (he appeared on the day of the fight and gave me the tibia of an Arctic hare as a good-luck token—the biggest rabbit's foot I had ever seen); Tom Guinzburg, of the Viking Press;

Blair Fuller, the novelist; Bob Silvers, then an editor of *Harpers;* and, of course, George Brown, my trainer, the only professional among us, who of course had literary connections because of his friendship with Ernest Hemingway. None of them, except Brown, had anything to do, really. I asked them if they would have lunch with me the day of the fight. They could steady me through the meal and get me to eat something. They could distract me with funny stories.

On the morning of the fight, to get a flavor of what the boxer goes through on the day of his bout, I turned up at the offices of the Boxing Commission, just uptown from Madison Square Garden, to get weighed in with the rest of the boxers scheduled to fight on various cards that evening around the city. John Conden, of the Garden, who was in charge of the proceedings, had said he would see to it that I got weighed in along with everyone else. The room was crowded with fighters, their managers, and more press than usual—a boxer-policeman from New Jersey named Dixon had raised considerable public interest.

I got in line. The fighters who were scheduled to fight in the Garden that evening and were staying in local fleabag hotels came ready for quick disrobing—overcoats over a pair of underwear shorts. One or two of them were wearing shoes with the laces already untied, so that all they had to do was shuck their overcoats and step up out of the shoes onto the scales. The official at the scales jiggled the weights and announced the figures. We shuffled forward. I had my overcoat on my arm. I was wearing a Brooks Brothers suit, a waistcoat that I was affecting at the time, a button-down shirt with a striped regimental tie, and a pair of dark, scuffed shoes over long calf-length socks.

When I was within eight boxers of the scale, I began to take off my clothes. I removed my suit coat, tossing it and my overcoat on a chair as I passed, and I started taking off my tie, just picking at the knot. But then I saw someone staring at me—one of the journalists, probably—nudging the man next to him to attract *his* attention, the two of them staring at me, as surprised as if the boxing commissioner himself had decided to step out of his trousers. That was enough. I could not go through with it. My fingers slipped off the tie, and I rolled my eyes ceilingward to suggest how stifling I felt the room was.

I did not tell my corner men at lunch about my experience that morning at the commissioner's office. It was not appropriate to the temper of the day to dwell on bungles of any sort. We had the lunch at the Racquet Club. My friends stared at me with odd smiles. We ordered the meal out of stiff large menus that crackled sharply when opened. I ordered eggs Benedict, steak Diane, and a chocolate-ice-cream compote. Someone said that it was not the sort of place, or meal, one would relate to someone going up against the light-heavyweight champion of the world, but I said I was having the meal to quiet my nerves; the elegance of the place, and the food, arriving at the table in silver serving dishes, helped me forget where I was going to be at five that afternoon.

I took out Matthiessen's enormous rabbit foot. "How can I lose with this thing?" I said. We talked about good-luck charms and I said that in the library down the hall I had read that when Tom Sharkey was preparing for a fight against Gus Ruhlin, he was sent a pair of peacocks by Bob Fitzsimmons, the former heavyweight champion. Sharkey was somewhat shaken by the gift, because he said he had heard from an old Irishwoman that an owner of a peacock never had any good luck. But Fitzsimmons was such a good friend that Sharkey didn't want to insult him by sending the birds back. So Sharkey kept them around, walking past their pens rather hurriedly, and indeed, when he lost his fight to Ruhlin in the eleventh round, he blamed it on what he called his "Jonah birds."

"You trying to tell me you feel awkward about that hare's foot?" Matthiessen asked.

I had the sense that he had been reluctant to give it up in the first place. It was a *huge* foot, and it probably meant a lot to him.

"Perhaps you could hold it for me," I said.

"You better keep it," he said.

During lunch I kept wondering what Archie Moore was up to. I knew that he was in town, not far away. I thought of him coming closer all the time, physically moving toward our confrontation, perhaps a quarter of a mile away at the moment, in some restaurant, ordering a big steak with honey on it for energy, everybody in the place craning around to stare at him, and a lot of smiles because a month before, he had won an extraordinary fight against Yvon Durrelle, a strong poleaxer French Canadian, in which he had pulled himself up off the canvas five times, eventually to win, so that the applause would ripple up from among the tables as he left the restaurant; then he would turn uptown feeling good about things, people nodding to him on the avenues, and smiling, and then he might duck into a Fifth Avenue shop to buy a hat, and afterward perhaps he'd wander up by the Plaza and into the park, where he might take a look at the yak over there in the zoo. Then he'd glance at his watch. That might get him upset. It disturbed the equanimity of the day. Who *was* this guy? The nerve! This creep who had written him a letter. So the distance would be shortened; he was coming crosstown now, then up the stairs of Stillman's, just yards away from me in the labyrinthine gloom of the dressing lockers, and then finally in the ring, just a few feet away, seeing me for the first time, looking at me speculatively, and then, when he put a fist in my stomach, there wouldn't be any distance between us at all!

Later I discovered what he *was* doing. At the same time I was having lunch with my entourage, he was sitting in a restaurant with Peter Maas, a journalist friend of mine. Over dessert Archie Moore asked Peter who I was—this fellow he had agreed to go three rounds with later that afternoon. Maas, who knew about the arrangements—I had invited him to Stillman's—could not resist it: he found himself, somewhat to his surprise, describing me to Moore as an "intercollegiate boxing champion."

Once Peter had gotten that out, he began to warm to his subject: "He's a gawky sort of guy, but don't let that fool you, Arch. He's got a left jab that sticks, he's fast, and he's got a poleax left hook that he can really throw. He's a barn burner of a fighter, and the *big* thing about him is that he wants to be the light-heavyweight champion of the world. Very ambitious. And confident. He doesn't see why he should work his way up through all the preliminaries in the tank towns: he reckons he's ready *now."*

Moore arched his eyebrows at this.

"He's invited all his friends," Maas went on gaily, "a few members of the press, a couple of guys who are going to be at the McNeil Boxing Award dinner tonight"—which was the real reason Moore was in town—"and in front of all these people he's going to waltz into the ring and *take* you. What he's done is to sucker you into the ring."

Maas told me all of this later. He said he had not suspected himself of such satanic capacities; it all came out quite easily.

Moore finally had a comment to offer. "If that guy lays a hand on me I'm going to coldcock him." He cracked his knuckles alarmingly at the table.

At this, Peter Maas realized that not unlike Dr. Frankenstein he had created a monster, and after a somewhat hollow laugh, he tried to undo matters: "Oh, Arch, he's a friend of mine." He tried to say that he had been carrying on in jest. But this served to make Moore even more suspicious—the notion that Maas and the mysterious man with the "poleax left hook" he was describing were in cahoots of some sort.

39

At the time, of course, I knew none of this. I dawdled away the after-noon and arrived early at Stillman's. George Brown was with me, carrying his little leather case with the gloves, and some "equipment" he felt he might have to use if things got "difficult" for me up in the ring.

We went up the steps of the building at Eighth Avenue, through the turnstile, and Lou Stillman led us through the back area of his place into an arrangement of dressing cubicles as helter-skelter as a Tangier slum, with George Brown's nose wrinkled up as we were shown back into the gloom and a stall was found. George sat me down in a corner, and, snapping open his kit bag, he got ready to tape my hands. I worried aloud that Archie Moore might not show up, and both George and I laughed at the concern in my voice, as if a condemned prisoner were fretting that the fellow in charge of the dawn proceedings might have overslept. We began to hear people arriv-ing outside, the hum of voices beginning to rise. I had let a number of people know; the word of the strange cocktail-hour exhibition had spread. Blair Fuller arrived. He was the only one of my seconds who seemed willing to identify himself with what was going to go on. The rest said they were going to sit in the back. Fuller was wearing a T-shirt with THE PARIS REVIEW across the front.

Suddenly, Archie Moore himself appeared at the door of my cubicle. He was in his streetclothes. He was carrying a kit bag and a pair of boxing gloves; the long white laces hung down loose. There was a crowd of people behind him, peering in over his shoulders—Miles Davis, the trumpet player, one of them; and I thought I recognized Doc Kearns, Moore's legendary manager, with his great ears soaring up the sides of his head and the slight tang of toilet water sweetening the air of the cubicle (he was known for the aroma of his colognes). But all of this was a swift impression, because I was staring up at Moore from my stool. He looked down and said as follows: *"Hmm."* There were no greetings. He began undressing. He stepped out of his pants and shorts; over his hips he began drawing up a large harnesslike foul-protector. I stared at it in awe. I had not thought to buy one myself; the notion of the champion's throwing a low blow had not occurred to me. Indeed, I was upset to realize he thought *I* was capable of doing such a thing. "I don't have one of those," I murmured. I don't think he heard me. The man I took to be Doc Kearns was saying, "Arch, let's get on out of here. It's a freak show." Beyond the cubicle we could hear the rising murmur of the crowd.

"No, no, no," I said. "It's all very serious."

Moore looked at me speculatively. "Go out there and do your best," he said. He settled the cup around his hips and flicked its surface with a fingernail; it gave off a dull, tinny sound. He drew on his trunks—a knit pair like a 1920s bathing suit. He began taping his hands—the shriek of the adhesive drawn in bursts off its spool, the flurry of his fists as he spun the tape around them. During this, he offered us a curious monologue, apparently about a series of victories back in his welterweight days: "I put that guy in the hospital, didn't I? Yeah, banged him around the eyes so it was a question about could he ever *see* again." He looked at me again. "You do your best, hear?" I nodded vaguely. He went back to his litany. "Hey, Doc, you remember the guy who couldn't remember his name after we finished with him . . . just plumb banged that guy's name right out of his skull?" He smoothed the tape over his hands and slid on the boxing gloves. Then he turned and swung a punch at the wall of the cubicle with a force that bounced a wooden medicine cabinet off its peg; it fell to the floor and exploded in a shower of rickety slats. "These gloves are tight," he said as he walked out. A roll of athletic tape fell out of the ruin of the cabinet and unraveled across the floor. Beyond the cubicle wall I heard a voice cut through the babble: "Whatever he was, Arch, he was not an elephant."

Could that have been Kearns? An assessment of the opposition? Of course, at the time I had no idea that Peter Maas had built me up into a demonic contender whom they had good reason to check.

"What the hell was that?" I said. I looked at George Brown beseechingly. He shrugged. "Don't let it bother you. Just remember what we've been doing all this time," he said, smoothing the tape on my hands. "Move, and peck at him."

"At least he didn't find out about the sympathetic response," I said.

"What's that?" Brown asked.

"Well, it's that weeping you've noticed when I get cuffed around."

"Maybe he'll think it's sweat," Brown said cheerfully.

After a while he reached for the gloves and said it was time we went out.

The place was packed; the seats stretching back from the ring (a utility from the days when the great fighters sparred at Stillman's) were full, and behind them people were standing back along the wall. Archie Moore was waiting up in the ring. As I climbed into the ring he had his back to me, leaning over the ropes and shouting at someone in the crowd. I saw him club at the ring ropes with a gloved fist, and I could feel the structure of the ring shudder. Ezra Bowen, a *Sports Illustrated* editor, jumped up into the ring to act as referee. He provided some florid instructions, and then waved the two of us together. Moore turned and began shuffling quickly toward me.

I had read somewhere that if one were doomed to suffer in the ring, it would be best to have Archie Moore as the bestower. His face was peaceful, with a kind of comforting mien to it—people doubtless fell easily into conversation with him on buses and planes—and to be put away by him in the ring would not be unlike being tucked in by a Haitian mammy.

I do not remember any such thoughts at the time. He came at me quite briskly, and as I poked at him tentatively, his left reached out and thumped me alarmingly. As he moved around the ring he made a curious humming sound in his throat, a sort of peaceful aimless sound one might make pruning a flower bed, except that from time to time the hum would rise quite abruptly, and *bang!* he would cuff me alongside the head. I would sense the leaden feeling of being hit, the almost acrid whiff of leather off his gloves, and I would blink through the sympathetic response and try to focus on his face, which looked slightly startled, as if he could scarcely believe he had done such a thing. Then I'd hear the humming again, barely distinguishable now against the singing in my own head.

Halfway through the round Moore slipped—almost to one knee—not because of anything I had done, but his footing had betrayed him somehow. Laughter rose out of the seats, and almost as if in retribution he jabbed and followed with a long lazy left hook that fetched up against my nose and collapsed it slightly. It began to bleed. There was a considerable amount of sympathetic response and though my physical reaction, the jab ("peck, peck, peck") was thrown in a frenzy, and with considerable spirit, the efforts popped up against Moore's guard as ineffectually as if I were poking at the side of a barn. The tears came down my cheeks. We revolved around the ring. I could hear the crowd—a vague buzzing—and occasionally I could hear my name being called out: "Hey, George, hit him back; hit him in the knees, George." I was conscious of how inappropriate the name George was to the ring, rather like hearing "Timothy" or "Warren" or "Christopher." Occasionally I was aware of the faces hanging above the seats like rows of balloons, unrecognizable, many of them with faint anticipatory grins on their faces, as if they were waiting for a joke to be told that was going to be pretty good. They were slightly inhuman, I remember thinking, the banks of them staring up, and suddenly into my mind popped a scene from Conan Doyle's *The Croxley Master*: his fine description of a fight being watched by Welsh miners, each with his dog sitting behind him; they went everywhere as companions, so that the boxers looked down and everywhere among the human faces were the heads of dogs, yapping from the benches, the muzzles pointing up, the tongues lolling.

We went into a clinch; I was surprised when I was pushed away and saw the sheen of blood on Moore's T-shirt. Moore looked slightly alarmed. The flow of tears was doubtless disarming. He moved forward and enfolded me in another clinch. He whispered in my ear, "Hey, breathe, man, breathe." The bell sounded and I turned from him and headed for my corner, feeling very much like sitting down.

Lou Stillman had not provided a stool. "There's no stool," I said snuffily to George Brown. My nose was stopped up. He ministered to me across the ropes—a quick rub of the face with the towel, an inspection of the nose, a pop of head-clearing salts, a predictable word of the old advice. ("Just jab him, keep him away, keep the glove in his snoot, peck, peck, you're doing fine.") He looked out past my shoulder at Moore, who must have been joking with the crowd, because I could hear the laughter behind me.

For the next two rounds Moore let up considerably, being assured—if indeed it had ever worried him—of the quality of his opposition. In the last round he let me whale away at him from time to time, and then he would pull me into a clinch and whack at me with great harmless popping shots to the backs of my shoulder blades that sounded like the crack of artillery. Once I heard him ask Ezra Bowen if he was behind on points.

But George Brown and Blair Fuller did not like what was going on at all . . . I think mostly because of the unpredictable nature of my opponent: his moods seemed to change as the fight went on; he was evidently not quite sure how to comport himself—clowning for a few seconds, and then the humming would rise, and they would grimace as a few punches were thrown with more authority; they could see my mouth drop ajar. In the third round Brown began to feel that Moore had run through as much of a repertoire as he could devise, and that the fighter, wondering how he could finish things off aesthetically, was getting testy about it. I was told Tom Guinzburg, one of my seconds, came up to the corner and threw a towel into the ring . . . but whether he was doing it because he was worried or because he knew it would raise a laugh—which indeed it did—I never discovered. But long after the event I found out that Brown had reached down and advanced the hand of the time clock. The bell clanged sharply with a good minute to go. Ezra called us together to raise both our arms, and funning it up, he called the affair a draw. I can remember the relief of its being done, vaguely worried that it had not been more conclusive or artistic; I was quite grateful for the bloody nose.

"That last round seemed awfully short," I mentioned to Brown.

He dabbed at my face with a towel. "I suppose you were getting set to finish him," George said.

Much of the crowd moved with us back into the cubicle area. In my stall, I was pushed back into a corner. Moore stood in the doorway, the well-wishers shouting at him, "Hey, Arch, hey, Arch!" There was a lot of congratulating and jabber about the great Yvon Durelle fight. I heard somebody ask, "Whose blood is that on your shirt, hey, Arch?" and somebody else said, "Well, it sure ain't his!" and I could hear the guffawing as the exchange was passed along the gloomy corridors beyond the cubicle wall.

The character of the crowd had begun to change. The word had gone around the area that Archie Moore was up in Stillman's, and the fight bars down the avenue had emptied. A whole mess of people came up Stillman's stairs, some of them in time to see the final round, others pushing against the striped-tie crowd leaving. "It's over? What the hell was Arch doin' fightin' in Stillman's?"

"I dunno," one of the others pushing up the stairs said. "I hear he kilt some guy."

"A grudge fight, hey?"

They pushed back into the cubicle area. The cigar smoke rose. I caught sight of Lou Stillman. He was frantic. He had found two women, a mother and daughter, back in the cubicle area, which had flustered him; but the main aggravation was that his place was packed with people who had not paid to come through his turnstile. Someone told me that he had become so astonished at the number turning up for the exhibition, at the quantity of coats and ties, signifying that they *could* pay, that finally venality had overcome him; he rushed to the turnstile and the last twenty or thirty people who crowded in had to pay him two dollars a head. Later I heard that he had tried to recoup what he had missed by charging people, at least those wearing ties, as they *left*.

I sat on my stool, feeling removed from the bustle and the shouting. While I pecked at the laces of my gloves, suddenly in front of me a man turned—I had been staring at the back of his overcoat—and he said, "Well, kid, what did you get out of it?"

He was an older black man, with a rather melancholy face distinguished

44

by an almost Roman nose; his ears were cauliflowered, though very small.

"So far, a bloody nose," I said.

He smiled slightly. "That's the good way to begin; that's the start."

"I guess that's right," I said.

"There's a lot more to it," he went on.

I must have looked puzzled.

"Stick to it," he said. "You've got a lot to find out about. Don't let it go, hey?"

"No," I said vaguely, "I won't."

I never discovered who he was. I thought of him a couple of times later that evening.

Stillman's cleared out, finally. The fighters, who had been standing along the back wall to watch the strange proceedings, took over the premises again; they climbed up into the rings; the trainers sat down in the front seats, gossiping; things returned to normal.

I was told that at seven o'clock or so the duchess d'Uzès had arrived. She was not a duchess then (she had a marriage or so to go before she became one) but she had the airs: she was delivered to the door of Stillman's in a Rolls-Royce. She stepped out and hurried up the stairs. She was famous for being late—even at her own extravagant parties, where her guests stood yawning with hunger, waiting for her to come down the long, curved stair and make an entrance—and she paused at the turnstile, a lovely, graceful girl who always wore long, light blue chiffon to set off her golden hair.

She peered into the gloom. "Where's everybody?" she called. She had a clear musical voice, perfect for cutting through the uproar of a cocktail party.

Lou Stillman approached. I don't know if he produced one of his infinitesimal spittles. Let us say he cleared his throat.

"Everybody is not here," he said.

I wrote to six teams in the National Football League, as I recall, in the hope that one of them would take me on as their last-string quarterback during the training season. The Detroit Lions finally accepted me—an older and experienced team, imbued with a lot of the devil-may-care attitude of Bobby Layne, the roustabout quarterback who had been there a few years before. The pivotal moment came when George Wilson, the coach, just outside the classroom into which the team was filing, was pondering whether to give me a playbook. The playbook is the symbol of acceptance, of belonging. As long as a player has one in his possession he is a member of the team. It is what he must give up if he is cut. The assistant coach tells him, "The coach wants to see you. Bring your playbook."

At first, by the classroom door, Wilson had said, "No, you can't go in there."

I must have looked agonized. "But don't you understand what I'm trying to do?"

So he thought about it, just for an instant, everything hanging in the balance, and then he smiled and handed me the playbook. If he had not, I would have been as far removed from the Lions as a reporter sitting up in the press box.

The game described is a nighttime preseason scrimmage in Pontiac, Michigan. I had a repertoire of five plays.

Football

Jack Benny used to say that when he stood on the stage in white tie and tails for his violin concerts and raised his bow to begin his routine—scraping through "Love in Bloom"—that he *felt* like a great violinist. He reasoned that if he wasn't a great violinist, what was he doing dressed in tails, and about to play before a large audience?

At Pontiac I *felt* myself a football quarterback, not an interloper. My game plan was organized, and I knew what I was supposed to do. My nerves seemed steady, much steadier than they had been as I waited on the bench. I trotted along easily. I was keenly aware of what was going on around me.

I could hear a voice over the loudspeaker system, a dim murmur telling the crowd what was going on, telling them that number zero, coming out across the sidelines was not actually a rookie, but an amateur, a writer who had been training with the team for three weeks and had learned five plays, which he was now going to run against the first-string Detroit defense. It was like a nightmare come true, he told them, as if one of *them*, rocking a beer around in a paper cup, with a pretty girl leaning past him to ask the hot-dog vendor in the aisle for mustard, were suddenly carried down underneath the stands by a sinister clutch of ushers. He would protest, but he would be encased in the accoutrements, the silver helmet, with the two protruding bars of the cage, jammed down over his ears, and sent out to take over the team—that was the substance of the words, drifting across the field, swayed and shredded by the steady breeze coming up across the open end of Wisner Stadium from the vanished sunset. The crowd was interested, and I was conscious, just vaguely, of a steady roar of encouragement.

The team was waiting for me, grouped in the huddle, watching me come. I went in among them. Their heads came down for the signal. I called

47

out, "Twenty-six!" forcefully, to inspire them, and a voice from one of the helmets said, "Down, down, the whole stadium can hear you."

"Twenty-six," I hissed at them. "Twenty-six near oh pinch; on three. *Break!*" Their hands cracked as one, and I wheeled and started for the line behind them.

My confidence was extreme. I ambled slowly behind Whitlow, the center, poised down over the ball, and I had sufficient presence to pause, resting a hand at the base of his spine, as if on a windowsill—a nonchalant gesture I had admired in certain quarterbacks—and I looked out over the length of his back to fix in my mind what I saw.

Everything fine about being a quarterback—the embodiment of his power—was encompassed in those dozen seconds or so: giving the instructions to ten attentive men, breaking out of the huddle, walking for the line, and then pausing behind the center, dawdling amid men poised and waiting under the trigger of his voice, cataleptic, until the deliverance of himself and them to the future. The pleasure of sport was so often the chance to indulge the cessation of time itself—the pitcher dawdling on the mound, the skier poised at the top of a mountain trail, the basketball player with the rough skin of the ball against his palm preparing for a foul shot, the tennis player at set point over his opponent—all of them savoring a moment before committing themselves to action.

I had the sense of a portcullis down. On the other side of the imaginary bars the linemen were poised, the lights glistening off their helmets, and close in behind them were the linebackers, with Joe Schmidt just opposite me, the big number fifty-six shining on his white jersey, jumpjacking back and forth with quick choppy steps, his hands poised in front of him, and he was calling out defensive code words in a stream. I could sense the rage in his voice, and the tension in those rows of bodies waiting, as if coils had been wound overtight, which my voice, calling a signal, like a lever, would trip to spring them all loose. "Blue! Blue! Blue!" I heard Schmidt shout.

Within my helmet, the schoolmaster's voice murmured at me: "Son, nothing to it, nothing at all. . . ."

I bent over the center. Quickly I went over what was supposed to happen—I would receive the snap and take two steps straight back and hand the ball to the number two back coming laterally across from right to left, who would then cut into the number-six hole. That was what was designated by twenty-six—the two back into the six hole. The mysterious code words "near oh pinch" referred to blocking assignments in the line, and I was never sure exactly what was meant by them. The important thing was to hang on to the ball, turn, and get the ball into the grasp of the back coming across laterally.

I cleared my throat. "Set!" I called out, my voice loud and astonishing to hear, as if it belonged to someone shouting into the earholes of my helmet. "Sixteen, sixty-five, forty-four, *but* one, *but* two, *but* three," and at three the ball slapped back into my palm, and Whitlow's rump bucked up hard as he went for the defense men opposite.

The lines cracked together with a yawp and smack of pads and gear. I had the sense of quick, heavy movement, and as I turned for the backfield, not a second having passed, I was hit hard from the side, and as I gasped, the ball was jarred loose. It sailed away and bounced once, and I stumbled after it, hauling it under me five yards back, hearing the rush of feet, and the heavy jarring and wheezing of the blockers fending off the defense, a great roar up from the crowd, and above it, a relief to hear, the shrilling of the referee's whistle. My first thought was that at the snap of the ball the right side of the line had collapsed just at the second of the handoff, and one of the tacklers, Roger Brown or Floyd Peters, had cracked through to make me fumble. Someone, I assumed, had messed up on the assignments designated by the myserious code words "near oh pinch." In fact, as I discovered later, my *own man* bowled me over—John Gordy, whose assignment as offensive guard was to pull from his position and join the interference on the far side of the center. He was required to pull back and travel at a great clip parallel to the line of scrimmage to get out in front of the runner, his route theoretically passing between me and the center. But the extra second it took me to control the ball, and the creaking execution of my turn, put me in his path, a rare sight for Gordy to see, his own quarterback blocking the way, like coming around a corner in a high-speed car to find a moose ambling across the centerline, and he caromed off me, jarring the ball loose.

My confidence had not gone. I stood up. The referee took the retrieved ball from me. He had to tug to get it away, a faint look of surprise on his face. My inner voice was assuring me that the fault in the fumble had not been mine. "They let you down," it was saying. "The blocking failed." But the main reason for my confidence was the next play on my list—the ninety-three pass, a play which I had worked successfully in the Cranbrook scrimmages. I walked into the huddle and I said with considerable enthusiasm, "All right! All *right*! Here we *go*!"

"Keep the voice down," said a voice. "You'll be tipping them the play."

I leaned in on them and said: "Green right" (*Green* designated a pass play, *right* put the flanker to the right side), "three right" (which put the three back to the right), "ninety-three" (indicating the two primary receivers; nine, the right end, and three, the three back) "on *three . . . Break!*"—the clap of the hands again in unison, the team streamed past me up to the line, and I walked briskly up behind Whitlow.

Again, I knew exactly how the play was going to develop—back those seven yards into the defensive pocket for the three to four seconds it was supposed to hold, and Pietrosante, the three back, would go down in his pattern, ten yards straight, then cut over the middle, and I would hit him.

"Set! . . . sixteen! . . . eighty-eight . . . fifty-five . . . *but* one . . . *but* two . . . *but* three . . ."

The ball slapped into my palm at three. I turned and started back. I could feel my balance going, and two yards behind the line of scrimmage I *fell down*—absolutely flat, as if my feet had been pinned under a tripwire stretched across the field, not a hand laid on me. I heard a roar go up from the crowd. Suffused as I had been with confidence, I could scarcely believe what had happened. Mud cleats catching in the grass? Slipped in the dew? I felt my jaw go ajar in my helmet. "Wha'? Wha'?"—the mortification beginning to come fast. I rose hurriedly to my knees at the referee's whistle, and I could see my teammates' big silver helmets with the blue Lion decals turn toward me, some of the players rising from blocks they'd thrown to protect me, their faces masked, automaton, prognathous with the helmet bars protruding toward me, characterless, yet the dismay was in the set of their bodies as they loped back for the huddle. The schoolmaster's voice flailed at me inside my helmet. "Ox!" it cried. "Clumsy oaf."

I joined the huddle. "Sorry, sorry," I said.

"Call the play, man," came a voice from one of the helmets.

"I don't know what happened," I said.

"Call it, man."

The third play on my list was the forty-two, another running play, one of the simplest in football, in which the quarterback receives the snap, makes a full spin, and shoves the ball into the four back's stomach—the fullback's. He has come straight forward from his position as if off starting blocks, his knees high, and he disappears with the ball into the number-two hole just to the left of the center—a straight power play, and one which seen from the stands seems to offer no difficulty.

I got into an awful jam with it. Once again, the jackrabbitspeed of the professional backfield was too much for me. The fullback—Danny Lewis—was past me and into the line before I could complete my spin and set the ball in his belly. And so I did what was required: I tucked the ball into my own belly and followed Lewis into the line, hoping that he might have budged open a small hole.

I tried, grimacing, my eyes squinted almost shut, and waiting for the impact, which came before I'd taken two steps—I was grabbed up by Roger Brown.

He tackled me high, and straightened me with his power, so that I churned against his three-hundred-pound girth like a comic bicyclist. He began to shake me. I remained upright to my surprise, flailed back and forth, and I realized that he was struggling for the ball. His arms were around it, trying to tug it free. The bars of our helmets were nearly locked, and I could look through and see him inside—the first helmeted face I recognized that evening—the small, brown eyes surprisingly peaceful, but he was grunting hard, the sweat shining, and I had time to think, "It's Brown, it's *Brown!*" before I lost the ball to him, and flung to one knee on the ground I watched him lumber ten yards into the end zone behind us for a touchdown.

The referee wouldn't allow it. He said he'd blown the ball dead while we were struggling for it. Brown was furious. "You taking that away from *me,*" he said, his voice high and squeaky. "Man, I took that ball in there good."

The referee turned and put the ball on the ten-yard line. I had lost twenty yards in three attempts, and I had yet, in fact, to run off a complete play.

The veterans walked back very slowly to the next huddle.

I stood off to one side, listening to Brown rail at the referee. "I never scored like that befo'. You takin' that away from me?" His voice was peeved. He looked off toward the stands, into the heavy tumult of sound, spreading the big palms of his hands in grief.

I watched him, detached, not even moved by his insistence that I suffer the humiliation of having the ball stolen for a touchdown. If the referee had allowed him his score, I would not have protested. The shock of having the three plays go as badly as they had left me dispirited and numb, the purpose of the exercise forgotten. Even the schoolmaster's voice seemed to have gone—a bleak despair having set in so that as I stood shifting uneasily watching Brown jawing at the referee, I was perfectly willing to trot in to the bench at that point and be done with it.

Then, by chance, I happened to see Carl Brettschneider standing at his corner linebacker position, watching me, and beyond the bars of his cage I could see a grin working. That set my energies ticking over once again—the notion that some small measure of recompense would be mine if I could complete a pass in the Badger's territory and embarrass him. I had such a play in my series—a slant pass to the strong-side end, Jim Gibbons.

I walked back to the huddle. It was slow in forming. I said, "The Badger's asleep. He's fat and he's asleep."

No one said anything. Everyone stared down. In the silence I became suddenly aware of the feet. There are twenty-two of them in the huddle, after all, most of them very large, in a small area, and while the quarterback ruminates and the others await his instruction, there's nothing else to catch the attention. The sight pricked at my mind, the oval of twenty-two football shoes, and it may have been responsible for my error in announcing the play. I forgot to give the signal on which the ball was to be snapped back by the center. I said: "Green right nine slant *break*!" One or two of the players clapped their hands, and as the huddle broke, some of them automatically heading for the line of scrimmage, someone hissed: "Well, the *signal*, what's the signal, for chrissake."

I had forgotten to say "On two."

I should have kept my head and formed the huddle again. Instead I called out "Two!" in a loud stage whisper, directing my call first to one side, then the other. *"Two! two!"* as we walked up to the line. For those that might have been beyond earshot, who might have missed the signal, I held out two fingers spread like a *V,* which I showed around furtively, trying to hide it from the defense and hoping that my people would see.

The pass was incomplete. I took two steps back (the play was a quick pass, thrown without a protective pocket) and I saw Gibbons break from his position, then stop, buttonhooking; his hand, which I used as a target, came up, but I threw the ball over him. A yell came up from the crowd seeing the ball in the air (it was the first play of the evening which hadn't been "blown"—to use the player's expression for a missed play), but then a groan went up when the ball was overshot and bounced across the sidelines.

"Last play," George Wilson was calling. He had walked over with a clipboard in his hand and was standing by the referee. "The ball's on the ten. Let's see you take it all the way," he called out cheerfully.

One of the players asked: "Which end zone is he talking about?"

The last play of the series was a pitchout—called a flip on some teams—a long lateral to the number-four back running parallel to the line and cutting for the eight hole at left end. The lateral, though long, was easy for me to do. What I had to remember was to keep on running out after the flight of the ball. The hole behind me as I lateraled was left unguarded by an offensive lineman pulling out from his position and the defensive tackle could bull through and take me from behind in his rush, not knowing I'd got rid of the ball, if I didn't clear out of the area.

I was able to get the lateral off and avoid the tackler behind me, but unfortunately the defense was keyed for the play. They knew my repertoire, which was only five plays or so, and they doubted I'd call the same play twice. One of my linemen told me later that the defensive man opposite him in the line, Floyd Peters, had said, "Well, here comes the forty-eight pitchout," and it *had* come, and they were able to throw the number four back, Pietrosante, who had received that lateral, back on the one-yard line—just a yard away from the mortification of having moved a team backward from the thirty-yard line into one's own end zone for a safety.

As soon as I saw Pietrosante go down, I left for the bench on the sidelines at midfield, a long run from where I'd brought my team, and I felt utterly weary, shuffling along through the grass.

Applause began to sound from the stands, and I looked up, startled, and saw people standing, and the hands going. It made no sense at the time. It was not derisive; it seemed solid and respectful. Wha'? Wha'? I thought, and I wondered if the applause wasn't meant for someone else—if the mayor had come into the stadium behind me and was waving from an open-topped car. But as I came up to the bench I could see the people in the stands looking at me, and the hands going.

I thought about the applause afterward. Some of it was, perhaps, in appreciation of the lunacy of my participation and for the fortitude it took to do it; but most of it, even if subconscious, I decided was in *relief* that I had done as badly as I had: it verified the assumption that the average fan would have about an amateur blundering into the brutal world of professional football. He would get slaughtered. If by some chance I had uncorked a touchdown pass, there would have been wild acknowledgment—because I heard the groans go up at each successive disaster—but afterward the spectators would have felt uncomfortable. Their concept of things would have been upset. The outsider did not belong, and there was comfort in that being proved.

Some of the applause, as it turned out, came from people who had enjoyed the comic aspects of my stint. More than a few thought that they were being entertained by a professional comic in the tradition of baseball's Al Schacht, or the Charlie Chaplins, the clowns, of the bullfights. Bud Erickson, the public relations director, told me that a friend of his had come up to him later: "Bud, that's one of the funniest goddamn . . . I mean, that guy's *got* it," this man said, barely able to control himself.

I did not take my helmet off when I reached the bench. It was tiring to do and there was security in having it on. I was conscious of the big zero on my back facing the crowd when I sat down. Some players came by and tapped me on the top of the helmet. Brettschneider leaned down and said, "Well, you stuck it . . . that's the big thing."

The scrimmage began. I watched it for a while, but my mind returned to my own performance. The pawky inner voice was at hand again. "You didn't stick it," it said testily. "You funked it."

At half time Wilson took the players down to the bandshell at one end of the stadium. I stayed on the bench. He had his clipboards with him, and I could see him pointing and explaining, a big semicircle of players around him, sitting on the band chairs. Fireworks soared up into the sky from the other end of the field, the shells puffing out clusters of light that lit the upturned faces on the crowd in silver, then red, and then the reports would go off, reverberating sharply, and in the stands across the field I could see the children's hands flap up over their ears. Through the noise I heard someone yelling my name. I turned and saw a girl leaning over the rail of the grandstand behind me. I recognized her from the Gay Haven in Dearborn. She was wearing a mohair Italian sweater, the color of spun pink sugar, and tight pants, and she was holding a thick folding wallet in one hand along with a pair of dark glasses, and in the other a Lions banner, which she waved, her face alive with excitement, very pretty in a perishable, childlike way, and she was calling, "Beautiful; it was beautiful."

The fireworks lit her, and she looked up, her face chalk white in the swift aluminum glare.

I looked at her out of my helmet. Then I lifted a hand, just tentatively.

As I wrote in the opening pages of *Open Net* (from which this extract is taken), ice hockey was one sport I never thought I would participate in at the professional level. I am very poor on skates. I have weak ankles. Friends joke that I am the same height on the ice as I am off. Nonetheless, arrangements to train as a goaltender were made through *Sports Illustrated* and I found myself in Fitchburg, Massachusetts, where the Bruins have their training facility. Before going, I had my protective face mask decorated with a large blue eye in the hope this might distract the wings coming down the ice toward me. My roommate, a fellow goaltender, pointed out how much the mask looked like a target. So I discarded it for another model. The Bruins were in a constant state of merriment about my troubles on the ice— especially my inability to stop sharply. Often I would crash into the boards to stop. The Bruins joked that I was the only hockey player who would check *himself* into the boards. There in Fitchburg, over the course of a couple of weeks, they tried to prepare me to face the Philadelphia Flyers in the Spectrum.

Hockey

Cherry read out the lines: Mike Forbes and Al Sims at defense, and the McNab line, with Dave Forbes and Terry O'Reilly at the wings, would start. He read out my name as the goaltender somewhat perfunctorily, I thought, making nothing of it in any jocular way, as if it were a perfectly natural choice to make, and then he looked over at me and said: "It's time. Lead them out."

I put on my mask and clumped to the locker room door. I had forgotten my stick. Someone handed it to me. I was the first Bruin in the tunnel. I could hear the Bruins beginning to yell behind me as we started out.

The tunnel to the rink is dark, with the ice right there at its lip, so that one flies out of it, like a bat emerging from a cast-iron pipe, into the brightest sort of light—the ice a giant opaque glass. The great banks of spectators rose up from it in a bordering mass out of which cascaded a thunderous assault of boos and catcalls. Cherry was right. The Bruins were not at all popular in Philadelphia.

We wheeled around on our half of the ice . . . the Flyers in theirs. There was no communication between the two teams; indeed, the players seemed to put their heads down as they approached the centerline, sailing by within feet of each other without so much as a glance. My roommate, Seaweed, had told me: "In hockey you don't talk to the guys from the other team at all, ever. You don't pick him up when he falls down, like in football." He told me about a pregame warm-up in the Soviet–Canada series in which Wayne Cashman had spotted a Russian player coming across the centerline to chase down a puck that had escaped their zone; Cashman had skated over to intercept him and checked him violently into the boards. "Well, the guy was in the wrong place," Seaweed said when I expressed my astonishment. "He should have known better."

I skated over to the boards, working at the clasp at my chin to adjust my mask. The fans leaned forward and peered in at me through the bars of the mask—as if looking into a menagerie cage at some strange inmate within. "Hey, lemme see." A face came into view, just inches away, the mouth ajar, and then it withdrew to be replaced by another, craning to see. I could hear the voice on the public-address system announcing me as the goaltender for a special five-minute game. The Bruins were motioning me to get in the goal. We were a minute or so away. I pushed off the boards and reached the goal in a slow glide, stopping and turning myself around slowly and carefully.

The three officials came out onto the ice. The organist was playing a bouncy waltzlike tune that one's feet tapped to almost automatically, but I noticed the officials pointedly tried not to skate to its rhythm as they whirled around the rink to warm up, perhaps because they would seem to demean their standings as keepers of order and decorum if they got into the swing of the music. They, too, came up and inspected me briefly, glancing through the bars of my mask without a word and with the same look of vague wonder that I had noticed from the fans.

The Bruins began skating by, cuffing at my pads with their sticks as they passed. Tapping the goaltender's pads is perhaps the most universal procedure just before the game—in most cases, of course, a simple gesture of encouragement, like a pat on the back.

I wobbled slightly in the crease from the impact of some of the stronger blows from my Bruin teammates as they skated by. I felt a surge of appreciation and warmth toward them for doing it. Two of the Bruins stopped and helped me rough up the ice in front of the cage—this a procedure so the goalie gets a decent purchase with his skate blades. Invariably it is done by the goalie himself—long, scraping side thrusts with skates to remove the sheen from the new ice. It occurred to me later that to be helped with this ritual was comparable to a pair of baseball players coming out to help a teammate get set in the batter's box, kneeling down and scuffing out toeholds for him, smoothing out the dirt, dusting his bat handle, and generally preparing things for him, as if the batter were as unable to shift for himself as a storefront mannequin. However odd this may have appeared from the stands—the three of us toiling away in front of the net—it added to my sense of common endeavor. "Thank you, thank you," I murmured.

Other Bruins stopped by while this was going on, and peering into my mask, they offered last-minute advice. "Chop 'em down! Chop 'em down!" I looked out at Bobby Schmautz and nodded. His jaw was moving furiously on some substance. "Chop 'em down!" he repeated as he skated off. Slowly the other Bruins withdrew, skating up the ice toward the bench or their positions to stand for the National Anthem.

I spent the anthem (which was a Kate Smith recording rather than the real article) wondering vaguely whether my face mask constituted a hat, and if I should remove it. My worry was that if I tampered with any of the equipment I might not have it in proper working order at the opening face-off. The puck would be dropped . . . and the Flyers would sail down the ice towards a goaltender who would be standing bare-headed, facedown, fiddling with the chin strap of his mask, his big mitt tucked under his arm to free his fingers for picking at the clasp, his stick lying across the top of the net . . . no, it was not worth contemplating. I sang loudly inside my mask to compensate for any irreverence.

A roar went up at the anthem's conclusion—something grim and anticipatory about that welter of sound, as if, oh my! we're really going to see something good now, and I saw the players at the center of the rink slide their skates apart, legs spread and stiff, their sticks down, the upper parts of their bodies now horizontal to the ice—a frieze of tension—and I knew the referee in his striped shirt, himself poised at the circle and ready for flight once he had dropped the puck, was about to trigger things off. I remember thinking, Please, Lord, don't let them score more than five—feeling that a goal a minute was a dismaying enough fate to plead against to a Higher Authority— and then I heard the sharp cracking of sticks against the puck.

For the first two minutes the Bruins kept the play in the Flyers' end. Perhaps they realized that a torrid offense was the only hope of staving off an awkward-sounding score. They played as if the net behind them were empty . . . as if their goalie had been pulled in the last minute of a game they had hoped to tie with the use of an extra forward. I saw the leg pad of the Flyers' goaltender fly up to deflect a shot.

Well, this isn't bad at all, I thought.

There can be nothing easier in sport than being a hockey goalie when the puck is at the opposite end. Nonchalance is the proper attitude. One can do a little housekeeping, sliding the ice shavings off to one side with the big stick. Humming a short tune is possible. Tretiak, the Russian goaltender, had a number of relaxing exercises he would put himself through when the puck was at the opposite end of the rink. He would hunch his shoulder muscles, relaxing them, and he'd make a conscious effort to get the wrinkles out of his brow. "To relax, pay attention to your face. Make it smooth," he would add, the sort of advice a fashion model might tend to.

It is a time for reflection and observation. During a static spell Ken Dryden from the Montreal goal noticed that the great game clock that hung above the Boston Garden was slightly askew.

With the puck at the other end, it was not unlike (it occurred to me) standing at the edge of a mill pond, looking out across a quiet expanse at some vague activity at the opposite end almost too far to be discernible— could they be bass fishing out there?—but then suddenly the distant, aimless, waterbug scurrying becomes an oncoming surge of movement as every-thing—players, sticks, the puck—starts coming on a direct line, almost as if a *tsunami,* that awesome tidal wave of the South Pacific, had suddenly materi-alized at the far end of the mill pond and was beginning to sweep down toward one.

"A tsunami?" a friend of mine had asked.

"Well, it *is* like that," I said. "A great encroaching wave full of things being borne along toward you full tilt—hockey sticks, helmets, faces with no teeth in them, those black, barrellike hockey pants, the skates, and some-where in there that awful puck. And then, of course, the noise."

"The noise?"

"Well, the crowd roars as the wings come down the ice, and so the noise seems as if it were being generated by the wave itself. And then there's the racket of the skates against the ice, and the thump of bodies against the boards, and the crack of the puck against the sticks. And then you're inclined to do a little yelling yourself inside your face mask—the kind of sounds cartoon characters make when they're agonized."

"Arrrgh?"

"Exactly. The fact is it's very noisy all of a sudden, and not only that, but it's very crowded. You're joined by an awful lot of people," I said, "and very quickly. There's so much movement and scuffling at the top of the crease that you feel almost smothered."

What one was trained to do in this situation, I told my friend, was to keep one's eye on the puck at all costs. I only had fleeting glimpses of it—it sailed elusively between the skates and sticks, as shifty as a rat in a hedgerow: it seemed impossible to forecast its whereabouts . . . my body jumped and swayed in a series of false starts. Cheevers had explained to me that at such moments he instinctively understood what was going on, acutely aware of the patterns developing, to whose stick the puck had gone, and what the player was likely to do with it. The motion of the puck was as significant to him as the movement of a knight on a chessboard. His mind busied itself with possibilities and solutions. For me, it was enough to remember the simplest of Cheevers' instructions: "Stand up! Keep your stick on the ice!"

The first shot the Flyers took went in. I had only the briefest peek at the puck . . . speeding in from the point off to my right, a zinger, and catching the net at the far post, tipped in on the fly, as it turned out, by a Philadelphia player named Kindrachuk, who was standing just off the crease. The assists were credited to Rick Lapointe and Barry Dean. I heard this melancholy news over the public-address system, just barely distinguishing the names over the uproar of a Philadelphia crowd pleased as punch that a Bruins team had been scored on, however circumspect and porous their goaltender.

Seaweed had given me some additional last-minute tips at training camp on what to do if scored upon. His theory was that the goaltender should never suggest by his actions on the ice that he was in any way responsible for what had happened. The goalie should continue staring out at the rink in a poised crouch (even if he was aware that the puck had smacked into the nets behind) as if he had been thoroughly screened and did not know the shot had been taken. In cases where being screened from the shot was obviously not a contributing cause of the score, Seaweed suggested making a violent, abusive gesture at a defense man, as if that unfortunate had made the responsible error.

When the Flyer goal was scored, I had not the presence or the inclination to do any of the things Seaweed had recommended. I yelled loudly in dismay and beat the side of my face mask with my catching glove. I must have seemed a portrait of guilt and ineptitude. "I didn't see the damn thing!" I called out. As I reached back to remove the puck, the thought pressed in on my mind that the Flyers had scored on their very first attempt—their shooting average was perfect.

What small sense of confidence I might have had was further eroded when soon after the face-off following the Philadelphia goal, one of the Bruins went to the penalty box for tripping; the Flyers were able to employ their power play, and for the remainder of the action the puck stayed in the Bruins' zone.

I have seen a film taken of those minutes—in slow motion so that my delayed reactions to the puck's whereabouts are emphasized. The big catching mitt rises and flaps slowly long after the puck has passed. There seems to be a near-studied attempt to keep my back to the puck. The puck hits my pads and turns me around, so that then my posture is as if I wished to see if anything interesting happened to be going on in the nets behind me. While the players struggle over the puck, enticingly in front the crease, the camera catches me staring into the depths of the goal, apparently oblivious of the melee immediately behind me.

The film also shows that I spent a great deal of the time flat on the ice; alas, just where Cheevers and Seaweed had warned me not to be. Not much had to happen to put me there—a nudge, the blow of the puck. Once a hard shot missed the far post, and in reaching for it, down I went, as if blown over by the passage of the puck going by. The film shows me for an instant, grasping one of my defense man's legs, his stick and skates locked in my grasp as I try to haul myself back upright, using him like a drunk enveloping a lamppost.

Actually, my most spectacular save was made when I was prostrate on the ice . . . the puck appearing under my nose, quite inexplicably, and I was able to clap my glove over it. I could hear the Bruins breathing and chortling as they clustered over me to protect the puck from being probed out by a Flyer stick.

What was astonishing about those hectic moments was that the Flyers did not score. Five of their shots were actually on goal . . . but by chance my body, in its whirligig fashion, completely independent of what was going on, happened to be in the right place when the puck appeared.

A friend, who was observing from the seats, said the highest moment of comic relief during all this was when one of the Flyers' shots came in over my shoulder and hit the top bar of the cage and ricocheted away.

"What was funny," my friend said, "was that at first there was absolutely no reaction from you at all—there you were in the prescribed position, slightly crouched, facing out toward the action, stick properly down on the ice and all, and then the puck went by you, head high, and went off that crossbar like a golf ball cracking off a branch; it wasn't until four or five seconds, it seemed, before your head slowly turned and sneaked a look at where the puck had . . . well . . . *clanged.* It was the ultimate in the slow double take."

"I don't remember," I said. "I don't recall any clanging."

"Hilarious," my friend said. "Our whole section was in stitches."

Then, just a few seconds before my five-minute stint was up, Mike

Milbury, one of the Bruins' defense men out in front of me, threw his stick across the path of a Flyers wing coming down the ice with the puck. I never asked him why. Perhaps I had fallen down and slid off somewhere, leaving the mouth of the net ajar, and he felt some sort of desperate measure was called for. More likely he had been put up to it by his teammates and Don Cherry. Actually, I was told a *number* of sticks had been thrown. The Bruins wanted to be sure that my experience would include the most nightmarish challenge a goaltender can suffer . . . alone on the ice and defending against a shooter coming down on him one-on-one. The penalty shot!

At first, I did not know what was happening. I heard the whistles going. I got back into the nets. I assumed a face-off was going to be called. But the Bruins started coming by the goal mouth, tapping me on the pads with their hockey sticks as they had at the start of things, faint smiles, and then they headed for the bench, leaving the rink enormous and stretching out bare from where I stood. I noticed a huddle of players over by the Philadelphia bench.

Up in Fitchburg I had been coached on what the goaltender is supposed to do against the penalty shot . . . which is, in fact, how he maneuvers against the breakaway: as the shooter comes across the blue line with the puck, the goaltender must emerge from the goal mouth and skate out toward him—this in order to cut down the angle on the goal behind him. The shooter at this point has two choices: he can shoot, if he thinks he can whip the puck past the oncoming, hustling bulk of the goaltender, slapping it by on either side; or he can keep the puck on his stick and try to come *around* the goalie; in this case, of course, the goalie must brake sharply and then scuttle backward swiftly, always maneuvering to keep himself between the shooter and the goal mouth. I would always tell Seaweed or Cheevers, whomever I was chatting with about the penalty shot, that I had to hope the shooter, if this situation ever came up, did not know that I was not able to stop. All the shooter had to do was come to a stop himself, stand aside, and I would go sailing by him, headed for the boards at the opposite end of the rink.

Penalty shots do not come up that often. Gump Worsley in his twenty-one-year career had only faced two, both of which he was unsuccessful against—not surprising perhaps, because the goals came off the sticks of Gordie Howe and Boom-Boom Geoffrion. But Seaweed had told me—despite the Gump Worsley statistics—that he thought the chances favored the goaltender . . . that by skating out and controlling the angle the goalie could force the shooter to commit himself. Also, he pointed out that since the shooter was the only other player on the ice, the goaltender always had a bead on the puck, whereas in the flurry of a game he had often lost sight of it in a melee, or had it tipped in by another player, or passed across the ice to a position requiring a quick shift in the goal. Others agreed with him. Emile Francis believed that the goaltender should come up with a save three times out of five. He pointed out while the goaltender is under considerable pressure; so is the other fellow—the humiliation of missing increased because the shooter *seems* to have the advantage . . . the predator, swift and rapacious, swooping in on a comparatively immobile defender. The compiled statistics seem to bear him out. Up until the time I joined the Bruins, only one penalty shot out of the ten taken in Stanley Cup play has resulted in a score—Wayne Connelly's of the Minnesota North Stars in 1968 off Terry Sawchuck.

The confidence that might have been instilled by knowing such statistics was by no means evident in my own case. I stood in the cage, staring out at the empty rink, feeling lonely and put upon, the vast focus of the crowd narrowing on me as it was announced over the public-address system that Reggie Leach would take the penalty shot. Leach? Leach? The name meant little to me. I was told afterward his nickname is the Rifle. I had heard only one thing that I could remember about him from my résumé of Flyers players, which was that he had scored five goals in a play-off game, a record. I dimly recalled that he was an Indian by birth. Also a slap-shot specialist . . . just enough information to make me prickle with sweat under my mask.

I gave one final instruction to myself—murmuring audibly inside the cage of my face mask that I was not to remain rooted helplessly in the goal mouth, mesmerized, but to launch myself out toward Leach . . . and just then I spotted him, moving out from the boards, just beyond the blue line, picking up speed, and I saw the puck cradled in the curve of his stick blade.

As he came over the blue line, I pushed off and skated briskly out to meet him, windmilling my arms in my haste, and as we converged, I committed myself utterly to the hope that he would shoot rather than try to come around me. I flung myself sideways to the ice (someone said later that it looked like the collapse of an ancient sofa), and sure enough he *did* shoot. Somewhat perfunctorily, he lifted the puck and it hit the edge of one of my skates and skidded away, wide of the goal behind me.

A very decent roar of surprise and pleasure exploded from the stands. By this time, I think, the Philadelphia fans thought of me less as a despised Bruin than a surrogate member of their own kind. I represented a manifestation of their own curiosity if they happened to find themselves down there on the ice. As for the Bruins, they came quickly off the bench, scrambling over the boards to skate out in a wave of black and gold. It occurred to me that they were coming out simply to get me back up on my skates—after all, I was flat out on the ice—but they wore big grins: they pulled me up and began cuffing me around in delight, the big gloves smothering my mask so I could barely see as in a thick joyous clump we moved slowly to the bench. Halfway there, my skates went out from under me—tripped up, perhaps, or knocked askew by the congratulatory pummels—and once again I found myself down at ice level; they hauled me up like a sack of potatoes and got me to the bench. I sat down. It was a very heady time. I beamed at them. Someone stuck the tube of a plastic bottle in my mouth. The water squirted in and I choked briefly. A towel was spread around my shoulders.

"How many saves?"

"Oh, twenty or thirty. At least."

"What about that penalty shot?"

"Leach is finished. He may not play again. To miss a penalty shot against you? The Flyers may not recover."

I luxuriated in what they were saying.

"Is that right?"

But their attention began to shift back to the ice. The game was starting up again. The sound of the crowd was different: full and violent. I looked up and down the bench for more recognition. I wanted to hear more. I wanted to tell them what it had been like. Their faces were turned away now.

Sports Illustrated assigned me to do a long piece on George Bush and his athletic background. He was within a month of becoming the president. We met at the Naval Observatory, which is the official residence of the vice president.

Horseshoes

The atmosphere was very relaxed. The interview went well. The president-elect talked a lot about fishing—how it gave him time to relax from the rigors of work, and to do some contemplative thinking. He quoted Izaak Walton's line that says the day a man spends fishing ought not be deducted from his time on earth. He'd had only one long spell of government duty without fishing and that was when he served as chief of the U.S. Liaison Office in Beijing from 1974 to '75. At a Soviet embassy party he was invited to sit in a boat at one end of a ceremonial pool. At the other, an army of beaters got in the water and started driving a school of large carp toward him.

"Scary," Bush said. "Hundreds of these gigantic carp crashing around in the water. We waited for them with nets on the end of poles."

Barbara Bush remembered that what was caught was immediately cleaned by the Russian kitchen staff and prepared to take home. "The Russians had a beautiful complex built during the time of Peter the Great," she said. "They entertained a lot."

"Hockey games," the president-elect said. "On the lake. I was never much of a skater so I didn't go out on the ice. I don't like to do things I can't do well. I don't dance well, so I don't dance.

"See this scar here?" he asked suddenly. He pointed to the back of his hand. A six-pound bluefish off Florida had nipped him. "Then I've got a scar here close to my eyebrow from a collision trying to head a ball playing soccer at Andover. Can't see it? Well, how about *this* one?" He pulled his shirt away from his neck to reveal a prominent bump on his right shoulder blade. "Got that one playing mixed doubles with Barbara at Kennebunkport. Ran into a porch."

"His mother always said that it was my shot," Barbara Bush said. "I didn't run for it, so he did. She was probably right."

The president-elect smiled and shrugged his shoulders. "Popped the shoulder out," he said. "Separated."

"After that they moved the porch," his wife said with a smile.

Bush said that he had been playing tennis since he was about five. He had stopped singles not long after grade school and concentrated on doubles, largely because his ground strokes were "terrible" except for a backhand chip return of service that drops at the feet of the oncoming server and which he referred to as the "falling leaf."

"The what, sir?" I asked.

"The falling leaf." He went on to say that at the net is the only place where he feels completely at home and he will come in at every opportunity, even behind a second serve. "Or even the falling leaf," he added with a laugh.

A number of other homegrown phrases had developed in the Bush family over the years, and I was told what some of them were. A weak shot elicits the disdainful cry, "Power outage!" The most esoteric is "Unleash Chiang"—from the hue and cry in government circles to allow Chiang Kai-shek to invade the Chinese mainland from Taiwan and which, on the Bush court, refers to a potential source of power.

"George will look over his shoulder," Barbara Bush explained, "and urge his partner to 'unleash Chiang!' "

"The interesting thing about these phrases," she went on, "is that they get exported; people take them with them, and off in the distance, from someone else's court, you'll suddenly hear, 'All right, now, unleash Chiang!' "

When the interview was over, the president-elect looked at me and asked, "Hey, how about a game of horseshoes. You've done all these things . . . football with the . . ."

"Detroit Lions."

"Right. And the Boston Bruins and all that. You gotta try some horseshoes."

I nodded and said it would be a great honor.

On the way out to the horseshoe court, Barbara Bush stopped me. "You'll have to wear a cowboy hat," she said. "No one with any self-respect plays horseshoes without a cowboy hat." She rummaged around in a closet just inside the front door. On a top shelf sat an assortment of Bush's hats.

I tried on a few of the western variety. His head is a lot larger than mine, so the hats tended to slide down my forehead nearly to my eyes.

"These hats all seem to be the same size," I remarked, a somewhat lunatic observation since it implied Mr. Bush wore hats of different head measurements.

I finally picked a tall-crowned model with the president-elect's name stamped in gold on the inside. I wore it out to the horseshoe pit at a curious, raked angle so that I could see where I was going. The president-elect stared briefly at it. His was decorated with a braided Indian cord that supplemented the hatband. He held out some horseshoes.

"You got a choice," he said. "The drop-forged eight or the ten."

"I'll take the . . . ah."

The president-elect laughed. He looked down at the horseshoes, hefting them to judge their weight. "I don't know the difference myself," he said. "They tell me the harder the metal, the more it tends to be rejected by the stake."

Then he explained the rules—one point for the shoe closest to the stake and three for the ringer; the winner would be the first to reach fifteen. We took some practice throws. I threw my shoes so that they revolved, parallel to the ground, toward the opposite stake. This somewhat startled the president-elect since that is the style (though I was unaware of it) used by most top-flight pitchers.

"Hey, what have we got here?" he asked suspiciously. He prefers to hold the shoe at its closed end and toss it so it turns once, ass over teakettle, as it goes down the pitch.

"You played this game before?"

"Not for thirty years," I said truthfully.

The game began. The president-elect was supported loudly by his grand-daughter Jenna, who is seven, seated at courtside bundled up in a bright orange parka. There was considerable chatter during play—needling and a plethora of the homegrown expressions: "power outage" for a halfhearted toss, "SDI" for a throw with a higher arc than usual, and "It's an ugly pit" for those times when no one's shoe was close to the stake. Once, it was impossible to tell which of the two shoes had landed closer; the president-elect shouted, "The tool! Get the tool!"—a request that was echoed by those standing around watching.

The tool, which was fetched from the gardening shed, turned out to be oversized navigator's dividers. The president-elect knelt in the pit and brushed the dirt away from the two horseshoes. He handled the gadget with great relish. In fact, all aspects of the game were carried on with great élan. On occasion he would turn to me and ask the rhetorical question: "Isn't this game great? Have you ever had a better time? Isn't this just great? *Heaven!*"

I *was* having a good time. The iron felt cool and comfortable to the grip. I peered out from under the brim of my hat and suddenly, after a number of one-pointers, threw a ringer. I found myself with fourteen points and only one to go to win. The president-elect had thirteen. Cries of alarm rose from Jenna's chair.

I began to worry about winning. What would it do to the president-elect's confidence to lose to someone who hadn't thrown a horseshoe in thirty years? Would he brood? Suddenly slam the heel of his hand against his forehead at cabinet meetings? Stumble into the bushes in the Rose Garden? Talk out loud to himself at state dinners? Snap at Sununu?

I decided that I would credit my victory to the hat. "Beginner's luck," I was going to say. "And this hat of yours. If it hadn't been for this cowboy hat . . ."

It seemed the perfect solution. Gracious. Self-effacing. Just the thing to say.

"Listen, we can't let this happen," the president-elect was saying as he stepped up to throw. He sighted down the pitch. As he swung his arm back he produced one of his homegrown motivators; it wasn't "Unleash Chiang!" in this case. "Remember Iowa!" he called out, in reference to his recovery from political adversity there during the primaries. We watched the red horseshoe leave his hand, turn over once in flight, drop toward the pit with its prongs forward and, with a dreadful clang, collect itself around the stake. A ringer! Sixteen points and the victory for the president-elect. He flung his arms straight up in triumph, a tremendous smile on his face. From her chair Jenna began yelping pleasantly.

I said as follows: "Nerts!"

I can't recall the last time I had used that antique expression. The president-elect came toward me, his hand outstretched. "Isn't that great!" he said as I congratulated him. He wasn't talking about his win but the fact that the game had been so much fun. I agreed with him. *"Heaven!"* he said.

We walked back up to the residence. Up on the porch, Mrs. Bush suggested that we leave our shoes, muddy from the horseshoe pitch, by the front door so we wouldn't track mud on the carpets. I stepped out of my loafers. One of my socks had a hole in it. My big toe shone briefly until I pulled the sock forward so that it dangled off the front of my foot, flopping as I followed the president-elect into the house. He wanted to give me a tour of the premises. I followed him upstairs, first to his closet-sized office with its photographs of the cigarette boat *Fidelity,* which he takes out for bluefishing, and a mounted bonefish (TEN POUNDS, EIGHT OUNCES, reads the plaque under it), a little rubber shark riding its back, tossed up there by a grandchild.

We went up to a dormitory-like room at the top of the house where the older Bush children bunk out on the floor in sleeping bags when they come to visit. The nearest thing to a trophy case is up there—a shelf cluttered with the kind of shoebox mementos one might find in the back of a teenager's closet: scuffed baseballs, one of them, I noted, signed by Joe DiMaggio with the inscription, "You make the office look great"; a football autographed by Roger Staubach, who wrote, "Thanks for giving a darn about friends"; a Keith Hernandez–model first baseman's mitt; a Chicago Cubs pennant; a 1988 Dodgers World Series baseball cap; an NASL soccer ball; two construction worker's hard hats; and a blood-red Arkansas Razorback novelty hat shaped like a boar's head. The president-elect took the hat off the shelf and tried it on, the snout poking over his forehead.

"I'm not sure it suits you, sir," I said. "It would startle your constituency."

"Not in Arkansas," he said, putting it back.

He picked up one of the baseballs and began tossing it in his hand. "Now the only time I handle these is throwing out ceremonial balls." He began describing one of his more embarrassing moments when—apparently hampered by a bulletproof vest—at an opening-day ceremony he had bounced a ball halfway to the Houston Astros' catcher. "You tend to forget the distance," he said. "It's a question of raising your sights. You learn. Next time it's going to be right on target."

As we came down the stairs a small group was standing in the foyer—members of his cabinet-elect. I recognized Quayle, Sununu, the chief of staff, and Nick Brady, the secretary of the treasury. Scowcroft. Apparently the president-elect had scheduled a staff meeting. The toe of my stocking hung over a step. Sununu apparently knew something about my career as a participatory journalist. "Hey," he called up merrily. "A new cabinet member?"

The president-elect came to the door with me. As I stepped back into my loafers he urged me to come back for a rematch. "When the White House horseshoe court is ready, there'll be a ribbon-cutting ceremony. Got to come down for that."

I said I would. "I'm bringing my own cowboy hat this time," I said.

It was evident enough that participatory journalism could be extended beyond the world of sports. I did a number of these—some of them for hour-long television documentaries (all of them produced by David Wolper): playing a small role in a Western starring John Wayne, trying my hand as a stand-up comedian (at Caesars Palace in Las Vegas), practicing wildlife photography in Africa, performing in the Clyde Beatty–Cole Brothers circus as a trapeze artist and known among my fellow performers as "The Flying Telephone Pole." What follows is an account of playing with the New York Philharmonic orchestra. David Wolper's people filmed what went on for a Bell Telephone Hour special. What made this participation especially agonizing for me (and surely for Leonard Bernstein, the conductor) was that the performances in which I played were not rehearsals but the real thing. A mishap on my part would surely be noted by critics sitting in the auditorium and by those musically knowledgeable, and indeed by the entire audience if I did something major such as dropping the cymbals on the concert hall stage. I was intimidated not only by the importance of my role, but especially by Bernstein. I had known him before I joined his orchestra. He was a good friend of various members of my family, especially those involved in music in New York, such as my father, who was on the Board of Directors of the symphony. It was always such a pleasure to see "Lenny," as everyone called him, at various gatherings. But not so much afterwards. Part of it was having been in the presence of such genius. Whatever, now the sudden sight of him at a cocktail party, say, gets my heart thumping and I either sidle out the door or mosey up to the bar. What follows might suggest why.

Music: An Address at a New York Philharmonic Lunch

I am often asked which of the participatory exercises I have been involved in was the most frightening. People are always startled when I say that the one that frightened me the most was not playing football with the professionals, or basketball, or boxing, but when I played with the New York Philharmonic.

I played the triangle. And some of the other percussion instruments.

One reason it was terrifying was that in music you cannot make a mistake. Almost all sports are predicated on the concept of an error being a determinant in the outcome: in tennis you put a twist on the ball in the hope your opponent will make an error; in boxing you feint and hope the other fellow is going to drop his guard so you can pop him; football is an immense exercise in trying to get the other people to make mistakes—not be where they should be.

But in music you cannot make a mistake. It is not part of the *zeitgeist*. If you make a mistake, a big one, you destroy a work of art. The thought of doing this nags, of course, at the consciousness of all musicians, even the very good ones. In the rehearsal rooms of the great concert halls the musicians getting ready for an important concert have that same glazed look I have seen on the faces of professionals going out to face the Chicago Bears. In fact, I got to know a violinist with the Philharmonic who told me he was so frightened of making a mistake—especially in rehearsals, where the conductor can stop everything and glare at you and point out that it's a B-flat not a B—that he toyed with the idea of putting soap on the strings of his violin so that when he played it hardly any sound would emerge off it. The idea was to do this until he got a surer sense of where he was—got his confidence.

Well, you can imagine what all this did to *my* sense of well-being! My

74

knowledge of music is extremely skimpy. I'd gone to Leonard Bernstein, the great conductor, and asked him if I could join the Philharmonic on its forthcoming month-long tour of Canada . . . so that I could look into the workings of a world-class orchestra. Mr. Bernstein knew of my work. He'd read some of my things, I think; he used to refer to me as the "amateur professional." On this occasion he asked a rather obvious question. What could I play?

A word about this. I play a very sketchy sort of piano. I had taken years of the obligatory music lessons. Little snatches are left . . . a few bars of a Chopin étude, the opening scale of *Rhapsody in Blue,* the March from *Aida.* Some Wagner motifs (played with one hand). My two strong efforts are "Deep Purple" and "Tea for Two." Even here I often have to back up and rush my fingers, rusty from disuse on the keyboard, through the obscure parts in the forlorn hope they can find their way.

Sight-reading is beyond me—my manner at it to this day not unlike an early archaeologist working out the hieroglyphics on the Rosetta stone. At Christmastime my family drags out what they're singing while I search for the next chord. I told Mr. Bernstein about "Deep Purple" and "Tea for Two."

He said, "Well, we don't have much need for those things around here." He sent me off to learn percussion—to join the group far in the back of the orchestra in what he referred to as the "Shady Corner."

What a crew they were: Saul Goodman, the head tympanist, who taught me how to hold the triangle and to bounce the metal rod off the steel to get different effects; Buster Bailey, who wore a beret and was a circus buff: he sat in on the circus bands when they came to town, playing the long snare drum rolls when the trapeze artist was about to launch himself into the triple somersault; Walter Rosenberg, the baseball fan who listened to the games with a plug in his ear during rehearsals. He was the manager and coach of the Philharmonic's baseball team, which, appropriately enough, was called the Penguins. They played in the Theater League. You could tell which ones were the violin players. They had to worry about their fingers, so when a ball was hit toward them they turned and ran alongside until it had just about stopped; then they would pounce on it and throw the ball to second base. The violinists were always throwing the ball to second base.

Back there in the Shady Corner they helped me as best they could. During the rehearsals one of them would lean over and point to where we were in the score, or whisper how many bars before I was supposed to come in. They swayed toward me at the moment of commitment as if bodily willing me to pick up the conductor's cue and perform properly. I would stare bleakly at Bernstein over the top of the triangle, metal rod gripped tightly, and look for the slight roll of the eye, or some insignificant gesture in the whirlwind of his movements that suggested my time had indeed come. Then "ping!"

Bernstein waved his baton from side to side signifying he wanted to stop to go over things—first the violins, about the bowing at a certain point, then the woodwinds, a little adjustment here please, a certain phrasing, perhaps a little joke with Harold Gomberg, the great oboist, a vocal exhortation as to how he wanted the horns to sound—"Vaa-*room!*" or whatever—and then from the podium across all those heads he would look at me.

"Now, George."

This would be followed by the sound of chairs shifting slightly, the musicians turning, because they knew that Lenny, as everyone called him, was going to have a little fun.

"George, would you play that note for us again."

I picked up the triangle. "Ping!"

"Again, please."

"Ping!"

"Once more, please," cupping his hand behind his ear.

"Ping!"

A pause for effect. "Now which one of those do you mean?" he asked.

"They're all different."

Guffaws.

"Practice, practice, practice," Bernstein would call out, and turn back to his score.

I never had the sass to join in the fun ("Pick the one you like, Lenny") or anything like that. I stood ashen-faced, my heart pounding, and I'd think of my friends sitting at their desks at the publishing houses and the magazines with nothing really troubling their minds except where to have lunch.

Sometimes I would get an indication that I had played my part successfully. Musicians have a way of applauding each other while the music is still going on—a little quick shuffle of the foot on the floor of the concert stage. It's how they acknowledge another's brilliance. Harold Gomberg, for example, on completing an extremely difficult virtuoso passage, sets his oboe on his knee while all around him the feet shuffle—his fellow musicians saluting his artistry. When I would get past my entrances without error, all over the orchestra the feet shuffled, very likely out of relief. What an odd sight for an audience to puzzle over—the sudden convulsion of shoe shuffling as if an army of red ants, at some signal from a minuscule conductor, had attacked at ankle height simultaneously!

Well, off we went on the Canadian tour. We got to the town of London, Ontario, where we were scheduled to play Gustav Mahler's Fourth Symphony. That symphony starts off with eighteen strokes on the "sleigh bells"— an instrument in shape and size somewhat like a large corncob—with the bells (like the bells off a horse's harness) in rows along a center shaft. The musician holds the instrument by the handle (mine was a bright red) and taps or shakes it. The Mahler score calls for the percussionist to tap the sleigh bells with the tips of his fingers the requisite number of times, *diminuendo.* The notes are enormously important because they are the first thing one hears in the concert hall—crystalline, brilliant, rhythmic, and dying away at the end as the woodwinds come in.

The sleigh bells were in my charge.

Something happened in London, Ontario. To this day I have never known quite what. Mr. Bernstein walked onto the stage, a great accolade from the audience greeting him; he bowed; he turned to his orchestra, nodded at them, and then he looked across all those heads at me poised in the Shady Corner, holding the bells out in front of me, ready to tap them and get things going. I was petrified.

A curious expression crossed his face. I have thought about it since— slightly forlorn, wistful, pleading perhaps, as if hoping against hope that things would be all right. He raised his baton. The whites of his eyes shone as he peered up at the ceiling. His mouth went slightly ajar.

I began tapping away. I may have hit the instrument twenty-three times, carried away in my terror. Or not enough. Or raggedly. In any case, I knew something had gone wrong. First of all, there was no shuffling of feet. Anywhere. I looked. Not only that, but the shoulders of the musicians immediately in front were sort of curled forward. Not very encouraging. My fellow percussionists stared straight ahead. During the symphony on more than one occasion Mr. Bernstein glanced over—a tense, exasperated look on his face, almost accusatory, as if I had involved him in a monstrous practical joke of which he did not approve. Indeed, after the symphony ended he appeared backstage, looking for me. In a near shout he informed me that I had "destroyed" Mahler's Fourth, that he never wanted to hear such a terrible sound emerge from the back of his orchestra ever again, and that as far as he was concerned I was finished, *through!* And with that, this tortured man turned and rushed out into the Canadian night. I stared after him, appalled.

You can imagine my feelings at this point . . . told that I had destroyed a symphony, disgraced the orchestra: cast out from the Shady Corner into the wilds of Ontario, somewhere north of the Canadian border.

The percussion gang turned up. They crowded around. They assured me that I had nothing to worry about. "A typical conductor's tantrum," one of them said. "You'll be back with the orchestra tomorrow."

They took me out on the town in London to help me forget. We went to a number of saloons. They kept telling me stories about musicians, mostly percussionists, who had—as they put it—"gone wrong." They thought that would make me feel better. They told me one involving the loudest sound in music—which is purportedly the cannon-firing in Tchaikovsky's *1812* Overture. Outdoors this is done with real cannon, fireworks, and so forth. Indoors, the percussionist stands backstage, peering through a little hole in the backdrop, and when he gets the cue from the conductor he fires a kind of shotgun apparatus into a barrel—which produces the reverberating sound of cannonading that is called for in the score. On the occasion they described, which was back in the old Carnegie Hall days of the Philharmonic, the percussionist (his finger perhaps tightening on the trigger involuntarily) fired off this instrument *sixty* bars too early. Some of the musicians out in front thought a suicide had occurred back there!

There were other stories. They described how a cymbal player had clapped his instrument in some vast orchestral climax and one of the cymbals had fallen off and rolled among the musicians' chairs like a hubcap on a highway. They told me about a man playing the chimes—those cylinders that hang from an iron frame—and that rather than hitting the longest of the cylinders, the one that hangs right next to the framework, he stared at the conductor for his cue and then with his hammer rapped the *framework,* hit the iron, *clunk!* "Overture to *Romeo and Juliet,*" one of them said. "Brought down the house!" They told me about a pianist with the Swiss National Symphony who had come out onto the stage, sat down at the grand piano in front of the orchestra, twiddled with the knobs on either side of her seat to get herself comfortable, nodded up at the conductor signifying that she was ready, and then brought her hands down in such an enormous concussive opening chord that she somehow dislodged the piano from its chocks and got it rolling; it picked up a little momentum and began moving for the footlights. They said that she had hunched along behind it, trying to do her best under very adverse conditions.

I have no doubt that some of their stories were apocryphal, especially the one about the woman pianist. They were doing their best to cheer me up. But my mind kept reverting to earlier that evening . . . Bernstein's pleading look, the sound of the sleigh bells, *clink clink clink,* startlingly loud in the silence of that huge auditorium, the rows of people stretching back . . . his despair . . .

Then one of the musicians—I think it was Walter Rosenberg—remembered that in a few nights in Winnipeg the orchestra was scheduled to play Tchaikovsky's Second Symphony, the *Little Russian.* At its conclusion, he said, there was an enormous explosive shot on the *gong.*

"It's a great moment," he went on. "Right at the end; comes in like an exclamation point! Then the violins play for a couple of measures and it's over."

The other musicians chimed in. We would go to see the maestro, Mr. Bernstein, to see if he would let me play the gong in Winnipeg. It would be exactly the therapy needed after the sleigh bells trouble. "You've fallen off the horse," one of them said. "Got to climb right back on."

"Hey," I said. "I'm not so sure about this." I went on to say that I knew nothing about Tchaikovsky's Second Symphony, wouldn't recognize it if I heard it and were given twenty guesses. More important, I had never played a gong, and while it was grave enough to make a mistake with the sleigh bells, or the triangle, it was quite another to do something wrong with a gong. "They'd know about it in Massachusetts," I said.

They were insistent. They whispered among themselves like conspirators. The next morning they pulled me out of bed and we went to see Mr. Bernstein. I was very reluctant. Mr. Bernstein was wearing a terry-cloth bathrobe, as I remember. He wouldn't look at me. The percussionists sort of propped me up against a wall. They pleaded with him. They said it would be very bad for my psychic well-being if I weren't given another chance. They said they would prepare me. On and on they went.

Finally, Mr. Bernstein looked at me. "All right," he said. "You can play the gong in Winnipeg on a number of conditions." His voice was exceedingly stern. "First of all I want you to watch me through the entire symphony. Don't look down at the music. We all know that you can't read music. You don't fool anybody when you turn the pages. It's disconcerting, all that shuffling back there. So keep your eye on me. About nine minutes or so into the last movement I will give you a cue the likes of which no musician has ever seen before. At that point," Mr. Bernstein said looking at me sharply, "smack it!"

So a day or so later there I was in Winnipeg, back in the Shady Corner, in my white tie and tails, standing behind the gong, which hung monstrously from its chains. The place was packed—music lovers who had piled in to hear the greatest orchestra in the world . . . not knowing that one of its musicians could only barely get through "Tea for Two" and "Deep Purple."

Mr. Bernstein appeared from the wings. Prolonged applause. He turned to face us and the symphony began.

One of the terrors of orchestral music is that once it starts there is no earthly way that you can stop it. It is utterly unlike sports where, if you think about it, the athlete has an almost God-like ability to stop time itself. The quarterback makes a crossed X sign to call time-out and everything stops. The batter steps out of the batter's box and everything stops. An Olympic diver, poised on the board, can take her time, wriggling her toes and getting herself feeling just right before she commits herself to arch off into the water below.

But in music, as soon as the conductor's stick comes down, one is immediately put onto a treadmill that bears one inexorably up toward the moment of commitment and there's nothing that can be done about it.

Well, we got into the fourth movement. I had taken hold of the big mallet almost as soon as the movement started—just to be sure, and to indicate to Mr. Bernstein that he was not going to catch me napping.

Some percussionists—I was told during my preparations—like to get the gong shimmering slightly just before hitting it. A more mellow sound is produced. One gets the gong trembling by barely touching the mallet to it, the slightest rubbing effect all that is needed. I didn't bother. I wasn't going to take any chances fiddling around with that gong, any more than I'd fool around with a large bottle of nitroglycerin. It hung immobile.

As we got into the fourth movement it seemed to me that every once in a while Mr. Bernstein would give me just the quickest of glances—perhaps in the hope that his nemesis had disappeared and that in his place would be the more reassuring presence of one of the Shady Corner professionals. Alas!

The music rushed on. It sounded vaguely familiar because I had been playing a tape of Tchaikovsky's Second over and over in my hotel room, Walter Rosenberg with me to coach and count the bars, pretending to be Mr.

Bernstein, and when he gave me the cue I whacked a pillow with a rolled-up newspaper. I got it right about three-quarters of the time.

This time, back there in the Shady Corner in the Winnipeg concert hall, Walter was not there to help me. He had his own duties. I stared at Mr. Bernstein. Suddenly, out of a flurry of movement, he looked across at me; his eyes opened wide so that the whites of them showed alarmingly in his face, his mouth dropped open, his stick pointed at me, and I reared back and hit the gong much harder than I intended. It was hit with all that pent-up energy and emotion and fear let loose . . . so hard that an enormous wave of sound welled up and swept out across the heads of the musicians—many of them half-turning in their chairs to see what had happened back there—past Mr. Bernstein, whose eyes popped even further as it went by him, and out into the auditorium, where it slowly dissipated as the violins came in.

I stood panic-stricken. My God, I thought, I've gone and done it! I've destroyed yet another symphony, and this one truly in spades.

But then while the violins sawed their way to the finale the *feet began going,* the shuffling of accolade everywhere across the stage. It took a bit to sink in. Apparently, it was all right. The symphony ended. Some of the musicians turned around and smiled as Mr. Bernstein bowed to the audience. I beamed. I waved my mallet. Walter touched me on the arm. "You hit it right on the button!"

"Piece of cake," I said.

Backstage Mr. Bernstein came up. He had a towel around his neck. "No one has ever hit a gong that hard," he said. His face was wreathed in smiles. "If Tchaikovsky heard it—which I'm quite sure he *did*—why, he would have been delighted!"

The Philharmonic musicians still joke about the enormous noise I produced. They call it the "Winnipeg Sound." When Mr. Bernstein wants a really loud *fortissimo* during rehearsal, he calls out, "All right, I'd like the Winnipeg Sound, if you please!"

Someone from the front office called the other day. They said that the Philharmonic was planning to record the *Little Russian.* They hoped I would come down to the recording studio and (as they put it) "unleash the Winnipeg Sound."

So I did. I went down and whacked it again. They got me to tone it down just a bit. But not much. Perhaps they'll list my name on the back of the album cover as a soloist: *Gong . . . Plimpton.* That would be nice, wouldn't it? It would indicate that at least once in the parlous world of participatory journalism I had enjoyed a small success.

PERSONAGES

Marianne Moore

Until we went out to the Stadium for the second game of the World Series I had not met Marianne Moore. She had written some kind words about a baseball book I'd done a few years ago. I wrote to thank her, and a correspondence had ensued—her letters typed, always with a network of footnotes, asterisks, additional comments, and then her name—these in ink and in a spidery hand as if touched on the paper by a Persian miniature painter with his brush of a cattail hair. You had to turn the letter around a few times to be sure there wasn't a line or so you'd missed.

When the Dodgers won the National League pennant, I wrote Miss Moore that I would get some tickets, if she would come, and I would assist her—if with difficulty—in cheering her Dodgers on for the World Series against the Yankees.

She wrote back promptly that she would be delighted to see the second game of the Series. Her letter included careful instructions to get to her Brooklyn apartment house—"Am on right, middle of the block, with what look like mothballs on iron stands flanking the entrance." On the morning of the game I hired a large chauffeur-driven limousine and set out for Brooklyn. Her directions were excellent, though when I arrived in her street I saw that the mothball globes had been smashed off their stands . . . in a minor street rumble the night before, I was to learn. Miss Moore had noticed this, coming in that night, and she had tried to persuade the superintendent to put a bunch of flowers in the empty sockets, to help guide her escort coming to pick her up for the World Series. The superintendent was evasive.

Miss Moore lives on the fifth floor. The door opened almost as soon as I touched the bell. She is small, and I bent forward slightly to shake her hand, and then followed her down a long, narrow corridor into the front room of

85

the apartment. I only had a moment to glance around. Piles of books were everywhere, tea-colored oils on the walls, and a fine clutter of memorabilia, of which she pointed out a marlinspike from Greely's expedition to the Arctic. She talked a while about that, and then, as we were moving for the front door, paused in the corridor and said, "I have a present for you." She held out an envelope.

Flattered, I took it. I asked, "Shall I open it here?"

"Certainly," she said. She has light eyes, the eyes of birds, and they glanced quickly.

Inside the envelope was a postcard of a scaly anteater, a pangolin walking in the sands of the Antwerp Zoo. He is an interesting animal, and Miss Moore, in the thirties, wrote one of her more famous poems about him. It is hard to know what to say, presented with a postcard of an anteater.

"Well," I said, "very kind of you."

She nodded with a faint smile and handed me an enormous fur coat to hold for her to get into. She was wearing a very smart aquamarine suit—of wool, I think—and at the throat of a white blouse she wore a short tie, a cravatlike thing of small polka dots which was cut off short as if a practical joker had been at it with a pair of shears. It was secured with a pin. On her left wrist she wore two watches, one on a gold strap, the other on a black band. To protect herself against the elements (it was balmy outside, in the low seventies) she had this heavy and very bushy fur coat, nearly ankle-length, and at an estimate weighing, without her in it, about fifteen pounds. She'd ordered it from winter storage a day or so before, she told me, and had difficulty getting it at such short notice. "I must have it," she told the manager, "because I'm going to the World Series." So they got it to her on time, and it was with us for the day, sometimes encasing her, and sometimes in my charge, under an arm, quite material enough in its bulk to pass as a third person in our party. Miss Moore herself referred to it as a "large piece of upholstery."

As for her hat, the famous Marianne Moore hat, I was not disappointed. It wasn't the tricorner hat of the photographs. What she put on, pushing a long hatpin through it as we stood briefly at the front door, was a cartwheel-sized beret—rich black in hue, and of stiffened crinoline, I guess, so that it stuck out around her as if she were balancing a large plate on her head. Walking with her and being angular, six feet four, and she only five feet tall or so, I would look down on an expanse of black beret beside me, with only an occasional glimpse of a foot stepping out from it, or an arm swinging, to indicate she was underneath. She likes to talk as she moves along and, hearing the faint hum of her voice under the beret, I would bend far down, as if picking up something, to get under the sweep of the hat: it was quiet in there, like being under a parasol in summer, and I'd listen and say, "Yes, yes, hmm."

We got into the limousine, and here, seated in what she referred to, looking around, as a "super-capacious car," we were at eye level, and it was easier to listen. She is an engrossing talker—a soft, even voice which shifts and slides through topics with the erratic motion of a snipe—her talk almost as anarchic as that of Casey Stengel, the Mets' manager, who is four years her junior and could take some lessons. During the relatively short trip to Manhattan she talked briefly about her Brooklyn neighborhood, which is rough ("They come in sometimes and tell me about murders"), again about the Greely expedition to the Arctic, then a sudden diatribe against the Aero Shave girl, the wispy sprite who hovers around a heavily soaped beard in a shaving television commercial ("I hate that girl! I am against her!"), then an appraisal and criticism of the Beinecke Rare Book Library at Yale, followed in turn by a short eulogy of Willie Mays ("You can feel his enjoyment—the expectation when he hits that everything's going to be all right"), then a long and very funny account of her experiences two or three days before with a Hungarian professor. Endowed with Old World manners, he had insisted after a ten-minute meeting in Manhattan on taking her home to Brooklyn, could not be dissuaded, and so was introduced to the New York subway system. Miss Moore is a great subway traveler ("I am inured and go on down into it out of habit"), but the professor, sitting bleakly in his seat, was new to the city, with absolutely no conception of where his courtliness was taking him.

Up front, the chauffeur was particularly interested in this story—it being his sort of thing: misunderstood directions, citizens lost in the metropolis— and he pushed back from the steering wheel, his arms straight out like Stirling Moss's on a straightaway, his head turned slightly, and I could see his shoulders shake with mirth. We moved very slowly across the Manhattan Bridge. Miss Moore inspected the New York skyline and announced that if she ever left Brooklyn, which she wouldn't, she'd like to live in the loft of a New York skyscraper. Then she talked about Sandy Koufax, who had pitched his fine game the day before, which she had seen on television. She said Koufax a number of times, working on the name, repeating it often that day, as if what she as a poet would finally sort out of what she had seen of his artistry, and would write about, was somehow locked up in the name itself. Ballplayers' names did intrigue her. "Vinegar Bend Mizelle," she said suddenly, in reference to the ex-Met pitcher. "A wonderful name."

We turned off the Drive in mid-Manhattan. I had a small lunch arranged for her—at home, just off the Drive. An editor or two and some poets were there, including Robert Lowell. Marianne Moore sat on a sofa amid them, her fur coat open, draped at her shoulder. I could only get a snatch of their conversation, since I was laying forks and such things out on a table. I overheard her say about the poet Robert Graves, "I'm not sure about those honeycomb curls on the back of his head, but I've always liked him. He's always had his own way . . . he's reciprocal, however, and I like that."

I announced the lunch, urging everyone on since game time was not far off, and Miss Moore, pulling her fur coat around her, inspected the buffet table, the chickens lying there, a roast beef, some salads, and she took a small piece of cheese and that was her lunch. She refused more. Still nibbling on the cheese, she said good-bye to the others, and we went back down to the car. Robert Lowell came with us. He didn't have a ticket to the game, but the idea of going to the World Series struck him suddenly. He thought he'd come along and take his chances at getting in. I outfitted him with a pair of powerful field glasses. He is a man swept by enthusiasms.

The talk on the way to the game was not about baseball but football. We talked about coaches and players, and Miss Moore told us about Jim Thorpe—*James* Thorpe she called him: "He was always James to me, nothing else." She taught this extraordinary athlete at the Carlisle Indian School— taught him English, and she remembers him as slow, but that he possessed an astonishing decorum and wrote a fine Spencerian hand. He was shy and very polite. "Once," she said, "we were walking along railroad tracks in the heat. I had a gloria man's umbrella. 'Could I carry your parasol for you?' he said. 'Thank you, James,' I said, 'by all means.' He was courteous, you see, and very gentle. I liked him. . . . Of course he had his troubles."

Robert Lowell got us back on baseball. How had Miss Moore become interested in the game? he wanted to know. "Ah, Robert!" she said. She told us that in the summer of 1949 she had been invited to Ebbets Field and saw Roy Campanella walk out to the mound to calm down a pitcher named Carl Spooner. He had stood there on the mound, resting the big catcher's mitt on his hip, the mask pushed back on the top of his head; and his earnest demeanor, his "zest"—as she put it—something of that moment, and how he imparted his encouragement with a pat to Spooner's rump as the pitcher turned back to the mound, caught her fancy, indeed made a baseball addict of her—this when she was sixty-six—incurably afflicted with what gets most people about the time they first come down with an attack of mumps. I appreciated that what had ignited her interest had not been a stupendous moment in Brooklyn history—Gionfreddo's miracle catch of DiMaggio back near those monument stones in the Yankee Stadium, or Cookie Lavagetto's double against the right-field fence to break Bevens's no-hitter, or even the jokes, the Brooklyn jokes, the baseballs that came out of the sun and conked Babe Herman on the head, none of these but a moment of suspended activity, just a mound conference going on, a dull thing, many people think. Of course, I don't mean to suggest that appreciation of the game rests with such static situations as mound conferences. Nor would Marianne Moore. She spoke later that day of a great catch she'd seen Don Zimmer make, and she once wrote that she didn't know how to account for people who could be indifferent to miracles of dexterity. But to concentrate entirely on those moments when a play is in progress would be to appreciate only skill and not emotion.

The catalyst for my own emotional involvement with baseball was the same sort of thing that caught Marianne Moore. In my case it wasn't even a mound conference. Just the pitcher alone—he was Carl Hubbell—and he was standing on the mound with his jaw moving slightly on a chaw, or gum perhaps. It wasn't an important moment in the game. Before he got the sign from his catcher he turned his back, tucked his glove under his arm and began polishing the ball, kneading it, a somewhat vacant look under the long bill of his cap which then suddenly tilted back, and he was looking *up* at something—an airplane, perhaps, or the flags on the rim of the stadium to see how the wind was turning them, or the slant of a pigeon against the air currents, something like that, whatever it was interesting him sufficiently so that his chewing stopped, just momentarily. He took his time about it, staring up, his jaw slightly dropped, before he then tugged at his cap, turned, and read-dressed himself to the situation at hand. I watched, quaking with excitement, not quite knowing why, but in some vague appreciation of seeing someone with the power to refuse to deliver himself, or anyone else, for that matter, to the future—keeping everything in suspension while he indulged himself in whatever it was—flag watching, or pigeon watching—and, of course, being Hubbell, he carried it off with *style,* so that you didn't begrudge him his self-indulgence, and indeed admired him for it. I did. And others perhaps? What was it? The evocation of self? Of power? Long after, remembering back, I thought I knew what Robert Frost had in mind, at least partly, when he said he had always wanted (riding alone in trains particularly) to be taken for a baseball pitcher.

Miss Moore began talking about the responsibilities of each player and how one could be awed by what the humiliation and the consequences must be when they failed. "It is not easy. Elston Howard can't eat supper if he strikes out. To strike out is the height of embarrassment. But he and Tom Tresh are my favorite Yankees. It's the way they *take* their defeats. They don't show it to you—no sign of fatigue or annoyance. Elston Howard has a light walk, and yet he's heavy." She adjusted her fur coat around her. "I have named my alligator after him—after Elston Howard. He's a very flexible animal, and popular in my building. One of the children rings my bell regularly. 'Could I see your crocodile?' she asks."

I wanted to ask Robert Lowell if he had had a moment that ignited his interest in baseball, and what it was, but we were in the fringes of the crowd by then, the loom of the Yankee Stadium coming up, and the flags, and he was beginning to fidget about getting his ticket.

"Mister," said the chauffeur from the front. "Ticket's going to set you back one hundred bucks."

Lowell was aghast.

"Robert," said Miss Moore brightly, "I have ten dollars you can have . . ." She opened her handbag up and began to rummage in it.

Lowell murmured "No, no, no." You could see he'd set his mind on the game. He was very anxious to go.

"Maybe *fifty* bucks'll get you in there," said the chauffeur. "But no less." He had a booming, assured voice.

Marianne Moore found a ten-dollar bill. She pressed it on Lowell, but he waved his long arms, refusing it, and began, mournfully, to wonder about going home. I suggested that certainly the bleachers would be worth a try, and if there weren't any seats available, he could walk around the outside of the Stadium to *see* what the scalpers wanted for a ticket.

The chauffeur jockeyed us up opposite Gate Two, the crowd now heavy around the car—game time not far off and the excitement beginning to fetch us—and Lowell agreed he had to try. We climbed out of the car and stood with him momentarily.

"The scalpers will come to you," said the chauffeur. "Bargain with them and don't get yourself short-changed."

Lowell looked worried. We were being jostled by the crowds moving for the gates. "I'm not very good at this sort of thing," he said.

"Robert," said Marianne Moore. "You have great resources, and you will succeed."

We watched him move off. In fact, he was the perfect mark, a tall figure, hunched shoulders, looming above the crowd, my field glasses dangling from his neck, his melancholy, patrician face set with horn-rimmed spectacles, and he looked truly bewildered, pushing a foot one way, the other splayed off another way, so that between them he teetered with such uncertainty that the scalpers, the program salesmen, the hotdog and beer people, the vendors who sell autographed baseballs in cellophane, miniature bats, and trays of bobbing Kewpie baseball dolls, all these people must have been twitching to get at him. As it was, in his manner he was so good that the scalpers shied away from him. They must have assumed that anyone of such apparent susceptibility must be an authority in disguise—a plainclothes policeman, perhaps. He was able to do almost a complete circuit of the stadium without running into one scalper. But he tried the bleachers ticket booth. There wasn't a line there, so he didn't hold much hope. He leaned down and put his face up to the ticket window.

"Any tickets?" he asked.

The man behind the wicket said, "About fifty."

"I mean for today—for today's game," said Lowell.

"Like I said—about fifty."

"Well," said Lowell. It seemed too easy. "Well, I'll have *one,*" he said and he got it, and was up there in the bleachers for the game where he had a fine time and a seat in a much better location, it turned out, than ours.

Miss Moore and I were passed from aisle to aisle, directly away from home plate, by ushers who looked at us curiously and sent us on, until we were finally nestled down in the left-field corner. Miss Moore looked around with evident pleasure. She admired the mitten the usher had used to dust off her seat. She looked out into the vast enclosure, full now, the teams off the field, and last-minute ministrations being done to the infield by the grounds keepers—all this to be seen through a thick curtain of haze and cigarette smoke. I apologized for the bad seats. "We have the same advantages as the left fielder," said Miss Moore tactfully. "Besides," she said, "I have opera glasses." She looked in her purse, found them after poking about, and we tried them out. They were a little pair, very little, and you held them between the fingers, carefully, rather than in the hand. Perhaps there was some magnification, but the field was very restricted so it was like looking through a small pipe. Writers seem to affect strange eyepieces: I went to a New York Giants football game not long ago with Norman Mailer, the novelist, and a Brooklyn neighbor of Miss Moore's, and he produced a pocket telescope that snapped out, section by section, until it was as long as a baseball bat. It did not endear us to the row of people in front, who had it over them, moving back and forth, like an overhead crane. It, too, had a small field, but it was very powerful, so that when you looked into it, if it was properly focused on the field, you'd find yourself staring into the interior of a football helmet with someone like Andy Robustelli, say, the Giants' defensive end, inside, looking back through the bars of the noseguard.

I had brought a program for Miss Moore. I called out the starting lineup, reading names off the electric scoreboard, which she wrote down, with an occasional nod at the familiarity of a name, and often with a comment, concise and accurate, as one would expect from her.

Of John Roseboro, the Dodger catcher, she noted, "He is a sober fellow and does his duty." That is Roseboro exactly.

She nodded at Frank Howard's name, writing it down carefully with her pen, and she said, "He's a giraffe, of course, with those long strides, and I am not sure he can get in a subway."

She mentioned two Yankees—Hector Lopez ("He's reliable—saved many a game but lacks Cletis Boyer's spectacular uniqueness") and Mickey Mantle, about whom she said, "He is not graceful—one trouble; stodgy in fact, except on a catch way off center. But then he has taken a great beating, and I like him more now."

She watched him carefully as he lead his teammates out of the Yankee dugout—into the roars and brays of encouragement and discontent from the crowd—and trotted, then, heavily to his center-field position, where he stopped, holding his cap to his chest, and we stood for the National Anthem.

"My mother insisted that we stand for it—'The Star Spangled Banner' on the radio," said Miss Moore when we'd sat back down, "and even if we'd sat down too early, just sat down, we had to get up again, none too pleased."

The game was decided in the first inning. Maury Wills, the first man up, bounced a single past Al Downing, the Yankee pitcher, who moments later in a fine vengeful move had his man picked off first base but lost him when Wills fled down the base paths and reached second with a long, twisting belly slide, looming high over him the base umpire, Shag Crawford, with his arms outstretched in the safe signal. Miss Moore thought the umpire's *prénom* Shag was fine. She looked him up in the program. She also liked his decision, and particularly admired the speed with which it was made. "It's instantaneous opinion," she said. "Very odd but quite acceptable."

Junior Gilliam was the batter at the time, standing back from the plate and leaning easily on his bat as the action developed at second base. "He is simulating sangfroid," Miss Moore said of him, surely the first time that phrase has been used in Yankee Stadium. The man in front of us, a beefy man wearing a porkpie hat, turned laboriously and stared once at Miss Moore, looking at the small, pale, lively face under the cartwheel hat, the fur coat, taking all this in (she was concentrating through the tiny opera glasses on the distant Gilliam) before turning back to the game.

"Simulating," Miss Moore repeated, still with the glasses at her eyes. "They say the Gilliams are very peppery and high-strung in their family. He's resourceful—Junior is—hates to fail, and *hates* to be called Junior."

Gilliam promptly singled, Wills scampering for third, and moved to second himself when Roger Maris, far across from us in right field, uncorked an ill-considered throw to the plate. Willie Davis then hit a lofty drive, once again out to Maris, who suddenly sat down as if a stool had been snatched out from under him; the ball sailed over his head, and by the time he had it back to the infield two runs had scored. "Well," said Marianne Moore, "it's not dull."

Johnny Podres of the Dodgers came out to pitch his half of the inning. He got the first two batters, Kubek and Richardson, and seemed to be working effortlessly. Miss Moore, looking at him carefully, said, "Podres affects a great insouciance, but I really doubt he has it." In front, the man with the porkpie hat stiffened, but just at that moment Tom Tresh singled sharply, bringing everyone up out of their seats, and we all concentrated on Mickey Mantle moving for the batter's box. Podres' "insouciance" no longer showed. He stalked around the mound, fiddling with it, getting it to his liking, as if tidy surroundings would ease the unseemly sight of Mantle waiting for him down at home plate. He got him too, on a hard-slugged ball that went deep enough to go into the stands in most parks. "Yes, he had room," Miss Moore said of the fielder who caught the ball. "He did not run out of room."

I wasn't sure what she had said. I leaned in under her hat and she said, "That phrase—'He ran out of room'—I have always liked that phrase."

After the first inning things quieted down. Miss Moore's attention began to wander . . . no that's not it—her *concentration* went elsewhere, often away from the focal point of the play. It was worrying. She had said, "I am in a ballpark so seldom I hardly know where to look." So the temptation, after the first inning, was to direct her attention to what was going on. I was assisted in this by two men in adjoining seats, not the porkpie fellow in front—young executives, I would guess—who recognized Miss Moore and introduced themselves. They said they were honored to be sitting next to her, and they were nervous, too—one of them tipped his hat and it toppled down off his fingers and rolled under the porkpie-hat fellow's seat. He didn't turn, but you could tell from the set of his neck muscles that he knew someone was fishing around under his chair among the peanut shells.

The two men were very solicitous with Miss Moore, and so was I, answering questions, offering general comments, and when something of particular interest occurred, we all pointed at it, leaning in on her, a sudden copse of stiffened arms.

Midway in the game, Mickey Mantle hit another long drive, out toward the fence, and our little group rose shouting, arms full length, pointing at the ball's high long arc—like a Bofors antiaircraft battery—calling Miss Moore's attention to the ball, then sighting her down to Frank Howard, her "giraffe," moving back untidily but successfully, catching the ball over his right shoulder up near the wall. Despite her three spotters I'm not sure Miss Moore saw what we were pointing at—either the ball or Howard. She seemed to me to be peering out from under her beret at something behind second base, very intently, and though I followed the line of her concentration I couldn't tell what it was. She once said, "The accuracy of the vernacular. That's the kind of thing I'm interested in." Perhaps that was what she was doing, listening, with an ear cocked. No, she brought up her opera glasses. Something out there being moved by the wind? A pigeon perhaps? She was interested in them. Was there something there that told her more about Mantle and that long fly ball than we saw, watching directly? Certainly that was a poet's trick—to look away from the focal point and study what was peripheral. Hemingway talked about it in writing descriptive prose—to concentrate at moments of apparent inactivity, that the key, the emotion might be uncovered there, far removed from the action itself.

Similarly, Marianne Moore—you knew it from her work—looked at things from an odd angle. Given the sketches of the 1956 Ford car (the Ford company hoped she might come up with a name for their new line) she wrote: "They are indeed exciting; they have quality, and the toucan tones lend tremendous allure . . . looked at *upside down* furthermore, there is a sense of fish buoyancy."

Who would have thought to judge a car's lines by looking at them upside down? Some of Miss Moore's suggestions had aquatic overtones obviously derived from looking at the sketches that way: "The Intelligent Whale," "Varsity Stroke," and of course her famous offering, "Utopian Turtletop," which elicited a floral tribute from the Ford Motor Company. "Edsel" was the name finally selected for that ill-fated line—not from Miss Moore's remarkable list, which was primarily based on physical phenomena, but by Ford officials who felt compelled to turn somewhat closer to home.

So in the Yankee Stadium perhaps there was no need to be so solicitous. It was interesting, though, to listen to her on what did catch her fancy. She liked the bills of the baseball players' caps and remarked on them, particularly the double-bill effect, like a duck's head, when they were wearing the snap-down sunglasses; she had some things to say about the pigeons, the height of the pitcher's mound, a fine Zen Koan observation on Mantle being run out in the third inning ("The distance between home plate and first base is too great"), the double play ("It is a cruel thing but necessary"), on the practice of trading players ("It is scandalous and I don't approve of it. If a player is good enough for one team he's good enough for another"). The opera glasses would come up and she'd look through them, and sometimes she gave a little "Huh" of surprise. She never tried a hot dog or a beer. But she watched the vendors go by with their trays.

"I don't know about the traffic in signed balls," she said. "I'd rather catch one." "Very often," said one of the executives, leaning over, "the right-hand batters pull them into this section, right in this corner where we are, coming around too fast on the ball, letup pitches mostly . . ."

"I'm quite prepared," said Marianne Moore.

In the seventh inning it began to rain—a soft unseasonal rain, a summer shower, fine so that you could see it swayed by the wind as it came down. Newspapers were raised, folded intricately and used as hats, and so were magazines and scorecards. The game continued. A few people in the exposed seats moved back under the overhangs of the stadium—including the man in the porkpie hat, who gave us one quick look as he turned and went up the aisle. We stayed. One of the executives offered Miss Moore his raincoat. She raised a hand and murmured, but he insisted. So she took it, thanking him, and then, drawing the hatpin out, she removed her big, black beret, set it on her lap, and over it she spread the raincoat.

The executives and I looked at each other. The rain fell slightly about our shoulders, and on Miss Moore's bare head. People began coming back to their seats wearing blue Dodger baseball caps for protection against the rain. A priest went by with one on. These caps are modeled for small boys, and on adult heads they have a tendency to ride quite high. "Well, it's all right," said Miss Moore. "You get a very small Dodger hat on a large Dodger head and the rain doesn't seem to bother them at all. Very little else does, either."

The rain, soft as it was, seemed to reflect the Yankees' lot. They put up a mild flurry in the ninth inning. They were behind 4–0 at the time. With one out, Hector Lopez doubled, and Ron Perranoski, the brilliant Dodger relief pitcher, was brought in. He walked by in front of us on his way in from the bullpen in left field. Miss Moore watched him carefully. "I like the improvement in the way they wear their stockings," she said, "much neater than I was expecting, though they oughtn't to have uniforms of that depressing prison color." She followed Perranoski with her glasses and watched him warming up. "He's slim coming in," she said, "but heavy on the mound." Perranoski lost his first man: Howard singled sharply off him, bringing home a run—the only Yankee run, as it turned out, to cross the plate that afternoon. Perranoski got Pepitone on a fielder's choice, and then he struck out Boyer, and the game was gone.

We sat for a while, waiting for the crowd to thin. Miss Moore said good-bye to the executives. I could hear her humming. She made a notation on her scorecard. "Well, it's too bad—a shame!" she said suddenly.

What could she have meant? I leaned under her beret and she said it again, somewhat sorrowfully. Could she not have known her Dodgers had won? Possibly. She had her own *privé* way of looking at things. It must have been strange seeing a game from those seats without a commentator to keep things straight. One did not sense that the score was of much interest to her—but that the specifics were: dexterity, emotion, speed, a ball player's "zest" . . . and that perhaps *that* was what had sorrowed her, that she had not caught examples of these that afternoon.

We found our car. Robert Lowell was there waiting. We moved off slowly, up into a traffic jam on the Major Deegan Expressway. Lowell was full of excitement. He'd had a fine afternoon in the bleachers. We dropped him off midtown, and continued on across the Manhattan Bridge to Brooklyn.

"I have had such a number of adventures recently," Miss Moore said, as we were getting near her home. "I made a few suggestions about a script some time ago for the Port of New York Authority—for their World's Fair show, which is to be a color film of New York. They took me up in a helicopter, to see the bridges and docks—they've some beautiful new docks in Brooklyn—showed me the parks and fairgrounds, ships, and Ellis Island so I could see what it was all about. I enjoyed it hugely."

"And the helicopter?"

"An interesting machine. It *feels* its way down, settles in a swirl—like a lady curling a train around her feet before sitting. Noisy. We flew quite near the Statue of Liberty, looking at her from above. Very handsome. The pilot asked—in fact shouted—'Did I see the chains of tyranny, broken at her feet?' 'No' I said, 'I hadn't seen them,' looked and *did* see them—big narrow parallelogram-shaped links."

"What's the next adventure to be?" I asked.

"I do hope I can see John Teale's musk-ox in Vermont sometime," she said, quickly as if she'd had it on her mind most of the day. "He has them on his farm up there, the young ones he captured and flew there to raise. They love jumping in and out of holes. They've been maligned about their smell—the musk-ox smell—because if you put your nose in one when he's been rained on and is wet, he smells of water, nothing else. They are vastly superior to cashmere goats. Do you know about them?" she asked.

"No," I said.

"I *must* see them," Miss Moore said, "if I can get someone to take me—I was invited by Mr. Teale. Perhaps it's my duty to forget it; too many visitors do become a problem, I believe."

"It would be something to look forward to," I said.

She nodded and began collecting things, folding her scorecard and stuffing it in her handbag. The car turned into her street. We pulled up and the chauffeur jumped out very adroitly to hold the door open for her. I walked her to the front door of her apartment house, a heavy iron-cased glass door you had to lean against to swing open. We chatted on the stoop there for a minute. I said what a fine afternoon I'd had, and she said she'd had one too, and she turned and was gone.

In the limousine the chauffeur was all hopped up. "My God!" he said as we drove away, "who was that lady?" I settled back in the seat. The car seemed enormous without another passenger in it, and being in it was a little embarrassing on that Brooklyn street.

"Well, she's a great American poet," I said.

"*Great?* Listen," he said. "I had many kinds of customers driving all these years—y'know, important people, Richard Nixon—but she's got them all beat."

He thumped his palms on the steering wheel as we moved slowly down the street.

"Just great!" he said.

I repeated her name for him a few times. He was going to go down and buy her books. He had one book of poems in his house—*Spoon River Anthology*. Someone had left it in the back of his limousine. He hadn't looked at it yet, but he was going to one day. And he certainly was going to look at Miss Moore's poems. Did she like the game? he wanted to know.

"Yes," I said. "I think so. She was wonderfully perceptive. It was new for her, going to the game itself. She watches on television. She may have been puzzled by the score. She was seeing everything from an odd angle—not at all what she sees on a TV set."

"What the hell!" said the chauffeur. "Why *should* she know the score?" He was absolutely furious. He blew the horn—at nothing that I could see. "It's what she *sees* that counts. I mean, take those oxes, them goats she was talking about. Who would think of putting his nose to a wet ox—I mean, that's *great.*"

"She wrote a poem about them," I said.

"Well, I hope so," he said. "And I hope she gets up there to see them. You know something? *I'd* like to take her up there. Why not? She's going to need a driver and a car . . . so why not me?" He half turned in his seat. "You tell her if she ever wants to go anywhere, I'll make myself available."

"I will do that," I said.

Who was the tall guy, he wanted to know after a while, the guy with the specs?

"Another poet—Robert Lowell," I said. "A very good one too."

"You could tell he knew he was in there with the best."

"He is a Bostonian and very polite," I said.

"That was *respect,*" he said firmly. "You could tell by the way he was talking to her. What do you think?" he went on. "Do you think that coat of hers might've come off one of them oxes?"

"I'm no good at materials," I said. "But I'm sure a type of *wool* would come off those animals, not fur."

" 'S right," he said. "She was wearing fur, so she hadda be wearing *bear,* or a helluva big fox, something like that."

He began to get excited again. "Nixon," he said, "Nixon I had in this car." He shook his head, and would have gone on about her some more, but we got into the Midtown Tunnel about that time, where the noise stopped him. I had to get out close to the Manhattan exit, so I didn't hear him talk about her again. But when he drove off, I could see him whacking at that steering wheel with his palm. It would be a long time before he'd forget. And perhaps he'd go down and buy the poems.

Alex Karras

The year after my participation with
the Detroit Lions I went down to Philadelphia one weekend to watch the
team play the Eagles. After the game-day breakfast with them in the hotel,
John Gordy took me up to his room. Alex Karras was his roommate.

Gordy said, "Alex will be telling stories, or doing some damn thing
that'll keep our minds occupied. There'll be a bunch of guys up there."

"He takes the day of the game calmly?" I asked.

"Hell, no," Gordy said. "He gets sick before every game—violently."

"Well," I said tentatively, "why don't we drop in on Friday Macklem,
or somebody else." Friday was the equipment manager. "Friday, if pushed,
can talk enough to keep one's mind occupied . . ." I said.

"Alex will be all right," Gordy said.

There were some other players sitting around the room—Terry Barr,
Jim Gibbons, and Gary Lowe. Karras was lying on his bed staring up at the
ceiling through his big horn-rimmed glasses. His torso was enormous. In his
self-deprecatory manner he used to say that if the rest of him was in proper
proportion to his torso he'd be eight feet tall. On the field he ran, his
teammates said of him, like a "mad duck," but they used to swear softly
thinking of his ability.

Gordy introduced me to him, and Karras stuck out a hand, remaining
absolutely flat where he was on the bed.

I wished him luck that afternoon in the Eagle game. I found a chair in
the corner and sat down. He raised up slowly and looked down between his
feet at the television set against the wall opposite the foot of his bed. It was
on. The sets were almost automatically turned on as soon as one walked into
a hotel room, flicked on like pulling up a window shade, not because there

100

was a specific program to see but to create a second window in those airless rooms to glance at as one might glance out the real window at the walls of the air shaft opposite. "Look at that," Karras said. He was staring moodily at the image. An advertisement was showing—a young man in sharkskin trousers and a yachting jumper sitting on a boulder with the surf piling around, with a girl in close to him, and he was inhaling deeply on a cigarette. "Look at that guy," said Karras. He said he reminded him of Milt Plum, the Detroit Lions quarterback. "They always have good-looking guys puffing on cigarettes. They put cigarettes in Milt Plum's mouth and color snapshots of him for the big magazines and Milt doesn't even smoke—he hardly knows how to hold a cigarette. They had to *teach* him. What about me? I'm a longtime smoker, known how to hold a cigarette since I was eight, I inhale and all, and when the wind's down and I get a little practice, with the pressure really on me, I can put together a smoke ring, think of that. Why not me, then, instead of Plum? The reason is they only pick the good-looking guys, and the good-looking girls. They look at me, blowing away on those smoke rings, and they think, well, he's okay on those rings, but he's got the face of a mechanic who's gotten squashed working under a large touring car. There ought to be a union of us ugly cruds. I'd like to see an ad, a TV ad, in which this great mountain of a girl comes out, just horrible-looking, with a name like Betty Home, and she's advertising nylons, y'see, and she draws on a pair of nylons over these enormous fat thighs. 'Sheer,' she says, working her lips up the way those thin models do."

"You're beautiful, Alex," someone said.

"Who am I kidding?" Karras said. "I know I'm not very pretty, but then the girls I talk to aren't very pretty either." He groaned. "Even with them I can't make out. I couldn't make out if I had the Hope Diamond hanging from my neck." He dropped back on the bed and stared up at the ceiling. "It wasn't always like that. In my other lives I had some grand times."

It was Karras's fantasy that he had lived a succession of different lives—stretching far back into the past. He had been, among other things, an aide-de-camp to both General Washington and Adolf Hitler.

"What about Hitler?" one of the players asked. "What was your impression?"

"Hitler was not an ordinary joe," Karras said expansively. "You knew that when you were around him as much as I was. He had this obsession to hold his breath for more than three minutes."

"No! Could he do it?"

˙ "Nowhere near. He got red in the face very quickly, and there'd be this little popping sound when the air came rushing out. He never lasted more than eight or nine seconds—shortest-breathed man I ever saw."

"How about the others? Did you know Rommel, Hess, Goering, and all those . . . ?"

"Certainly, I knew all those cats, Rundstedt, Goering—Bavaria Fats, we called him—and Rommel. He had a terribly weak stomach, Rommel did. He used to get sick all the time. I'd come rushing up to him in the morning to fling the salute at him, and say, 'Hello, hello, *heil, heil,* good *morn*in', gener'l,' and he'd get sick. Hitler never trusted him for that reason. Why, he'd come striding up to Rommel at headquarters and say, 'A fine day to mount ze attack against the filth *Schweinhund* Monty, the Britisher.' Rommel, he'd lean over and get sick into one of those tall nickel-plated upright ashtrays you find in the smoking section of railroad coaches—the kind with a button on the side of the stand you push and the trapdoor opens and the cigar falls down. I carried one of these things around for Rommel when he was at headquarters, ready with my thumb on the button. Hitler was suspicious of those ashtrays. 'What is that thing?' he'd always say. I think he had an idea it was a bomb. 'It's an ashtray,' I'd say. 'It's General Rommel's ashtray.' Hitler'd take a long look, and he'd say, 'Why doesn't the general carry a smaller model around— that thing's three feet tall. What's wrong with those little *pocket* ashtrays, the kind with a hotel name on the bottom? Besides,' Hitler said, 'he doesn't smoke, Rommel, what does he need a big thing like that for if he doesn't smoke, answer me *that*!' 'Well,' I said quickly, 'the general smokes *hemp.*' 'Oh, well, no wonder,' Hitler says. 'Why not say so in the beginning?' "

"What about Eva Braun? Tell us about her."

"Eva Braun was my sister."

"No!"

"She was. You may not think so, my looking the way I do, but in that life I was smart-looking, a blond cat, with boots that went up clear to the crotch, shiny as brass, and in company people was always saying, 'Who's that good-looker?' Real Aryan I was."

"Tell us more about Eva."

"She and Hitler didn't get along at all."

"No!"

"My sister had this terrible laugh, a sort of cackle, and when Hitler came fooling around, pushing that mustache at her, why, she'd let out this cackle. Hitler could never figure why she was laughing. 'What's wrong?' he'd ask, looking behind him, thinking some clown back of them was making faces. Her cackling was horrible. 'You laughing at one of Bavaria Fats's jokes?' he'd ask."

Gibbons said, "History books say they were quite a pair."

"That was for appearances," Karras said. "They had to show that Hitler had normal feelings for women. So the public-relations people took a bunch of pictures of the two of them together, she standing under a waterfall bare-ass, and Hitler next to her, getting his uniform wet. You ever see Hitler bare-ass? The answer is no. The fact was, and everybody around headquarters knew it, that Hitler was a woman—my aunt, if you really want to know, Aunt Hilda, and quite a trial she turned out to be to the rest of the family."

"Did Eva know about that?"

"The fact is she *didn't*. And you know what fooled her?"

"What?"

"That mustache. You'd think it was false, Aunt Hilda being a woman and all. Well, that mustache was absolutely real. Aunt Hilda shaved five times a day. After a while Eva got over her cackle, and toward the end she fell for Aunt Hilda. No one wanted to disillusion her, so they got a marriage going there in the Berlin bunker. The Russians were turning up, so the pair committed suicide, which was maybe good for Eva. She'd have found out—"

"That Hitler was Aunt Hilda."

"Her own *mother*!" said Karras. "Aunt Hilda was Eva's mother, you see. Eva didn't know that, of course. She thought she was an orphan. And guess who Eva's *father* was?"

"Who? Bavaria Fats?" someone suggested.

"You're looking at him," said Karras comfortably from his bed.

"You! Come on," said Gary Lowe. "Eva Braun was your sister."

"Both sister *and* daughter," Karras said proudly. "Adolf Hitler was my wife."

"That's horrible," said Gordy.

We sat there reflecting on the tangled family tree of the Nazi hierarchy, the television set murmuring slightly in the background.

"Well, I hope things weren't as horrible as that in General Washington's time," Gordy finally said.

Karras stirred. "General Washington was beautiful. I was at Valley Forge, you know, real cold there, feeding on owls' heads, we were, and such things, and the general would come through the camp fires and strike these poses and he'd say, 'Men, we will endure,' things like that. He was just beautiful. But they get a lot of things wrong about him. You recall the cherry-tree story?"

We nodded.

"He *had* to cut that tree down. What did it have but the Dutch elm disease, easiest thing in the world to see, that cherry tree was top-heavy with it, and if Washington hadn't fetched an ax to it, everything around would have been infected."

"Why didn't George tell his father that?" Gordy asked. "He'd have saved himself a whipping."

"Young George had false teeth, you know, a full set, even as a young boy, and when his daddy called him in to ask him about the cherry tree, he *tried* to explain about the Dutch elm disease, but out came a lot of clacking. Washington's teeth fit badly, and when he spoke, he either did this clacking, or sometimes a whistle, a high whistle." Karras demonstrated the whistle. "So when his daddy said, 'Who cut that tree down?' he was only able to understand through all that clacking and whistling that his son, George, had, but he couldn't understand the *reason.* So he took a switch to him. Beat him half crazy."

"How could you understand him saying 'We will endure,' and things like that at Valley Forge," someone asked, "if Washington had this speech difficulty?"

"We *couldn't* understand him," explained Karras. "But he got into all these poses, you see. He'd stand around among the campfires, and when he crossed the Delaware, he struck a fine pose *that* time, with his foot up there on the bow, so you always knew what the guy had in mind. You know actually who spoke the Farewell Address?"

"Who?"

"You're looking at him," said Karras. "What happened was that I stood right behind the general up there on the platform and I spoke the words for him. He was like a wood dummy, clacking his jaw, but you couldn't tell unless you were right up close that it was me."

"How about his staff? How did they understand his orders?"

"Well, lip reading—they were all deaf mutes," Karras went blithely on. "That's not generally known, but Washington's closest people—Lafayette (French Fats, we called him), General Gates, and the rest of them—they could hear nothing; but they could *lip-read.* That's why in the portraits of Washington all the generals and the staff people are standing around staring at him. You hear that's devotion they was showing. Crap. They was looking at his mouth in case Washington had it in mind to say something, so they could begin their lip reading and hop to it if there was something to be done."

There had been some other lives Karras hinted at: he had been something during the Civil War—he wasn't sure what. Something low, he thought—a camp follower, perhaps.

Between lives, he told us, he would find himself on an airliner flying in heavy cloud banks, or often above them, with the sun shining. The ground was always out of sight, though he would press his forehead against the windows to look for it far down through the clouds, never succeeding, though often the clouds fell away into deep valleys that seemed to drop for miles. The flight was always very smooth and long, with pretty stewardesses coming by and leaning over to offer beef bouillon, and when the evening came, their trays had tall drinks on them. He was always very tired on these flights, utterly relaxed; through half-closed eyes he would watch the stewardesses in the aisle, and when they came by, he would hold out his cup for the bouillon, or the tall drink if it was in the evening. On the third day, perhaps the fourth, when he was beginning to feel more lively, a mist would suddenly settle in the cabin, increasingly thick, so that it began to take on the same consistency as the clouds outside, the walls of the cabin disappearing in it, and finally the back of the seat in front of him, so that in its thickness he felt himself in the clouds themselves, the wind beginning to sweep across his face, and as he felt himself begin to fall and turn, he knew his time was coming to be someone else and he would cross his fingers and hope to Christ he wasn't going to be a goddamn jockstrap athlete again.

"Well, what would you hope to be?" Gary Lowe asked.

"How the hell do I know?" Karras said. He seemed ill-tempered suddenly. "I tell you nothing can be worse than this—lying around in a little hotel room like a bunch of cruds. Then we get out on some field and knock some guys around for a lousy pile of pennies. What sort of a life is that? It's crud," he said. He raised up off the bed. He looked very sour.

"Let's clear out of here," he said. "I got to find me a place to puke."

When we got out in the corridor, he hurried on down in front of us and began punching at the elevator button.

"That's a mood, isn't it?" I said quietly to Lowe.

"Alex is ready," Lowe said happily. "He's right as rain. He's up for the game."

"Does he mean it when he says he's going to get sick?"

"Sure he will," said Lowe. "Just as George Wilson tells us to go out there and rock them, out in the can we'll hear Alex lose his lunch. Sure. And then in five minutes he'll be out there on the field making the poor fellow from Philadelphia opposite him pay for it."

We crowded into the elevator. No one said anything going down. Karras would sit alone in the bus.

One of the persistent problems facing sportswriters, especially at Big Events, is to find a fresh angle. Sealed in with two hundred writers in a press box I have always felt as if I were taking a final exam, competing with my peers. I feel I do much better out on my own. In the 1984 Olympics, on assignment from *Time* magazine, I tried to persuade the authorities to let me take the place of the scuba diver in the bottom of the diving tank who is there to help if any of the athletes gets in trouble. It would provide me with copy from an original point of view. No, it was impossible, I was told. One reason was that the scuba diver, a dark shape in the corner of the pool, was a woman—this because the tank suits of the women divers often "pull away" as they plunge through the water, and must be readjusted on the way to the surface. A male frogman might be intimidating, I was told.

"Oh yes," I said.

As it was, I wrote a column about what fell out of people's pockets sitting in the high wooden stands and watching the swimming events. I went under the stands with my notebook. I wore a hard hat poking around down there.

I can't remember how I arranged to be in Muhammad Ali's dressing room before the Jerry Quarry fight—very likely through the influence of Bundini Brown, Ali's corner man, himself a flamboyant figure who had coined the famous description of his fighter, "Float like a butterfly, sting like a bee."

The fight marked Muhammad Ali's return to the ring after being barred from it for three years by the boxing commissions for refusing to join the army ("I ain't got no argument with them Vietcong").

Muhammad Ali

Muhammad Ali's dressing room at the arena was small, not much wider than the length of the rubbing table set at one end, and only three or four paces long—hardly enough room, as Bundini said when he saw it, for Ali to "exercise up some sweat." Dressing tables were set against opposite walls, their mirrors outlined with light bulbs.

Ali arrived with an hour to go before the fight. Even before he got out of his streetclothes he was moving around the room, snapping out the jabs, and staring at himself in the mirrors. "This room's too crowded," he said. "I want room to rest."

The room was cleared except for the entourage he would take to the ring, along with two interns assigned to the fight, and the Reverend Jesse Jackson. I was allowed to stay. I crouched in a corner with a notebook open. Ali stripped quickly. He pulled on a pair of white boxing trunks and turned slowly in front of the mirror. "I am the champ," he said softly. "He must fall." He tried out the Ali shuffle, his white gym shoes snapping against the floor.

"Angelo," he said. "I'm not wearing the foul-protector tonight."

Angelo looked up. He and Bundini were having words in the corner. In the days immediately before the fight there had been considerable argument about the regulation foul-proof belt. Ali wanted to wear a small tin cup rather than the leather device which bulked out his boxing trunks and made him look, at least to his eyes, fat. But Dundee had insisted on the regulation belt. He warned Ali that Quarry not only was a body puncher but had nothing to lose: he had been known to hit "south of the border," and it was just crazy to take chances.

Bundini had packed the equipment suitcase two days before and

109

checked it out twice to see if everything was there, especially the foul-proof belt, which was red and had Ali's name on it. To his astonishment, the belt was missing when he opened the suitcase in the dressing room. So he and Dundee, who thought Bundini had simply forgotten it back at the cottage, had a low but harsh exchange. The champion, shadowboxing in the rear, gave no indication of being aware of what was going on: perhaps there was no need to, since the belt was found under his bed the next morning. Dundee opened the suitcase, which belonged to Rachaman, Ali's brother— who had fought on the card earlier that evening—and produced *his* protector, a black model marked STANDARD. Ali looked at it warily. He turned to the mirrors and began some light shadowboxing, always exhaling sharply with each punch thrown—a hard, distinctive, explosive snuffle; after a minute or so he stopped and left the dressing room for the lavatory. There were forty minutes left to go. I went racing along with my notebook. On the way back Ali passed his opponent's dressing room, just a step down the corridor from his own. It had a hand-lettered notice, QUARRY, tacked to the door. Ali could not resist the temptation. He pushed the door open and peered in. Over his shoulder I could see Quarry sitting facing him, his knees jiggling.

"You, fellow," Ali said in a sepulchral voice, "you best be in good shape, because if you whup me, you've whupped the greatest fighter in the whole wide world."

He clicked the door shut before Quarry could come up with a reply, and back in his own dressing room he described what he had done with impish pleasure. It had been a ploy of the type which delighted him—the unexpected materialization. I remembered on one occasion, the year before, driving through Queens with a reporter, Ali had stopped the car and tiptoed up behind a truck driver who was changing a tire. "I hear you're talking around town that you can whup me," the fighter said. "Well, here I is."

The truck driver's ears had turned a quick red and he spun on his haunches to stand up; and then, seeing Muhammad, and recognizing him, his jaw dropped, and he froze in a curious half stoop, the tire iron clattering from his hand as the fighter grinned at him and stepped back for his car.

With a half hour to go a representative from Quarry's camp turned up in the dressing room to oversee the taping of Ali's hands. His name was Willie Ketcham, an older man, a towel over one shoulder of his jacket, and his jaws working evenly on a piece of gum. Ali's eyes sparkled. "Well, look who's here," he said. "You all in trouble tonight."

"Who's in trouble?" Ketcham said. He knew he was in for some badgering.

"Your man's in for a new experience," Ali said. "He's against the fastest heavyweight alive, quick and trim. Look at that." He slapped his belly. "Look how pretty and slim."

"You won't be when Jerry finishes," Ketcham said. "I know he's going to hit *you*."

"How's he going to do that?" Ali looked genuinely surprised. "Angelo, how can he get away from the jab? How will he ever see it?"

Dundee shrugged. He motioned Ali to the rubbing table and began the taping of his hands.

Ketcham challenged him. "And if Jerry move in on you, throwing the big ones? Ho ho."

"He's going to get hit right in the banana," Ali said crisply. "He never seen a right like that."

"If you beat Quarry tonight, you are the greatest heavyweight who ever lived," Ketcham said. And he added with attempted sarcasm, "Yeh, and if that happens, I'll come in here and kiss you."

"Oh, my, no," said Ali. He looked at the taped hand Dundee had finished. "Hey," he said. "We will give you guys five hundred thousand dollars *cash* . . . if you let me put a horseshoe in my gloves."

Ketcham blinked. "Aw," he said.

Dundee finished the taping and Ketcham leaned over and crisscrossed the tape with pen strokes. When he stepped back, Ali stood up and moved close to stare into Ketcham's eyes. Ketcham is a tall man; standing, the two of them braced each other like fighters while getting instructions from the referee. "Look into my eyes," Ali said. "I'm the real heavyweight. I am the fastest heavyweight that ever lived."

Ketcham didn't back down. His jaw kept moving impassively.

"I won some money on you once," he said. "I bet fifty dollars at seven to one that you'd whup Sonny Liston."

Ali began to turn away. "We'll give them a good show tonight," he said. "I couldn't pick no better contender."

"Okay, pal," Ketcham said. He cuffed Ali affectionately alongside the head and turned to go.

"Twenty minutes," someone said.

"We're going to warm up on the ropes," Ali said. "We're going out there and lay on the ropes. . . ."

"Don't say *we* when you say that," Bundini said. "You stick him *fast,* you hear?"

"Who goes into the ring first?" Ali asked.

"Quarry," he was told.

He lay down on the rubbing table, his head to the wall. One of the young interns leaned forward and brashly asked Ali what he was thinking, just at that instant.

Ali began his litany. He said he was thinking about the people in Japan and Turkey and Russia, all over the world; how they were beginning to think about the fight and about him; and the television sets being clicked on; and the traffic jams in front of the closed-circuit theaters; and how the big TV trucks out in back of the Atlanta arena, just by the stage door, were getting their machinery warmed up to send his image by satellite to all those people, and how he was going to dance for them. "I got to dance," he said, all this in the soft silky voice he uses when he does this sort of thing, almost the voice of a mother soothing her child to sleep with nursery rhymes.

"How about a verse?" the intern asked.

"Quarry/sorry," Ali said.

The intern was delighted. "Hey, that's pretty *short,*" he said. "How about another?"

"I don't have time/to find a rhyme," Ali replied gently, and he went on with his thoughts, how finally he was thinking most of all of Allah, his God, the Almighty Allah, who had given him so many gifts. He began to enumerate them in his singsong voice—a long free-verse ode to carrot juice, to honey, to the things which grew in his garden and which he ate, never anything manmade that came in tin cans, none of that stuff, but only what came fresh from the gardens; and then the woods in which he would run "before the cars were up, and their poison"; and he talked about how he would face east and thank the Creator for all of this which had given him the strength to live right and to pray right. He said that thinking of all that the Creator had done made it simple for him to look at Quarry and see how little he was and how easy he could be whupped.

Ali swung his feet to the floor and stood up. Fifteen minutes were left. His corner man, Sazriah, applied a smear of Vaseline to the fighter's shoulders and started rubbing it into his torso. His body began to shine. A policeman stuck his head in and the crowd noise, roaring at the entrance of some celebrity, swept in for an instant and made the blood pound before it was shut off by the door.

"They're waiting for me to dance," Ali said. His feet were shuffling. Jesse Jackson put up a hand as a target and Ali popped a few jabs, snorting his sharp exhalations, and then he stopped and looked at himself in the mirror. "The Temptations are out there," he said. "The Supremes are out there; Sidney Poitier's out there."

He peered at himself closely.

"A hair comb, somebody." He held out his hand behind him blindly as he continued looking into the mirror, and it was filled by someone's slapping the comb into his palm as one might supply a busy surgeon.

He moved the comb through his short brush, flicking at some wayward tuft, until Dundee approached with the foul-protector and the boxing gloves, new and gum-red from their packing case.

Ali balked. "I'm *not* wearing that thing," he said. A chorus of dismay rose from around the room.

"Just try it on and see," someone urged. Sulkily Ali skinned out of his trunks and shimmied the protector up over his thighs. He pulled the trunks back up over them. A babble of voices rose.

"It looks just fine."

"Trim, man, beautiful. Trim."

Ali began some knee bends, hands out, and every time he came up above the level of the dressing tables he turned to look at himself in the mirrors. Then he stood up and slapped at his trunks disgustedly.

"Where are my brother's trunks?"

"Champ, those trunks look just *boss.*"

"Slim and trim, champ, slim and trim."

A pleading chorus rose from those around the room. Ali skinned off the trunks. Dundee opened up Rachaman's suitcase, and, rummaging through it, he produced a pair of white trunks with a black stripe down the side. Ali reached for them, put them on over the protector and turned slowly in front of the mirrors. Everybody stared at him.

"This is better," he said after a while. A quick chorus of approbation came from around the room.

"Right on, man."

"That's real trim."

"It brings your ass down just right."

Everyone was sweating.

"How much time?" someone asked.

"Ten minutes."

113

Ali began to shadowbox in earnest, throwing quick long jabs, flurries of combinations, and big hooks that seemed to shudder the air in that tiny room; the onlookers flattened themselves back against the wall to give him room. He stopped to tape his shoelaces against the top of his shoes so they wouldn't flop. "Too loose," he said. "In late rounds they can get soggy; and man, I want to dance."

The gloves were put on. He began another flurry of punches. Murmurs rose from those standing along the wall. "Hmmm, cook," called Bundini.

Hearing him, Ali stopped suddenly and turned to Bundini. "Now, I don't want you to be hollering in that corner, Bundini, and start to get all excited and shout things like 'cook' and all that. It takes my mind off things."

Bundini was furious. "What you expect?" he shouted. "You expect me to keep my mouth shut when the cake is put in the oven, when all the preparation and the mixing is done and it's time for the fire and you expect me to stand around with my hands on my hips? If'n you expect me to keep my mouth shut, you better kick me out of your corner and keep me in *here.*"

"All right, then, you stay out of the corner," Ali said. "You *stay* in here."

The two stared at each other, the enormity of what Ali had said beginning to hit. Bundini pressed his lips together and seemed on the edge of tears. "Aw come on," Ali said after an instant. "You can come on out," he said gently.

He started up his shadowboxing, once again concentrating on himself in the mirrors. Bundini wouldn't look at him for a while. "My goodness," he said. Sweat began to shine on Ali's body. "I'm warm now," he said, looking at Angelo.

The door burst open and Sidney Poitier, the actor, rushed in. The champion jumped for him and the two spun around the room in an embrace. "Sidney's here. I'm *really* ready to rumble!" Ali shouted. He held him off at arm's length and looked at the slim actor, elegantly dressed up in a tight form-fitting gray suit. "Man, you exercise?" he asked admiringly. "Hey," he said, "give me a rhyme to psych Quarry—when we're getting the referee's instructions." He held up an imaginary microphone. Poitier bent his head in thought; he had been caught by surprise. "You met your match, chump," he intoned in his soft voice. "Tonight you're falling in . . ." He cast an arm desperately for a rhyme for *chump.* "You're falling in *two,*" he cried, giving up.

"That's terrible," Muhammad Ali said. "Man, you stick to acting and leave me the rhyming and the psyching."

Poitier wished him luck amid the laughter and disappeared.

Ali reached for a towel and began to rub off the Vaseline. "Is the ring nice?" he asked.

"Perfect," Dundee said.

"Is the closed-circuit system okay?"

"They say it is."

Outside, the voice of the crowd, impatient now, began to beat at the door. A big roar went up. "Quarry," someone said. "Quarry's gone."

Seconds to go. Ali stood immobile for a second, perhaps to pray, which is his habit, and Jesse Jackson hopped off the rubbing table and embraced him, almost trembling with emotion.

A knock sounded on the door. "It's time," a voice called. Muhammad Ali gave one last peek at himself in the mirrors and he went out into the corridor, his people packed around him.

The writer who did the major articles on boxing for many years for *Sports Illustrated* was a gentleman with a palindromic name (the same backward as forward): Mark Kram. Another curiosity about him was that he found it almost impossible to get on airplanes. If he couldn't get to the big fights overland, the editors had to send a substitute, on occasion me. The phobia must have frustrated him. Muhammad Ali, the champion for much of Kram's tenure at the magazine, often fought in distant and exotic countries—Malaya, Zaire, Japan. Kram did finally make it to the Philippines, the site of the last of the great trilogy of Ali–Frazier fights. He arranged to sit next to Ali on the flight out because he felt that would enhance his chances of getting there. After the fight he stayed on in the Philippines. Indeed, he got divorced and married a young Philippine woman. I always wondered if all this happened in lieu of getting back on a plane.

In any case, his phobia gave me the chance to cover the George Foreman–Muhammad Ali fight in Zaire. Billed by Ali as the "Rumble in the Jungle," the occasion drew all the major sportswriters along with one or two luminaries from the literary world.

Hunter Thompson
and Norman Mailer

Some of the correspondents had stayed on in Zaire through the postponement of the Ali–Foreman fight while Foreman's cut healed—the "old hands"—and the experience seemed to affect them as it might Conradian characters bogged down too long in a strange culture. They stalked about like colonial planters, their khaki clothes, bought so long ago at Abercrombie and Fitch, hanging off them in folds. Their conversation tended to be abrupt, as if to concentrate on a whole sentence or a complete thought were too difficult, or perhaps boring, so that listeners were stuck with a few cryptic sentences, an occasional Lingala word thrown in, often punctuated with a sharp, disconcerting guffaw. Hunter Thompson had a theory that collectively these correspondents had found a grand Medicine Man who kept them supplied with various pills and concoctions. One of them was Bill Cardoza, who was in Zaire for *New Times*; he had stayed through the postponement. He was certainly a pepped-up character. "There are great stories here," he shouted at me. "I'm told there's a house somewhere in town that's full of pygmies. I don't want to go in there. I just want to lie in front of the house and watch them go in and out." He scarcely paused for breath. "Yesterday I heard about a cobra in town. Not far away. He lives near a sewer and from time to time he puts his head up and looks around. I'm thinking of including a good look at him as one of the requirements in an Easter-egg scavenger hunt we're going to have. I'll give a hint. There are twenty-eight zones in this city and he is in Zone Limba! Right. M'Bele!"

Cardoza and Thompson talked in an odd pidgin English they had developed: "He very m'Bele. He okay. Very, very m'Bele." Cardoza said that his English had disintegrated, since his arrival back in September, into an amalgam of Lingala, French, and English, plus a little Portuguese in deference to his own blood (he has a sharp face with a mole on one cheek), and his and Thompson's behavior around town was almost as puzzling as their language. In the bars Hunter signed a number of his checks Martin Bormann and Cardoza signed his Pottstown Batal Bogas, a name he had made up for an imaginary football team. Occasionally, Cardoza would lean forward and grasp two black miniature hands hanging from a thin gold chain around Hunter's neck and shake them at people in the bars. He introduced Thompson as Chief N'Doke from the Foreman camp—Big Doctore. Thompson let himself be pushed around by his small, agile friend, his necklace shaken at people; he seemed very abstracted. It was often apparent he had Martin Bormann on his mind. He felt the Nazi criminal was hiding in Brazzaville, across the river; he talked of renting a plane to fly over there and roust him out.

The true sportswriters hung around the lobby. Some of them did not like the assignment at all. Dick Young, the columnist from the New York *Daily News*—well, if you got within earshot of him he would be saying, "Johnny Bench hit two home runs and knocked in six," information he had picked up from a three-day-old *Paris Herald* box score, or maybe from a phone call to the States, just plain homesick he was and not liking anything about Kinshasa, and I had the sense of him hanging around the lobby wearing his snappy hat with its shaving-brush decoration, wishing he were in the Pfister Hotel in Milwaukee with a couple of hours to spend before the visiting Yankees left the hotel for batting practice. When he got back to the U.S. from Zaire, he wrote in his column that he "kissed the ground" to be where such things as Johnny Bench's run-producing feats were going on. The complaints were constant. The most interesting one I heard was that one reporter, from the UPI, had filed his story to his home office over a Teletype only to discover that it had been received by the Teletype machine in the Pan-American Plastics Corporation, in Forest Hills, New York.

The most idiosyncratic journalist on hand in Kinshasa was Hunter Thompson, who had been on hand to cover the fight for *Rolling Stone.* I had always felt a close relationship with Thompson, for though he was called a gonzo journalist for his personalized reportage *(Fear and Loathing in Las Vegas),* I had always thought of him as a participatory journalist, especially for his extraordinary book *Hell's Angels,* in which he joined a motorcycle clan, much in the spirit with which I had joined the Detroit Lions, except that the motorcyclists turned out to be extremely disagreeable company, beating him up, finally and quite severely.

I had met him on the plane coming down from Europe. He had arrived on board at Frankfurt—a big, loose-limbed figure wearing a pair of dark aviator sunglasses, a purple and strawberry Acapulco shirt, blue jeans, and a pair of Chuck Taylor All Star basketball sneakers that seemed too large for his feet, as if he had snatched them from the back of a Los Angeles Laker's locker. They took him this way and that, sashaying him around so that he bumped into people a lot. With him he carried a large leather flight bag with a *Rolling Stone* identification decal and a badge which read PRESS; he referred to it sometimes as his purse and often as his kit—full of pills and vials and bottles, judging from the way it clinked when he moved it. He carried a very expensive tape recorder, and also a portable radio set, a German model which he had bought on impulse the day before—military onyx, very fancy— and which he said could receive twenty-seven stations including WBSP in Spokane, Washington. "I can tell you a white sale is going on in Liberty's or some such shop down on Green Street—big news in Spokane," he said to me. "It came through clear as a bell. It's going on tomorrow, Tuesday, if you want to do anything about it."

He sat with me during the flight. He said he was trying to recover from a humiliating evening back in the States a few nights before when, lecturing at Duke University, he had been given the hook for being outlandishly drunk on Wild Turkey bourbon and making a fool of himself in front of a large and muttering audience. The representative who met him at the airport had offered him some hashish. He had taken it. Back in the motel, he felt the day begin to slip away. He poured himself a couple of shots of Wild Turkey. He kept his audience waiting for forty-five minutes. When he walked out with his glass in front of a large velvet curtain in the university auditorium, he got himself in a further state of belligerency with the crowd by starting off, "I'm very happy to be here at the alma mater of Richard Nixon."

"That did not exactly put them in my pocket," Thompson told me. "He went to the law school there, which they were either trying to forget or were proud of, and my telling them that truly stiffened them up. The questions began. They asked me if I thought Terry Sanford was going to run for the presidency in 1976. I said that he had been party to the Stop McGovern movement and that he was a worthless pig fucker. I didn't realize that he was the president of Duke. Not long after I was given the 'hook.' "

The "hook" had been a small blond girl sent out by the head of the lecture committee; when Thompson saw her coming, he tossed the Wild Turkey, along with the ice cubes, high in the air, a fountain of resignation, and he walked off with her. He said that the booze had fetched up against the velvet curtain behind his head and left a noticeable stain that he hoped was still there . . . to backdrop future speakers as they leaned solemnly against the lectern. Especially when Terry Sanford spoke to the student body. He asked me if I thought he was going to get paid.

"I don't know," I said. I asked how long had he been out there on the stage before the hook arrived. He couldn't remember. "Did I say it was Duke?" he asked.

"Yes," I said.

"Well, I *think* it was Duke."

He said that after his removal he had gone out into the parking lot and had talked to a circle of students in a pool of light under a neon standard, but he wondered if that was sufficient representation of his role as a lecturer. He usually read his lecture contracts very carefully. On one occasion he had been asked to lecture in Miami, but he noticed that proviso number seven of the contract stipulated that if the lecturer was under the influence of alcohol, all agreements were off. Hunter told me that he had not gone to Miami.

In Kinshasa I rarely saw Thompson. He never turned up at the press conferences or sparring sessions. But he always seemed very busy—mysterious missions, looking this way and that through his big aviator glasses as he rushed through the lobby of the Hotel Inter-Continental, and one half expected him to raise a finger to his lips to warn us to keep mum. He walked along with his toes cocked out at an angle, moving along at a jackrabbity, somewhat zigzag clip, not unlike the bouncy lope of Jacques Tati, the French comedian of *Monsieur Hulot* distinction. He seemed incapable of taking a small step, so that if he happened to come up to say hello, he would take one last big sideways step to keep from crashing into you. Walking somewhere with him was difficult—his feet carrying him off at the oblique one minute, *bang* into you the next—and it was quite easy to trip over him. Since he wore sneakers, all this backing and filling and sashaying and bobbing and weaving was carried on in cat-burglar silence—which lent considerably to the conspiratorial aura he affected.

His focus of interest was never on the upcoming fight, so far as I could see; and almost out of perversity he scorned those single-minded reporters who talked shop and gossiped about what had happened that day in the two fighters' camps. "They're blind," he said. He told me that he had "tested" one small group standing in the lobby of the Inter-Continental by leaning into their conversation and telling them he had uncovered a tremendous *news* story—to hell with the fight. He told them that he had snuck into the Republic of the Congo, across the Zaire, the night before and had discovered that the Congolese were working on some huge device down by the water, a sort of *torpedo,* he thought it was, damn near half the length of a football field, and it was his opinion that they were going to point this thing at Zaire and *put-put* it across the river and blow a great hole in the waterfront section of Kinshasa. "They turned away mumbling," Thompson said of the group he had buttonholed.

"No kidding," I said.

Then he would be gone, rushing off on some strange self-imposed quest.

Any time spent with Hunter Thompson seemed to generate its own carnival lunacy, especially when he was with Ralph Steadman, his cartoonist cohort who was with him in Zaire and who served to pep things up and inspire a corporate rather than an individual madness. Once, I got Hunter seated and reminiscing (God knows where Steadman was!) at the outside bar of the Inter-Continental (he sat under a sun-sheltering thatched roof drinking planter's punch, which he thought appropriate to the colonial atmosphere of the hotel), and he began telling me about the time he and Steadman were sent to cover the America's Cup yacht races at Newport, Rhode Island, the year the Australian twelve-meter *Gretel* raced against *Intrepid*—I can't imagine what sort of report their editor expected to come out of it—and the decorum and dignity of that occasion with the blazers with the yacht club insignias and the gray flannels and the pipes and so forth prompted a flagrant counterreaction on the part of Thompson and Steadman. The two of them "borrowed" a rowboat and with Hunter at the oars set out across the harbor late at night toward the *Gretel* at her berth. Aboard they had an aerosol can of black paint. Their intent was to range up along the *Gretel* and paint "Fuck the Pope" on her sides.

"We planned it quite carefully," Hunter told me. "We were truly inspired by the thought of that yacht setting out the next morning for the trials without anyone noticing, so that it would appear in Narragansett Bay in front of the vast spectator fleet with those terrible words brandished like a seagoing advertisement, for chrissake, and these little yachts would dart out of the spectator fleet, and the skippers' faces red with rage under their braided yachting caps, and they'd point and sputter, and yell against the wind, before falling away as if they were too affronted by the message to stay close. The great thing," Hunter continued, "was that being up on the deck, *no one on board the Gretel would know what the hell the matter was.* They would look at each other, knowing that something was wrong, and they'd check the rigging, and someone would say, 'Do you suppose it's the spinnaker pole *lift,* or something, they're trying to tell us about?' and they'd check *it* out, and there'd be a lot of shrugging of shoulders under the wet-weather gear while all the time those awful three words were being carried along through the seas on the sides of that long white knife. . . ."

"Well, of course," I said. "But what—"

"We were truly prepared," Hunter told me. "In the rowboat that night I even had these parachute flares along—cost me six dollars apiece—to shoot up and create a diversion if we needed one. Our idea was that if something went wrong, we'd shoot off a flare and the guys on board the *Gretel*'d look up. 'Jesus, what the hell's going on, *look* at that thing!' and in the confusion we'd finish painting our message and clear off."

The adventure turned out to be traumatic from the start. Thompson was not especially adept with oars, and on the way to the *Gretel,* ahead in the darkness, they spun around a bit in the harbor, everything deathly still out there, the black water with not a ripple on it, so that the oarlocks, the crack of oars against the hull as Thompson caught a crab, the "whoop" from Steadman as the rowboat lurched under him echoed, Thompson said, across the bay "like gunshots."

Somehow they got to the lee of the *Gretel,* shipping oars and gliding up to her as she lay alongside the wharf. Hunter was entranced by the great white expanse of the twelve-meter's flanks in front of him. "I felt like Gully Jimson." He reached for the aerosol can and handed it to Steadman, who was, after all, the artist of the two.

"Well, right from the start we had our troubles," Hunter told me. "First of all, those aerosol cans have these steel ball bearings in there to stir up the paint, and they clatter when you shake the can up to get it operative. Not only that, but it makes a kind of hissing sound when the plunger is pressed down to apply the paint. Well, as soon as Ralph shook the can, things began to happen. Maybe they knew we were coming . . . overheard our planning, which we had done in a number of bars quite loudly that week. All around lights went on. A couple of jeeps parked on the wharf turned on their headlights. Guys with flashlights began to move around on the deck of the *Gretel.* Time for a diversion. I set off a parachute flare. It went right up past the nose of the guy who'd just happened to peek over the rail and look down at us . . . *whoosh,* within a foot of him going up, and then it popped open above the *Gretel* and began swaying. It lit up the whole scene. There was enough illumination, what with the flare and the jeep headlights and the rest of it, to read the instructions on the damn aerosol can. We had to pull out. I don't remember that Steadman ever got even an *F* of his slogan on the side of the *Gretel.* He was very badly upset—the frustrated artist, spaced out and all, and the excitement made a heavy reaction on the both of us. We abandoned the rowboat and fled along the streets. One of us left a pair of shoes in the boat. We had to get out of that town. We couldn't even go back to the hotel to get our stuff. We argued about the shoes—Steadman said they were his. I suggested he buy a pair the next day. He said it was Sunday. Then I told him I had an important appointment in New York the next morning, which was true, and it was more important for me to wear the shoes than him. Besides, I told him with great sincerity that many New Yorkers went barefoot in the summer, no one would notice when he got there, even in the evening, if he wanted to go out to the theater, or the Empire Room at the Plaza. It was quite common to see guys who were shoeless. How would he know? He was English. I told him the fastidious ones wore black socks. Perhaps he didn't believe me, but by that time I had the shoes on my feet. He couldn't dispute that. He didn't even ask for *one.* He gave up."

Thompson finished off his planter's punch with a noisy pull on the straw. He stood up and walked out by the pool, where he gazed up at a small biplane, barely moving against a wind coming down from the north across the Zaire; it was towing a long sign sweeping behind it which read ASHIMA, advertising, apparently, a local travel agency. Thompson gazed at the sight with longing. "I wonder," he mused when he came back to the table, "if I could get a sign made. Some local guy. Quick-order job." He told us that the message he wished to have hauled across the skies of Kinshasa was to read: BLACK IS WEIRD.

Norman Mailer talked about Hunter Thompson somewhat disparagingly. He felt the Thompson constituency was too easy to please. It was like playing tennis without a net. Thompson's readers were not interested in the event at all—whether it was the Super Bowl, or politics, or a championship fight in Zaire—but only in how the event affected their author. So, in fact, the only reporting Thompson had to do was about himself: the more he disdained the fight and stayed around poolside bombed and absorbed by his own peculiar paranoias (as long as he could remember them and get them down on paper), the better his readers liked it.

Mailer was in Kinshasa to cover the story in his more straightforward, if inimitable, style. I could never see him in town, covering the same event as I, without wanting to snap the top back on my felt pen and flop my notebook shut. I glanced at his notebook (often we sat together at the press conferences or the sparring sessions), which had the most childlike, illegible scrawl helter-skelter on the pages, little pips and whirls, as messy as the smudge of a thumb, page after page, because he worked very hard on these assignments, and with an intensity that I felt was stoked by his knowing two hundred other journalists were on hand challenging him.

His competitiveness! I had known him for years and marveled at it. It consumed him. The oddest and most touching instance of it—at least that I ever saw—had happened in a venue in startling contrast to central Africa: at a country party arranged by Drue Heinz for her husband, Jack, the head of the Heinz empire, for his fifty-seventh birthday on a chilly spring night in Bedford Village, New York. To honor the parity of her husband's years and the number of varieties of Heinz products, his wife had gone to considerable trouble. Everyone was supposed to come in costume appropriate to the year the host was born. A lot of people wore boaters and white flannels. I remember how cold and clear the night was. Down on the lawn among the apple and dogwood trees behind the house, the midway of a fair had been set up—a merry-go-round with a bandstand in the middle, and a Ferris wheel, and a row of concession booths lit with lanterns, where guests could have their palms read or throw baseballs at wooden milk bottles, and there was even a shimmy dancer "from Egypt" and a stage with a red velvet curtain for her to go behind. The concession that particularly attracted Mailer was a strength-testing machine—a tall column rising up twenty-five feet or so, lit by an overhead light, so that the length of it glowed in the night, and it was worked by banging a big mallet-headed sledgehammer against a flat trigger device that sent a plunger up its runners toward a fire-alarm bell at the top. Levels were marked off to indicate how strong the wielder of the hammer was—a perfect blow would send the disc roaring up past MR. PIPSQUEAK, MR. HENPECKED, MR. AVERAGE, MR. BIG SHOT, MR. MUSCLES, on up to SUPERMAN! which was synonymous with hitting the alarm bell. *Clang!* Very satisfying indeed. Many of the guests tried it. I remember Charles Addams, the *New Yorker* cartoonist, rang the alarm bell with his first swipe, and everyone clapped. Then Mailer stepped up. I've forgotten what Addams was wearing for a costume, but Mailer had got himself up in a frock coat, pantaloons, and shoes with silver buckles on them; he wore a pair of small spectacles with square rims and it was apparent that he wished to be taken for Benjamin Franklin. He hadn't realized he was supposed to dress circa 1910. He looked very benign. He hefted the sledgehammer. With a little grunt of effort he brought it down on the trigger pan; the disc flew up three quarters of the length and stopped just a bit above MR. AVERAGE MAN and quite a bit below MR. BIG SHOT; the little crowd went, "Oh."

Mailer toiled at the machine most of the night, trying to clang the bell—going off to rest after a while, but then irresistibly drawn to it once again, a curious sight in his Ben Franklin specs, and the black prayer-meeting frock coat, his body swaying back, the hammer poised, then down, and the disc would fly up just about to the spot where it had when he had first tried it. Sometimes a knot of people would collect behind him in their strange costumes, one a girl in a hen's head with russet feathers, and encourage him; he had become one of the more or less permanent sights on the midway, along with the shimmy lady "from Egypt"; but they left him, sad because the disc would never seem to get any higher, and indeed, as the night wore on and he got tired, it began to sag toward MR. HENPECKED. Most of the time I remember him alone, the frock coat off sometimes, and he swung the mallet in a fancy ruffled white shirt that shone in the light like a moth's wings; you could see him through the trees and hear the thunk of the hammer.

Since that time much had happened to him, trauma on trauma, but in Africa I had never seen Mailer in such a relaxed mood and at ease with himself, which always meant that he was splendid company. I remember being slightly surprised because he had spoken of the country as Hemingway's territory, which was going to require him to be on his mettle.

I could never think of the two writers without thinking of the competitive streak in both that was so apparent, and without wondering, with a certain amount of despair, if such intensity was a necessary adjunct to one's craft. They had never met, though it had been close. I remember once when Hemingway was passing through New York, he called up and asked if I would like to join their party for dinner; Miss Mary and George Brown, my trainer, would be there, and A. E. Hotchner, and Antonio Ordoñez, the great bullfighter who was seeing the U.S. for the first time, and Hemingway said they were going to begin by showing him the Colony Restaurant, which was perhaps not a genuine U.S. landmark but a good enough place to start from.

I said that I had arranged a dinner with a girl named Joan that evening.

I was going to say that we planned to meet Norman Mailer later but he broke in and said, "Fine, fine, bring her along." He sounded in great form. Yes, that would be fine indeed. I never had a chance to explain that we were supposed to meet Mailer.

I called Norman after Hemingway had hung up. I explained things. Mailer was very anxious to have the meeting happen. I said I thought it could be arranged. So I brought it up when we met before dinner at Willie Hearst's pied-à-terre at the top of a brownstone on Sixty-third Street off Fifth Avenue. Hemingway stood in front of a big marble fireplace, looking at Joan, the girl I'd brought, perhaps deciding whether to call her Daughter, which was his particular term of affection for girls he liked. I said that Mailer was in town; I knew he'd always wanted to meet Hemingway . . . perhaps this would be a good time. "He'd be delighted to join us. He's expecting to hear."

Hemingway was interested. "Well, yes. You call him." But Hotchner—who perhaps then was beginning to note the suggestions of paranoia, the dips of the decline, that would eventually appear in his biography *Papa Hemingway*—had overheard. He came up and shook his head; apparently he felt the mix wouldn't work, and he was quite solemn and rather worried about it. "Well, I'm not sure, Papa," he said. He sounded like someone counseling against having another drink. "No, really, I don't think so."

"Oh, well, forget it."

But Hemingway kept bringing up Mailer's name throughout the evening. We arrived at the Colony carrying our own wine in brown paper bags because it was election night and the bars were shut down until the polls closed. In deference to the Colony's rule about coats and ties, Hemingway wore a sportcoat, a pair of khaki safari trousers, and I remember a plain woolen tie knotted hugely at his throat. There was a lot of excitement at the door; the management was honored. Hemingway picked out a table in the back of the restaurant next to the swinging doors to the kitchen, and he settled himself with his back up against the wall so he could look out at what was going on: a "good *querencia*," as he put it—the bullfight term for the area in the ring the bull repairs to and fights best out of—and besides, he said he felt comfortable with the waiters coming by, and the clatter of the kitchen so close at hand. It was in fact the worst spot in the house and there was quite a lot of fluttery concern on the part of the captain who seated us there. Tables had to be pushed together; extra chairs had to be provided. Joan was settled in on Hemingway's right; I sat on his left. The waiters stared at Hemingway from under the weight of their dishes, as they went by, and the chefs, in their hats, peered at him through the diamond-shaped panes in the swinging doors.

Almost immediately he began asking about Mailer. I found myself telling him about the "contests" that Mailer at that time seemed to engage in with near manic intensity; there was hardly a social occasion at which he did not challenge someone to a confrontation of some sort. With females, he involved them in a staring contest in which he and the person opposite stared into each other's eyes until one or the other gave way. Mailer always seemed to win, the girls never knowing quite how to react, usually glancing away out of embarrassment, or because they were bored and wanted a fruit punch, or more often simply from giggling. As for Norman, I supposed he did it to establish his dominance, like Mowgli staring down Shere Khan, and he apparently got a lot of satisfaction out of it. At cocktail parties it was not an uncommon tableau to see his somewhat chunky figure, legs slightly akimbo, a drink in one hand, swaying slightly as he engaged in this sort of ocular showdown with the girl opposite.

"For chrissake," Hemingway said.

With males, I went on quickly, the confrontation was much more spectacular. The most physically awesome was a knock-the-heads contest, in which he and his opponent stood opposite, perhaps five feet apart and, at a signal, came together like a pair of rams fighting during the rutting season, bopping each other with the crown of the skull—harmless, apparently, but producing a booming sound, like a pair of gourds *thonked* together—an alarming sound to hear at a cocktail party, especially if one of them had been knocked to the floor among the chair legs. Big banging sound, and then a groan.

"Hmm," Hemingway said. He reached down and pulled the wine bottle from the paper sack by his chair.

The one who had been knocked down would get up, shake his head, and the two of them—absolutely oblivious of what was going on around them— would go at it again. In fact, the guests got rather accustomed to it, as if what they had in the midst of their party was a bizarre piece of sculpture by Tinguely that had parts, and a motor to work them, so that if people arrived late and saw the two of them coming together with the *thonk* of the heads, and asked, "My God, what's that?" the response could indeed be, "What? Oh, that . . . well, that's our . . ." You know, very blasé about it.

Of course, not many people played this game with Mailer. I had been asked but declined. Of course, there were other contests, quite a bit of arm wrestling, but Mailer's favorite *mano a mano* at the time of my dinner with Hemingway was thumb-wrestling, in which the contestant grasped the other's hand so that the two thumbs faced each other on top of the two interlocked fists; the idea at the word *go* was to try to pin the other's thumb down for three seconds. The thumbs wave around a lot like snails' antennae. Mailer was pretty good at it. There was a period of time when he got his friends doing little else, sitting around bars or after dinner, and one woke up in the morning with the thumb so sore from exercise that it was hard to handle a fork at breakfast.

"How do you do it?" Hemingway suddenly asked. "What do you have to do?"

I showed him—our hands clasped over the tablecloth, elbows between the wineglasses, and his thumb began to weave back and forth. But it moved very slowly and awkwardly, and I could see that he was going to be bad at it; someone told me later that his hand had been crippled in some long-past accident.

So Hemingway, who himself could see that his thumb was outclassed and was mumbling under his breath about it, swiftly changed the rules of the game, simplifying it considerably to a purer test of strength: now let's just see who can *squeeze* the other's hand hardest. All of this was done without explanation: he simply began to apply pressure. His grip was enormous, quite belying the relative passivity of that thumb of his. I could feel his nails bite into the palm of my hand. His arm trembled from the force flowing through it, and I could see his face begin to mottle under the white of his whiskers. I looked at him blankly, quite terrified. There was nothing I could do: I could not detach myself from Hemingway's grip.

Then under the table George Brown began to kick at my shins. He told me later that he had seen what was going on and was trying to get me to stop—Hemingway was no person to get involved in duels of this sort; it got his adrenaline going and often built up into the kinds of punch-outs Brown had seen enough of down at the *finca* in Cuba.

He began to kick quite hard, and I stiffened abruptly a few times in my chair, jolted, my eyes widening in surprise, a reaction which Hemingway must have assumed was related to the power of his grip. He was encouraged. He increased his efforts. The table jiggled; ice cubes *chinked* in their glasses.

I do not know what this would have escalated to had not Joan, sitting on Hemingway's right, leaned over and said, "Say, what's going on?"

Hemingway turned his head. She was an uncommonly pretty girl, with blond hair that framed a wide Scandinavian-boned head with big intelligent eyes in it. She was looking at him with such genuine curiosity—as if puzzled by some sort of rite she did not understand—that Hemingway responded.

His grip relaxed. "We're just horsing around," he said. He flexed his fingers. He went on. "We're pretending we're a pair of Norman Mailers."

"Oh," she said. She seemed perfectly satisfied. She turned back to Hotchner, or Ordóñez—whoever was on her right—and picked up where she had left off.

But the spell had been broken; Hemingway was affable enough after that. He talked of his admiration for Mailer, though he wasn't so sure about the parlor games. When I got a chance, I glanced at my hand under the table; there were purple half moons where his nails had gone in, deep enough to last for five days afterward. . . .

I looked at them from time to time. I mentioned them on occasion. I was having dinner with a girl I thought might be impressed. She was telling me about a ritzy weekend she had spent somewhere. "Everything there was *flambé.* My God, you'd come down for breakfast and there'd be this sizzling sound and sure enough, coming through the pantry door, the something being carried in on a flambé platter was a grapefruit, for Pete's sake."

"Have you ever read *The Sun Also Rises?*"

"What?"

"Take a look at this hand of mine. You see these marks here?"

"Where?"

"Right here. In the palm of my hand."

"Are you talking about your life line or something?"

"No, I mean these little half-moon things. Wait a minute. Let me hold them up to the light."

I could not see them myself. I turned my hand in the candlelight but they had vanished. The girl, after a puzzled look at me, had hastened on to talk about something else. I remember looking at my hand a few times afterward just to be sure, but the marks had truly gone.

Norman Mailer never met Hemingway. He had stayed by a phone most of the night Hemingway was in town, waiting for my call—both scared and excited (he told me afterward) and then both disappointed and even a bit relieved when the call never came through. He had an idea that it would have been like visiting a South American dictator—not that Hemingway behaved like one, but there would have been a considerable entourage: Ordóñez and

George Brown and Ingrid Bergman and some other famous friends—and the meeting would have been unnerving and perhaps difficult. He had a feeling Hemingway would have been pretty mad at him. "I had been impertinent," he said.

I wondered. Hemingway always seemed very polite to people at first, especially those he had admiration for, however grudgingly.

"I would have gone anyway," Mailer said. "Of course, we know that he was a man of many moods. I would have been 'Mister Streak' to get up there. I was dying to meet him."

"What would you have talked about?" I asked.

"After a while I probably would have criticized him for not being in the country when we needed him—spending so much time out of it when we were slipping into totalitarianism. What seemed to concern him were insignificant private preoccupations that bored the hell out of us . . . the feuds between his friends Leonard Lyons and Walter Winchell. I would have said, 'Stop perfuming your vanity, get your hands dirty; we're tired of you and your little hurts . . . ' The sort of criticisms I had made in *Advertisements for Myself*."

" 'Perfuming his vanity.' Well, that would have been a hell of an evening," I remarked.

"Oh, I think so," Norman said.

Some years after playing football with the Detroit Lions I came back into the game to make a television special entitled *Plimpton, the Great Quarterback Sneak.* This time playing with the Baltimore Colts, I went in for four plays against my old teammates, the Lions, in an exhibition at Ann Arbor before 106,000-odd spectators, the largest crowd, I believe, to see a professional game up until then. I improved upon my performance with the Lions—making eighteen yards when I was in there for the Colts, fifteen of them on a roughing-the-passer penalty!

The All-Pro center on the Colts team was Bill Curry, articulate, thoughtful, observant, a man who could have gone on into some area of communication, or politics, but chose instead to continue in football as a coach (Georgia Tech, Alabama, Kentucky). What I particularly remember about him at the Colts training camp is that he was one of the few players who moved around and sat at a different table during meals as if to check out his constituency and his relationship to it. He behaved like an excellent reporter on a long assignment. Blessed with astonishing recall and a born storyteller, he struck me as a perfect collaborator. We did a book together—*One More July.* The framework of the book is an auto journey from Louisville, Kentucky, up to Green Bay, Wisconsin, where Bill was going back for one last crack at it—"one more July" as players refer to it—with the Packers, where he had started his football career a decade before. What follows is a remarkable portrait of his first professional coach.

Vince Lombardi

As we drove north from Louisville, Lombardi's name began to crop up increasingly—not surprising, since Curry had gone through a near traumatic relationship with him (which was probably true of any Green Bay Packer), and the more I heard about him, the harder I pressed for details. I spent quite a lot of time saying, "What?" or "That's hard to believe," or most often, "Well, I don't see how you went on with someone like that."

Curry was patient. "You see, the key to him was that he believed that games are won not by systems or superstar players but by execution. So a player had to suffer the consequences of being driven to execute. Everything was directed at that. It was brilliantly simple. In fact, the technical part of football was much simpler than I thought it was going to be—the simplest of all the systems I played under. When I first got to Green Bay, Ken Bowman, who was the other center, went through all the plays with me in one afternoon. Then the next day, Lombardi himself sat down with me and on one sheet of a yellow legal pad he drew up every single play that the Green Bay Packers had. I think of all the documents, the awards, all the memorabilia of my career, and I'd give them up for that one sheet of paper, which I lost, or never thought was worth keeping. The famous one on the paper, of course, was the power sweep. Lombardi's theory was that nobody could stop the power sweep without giving away something else. So if they could stop forty-nine, then you ran thirty-seven, which was an off-tackle play, because in order to stop the sweep they had to move the linebacker out. So then you ran inside him. There was no need for any fancy deception or anything of the sort, in his way of thinking. We had a reverse in our playbook. I don't think we ever ran it while I was there.

"So Lombardi's main theory was, 'You don't win games with systems; you win games with execution. Whatever the system is, you do it the same way every time.' So we would run the Green Bay power sweep five, ten, fifteen, twenty times in a row. The same play over and over. In the huddle the call for it was simply forty-nine or forty-eight, depending on which direction we were going to run it. It was the play that made Jerry Kramer and Fuzzy Thurston famous, because they were the pulling guards and they'd come out around, leading Paul Hornung or Jimmy Taylor. If Jimmy was carrying the ball, it was called thirty-eight or thirty-nine.

"Given this theory, everything depended on how you could execute. If you couldn't fit into the way he thought you should execute, well, then, that was the end of you there."

"How did he let his men go?" I asked. I had always been appalled by the methods of dismissing players in the NFL.

"If people went—were cut," Curry said, "there was no explanation. None needed. Lombardi never said, 'Well, we had to cut Joe Smith and John Black today.' They were just gone. The locker next door would be empty, like the guy had disappeared into thin air. Pat Peppler did the cutting for him. He was a big, bald, jovial guy, always with a grin on his face, who could do the painful job and I'm sure make it as painless as anybody. He'd look in after breakfast and he'd say, 'The coach wants to see you, and bring your playbook,' which meant 'So long, Charlie.' On the day of the last cut my rookie year, I was sitting alone in my room. My roommate had been injured; he was in the hospital. I hadn't made the team for sure—there were some other good centers in camp—and I was sitting by myself, just apoplectic . . . waiting. Sure enough, there was a rap at the door. My heart jumped. I opened the door and it was Peppler. I could feel the blood just drain from my face.

"He said, 'Bill, my wife, Lindy, wants Carolyn to go to a luncheon with her tomorrow. Have Carolyn call her, would you?' and he turned and started to walk off.

"I leaned out the door. I said, 'Mr. Peppler, if you ever do anything like this to me again, I'm going to break your neck!' He turned around, bewildered. He didn't realize what he'd done. We laugh about it today. He scared me to death. I could've killed him.

"With that there was a huge letdown. I'd made the Packers . . . what I had aimed for all those years. I was a professional athlete. I had made the team, one of the best teams in the business. Then my good friend Rich

Koeper, who had been the other rookie center and who had been moved from center to offensive tackle when I showed up from the All Star game, came to my room and he said, 'Bill, could you help me load my stuff in the car?'

" 'What do you mean?'

" 'I'm leaving,' he said.

"He saw how low I looked. 'Hell, man,' he said, 'you've won the battle; you've defeated someone else. You've taken the job, and *you're* there instead of them.'

"But I felt none of that. I helped him load his things, and then I began to drive him to the motel where he was going to catch a limousine for the airport. I began to *weep*. I cried and cried and I couldn't stop! It was just humiliating . . . finally a big hero, stud athlete, and here I was making an ass of myself. Rich Koeper was crying too. That was a real scene."

"I'll say," I remarked.

By this time we were miles up Route 65, long past the great curve of the expressway above the candy-making factories in the north section of Louisville . . . out in the country with the heat beginning to build up, the air waves beginning to shimmer over the fields.

I asked Curry if there was a way one could distinguish a Green Bay Packer other than their habit of breaking down and weeping occasionally.

Curry grinned and said that one of the earmarks of the Green Bay Packers was their tremendous physical condition . . . that driven by Lombardi, a player had to be in shape, in *great* shape, to survive. "Take Jimmy Taylor, the great fullback," Curry explained. "He was just about the best-conditioned athlete I've ever seen. He knew that I had a background of having worked a little with weights. Not much; I'm not a power guy at all. But Jimmy would get me to lift weights with him between the morning and the afternoon practices. It'd be ninety-nine degrees and like a furnace outside. My locker was next to his. He'd say, 'Come on.' I'd say, 'Well, gee, Mr. Taylor, we've got to go back out and practice this afternoon.' 'Well, we're going to do our bench presses, kid.' And we'd go and do bench presses.

"It was worth it. Lombardi would just *destroy* you physically if you weren't in shape. The calisthenics period before practice was incredible—not fifteen side-straddle hops but a *hundred*. Then at the conclusion of these calisthenics, which were led by a coach, Lombardi would walk up to the front of the group with a sadistic grin on his face and he'd say, 'Okay, let's go.' It was time for the grass drill. We'd start running in place. He wanted you

135

to pick up those knees to your chest, and when he said 'Down,' you'd dive on the ground; he'd say, 'Up,' and you'd jump to your feet, running in place. He would make you do them until you literally could not get off the ground. I've seen our offensive captain, Bob Skoronski, pass out. Guys were vomiting on the field, other guys could not get up off the ground, and he'd go over and say, 'Get up! Get up!' and they couldn't. That kind of thing.

"We'd just keep going. One time we did seventy-eight of them, up and down, which is an *awful* lot. Ken Bowman and I used to count them to keep from going insane with the pain. Willie Wood was famous for not . . . he would just quit! Lombardi'd say, 'Stop the drill!' which thrilled us because we could puff a bit. 'Willie, you're going to do those right! Now get going, you're going to do it for everybody.' Willie still couldn't do them. He'd fall down on the ground and he'd push himself up on one knee and then fall over again. You had to be as good a football player as Willie to be able to get away with that sort of thing. Finally Lombardi'd say, 'Oh, God, that's okay, okay,' and then we'd go on.

"Then, at the end of the grass drills, when everybody was just literally staggering, Lombardi would blow the whistle and we'd sprint around the goal post and back to the far end of the field . . . probably two hundred and fifty yards, and you had to *sprint*. If you were last you were in big trouble. When you'd start to run after those grass drills, your legs wouldn't work! Literally would not function! They'd just wobble, and it took a conscious effort to get one in front of the other. Then you'd recover a bit and you'd get to where you were actually running and you'd get around to the far end of the field, when you'd get about thirty seconds to get a breath of air; everybody'd just drop to a knee and just gasp and pant . . . even losing an occasional breakfast and that sort of thing.

"I always took great pride in being in good shape and doing every grass drill. Some guys would watch Lombardi when he'd walk by them, and when he had his back to them, they'd quit. When he'd come back, then they'd get going again. Well, I always did every single one of them, and when he blew his whistle for the sprint, I ran just as fast as I could. I wasn't fast enough to be first in from running around the goal post, but I always would *try* to be near.

"One day in my second year with the Packers, Jimmy Taylor came up to me and said, 'Now, Bill, you know you're a veteran now.' 'Yeah, that's right,' I said. 'You know you've gotta help set a good example for these young guys, these rookies.'

" 'Right.'

" 'Now, you know when we do our grass drills and run around the goal post?'

"I thought he was about to compliment me on how hard I tried.

" 'Well, when you get back over to the far end of the field . . . when we get to our little break, you know? Don't breathe so hard.'

" 'What?' I said. 'What do you mean, don't breathe so hard? I'm dying!'

" 'Well, you're in good shape,' he said, 'but you shouldn't be breathing so hard. These new guys, these rookies, will think you're tired and that you're not tough. Gotta be a tough guy.'

"I thought he was kidding. I started to laugh.

" 'I mean it,' he said. 'When you get back, blow it out. Then you'll feel all right. You don't have to be huffing and puffing.'

"Well, I thought, this man's crazy! The next morning I watched him. He did every single grass drill. He hit the ground, he picked his knees up higher than anybody else. In fact, Lombardi'd watch him and go crazy: 'Attaboy, Jimmy, attaboy! Look here, everybody, here's somebody in shape. Jimmy Taylor's always in shape!' That kind of thing. And he'd sprint around the goal post and come back. Sure enough! Everybody's dying and Jimmy Taylor was not breathing hard! He was just superbly conditioned. I thought I was in shape and I was just nothing compared to him. And then, to match his physical heft, he had this supreme self-confidence. At meetings, during the film critiques, Lombardi would jump on him, and he'd just sit in the back of the room with his cigar and grin. He'd take a couple of puffs on that big cigar."

I interrupted. "Do you mean with all that emphasis on conditioning he'd let people smoke?"

"Yeah," Curry said. "You could even smoke in the locker room. This was one of the great shocks to me . . . when I'd come in and Hornung would light up at half-time. . . . Well, Lombardi'd jump on Jimmy for making a mistake that showed up in the films, and Jimmy would take a drag off his cigar, a big puff of smoke would drift up, and he'd look around and grin and flick the ash off the cigar like Groucho Marx and he'd say, 'Guess I'm washed up, Coach.' Unbelievable self-confidence.

"In practice he'd sneak off to the field where the kickers were. Lombardi'd yell at him, 'Taylor, get over heah—what you been up to?' and Taylor'd raise his arms up over his face defensively and he'd say, 'Coach, I was working on my field goal block.' He could get away with it because he was such an extraordinary football player. But then, of course, Taylor played out his option and went to play in New Orleans. It destroyed their relationship."

"I remember that," I said. "They never spoke again, did they?"

"Loyalty was such a big thing," Curry said. "Jimmy was a very tough negotiator on contracts, but Lombardi was too. Sometimes he would just tell a guy, 'You get your ass up there and sign that contract.' And they'd do it. Because of this one-on-one relationship with players, Lombardi hated agents. He told the guys, 'Don't send some agent in here to negotiate for you.' This was a long time before the lawyer-agent kind of representative got to be the vogue. Well, Jim Ringo thought he could take the chance. He was a great center for the Packers, and he probably regarded himself as almost indispensable because he called all the blocking—a key figure in the offensive line—and besides, he had this phenomenal reputation around the league. So he sent a lawyer, an agent, into Lombardi's office to negotiate for him. The gentleman walked in and said, 'Mr. Lombardi, I'm here to represent Jim Ringo in his contract negotiations.' Lombardi said, 'You'll excuse me for a moment,' and he got up and left the room. About five minutes later he came back and he said, 'I'm sorry, you're talking to the wrong person.'

" 'I don't understand,' the agent said.

" 'Well, Jim Ringo now plays with the Philadelphia Eagles,' Lombardi said. 'You'll have to talk to them.' "

"And that's what happened with Taylor?" I asked.

"Something like that," Curry said. "Lombardi could not intimidate Jimmy into signing. He played out his option and went to play for New Orleans. I'm told Lombardi never forgave him. He never referred to him again by name. He called him 'the other guy.' They put Paul Hornung's jersey up in the Packer museum showcase, but not Taylor's. Lombardi said, 'We miss Hornung around here, but we could always do without the other guy.' "

I shook my head and remarked that I didn't understand how all that effort Taylor had made in his behalf—all those years of painful effort tearing through the middle of opposing lines—would not balance out just about *anything* that Lombardi could have held against him.

"He just wasn't an easy man," Curry said simply. "At times I couldn't stand the sight of him. Neither could the rest of us. I remember Gale Gillingham, his first week at Green Bay, was sitting in the backseat while somebody was driving us from practice back to the locker room. Gillingham had never said a word. In fact, I don't think I had heard him say a word since he'd arrived. He'd broken his right hand in the All Star game, and he had a big cast on it. We'd had those awful grass drills. Of course, to Lombardi, there was no such thing as an injury. Gilly did every one of those grass drills with one hand. Everybody noticed him and realized: We've got one here; he's going to be all right! The rest of us were struggling to do them with *two*. Well, on the drive back somebody said, 'Lombardi was *so* bad today.' You know the term that's applied when somebody's in an especially bad mood? 'He was on the rag today.' That was usually the comment somebody would make about him on an especially tough day. Well, Gillingham was sitting in the backseat and he suddenly said, unsolicited, the first words any of us had ever heard him say: 'That is the most disgusting man I've ever seen in my life.' I said, 'Boy, that sums it up.' "

"I would have sulked," I said. "I would have hangdogged around just to show him how awful I thought he was."

Curry laughed. "There was no way you could manipulate him. And yet the devastating thing about *him*—which caused the love-hate relationship the players had with him—was the way he used his ability to manipulate *you*, to make you do whatever he wanted you to do. He could ruin your whole day in a matter of seconds. In the morning I'd be starting on my weight program and he'd walk in and scowl. I'd try to speak to him. He'd ignore me, or mumble something, and I hated him even more, and he'd get me thinking: What the hell am I *doing* in this business? And then ten minutes later he'd walk up and put his arm on my shoulder and say, 'I like the way you work. You're doing a good job, and I'm proud of you,' and I'd *die* for him! Do anything for him! Then the realization would come: My God, I'm being manipulated like a piece of Silly Putty. He flattens me out when he wants me flat. He makes me round and bounces me when he wants to bounce me. He *makes* me. . . . It was somehow demeaning, and yet at the same time it was exhilarating to be a part of all this because you knew—and I don't care what anybody says about him—that you were in the presence of greatness. Anybody who can move men like that.

"He completely dominated me for two football seasons, and to this day, anytime I'm in a bind with a difficult problem to overcome, without exception I always think of him. Always! I think of him telling me, 'Son, the only thing you can do is to get off your ass and stop feeling sorry for yourself and overcome the pain and *do it*. Work out your method. Work out your system, and execute it. And don't tell me about a sprained ankle, and don't tell me that somebody's not being fair to you. I don't want to hear *any* of that. Do it!' That *always* rings in my mind."

"Well, was he fair?" I asked. "I mean in the sense of being equitable."

"Not especially," Curry said. "I remember one day in 1966, we were watching a film of a great game we had played the previous Sunday against the Cleveland Browns. It was the year after they had won the title. They just ate us up in the first half. The score was 14–0 when we went into the locker room. . . . Frank Ryan, their quarterback, was having a big day. We came out in the second half and began to peck away. Finally, with about two minutes left, the score was 20–14 in favor of the Browns. Lou Groza had kicked this mammoth forty-nine-yard field goal, which had hit the crossbar and bounced over for three points for them. With a couple of minutes left and six points behind, we started from our own twenty and gradually moved down the field. Finally, on their nine-yard line, it was fourth and goal, and time for a last play. Bart called a pass play. The wide receivers were covered, so he dumped it off to Jimmy Taylor in the flat. There were three tacklers— you've got to see this to believe it—and all they had to do was get him on the ground and the game was over. Well, he went by the first, around the second, and he ran over a third, and got into the end zone. We kicked the extra point and won the game 21–20. You can imagine the satisfaction. It was very hot. When I weighed in after the game I weighed two hundred and eighteen pounds. I had lost fourteen pounds.

"But in the film Lombardi began to notice *my* afternoon. I had been playing against Vince Costello, who was a very good middle linebacker. He was a very cagey guy. The week before, Lombardi had told me the way to work on him when we ran our sweep was not to take a sharp angle to cut him off, because he'd get around behind me to make the play. He wanted me to take an angle more directly at him, which is an unusual way to do it. Well, I did what the coach said. Costello beat me all day long. It was painfully obvious in the film that Tuesday. I'd go flying straight at him. He just ignored me. I'd miss him completely, and he'd make the tackle on Hornung or somebody. Lombardi stopped the projector and ran it back again. He didn't say a word. Ran it back again. Ran it back once more. Finally he stopped the projector, and in the dark I could see those glasses turn toward me. He said, 'Curry, you know that's God-awful.' All my teammates were sitting there. He said, 'How would you describe that?' Well, I was just burning. I was just *dying* to say, 'Coach, you *told* me to do it that way!' But of course I didn't. He went on, 'We're going to look at this again.' He ran it again, and then he went into one of his tirades. 'That's God-awful! You stink! *You* stink! And you know something else? Your snaps for punts have been stinking, too.' It went on for five minutes or so."

"I don't understand why you didn't get up and tell him, 'Well, you told me to, Coach.' " I said.

"Because," Curry replied, "all this time it kept running through my mind that though I kept excusing myself because, really, he *had* told me to use that technique, the point was that the only thing that matters is: Did you accomplish your mission? And if you didn't, there's no such thing as an excuse."

"Did anyone stand up to him?" I asked.

"Just about the only person who could handle these critiques was Fuzzy Thurston. Fuzzy would sit up in front, and when he knew that one of his bad plays was coming up, he'd begin to rant and rave before Lombardi could. It was really a riot. Some behemoth would thrash by Fuzzy, who'd missed his block—someone like Roger Brown of the Detroit Lions, who weighed three hundred pounds, and even before Roger could get into the backfield and crush Bart to the ground, Fuzzy'd be saying, 'Oh, look at that! Isn't that the worst block you've ever seen! That's awful!' Lombardi, in spite of himself, would have to laugh. He'd say, 'Fuzzy, you're right. That's *bad.* Okay, next play.' And Fuzzy could get away with it!

"Really no one was immune. The great veterans, everybody—it didn't make any difference. I remember him saying things to Jerry Kramer, who was an All-Pro guard. 'Did you see that, Jerry? Do you think that you're worth what we're paying you? Do you think for a minute that your football deserves the kind of dollars that you're getting?'

"Jerry'd be sitting there, a huge, powerful guy, literally leaning backward and bending the back of his metal folding chair in anguish. Just a devastating kind of thing! You asked about Lombardi being fair. Henry Jordan's great contribution about playing under Lombardi was: 'Lombardi is very fair: he treats us all alike—like dogs.'

"As he moved around the practice field, it was a presence that you could sense. It motivated people to perform. It wasn't malevolent. It scared. It was unique. Joe Thomas, when he was general manager of the Colts, had a presence when he appeared on the field . . . but it was sort of debilitating; everybody got tense and angry when he came around. When Lombardi came around, everybody got afraid . . . but highly active. The voice, like the personality, had just the most indescribable intensity. Everything he said was for effect. One day while we were practicing, a little dog came out and started prancing around the practice field. Nobody could concentrate because he was running in and out between people's legs. Just a cute little setter dog. Guys were trying to shoo him away—'Go! Go!'—and he'd scamper off and then run back, wagging his tail and having a good time. Lombardi was about sixty yards away at the other end of the field and suddenly this voice came booming from down there: *'Get the hell off the field!'* I swear I saw this happen: the dog tucked his tail between his legs, and the last time we saw him he was rounding a corner two blocks away from the field."

We drove on for a while through the Indiana countryside; the green overhang sign announced that we were coming up on a state road that swung off to a town called Franklin. We started chatting about other matters. Curry began talking about stereo equipment, but abstractedly, his mind still on Lombardi, and suddenly he said, "The difficult thing to articulate is how really forceful his presence was. Jerry Kramer didn't get it in his book, *Instant Replay.* He just didn't capture it. Nobody has. They did a TV show with Ernest Borgnine and it was just pathetic. Borgnine wasn't pathetic—Borgnine was superb. But they decided the Lombardi story was about a man going from New York, where he'd hoped to be a head coach, to an obscure town in Wisconsin that his wife didn't like. Crazy. The real story should have been about this man's ability to shock, to frighten, to overpower other people with whatever means he had to use. On the first day he gathered the team together he always showed the film of the championship game from the year before. He didn't comment on it; he just showed it, whether the Packers were in it or not. And then he'd turn off the projector and he'd say, 'Gentlemen, I have no illusions about what's going to happen to me if I don't win. So don't you have any illusions about what's going to happen to you if you don't produce for me. . . . There are three things that're important in your life: your religion, your family, and the Green Bay Packers—in that order.' And then, as soon as we'd get on the field, he'd get the order mixed up in his own mind. What was paramount was—by whatever means—to build in you that sense that you had to be the best ever. When I first came to pro ball I just wanted to make the team; then when I did I decided I sure would like to be first-string; then after that I made All Pro, and I thought: Now I want to be All Pro every year. The obsession to be best was precisely Lombardi's. Time and time again he'd say things like this: 'When you go on the field, I want you thinking about one thing—that is, for this day I'm going to be the greatest center in football. When those people walk out of the stands, I want that guy to turn to his wife and say, "We just saw the greatest offensive center who ever played." '

"So he had this uncanny talent for manipulating people to be exactly what he wanted them to be. He would select a role for each player. He wrote the play, he did the choreography, and if you didn't fit the role, he would change your personality so that you could play the part. If you didn't like the role, it didn't make any difference; he manipulated you and made you what he wanted you to be until you could play it better than anybody else in the National Football League. *Or* he would get rid of you. I heard him tell Steve Wright, who was a guy who grinned a lot—he'd miss a block and come back to the huddle with a smile on his face, which would drive Lombardi insane. 'Goddammit, Wright, you think that's funny! You're never gonna be a man! You're never gonna make it! *Yes,* you are! *I'm* gonna make you, I'm gonna create you. I'm gonna make you into something before I'm through with you.'

"I heard him tell another guy, 'I'm gonna make you work. I'm gonna make you hurt before I get rid of you!' And he did get rid of him. That was Rich Marshall. He had this forefinger cut off at the knuckle so that when he took his stance it looked like he'd stuck a finger in the ground. He got a lot of kidding about it. 'Git your finger out of the ground, Marshall!' "

"How Lombardi treated him just seems arbitrarily cruel," I commented. "What do you truly think he thought of all you players?"

Curry thought for a while, and then he said, "This will be argued by some players, but I believe that Lombardi really did love us. I don't think he could've appealed to our better instincts if we didn't feel that he really cared about us. I've seen him cry when we lost a game. Here we go again—those weeping Packers. It wasn't for appearance's sake. I mean, I've just seen the tears in his eyes. Of course, it was foremost because *he* had lost. But he also had genuine affection for . . . he liked to be around 'the guys.' He wanted to be accepted. When he was admonishing us about our behavior, he used to say things to us like: 'Don't you think that I'd like to go get drunk downtown too? Don't you think I'd like to go out and do that? Don't you think I'd like you guys to like me? I know you don't like me. But I don't give a crap about that. We're here to do a job. Your liking me is not near as important as winning football games. So I don't *care* if you like me.' That kind of thing. Every now and then it would surface, but it was very rare. He was such an odd contradiction. He was very profane, yet he went to church every day; he was a daily celebrant, Catholic, very devout. He considered the priesthood at one point. Bart Starr said, 'When I heard about this man taking over the team in 1959, I could hardly wait to meet a man that went to church every day.' Then he went on to say, 'I worked for him for two weeks and then I realized this man *needs* to go to church every day.' "

Curry shifted slightly in his seat behind the steering wheel. "You were asking me a while back if anyone stood up to him. I remember Starr one time. We were in Cleveland playing an exhibition game. Lombardi was into one of his tirades up and down the sidelines. Our offense was driving—Bowman was the center—and they got to Cleveland's four-yard line with a first down when Bart took too long in the huddle and they marched off a delay-of-game penalty against him. Lombardi went insane. He started *screaming:* 'What the hell's going on out there?' This terrible voice that everyone in that huge stadium—there were eighty-one thousand people there—could hear. I saw Bart slip back out of the huddle to glare at Lombardi; then he called the play and threw a touchdown pass to Boyd Dowler.

"At this point I started out on the field, trotting past Lombardi, to snap the ball for the extra point. That was my job. But to my surprise I saw Starr coming toward us, which was odd because he was supposed to be the holder for the extra-point play. So I stopped . . . baffled. I thought perhaps he was hurt. As he got alongside me, about fifteen feet from Lombardi, he yelled out at the top of his lungs and just *laced* him with the most incredible verbal barrage."

"I almost went to my knees. Bart Starr! This kind and decent churchman, one of the gentlest people, never a word of profanity or anything of the sort, and here he was yelling these things at Lombardi in a big, booming, resonant voice. I turned around and Lombardi was standing there, just agape; he couldn't believe it, either. Well, we ran on the field, kicked the extra point, and nothing was said about it. Lombardi didn't say another word the rest of that game—truly stunned, probably—and he was nice to us for about two weeks after that. Then he began to get mean again.

"We had a sort of war council, in which there were about six guys—Bob Skoronski, who was the offensive captain, and Tom Moore and Bart and Paul Hornung, guys like that—and every now and then when things got really bad, about once a year, they'd go to Lombardi and say, 'Coach, you're going to have to let up. You're driving us all crazy! We can't function under this withering kind of abuse.' Maybe he'd let up for a day or two. Maybe we'd have a good game, and he'd be nice for a few days. But then we'd have a bad game, and he'd stomp back in on Tuesday morning and everybody'd just be sitting there aquiver. He'd say, 'I tried it your way. I'm sick and tired of being father confessor for a bunch of yellow, no-good punks. The whip! That's the only thing you understand. And I'm going to whip you again, and drive you, make you! Why do I always have to make you? Don't you think I get tired of being this way?' Once again everybody would squirm and feel that somehow they'd made the wrong choice for a profession: What am I doing with this person here? Why? But invariably he would come back in the next breath and win everybody over again . . . although sometimes you couldn't imagine how he could do it.

"Once in 1965 we had been to Los Angeles and had lost a game to the Rams that we *had* to win. Los Angeles was the last-place team in the league and they just *stomped* us. On the way back, Lionel Aldridge—the big defensive end—began to sing. A couple of beers and he was singing! Lombardi heard about it. Well, on Tuesday morning he came into the meeting and he began to question Lionel's ancestry. He got into such an emotional shouting binge that it was like one of those tirades you'd see in films of Hitler going through a frenzy—though I don't mean to draw any parallel. I'm talking about awesome, forceful personalities, not the quality of what they did or the kind of people they were. Finally Lombardi said, 'I want all the assistant coaches out of this room and all the doors shut. I want to be here with these football players . . . if that's what you can call them.' So everybody cleared out. Scurried out."

"The assistant coaches?" I asked.

"Oh, yes. The assistant coaches were terrified of him too. Absolutely. You could hear him in the next room dressing *them* down the same way he did us, though of course he never did it in front of us.

"When the coaches were out and the doors were shut, Lombardi really went at it. The meeting seemed to go on for an hour and a half, with Lombardi screaming, shouting: 'Goddammit, you guys don't care if you win or lose. I'm the only one that cares. I'm the only one that puts his blood and his guts and his heart into the game! You guys show up, you listen a little bit, you concentrate . . . you've got the concentration of three-year-olds. You're nothing! I'm the only guy that gives a damn if we win or lose.'

"Suddenly there was a stirring in the back of the room, a rustle of chairs. I turned around and there was Forrest Gregg, on his feet, bright red, with a player on either side, holding him back by each arm, and he was straining forward. Gregg was another real gentlemanly kind of guy, very quiet. Great football player. Lombardi looked at him and stopped. Forrest said, 'Goddammit, Coach . . . excuse me for the profanity.' Even at his moment of rage he was still both respectful enough and intimidated enough that he stopped and apologized. Then he went on: ' 'Scuse the language, Coach, but it makes me sick to hear you say something like that. We lay it on the line for you every Sunday. We live and die the same way you do, and it hurts.' Then he began straining forward again, trying to get up there to punch Lombardi out. Players were holding him back. Then Bob Skoronski stood up, very articulate. He was the captain of the team. 'That's right,' he said. 'Dammit, don't you tell us that we don't care about winning. That makes me sick. Makes me want to puke. We care about it every bit as much as you do. It's our knees and our bodies out there that we're throwing around.'

"So there it was. The coach had been confronted, the captain of a ship facing a mutinous crew, with the first mate standing and staring him down face-to-face, and it truly looked as though he had lost control of the situation.

"But then damned if the master didn't triumph again. After just a moment's hesitation he said, 'All right. Now *that's* the kind of attitude I want to see. Who else feels that way?'

"Well, at this very moment Willie Davis was nervously rocking back and forth on his metal folding chair. Willie was known as Dr. Feelgood on the team because every day at practice, with everybody limping around and tired and moaning and complaining, somebody always looked over, and asked, 'Willie, how you feel?' He always said the same thing: 'Feel *good*, man!' So there was Dr. Feelgood rocking back and forth and you know how those chairs are. He lost his balance and he fell forward! He fell right out into the middle of the room . . . onto his feet; it looked as if he had leapt from his chair just as Lombardi asked, 'Who else feels that way?' And Willie sort of grinned sheepishly and he said, 'Yeah, me, too! I feel that way, man!' Lombardi said, 'All right, Willie, that's great.' And it swept through the room; everybody said, 'Yeah, hell—me too!' and suddenly you had forty guys that could lick the world. That's what Lombardi created out of that situation. He went around to each player in that room with the exception of the rookies— he skipped the four of us rookies—and as he looked in each man's face he said, 'Do you want to win football games for me?' And the answer was 'Yes, sir'—forty times. He wended his way through that mass of people sitting around in that disarray of chairs and looked each guy nose to nose two inches from his face and he said that thing: 'Do you want to win football games?' and every man said, 'Yes, sir,' and we did not lose another game that year."

A golf adventure was a continuation of the participatory journalism series for *Sports Illustrated.* The magazine had been able to arrange invitations to the pro-ams in the three major West Coast tournaments that occupy the schedule in late January and February—the Bing Crosby (now the cumbersomely titled AT&T Pebble Beach Pro-Am Tournament), the Lucky International in San Francisco, and the Bob Hope Classic in Palm Springs. I expanded the articles into a book entitled *The Bogey Man,* a title that should give a fair indication of my golfing skills.

Golf Caddies

Just about the liveliest place to listen to golf talk, though of a slightly different nature, was along the rail fence where the touring caddies gathered out behind the clubhouse—just off the practice putting green—where they perched upon the fence between the big golf bags they tended, many of them in white coveralls with the identifying numbers and names of their professionals across the shoulder blades. Their rialto was here, and they rocked back and forth on the fence and compared notes and swapped yarns and gossip, and talked of their rounds, particularly about money and how their pro had let them down: "Oh my, we're doin' jes' fine and then my man he goes an' *dies* on me," etc., etc.

There are about forty professional caddies—touring caddies, they're called—some of whom, the fortunate ones, stay with one golfer throughout the winter tour (the PGA does not allow the touring caddy system during the summer months when the high schools are out—at that time a caddy must stick to a home course) while the others, less fortunate, travel uncommitted and hope to pick up a bag, or "pack a bag" as the phrase goes, when they turn up on the eve of a tournament and look to catch a pro's eye and sign up with him for that particular event.

The touring caddies are a wildly individual clan, not at all to be confused with the local caddies. They are a nomadic group (some of the more disapproving professionals refer to them as "The Traveling Brewery") that moves from tournament to tournament, usually four or five to a car, and they suddenly appear around the caddy shacks with the abruptness and aplomb of extremely competent men sent to do an expert job. The local caddies stare at them with as much awe as they work up for the professional golfers. Johnny Pott once told me: "I can't imagine what it's like to travel with the touring

148

caddies. I remember once a car with six of them in it—going cross-country—came through my hometown, and they stopped by to pick up an open-faced driver I had promised one of them. Well, I opened up the trunk of their car to put in the driver and there wasn't anything in there at all—no suitcases, kits, anything. Real Gypsies. They travel in just their shoes."

During the tour I got to know some of them by wandering down and leaning up against the fence and asking questions from time to time. It was very lively listening. Most of the touring caddies are blacks, though there were exceptions, notably Arnold Palmer's caddy, Bob Blair, a loner I never saw with the others, and Jack Nicklaus's regular caddy, Angelo Argea, who was quite a different sort, being a soft-spoken Italian with a pleasant grin who was very popular with the others. In joshing him, they had a number of derogatory nicknames, which he took in good humor. The caddies, as a whole, owned a splendid variety of nicknames: Cut Shot, Violence, Texas Sam, the Wolfman, the Rabbit, the Baron, Cricket, the Rock, Big Ted, the Golfball . . . their names peppering their conversation, as in, "Hey, Cricket, you seen the Golfball?" "Hell, no, ask the Wolfman."

Ted Randolph was the one called the Wolfman. He was given that nickname in the Boy Scouts where he had once made, he told me, a very impressionable imitation of a werewolf. The name stuck for a while and was about to fade away. "Then," he said, "I grew me a long beard and I damn near *looked* like a werewolf. So the name stuck for good."

Walter Montgomery was the one they called Violence. He had had his hair straightened. He kept it flattened slick against his skull, so that the sheen of black seemed newly painted on. He was named after his short temper—a characteristic he had worked in recent years at curbing.

"What did you use to do, Violence?" I asked, relishing the odd nickname and the strangeness of it on the tongue. "Hey, Violence?" I asked, grinning at him.

"I've cooled it, baby. It don't make no sense. It don't do no help to the guys I was packing for."

"You mean you took it out on the golfers?" I asked.

"A cat'd make some crazy play like miss a putt of two foot. Now a cat like that, why he's cuttin' my money, making a bad shot, dig? So I go up and kick his bag. I really bang it."

"Well, how did they take that?"

"Like I say, it don't make no sense, 'cause it don't do no good. They start keepin' a side eye on me, like maybe I'm fixin' to lift a shoe into *them* the next time, druther than the bag. It don't do no good for their golf, and then I . . . well, they ain't fixin' hard to have me pack for them again.''

"What else did you do?"

Violence frowned slightly. "Oh," he said, "I slam the pin back in the cup real hard, jes' to show the guy, y'know, what I think of his messin' up the shot. Threw my cap quite a lot. Once I sailed it across the green and it hit Doug Sanders in the back of the head. But then, like I say, I cool it. I pack for Julius Boros and he like me and he say, 'Man, act like me, very calm, all the time, and you do okay.' So I do what he say. I'm goin' fine for a good long time now, and it pays good, it's an honest livin' an' I'm gettin' on fine. But the guys remember what I done—y'know, like in San Diego, when we go there for the Open, they say, 'Hey, Violence, baby, so you goin' out on the town? Well, you broke a guy's jaw in this town, you re-call,' and they grin, and I say, 'Sure, man, but that was las' year.' They waiting for me to bust someone, they al'ays *lookin'*, but I ain't done nothing like that for a time. 'Course I ain't sayin' when a guy messes a shot, the juices don' get worked up. . . ."

I said that frankly I was glad he wasn't packing my bag, if he didn't mind my saying so.

He laughed and said oh, yes, he had heard about my golf.

Alfred Dyer, out of New Orleans, was called the Rabbit. He was very self-assured. "You talk to the Rabbit," he said, "an' you're getting the stuff straight from number one. If it's caddyin' you're talkin' 'bout, the Rabbit's your man. Why, at those big Jewish country clubs in the East, it's the Rabbit they's always calling for. 'Where's the Rabbit? Where's the Rabbit?' They say, 'You think I'm takin' one step on this course lessen the Rabbit's packing my bag, you is loco in the *head.*' Why, I make forty dollars a day in the East jes' on my name alone. Autographs? Man, the Rabbit's always signing autographs. . . ."

At this there was a bit of good-natured hooting from the others down the fence. Someone shouted: "Rabbit, you can't write, man, an *X,* much lessen your name."

I asked: "Rabbit, what do you think you do best as a caddy?"

The Rabbit thought and he said: "Well, calm my man down, I think that's what I do very good. Pull him off to the side when he's got a lot of pressure on him and I tell him, let the Rabbit share it with you. Maybe I get him telling what he done the night before—jes' to get his mind off the pressure and make him relax. 'Course sometimes you got to do jes' the opposite—fire yo' man up. Now take Tom Weiskopf in the Colonial. We're comin' down the stretch with a jes' fine lead, but then Tom bogeys three holes in a row and he comes up on the thirteenth jes' 'bout ready to fall to pieces. He's chokin'. He's got this big ball in his throat. He says, 'Rabbit, we're going to have to play for second place. I'm playing it safe in here.' So the Rabbit says, 'Man, I'm dropping yo' bag right here if you don't go for the flag. You take a two iron and put the ball up there nice an' easy. Smooth,' I said. I can say 'smooth' like you never heard nobody say that word, like silk. Well, he done it.''

Quite another different sort of touring caddy was Dale Taylor, Billy Casper's caddy—a soft-spoken polite man in his forties, I would guess, and with very much of a no-nonsense attitude about his profession. He was an excellent golfer, I was told. He told me that he caddied for his man with pleasure because Casper always tended to the business at hand—their rounds together on a golf course had no other purpose.

"That's the point," Dale said. "If you're in the business and you want to make a dollar, you got to play with a man who's got a right attitude. Billy Casper's got a wife and two kids. He goes out on a golf course and he's got their support in mind. He isn't thinking about anything else but his business. That's the attitude I got to have too. We think alike. I'm good for him to have around. He keeps me on the payroll and I baby-sit for his children, things like that.''

I asked: "But don't all golfers go out on the course with that same attitude—that they're going to win?"

"They should," Dale said. "But then you get a golfer like Ken Still, who has this really great talent, this fantastic potential. . . ." He looked around at the other caddies. "That's right, isn't it?" They all nodded. "And yet when he goes out on a golf course, his mind just isn't on what's what. He's interested in sports, Ken Still is, and if there's a ball game going on some-where, he's thinking about it. He's like to have a transistor plugged in his ear, and sometimes he yells things like, 'Come on, Duke, belt one for ol' Ken.' You ever see Ken walk down a fairway?" The caddies all rocked back and forth, grinning. "Why, he's got that radio goin' in his ear, maybe one in *each* if they got two ball games on, and his feet come down *plop plop* like he's dizzy, and you got to see him wobble from one side of the fairway to the other, his arms waving, and his lips wobbling, too, and then he wanders off, and then his caddy, he's got to say, 'Man, we're over *heah*,' just to get his man back on the track.''

151

"You jivin'," someone said. They were all laughing.

Doug Sanders's caddy, who was called Cricket, spoke up and said that he wished he had transistors to worry about with *his* man, because it was girls, which was worse.

"He looks for 'em in the gallery, and man, he spots one, we gotta lose three strokes."

"It don't take much to make 'em a duck," someone said.

"A what?" I asked.

"A duck."

"Duck" turned out to be a word they used a lot for the young professionals rather than the word *rabbit,* which the golfers used. A caddy would say: "I got me a duck who *faints* on me at Napa—lies down on the course and goes to sleep with two holes to go and we got the cut made cold."

Some of the terms they used were rather arcane. One caddy referred to a golfer as a Union Oil.

"What's that?" I asked. "A Union Oil?"

"He's like those speculative oil stocks," I was told. "He goes up and down jes' like they do—man, he's a sixty-nine one day, and the next, he shoot up to a eighty-nine. So we call him a Union Oil. Or a drugstore pro. Sometime we call him that."

From the earliest days of golf, caddies have been the originators of golfing terms, and also masters of the quip, the laconic remark that seems so often the legacy of menial jobs. I particularly like the caddy's retort to the novice golfer who slices an enormous divot out of the ground, and asks, "What do I do with this?"

"Take it home," the caddy says, "an' practice on it."

Or the golfer who hits his drive toward the end of an imperfect day and peers off into the gloom.

Golfer: "Did that go straight, boy?"

Caddy: "Couldn't see it, but it sounded crooked."

Or this one.

Beginner (after repeated failures): "Funny game, golf."

Caddy: " 'Taint meant to be."

Traditionally, caddies have been great showboat characters. In recent times when Johnny Pott sank a chip shot to win the Crosby in 1968, his caddy, Scott, flung his arms up and fell down in a heap. The television cameras caught him in his prostration of pleasure, and he told me that his mother had seen him on national television, and most of the neighborhood, and he had become a celebrity with people coming around and knocking on his mother's window, and smiling in, some of them complete strangers, to indicate they'd seen him and now appreciated his status.

When I spoke to him, and he was reminiscing, he said that he thought he might *patent* his collapse and do it every time he came on the eighteenth with a tournament winner, or even with someone back in the pack if that golfer recorded a great shot on television. "Just throw up my arms," Scott said, "and fall in a heap on the green."

"Scott, do you ever throw up your arms and fall in a heap on an *early* hole—if your man makes a great shot on the third hole, say?"

I sensed his answer and was right: "Oh, I give a good yell," he said. "But for falling down, I save that for the finishing holes and the television. I mean it takes something out of you to fall down like that. It's a question of timing. Of course, the trouble is," he said, "you got to find someone to pack a bag for who's going to do *his* side of the act. I mean, make that shot, baby. I been all set to fall down for some months now but I ain't had no *kind* of cat to give me the opportunity. It seem like I'm fighting to make the cut every time. I dunno," he said mournfully. "Maybe the next time we make the cut I'm goin' to fall down in a heap jes' to keep my hand in. . . ."

I asked them about perhaps the most famous contemporary caddy—the one the golfing public would know about from watching TV—Arnold Palmer's Iron Man, the tall, gaunt dean of the caddies at the Masters in Augusta, the caddy everyone remembered for his long, slow, loping walk up the last fairways in the white coveralls, the old, thin face under the cap, and how he sat on the bag at the edge of the green with his knees drawn up under his chin, or stood out behind Palmer where he leaned over and spoke his notions into Palmer's ear as the two of them inspected the lie of the putt on those last huge greens.

A chorus of disapprobation rose, particularly from Scott.

"Iron Man? What he know 'bout packing a bag. He know nothin', man."

"That's right. You get the Iron Man offen the Masters course, an' he *lost*—why he stumble 'round like he gonna be *bit* by something."

Another caddy chimed in: "He been confused since he was two year ol'—shit, man, how you talk about Iron Man?"

"Well," I said, "what about all that advice he gives Palmer. On the green. You see him there, leaning over, advising . . . at least he's whispering things for Palmer to hear."

"He's jes' movin' his lips. He don't know what he sayin'."

"Why, he ain't *got* nothin' to say. He don' know golf enough to say beans."

One of them leaned forward. "I'll tell you what he's sayin', man. He's leanin' into Palmer's ear an' he's saying: 'Jes in case you wanna know, Mis' Palmer, it's gettin' on 'bout fo'-fifteen in the afternoon."

The caddies all grinned and hee-hawed.

The one caddy all of them spoke creditably of—a hero among them, apparently—was Hagan, semiretired now, they said, who worked out of the Riviera Country Club in Pacific Palisades, California. They spoke of him as being the first caddy who made a scientific art of the craft, checking the course early in the morning for pin positions and pacing off the course and marking distances on a card so that if a golfer asked what the distance was, Hagan would say, looking at his card, "Well, from that tree it's exactly one hundred and thirty-five yards to the center of the green." All of this, when Hagan began the practice, was unknown, and was now widely practiced, not only by the caddies, but by the golfers themselves. Nicklaus relied largely on a card he pulled from his hip pocket with the distances carefully tabulated.

"Tell me more about Hagan," I said.

"He really knew what he was doing," one of the caddies said. The others nodded. "Big pride in his work. There was this time he was working for Tommy Bolt. So Bolt says, 'What do you think?' and Hagan says, 'It's a six iron.' Bolt says, 'No, it's a five.' Hagan says, 'No, it's a six and when you hit it, just hit it firm and don't press.' Bolt says, 'You're crazy, Hagan,' and he takes a five iron and hits it twenty yards over the green. So Bolt takes the five iron and he breaks it over his knee. Well, Hagan, who's been holding the six iron, *he* breaks *it* over *his* knee, and he drops Bolt's bag right there and begins striding off down the fairway. He's done with him. But Bolt comes hurrying on down after him and he's all full of apologies. He says, 'Wait for me, Hagan; ol' Tom's right sorry. You was right. Listen, I'm on the tournament committee and I'm fining myself one hundred and fifty dollars for what I done.'"

"Do caddies ever get fired?" I asked.

The caddy called the Baron spoke up and said that Bob Goalby had fired him three times on one hole.

"He says to me, 'How far is the flag?' I tell him, and he says, 'You're fired.' Well, I stand around and he comes up with a bad shot and he sees I was right and he looks around and he hires me again. But he's all riled up inside, and when he misses his next shot he bangs his club around and his eye lights on me and he fires me again. So I drop his bag. I stand around. I don't know who else he can hang the bag on. A couple of grandmothers. He don't have this big gallery. His wife maybe. She was there. Or maybe he'll pack the bag himself. He must be thinking the same thing, 'cause after a while he says, 'Hey, Baron, pick it up,' which means he's hired me again. We get up to the green and we confer on a putt and he misses it real bad—he don't *begin* to do what I tell him. So he wheels around and he fires me again in this big loud voice. That's enough for me. I drop the bag and I head for the caddy shop. His wife comes running after me. She don't want to pack the bag. She says, 'Come back, Baron, please, Bob don't mean none of that, he *needs* you.' She's a great girl. I know he don't mean no harm. Golf does things to people. So I tell her that and I go back and I pick up his bag."

"Does one ever really drop a bag on a pro?"

"Who was it—Tony?—who dropped Finsterwald's bag on the thirteenth at Denver in the Open in '60."

They nodded.

"Yah, Arnold Palmer won that one with a little short white caddy. You recall?"

I never could get a word out of Arnold Palmer's present caddy, Bob Blair. He reminded me of a rancher—quiet, strong-faced. I asked him a few times if he would talk about his job but he always declined, very politely. He kept to himself. The other caddies knew very little about him. Palmer had had some strange ones, one of the caddies told me. For a while he had a caddy who was a Marine Corps colonel on the lam—his wife was trying to sue him. The colonel thought he could lose himself in the nomadic life of the touring caddies, which he imagined, I suppose, as the American equivalent of the Foreign Legion. It worked for a while, until suddenly he was Palmer's caddy, appearing on television, and it rather went to his head. "He tried to pass himself off as a big shot," the caddy said. "Man, he had a terrific wardrobe. Then he begins signing Palmer's name to checks. I don't know what happened to him. He was a big good-looking guy. He turned up at the country-club dances in a tuxedo—man, he was more at home in a tuxedo than Arnie, the guy he was caddying for."

"Maybe his wife caught up with him," I said.

"Well, it was sure a funny place to hide," the caddy said. "With the touring caddies. I mean, every Sunday, if his wife catches a look at her TV set, there her husband would be, most likely—standing in the background there."

"Maybe she never made the connection," I said. "Maybe she saw him and said, 'Well, that reminds me of somebody, that guy . . .' like that theory if you're going to hide something, set it right out in the middle of the room where it's so obvious everyone walks around it and ignores it."

"Well, I don't know about that theory," the caddy said. "More is likely she took one look at the TV set and said, 'So there you is, you mother,' and she jumped in the family car and took off after him. Hell, man, if my wife run off and I look in the TV set and there she is caddying for Jack Nicklaus, I ain't going to be saying to myself, 'Now, let's see, who that remind me of?' Hell, *no.*"

"Well, you sound very convincing," I said.

When I asked the caddies along the fence if there were any players they were not particularly anxious to caddy for, there was a quick reaction.

"Oh, my!"

A chorus of dismay went up.

"Frank Beard!"

"Man, Bert Yancy's got to head that list."

"Baby, I'll tell you, Bobby Nichols sure on that list, and there don't have to be no squeezing to get him on!"

"Cupit!"

"Tommy Aaron!"

"Shut yo' mouth. Richard Crawford, he's the cake. That man, why he's as tight as beeswax!"

"I'm telling you, Frank Beard! Nobody's alive like him—why, I'm telling you he pinches a penny and right between his fingers that thing turn into a BB pellet!"

"You know what Deane Beman give? Why, man, he give ten dollar a day and *three* percent of his winnings. And when he han' that ovah, he look at you like you done stab him in the knee!"

"How about the caddy's friend?" I asked.

The mood grew respectful.

"Dan Sikes, he's sure one, I'll tell you."

"Nicklaus. You know what he did for this caddy, this guy called Pappy?"

"What was that?" I asked.

"Pappy took his winnings at this Las Vegas tournament and he got hot on the crap tables and he had a pile—twenty-two thousand—sitting in front of him. He thought his luck was never going to stop. He was going to take that entire town and stuff it in his back pocket. Well, someone run and get Nicklaus and he come on the double and there's Pappy, the big crowd around him, with this big gleam in his eye and rolling the dice like crazy. Nicklaus says, 'Okay, hand it over, Pappy, 'fore it's gone.' He leaves Pappy two thousand and he takes that twenty grand and invests it for him in Arnold Palmer's equipment company. I tell you that fellow Pappy's sitting pretty these days."

"Dean Martin's a great caddy's friend," one of the others said. "There were these two guys last Fourth of July up to Bel Air Country Club, and they find Dean and they say, 'Dean, we got a good drunk goin' and we ain't got enough to *finish* it.' He looks 'em over and they were telling the truth, you could tell that right smart, and so he reckons twenty dollars ought to be enough to finish what they begun, maybe much less, maybe *two* dollars by the looks of them, but he takes out the twenty and he forks it over."

"I tell you my man Doug Sanders is a caddy's friend," Cricket said. There was general agreement.

"I tell you," someone said, "the caddies' best friends are the golfers who finish in the top fifteen. You don't pack a bag for one of those cats and you like to have troubles."

"You're talking," said Cricket. He reported he had made twenty-seven hundred in a month of Florida tournaments packing Sanders's bag.

They told me that if they finish out of the money, caddies get paid a hundred to a hundred and fifty. Usually they can rely on ten percent of their professional's winnings.

The caddy called Doc stirred and said that when it came to money they were all spoiled. He had been on the tour for twenty-two years. When he started to caddy he was lucky to get two dollars for packing a professional's bag for eighteen holes. Out of the first prize for tournaments in those days—maybe three thousand—why, a caddy'd be pretty lucky to clear a hundred and fifty. Doc's real name was Foster Eubanks. He was called Doc because he carried all his gear—his rainhat and so forth—in a doctor's satchel. He was one of the caddies with a car. Five other caddies drove with him, spelling each other at the wheel. He shook his head thinking of their conduct. "They don't know what a dollar is. The gambling! Those boys from Dallas, I tell you, they'll bet you a hoss fell out of a tree."

Most of the caddies certainly had first-class ideas about high living. Jack Nicklaus told me that Willie Peterson, who caddied him through his first Masters win in 1963, had suddenly, on one occasion, turned up in Columbus, Ohio, the golfer's hometown, to see him to borrow money—traveling first class on the plane and arriving at Nicklaus's door in a taxi with the meter ticking over and the driver waiting—very nattily dressed, according to Nicklaus, in an outfit which included a silk shirt in the twenty-dollar price range, with a straw boater set at a debonair tilt over one eyebrow. "Mr. Jack, I'm here for a loan," he said, just as easily as he might have said "good morning."

Nicklaus paid off the taxi, invited Peterson in, and sat him down to talk finance with him. "I told him I had some friends in Cleveland who could give him a hand, give him a good enough job to keep him going, and that I'd let them know. I suggested he cut down on his standard of living since he just wasn't in the financial bracket to keep it up. He nodded and he said certainly, but he'd better be hurrying on up to Cleveland to see those people I'd told him about. Well, he took a *taxi* to Cleveland—a hundred and forty-nine miles."

Nicklaus laughed and shook his head. "A great character. He was sort of a cheerleader for me—jump up and down and try to get some reaction from the crowds if there had been a good shot. He loved to get his picture in the paper and he was very proud about caddying. He'd say, 'Mr. Jack, I gotta have more than anyone's *ever* been paid.' "

The caddies themselves kept track of each other's fortunes. "You can tell if a caddy's doing okay on the tour by his shoes," one of them told me. "If he ain't wearing rubber-sole shoes to get a grip on the hills, and he's wearing his regular shoes with wax paper in them to keep the wet out of his socks and slidin' under those big bags—those big Haigs, hell, they'll weigh over a hundred pounds—and he's wearing a quarter in each ear to keep out the cold out there on the dew patrol—first golfers out in the morning—well, you got a caddy who hasn't got a deal, an' he'll be thinking real low. He'll be starvin' in *Florida,* man, packing for ducks who can't play the game, who won't stand up for you nohow."

A "deal" is what the traveling caddy craves—a steady arrangement with a golfer who finishes consistently in the high money.

I asked how they got started with their pros—those who packed for a pro regularly. One of them, called Leroy, who had talked about being fired, spoke up and said that he had been with Bob Goalby for nine years. He had gone through some tough times with him. And then, this one time, Goalby had this sixty-foot putt to win his first tournament. Goalby said: "Leroy, what do you think?"

"I took a look," Leroy said. " 'Bob,' I said to him, 'I think it's goin' to double-break this way, then hump over that way, but you got to make sure it *gets* there.' "

Goalby followed his advice. The putt dropped, and he leaped for Leroy and gave him a big hug, near hauling him down to the green. "You got a job for life!" he shouted.

Some of them got involved just by chance. Angelo Argea, who has been with Nicklaus pretty steadily since 1963, was assigned to him at a Las Vegas tournament in which Nicklaus was not expected to play because of a bursitis attack. Argea was assigned "just in case." Nicklaus did play and won the tournament.

The two had a ritual. Argea was always supposed to say, "Good luck," on the second hole. Sometimes, particularly if they started a round on the back nine, and the second hole was the eleventh, Argea would forget, and Nicklaus would fret and ask leading questions, until finally Argea would remember and say, "Oh, God, yes, good *luck!*"

One of the main topics that the traveling caddies talk about is the Rule. They inveigh against it at any opportunity, and one can hear such odd legal phrases along caddies' row as, "I'm telling you, baby, it's restraint of trade . . . and besides, it ain't fair practices."

The Rule is the condition enforced by the PGA that touring caddies cannot work the tour from June 1 to September 1 when school is out and the caddy forces are largely made up of kids caddying for their summer jobs. The PGA is sympathetic—excessively so, the professional caddies feel—to this group, administering, for example, a scholarship plan known as the Chick Evans Award, which benefits top caddies from each club; of particular dismay to the touring caddies is the PGA's insistence that when the tour arrives at a club in the summer season, its own club caddies should benefit.

Tommy Brown, a caddy they called the Kid, who had been on the tour for three years, said, "Yeh, it's a good life. You travel. You sit around in these nice country clubs. The company is good. You have just about every- thing. When the Rule hits, though—why these thirteen-year-old kids are depriving me of this good time and my income. The summer months—well, it's hard to sit in one place, in the East there; you count the time when you can get back moving."

"Those kids snap up our bread," the Rabbit said. "Why in San Francisco this one time when they play the tournament there in June, this kid from the Stanford University packs for Billy Casper who makes the playoff and wins it. Kid's name was Stark. Casper says, 'Stark, what's your fee for packing?' And the kid says, 'Seven dollars a day. Five dollars for the playoff 'cause that's extra.' Billy gives him two thousand dollars.''

A moan went up along the fence, and the clicking of tongues.

"What can you do to better your cause?" I asked.

"Well, let me say this," one of them said. "Them players, those cats who calls themselves the caddy's bes' friend, what they can do is say that if they can't have their own caddies for the summer months, why, they'll *strike*. Won't play. That's what those cats could do, dig?"

They all nodded their heads. "Man, you jivin'," one of them said.

"We're treated like dogs," one of the caddies said. "We got to park fifty miles over in the woods. The public don't understand this. We got a lot of trouble. We should have credentials just like the touring pros. We're worth it to them. In the seven years I been a touring caddy I can't think of a touring pro who's lost a penalty shot 'cause of some mistake."

It was true that many of the golfers were sympathetic to the caddies' woes. When I asked Doug Sanders about the Rule, he was very insistent.

"I wish they'd waive it," he said. "You have to be lucky to get a good caddy in the summer. I'd as soon put a hundred dollars in a kitty for the high-school kids for the chance to have a touring caddy packing for me. You don't want an intern operating on you; you want a doctor. A great caddy can help you maybe only one shot a week—but that adds up. Try that on the money list. It makes a big difference. An amateur caddy will lose you strokes. I don't mean that he's going to rake a trap with your ball in it, something against the rules that'll penalize you, but you can lose strokes worrying about him. Particularly if you're near winning a tournament. He's never been through an experience like that. It's like combat. You want someone you can really depend on."

Rod Funseth agreed. He said: "You get scared around a trap if your caddy doesn't know the rules. It's a two-stroke penalty if you hit your own bag. Most caddies don't know that. Two strokes if you hit an attended pin. Why I can remember T. B., who caddies for me a lot, having a pin stick on him with a long putt of mine rolling up toward him, and he wrenched at that flag, and he was so anxious he let out this yell, and finally he hauls the whole cup out, the entire metal thing, and just in time too."

"The only thing one can say against the touring caddies," Sanders said, "is that they drink and carry on too much—a bit crazy. Like if a caddy has five hundred dollars a week, he'll spend five-twenty. But then, that's *his* business. I tell you that for my business, which is golf, I want them around. Good caddies are confidence builders and great assets. In fact, if you've got a really good caddy you find yourself playing hard for him. My caddy, Cricket . . . you know him?"

"Yes," I said.

". . . well, this one time I made this really great recovery shot. Cricket says: 'That's a great save, Doug!' I say to him, 'Cricket, I'm right glad to hear what you say 'cause that's the first nice word I've heard you say this round.' And he says: 'Doug, up to now you ain't deserved any comment.' "

Some of the golfers disapproved of the touring caddy arrangement. Tom Nieporte, for example, told me that he thought a team of a professional and his caddy, if they had been together for a long time, might be tempted, well, to "try something." To give an extreme example, a caddy, with or without the knowledge of his pro, might be tempted to edge a ball into a slightly better lie. Nieporte had never heard of this happening on the tour, but his point was that an arrangement should not be condoned that could so easily lead to such a temptation.

I asked the caddies about this, and they were scornful. Cricket said: "It never happen. Man'd be crazy to take a chance like that. You get caught, that's the end, baby. I never heard of such a thing, trying to help or hinder a golfer. You ain't goin' to find any long-toed boys on the tour." When I asked, he said what he meant by "long-toed boys" was in reference to the old-time barefoot caddy who could envelop a ball with his toes and move it to a better lie. "You see these cats at the private clubs. These boys work the Eastern country clubs in the off-season, packin' those big-money amateur foursomes. You always give a good lie for those cats. It don't mean that much. If I step on a player's ball, man, I put it back. But you don' find nothing like that goin' on when the tour rolls aroun'. It ain't the same gig."

The main attribute of the caddy, almost all professionals seemed to agree, is to reinforce their pro's decisions, or even to dispute them, and make the golfer think hard before making his shot. Naturally some golfers feel a caddy's importance is overrated.

Claude Harmon was scornful of a caddy's advice. He said his instruction to them was always very simple: Clean the clubs and the balls and show up on time and be in the right place and always be quiet. "My idea of a caddy is the one I won the Masters with. Never said one word. Hell, he won two

161

other Masters that I know of—with Ben Hogan and Jackie Burke—and I think he won a fourth one. We compared notes and only Burke could remember him saying anything. That was on the seventy-second hole, the last of the tournament, and Burke, who was looking over his putt, heard this calm voice just behind him say: 'Cruise it right in there, Mr. Burke. Cruise it in.' And he did, too.''

Harmon said he never could recall asking a caddy's advice. He said: "How can a boy know what you spend your life learning? Take a ball's lie. Just how the ball's sitting on the ground, whether it's hunkered down or sittin' up can mean a fifty-yard difference in a shot's length using the same club. How's the caddy going to know? Is he good enough to make the right allowances for the weather—that a ball isn't going to go so far in the cold . . . that it's going to die up there—he's going to know *that*? And how's he going to know about adrenaline—that great power you get under pressure, that strength, y'know, that allows one-hundred-pound women to lift Cadillacs off children? That's why you get such great pitching performances in the World Series from those speed pitchers—guys like Gibson of the Cards. Why, he throws the ball faster than he ever *knew* he could. In golf the same thing . . . you come down those last fairways in contention and you find yourself hitting the ball thirty yards more than you know how. Well, how's a caddy going to judge *your* adrenaline quota? Think of Trevino in the '67 Open. He comes down the stretch just about ready to take the whole thing and he asks his caddy to club him and the guy suggests a five iron. Trevino's all hopped up, crazy strong, and he knows it, so he grabs himself an eight iron and hits the flag with it. Well, imagine where a five iron would have taken him. Right out of the whole caboodle, that's where.''

I asked: "Are there golfers who don't have the courage of their convictions? Who really rely on caddies excessively?''

"Well, Sam Snead's too dependent on his caddy, and he's gullible—which is a combination that can add up to a couple of mental errors a round. I can remember once at Oakmont on a round we come up to the thirteenth hole and we both hit the middle of the green with six irons. Well, the next day we come to the same hole and Sam asks his caddy, 'Boy, what do you think here?' He hasn't got his mind on it, I guess. His caddy clubs him with a five iron and Sam flies the shot over the green. He stares after it, and then he says, 'Hell, boy, that ain't no five-iron shot!' Well, hell, it's Sam should have known about that shot, not the caddy. It's typical of him, though. I always reckon I can have a good time with Sam on match play. I work up a little conversation with my caddy, just pretending to be all-fired confused about a shot, and I take out the three iron, and then the two, and then finally I choke up and hit an easy two that just clears the river and coasts up the green. The fact is, the shot's a natural four iron. Well, Sam steps up and he says, 'Boy, what do you think?' and his caddy, who's been keeping his ears open, knows that I used the two iron, so he says, 'It's a good two, Mr. Snead.' So Sam laces out a two iron and it clears the river, and green, and maybe some trees beyond. And Sam, he stares after it, and he says, 'Hell, boy, that ain't no two-iron shot.' Well, the fact is, you got to learn to depend on yourself. Hagen had the great system for penalizing opponents who eavesdropped on him. He had a jacked-up set of irons—the four iron was marked five, and so forth, and you could get into big trouble relying on him."

Gay Brewer, the 1967 Masters champion, also felt a caddy's value was overrated. It was fine to have his reassurance on club selection, but a professional would be foolish to rely on anything but judgment based on knowledge of his own game. Brewer had a different caddy every week on the tour, never really trying to keep one on a regular basis, and indeed he had won tournaments with boys who had never been on that particular course before. He took the Masters in 1967 but he couldn't remember the name of the caddy with whom he won.

"But I'll tell you when the caddy *is* important," he told me. "In England. The caddy seems more devoted there, and God knows he *has* to be. The weather is such a factor—weird stuff—that the courses can change overnight. You'll have a hole which one day requires a drive and an easy wedge, and the next day it takes a drive and a *three wood* to reach the green. So yardage doesn't mean a thing—I mean, unless the conditions are absolutely perfect and static, which in that country is rare, hell, *unknown.* So you rely more on your caddy. They not only know the course but also how your ball is going to act in the air currents above, and how it's going to bounce and move on the turf. I think I was clubbed on nearly every hole in the tournaments I played there. Those caddies are incredible."

Certainly the English caddies were self-assured. Bobby Cruickshank told me that on his first practice round at Muirfield in 1929 he had a seventy-five-year-old caddy, Willie Black. Cruickshank hit a good drive on the first hole. "Willie," he said, "give me the two iron." "Look here, sir," Willie said. *"I'll* give you the club, *you* play the bloody shot." I've always liked the story about the caddy at St. Andrews who interrupted his "boss" (which was the current term) at the top of his backswing, and shouted, "Stop! We've changed our mind. We'll play the shot with an iron!" Frank Stranahan had a terrible problem with such caddies in one of the British Amateur championships at Muirfield. He fired a number of them, mostly because pride on both sides got the best of the situation. The caddies were furious and sulking because their advice was ignored, and Stranahan was upset and oversensitive because he could not, under the circumstances, keep his mind on his golf game. The climactic moment in their strained relationship came on a hole with the green hidden behind a high ridge. Stranahan sent his caddy up on the ridge to point out the direction of the green, indeed to place himself so that a shot soared over his head would be on the correct line. The caddy went up there with the golf bag, moving around on the ridge, sighting between Stranahan and the green, his head turning back and forth, and finally he waved Stranahan on. Stranahan hit directly over the caddy and then toiled up the hill to discover that the caddy had lined him up with a thick patch of bracken, waist-high, where it would be a miracle if he found the ball, much less knocked it out; the caddy looked at him and very carefully, like a dog laying down a bone, he dropped Stranahan's golf bag at his feet and set out for the golf house, saying over his shoulder, "Now, sir, if you think you know so much about it, let's see you get yourself out of *there.*"

What a tradition caddies come from! I suppose the first of their number who achieved prominence was Scotland's William Gunn of the early nineteenth century. Caddy Willie, he was called—an odd and famous character referred to in the chronicles of the time as "peculiar but harmless." His habit was never to refer to those he caddied for by name, but rather by profession. Mr. Brand, for example, his landlord and an amateur gardener, he called "the man of the cabbage," as in "You'll be needin' a cleek, sure as not, man of the cabbage, to reach the green."

He wore his entire wardrobe on his back, one suit above the other—four or five of them at a time, including their vests. An old worn fur coat was outermost. He wore three bonnet-like hats, each sewed within the other.

He would leave his job for six weeks, hiking up to his Highland home, all those suits on his back, and the hats. One spring in the late 1820s he never came back. His one fear had been that he would end up in a pauper's grave—he had set all his money aside for a proper burial. Those for whom he had caddied comforted themselves that at least he had reached home and had his wish granted; they preferred not to think that he had succumbed on his long trek . . . a small tumble of clothes that could have been discarded from a passing coach.

There were others: "Big" Crawford, who caddied for "Wee" Ben Sayers and used to try to intimidate the opposition by rearing over them and making rumbling sounds in his throat. He once threw a horseshoe at Vardon. Pretense meant nothing to him. He referred to the Grand Duke Michael of Russia as Mr. Michael.

Max Faulkner, himself one of the most colorful personalities in golf, had a series of memorable caddies—Turner, who had a long red beard, and then for years he had a caddy who traveled with him named Mad Mac, who wore three ties but no shirt, and a long shoe-top-length overcoat which he kept on during the hottest weather. From his neck dangled a pair of large binoculars from which the lenses were missing and through which he would peer at the line of a putt and announce, "Hit it slightly straight, sir."

Then, Eddie Lowery, age ten, who carried Francis Ouimet's bag when the young American beat Ray and Vardon for the U.S. Open at Brookline.

Or Vardon's caddy at Prestwick in 1893, who was so disgusted when Vardon disregarded his advice that he turned his back and held out the golf bag behind him for Vardon to choose from.

Or Skip Daniels of Sandwich, who was Walter Hagen's caddy when he twice won the British Open Championship. Gene Sarazen had him in the year 1932—a stooped man who wore an old cap, a celluloid collar, and a black Oxford suit that had never been pressed. He was seventy years old when Sarazen won his 1932 Open with him at Prince's, a course next to Royal St. George's in Sandwich. He was almost blind and Sarazen didn't want to take him. He did more out of nostalgia than anything else, and when he won he had Daniels stand next to him while he accepted the trophy and he gave him a polo coat.

Or the caddy who is reputed to have said to Vardon when asked, "What on earth shall I take now?" "Well, sir, I'd recommend the four-oh-five train."

My favorite caddy, though, is a Frenchman—Vardon tells the story about him—who packed the golf bag of an Englishman playing the course at Pau, just north of the Basque country. The Englishman made a particularly fine approach shot, and he turned to his caddy with a wide smile for some indication of approval. "Well, good heavens! What? What?"

The caddy's English was very limited. He struggled, and offered what he had often heard uttered but did not fully understand. He said, nodding happily in reply: "Beastly fluke!"

Eddie Shore

The coaches tended to stay off by them-
selves after practice and they often had dinner at the Pickwick Arms, a few
miles outside of Fitchburg, where the light from overhead lanternlike fixtures
was muted and golden and the beer came to the table not in cans but in thick
crystallike glasses with handles. I went with them a few times—Don Cherry
and his associates, Tom Johnson, a former Bruins coach, and Harry Sinden,
who was then the club's general manager and also a former coach. The one
player I could never hear enough about was the great Bruins defenseman,
Eddie Shore, who played for the team in the 1920s and was the general
manager and coach of the Springfield Indians during the 1950s. Cherry was
the resident expert on him, having played for him on the Springfield squad.
It had been a traumatic experience. Shore was a man so bellicose and eccentric that in his coaching heyday, players had it written into their contracts that
they couldn't be sent to the Springfield Americans. Cherry had spent four
years with him in what he called "those pits."

"He called me Mister Cherry, the Madagascar Kid," Cherry was saying
one evening. "I never knew what he meant by the Madagascar Kid. I never
asked him why and he wasn't the kind of man you'd ask, and he probably
wouldn't tell you if you did. Nobody knew why. I hardly knew where
Madagascar was. Maybe it was because he thought so little of me he wanted
to send me there. As for the 'Mister,' he called everyone 'Mister.' That was
the only term of respect one ever heard (if it was respect), because the rest
of the time at Springfield it was all nightmare. We trained three sessions a
day, two hours each. We got only half an hour off for lunch. That wasn't
enough time for the goalies to get in and out of their equipment. So they'd
go across the street from the arena to the lunch counter and hoist themselves

166

up on the seats in full goaltending regalia, pads and all, and order up a hot chili. They'd gulp that down and get back across the street because you couldn't begin to guess what penalties Eddie Shore would dream up for you if you got back to the ice a minute or so late."

Cherry caught me shaking my head in disbelief. He grinned. "What a time you would have had there. He hated goalies who went down on the ice. To keep them in the habit of standing up he tied a rope around their necks that was attached to the crossbar of the cage so they couldn't go down."

"I would have hanged in the first minute," I said. "A suicide who'd picked a strange place to do it."

"It wouldn't have bothered Shore at all," Cherry said. "He was stuck on a stand-up style. We had a goaltender named Claude Evans . . ."

"You were telling me about him the other day," I said. "I reminded you of him—the motionless, stand-up style."

Cherry laughed. "Well, he wasn't *quite* motionless, though almost. This one time, he had a shut-out going, but then he made what for Shore was a cardinal sin—he went down to block a shot. Shore fined him fifty dollars on the spot, even though Evans had made a good save, and for the rest of the game Shore stood in the stands behind the net and every time there'd be a breakaway, he'd scream at Evans, 'Don't go down! Don't go down!'

"Shore had all kinds of crazy theories. He had an idea that you had to skate with your knees bent almost in a crouch. His image for it—which was hard to forget once you heard it—was that the proper skating position was like going to the bathroom in the woods. So his players tended to skate around like ducks. I mean literally. One day Jim Bartlett of the New York Rangers was sitting in the stands laughing at us and making remarks. Shore, skating by, noticed him, and a week later Bartlett was on the club. Shore had got him. He wasn't Jim any more. He was Mister Bartlett. He looked shell-shocked. He *was* shell-shocked. He began skating like a duck. Shore benched him for the entire finals of the Calder Cup and that was just about the end of Bartlett's hockey career."

"What did he look like?" I asked.

"Shore? Well, he walked upright, if that's what you're getting at. He looked like a cowboy. He wasn't a big man. A small cowboy. He wore the number two on his Bruins jersey and it looked as big on him as the numbers on a naval ship. But he had huge hands. He could grip a basketball in either palm. High balding forehead. Narrow shoulders. Never one to smile. He had lost half an ear to a hockey stick and the story was he held a mirror up to make sure the doctor was stitching it on right. Amazing athlete. He was close to seventy when I was with the Indians and he could skate faster backward than forward. He could take the laces out of his skates and tap dance on the ice."

"What was his play like on the ice?" I asked.

"In a hockey game, he played like a car out of control in a demolition derby. But he felt there was a connection between skating and tap dancing and the ballet. He invested in the Ice Capades, you know. One year he had his players lined up tap dancing in the hotel lobby."

"And they did it?"

"Of course, they did," Cherry said derisively. "What else? He was this crazy combination of finesse and tough. Tough! You can't believe how tough he was. They said he had over nine hundred stitches in his body. I never tried to count them, but I don't doubt it. I know he'd fractured his hip, his back, his nose had been broken flat fourteen times, and I don't think there was a tooth in his head that was his own. Maybe that was why he could dish it out the way he did. He'd been through those wars. So we respected him. But oh my God we hated him. A tyrant! He made me wear a puck around my neck because, playing defense, I had looked down at the puck and not at the forward's chest. Cardinal sin! Oh, we hated him.

"I tell you another. He once kept me out on the ice for four hours and twenty minutes because he caught me taking a peek at the clock. All this for thirty-five hundred a year. We used to drink to forget."

"Thirty-five hundred?"

"That's all we could get out of him," Cherry said. "He was the stingiest guy you ever heard of. To keep the light bills down, we had our practices in the semidarkness. We skated around in the gloom—these shadowy figures at the far end of the rink. You couldn't tell who was coming up the ice with the puck. When it was payroll time, you never knew quite what was going to happen. If the payroll was too high for the week he'd simply fine guys for poor play which would cut down on what he'd have to pay. He'd fine guys for poor play though maybe the guy hadn't been on the ice for a month!

"When he quit playing for coaching, he really ran that barn. In this one game against the Cleveland Barons a goal was scored which Shore did not think had gone into the nets. So he fired the goal judge just like that—you know, the guy that sits in the little glass cage and flicks on the red light. He *fired* this guy. You wouldn't have thought Shore had the right to do this, but he considered the Springfield arena his domain; the league didn't think he had the right either and he was fined a thousand dollars."

"Did he replace the goal judge with someone else?"

"He certainly did," Cherry said. "He put a state trooper in there who had apparently wandered into the arena to get out of the cold. This guy was suddenly pressed into duty. This guy didn't object, either," Cherry said. "This policeman didn't say, 'Well, I'm supposed to be out patrolling the street' or anything. He just stepped into that glass cage. You did what you were told when it was Shore who was doing the telling."

I asked: "Was he as terrifying to the referees and line judges?"

"Oh, yes. When he was playing, he'd occasionally plink them in the rear end with the puck. Once he shot the puck at a referee who had turned and was skating for the official's bench to report a penalty. The guy's name was Odie Cleghorn. Shore hit him in the rear end, which from short range was apparently rather easy to do. Cleghorn added two minutes to the penalty, and when Shore then flicked the puck up into the crowd, which was booing him, Cleghorn decided this act was far more outrageous than being plinked in the ass, and he gave Shore a ten-minute misconduct penalty.

"Shore once got so pissed at a penalty called by the referee, a brave guy named Frank Udvari, that he pulled his whole team off the ice. The only one who did not go to the bench was Don Simmons, the goalie, who was so busy housecleaning around the net, or something, that he was not aware he had been summoned. Udvari skated over to the Indians bench and told Shore he had ten seconds to get his skaters back on the ice, or he was going to drop the puck anyway. Shore turned his back on him. At this, Udvari, good to his word, dropped the puck in the circle. It was gathered in, of course, by the opposing team.

"Poor Simmons. He looked up from his crouch and saw I guess the ultimate goaltender's nightmare—his whole team vanished and five of the opposition sailing down on him, the puck clacking easily from stick to stick as they came. Incredibly, the first four shots missed—maybe these guys were weak from laughing—and the last one caromed out from the boards at an angle where Simmons was able to leap out and smother it. At this point, with play stopped, Shore somehow got himself under control and he sent his players back out onto the ice."

"Who brought him into the league?" I asked.

"He came in from Western Canada. Regina. I'm told he really hadn't played much hockey until an older brother told him he wasn't any good. He was a teenager already. Art Ross of the Bruins signed him. Art Ross was a great figure in the history of hockey—a coach and general manager of the Bruins. What a showman he was. He'd come out on the ice with Eddie Shore, pretending to be his valet. Eddie would be dressed in a big evening cloak. The band would play 'Hail to the Chief' or something, and Ross would take Shore's cloak like he was unveiling him, and carry it back to the bench. He was a great innovator as well. He invented the hockey cage shaped like the figure three in the back. Also the puck—standardizing its size, weight, and density. The old pucks used to bounce around like rubber balls."

"What was Shore's voice like?" I asked. I could not get enough.

"Well, he was very slow-speaking. And formal. For example, he'd refer to children as 'male (or female) offspring.' He'd get very personal. 'When's-your-wife's-period? What-was-period-day?' That was how he talked—a pause between every word. 'It-was-Wednesday? Then-you-do-not-have-relations-with-her-for-three-weeks.' He'd count on his fingers to emphasize what he was saying. "One-two-three-then-you-can-have-relations.' He had these strange ideas about sex and especially sex and the athlete. Once, when the team was going terrible, he called a meeting for all the players and their wives, and in this little steamy locker room, with the jockstraps hanging from the pegs, he proceeded to tell the wives they were allowing their husbands too much sex. It was affecting their play. 'Now you just cut that stuff out!' he yelled at them."

"He would get away with that kind of thing?"

"Oh, my, yes," Cherry said. "He once called in a player named Don Johns and told him to part his hair on the other side—thinking it might break him out of a scoring slump. Of course, the guy did it."

"How long did you spend with these people?" I asked incredulously.

"Four years," he said. "Oh yes. I came out of the trenches. When I was sixteen, I was getting my heart broken. Most of that time I spent on a kind of subsquad called the Black Aces. Those were the players who were in disfavor. It was also called the Awkward Squad. We had to do odd jobs around the Springfield arena for Shore. Painting seats, selling popcorn, and blowing up balloons. The Ice Capades were coming into the Springfield arena. So he had the Black Aces blowing up balloons for their show. They kept them in the locker room. So many balloons were blown up we could barely squeeze our way in to dress for the game. Shore did everything in that place. He had an assistant, but all that guy ever did was open the door. Shore even changed the lightbulbs. One night he was screwing in a lightbulb, way up on a ladder, when the ladder toppled away and left him hanging onto an iron rafter with one hand like a monkey dangling from a branch. Way up there at the top of the arena."

I winced.

"Yeah. Most people in a situation like that would start yelling. But Shore looked down, very cool, past his shoulder, and asked someone far below, 'Do-you-mind-moving-the-ladder-back-where-it-was,' just as calm as if he was asking for the salt to be passed at the dinner table."

I asked: "What did the League think of him?"

"He was the law unto himself," Cherry said. "For example, between the periods at the Arena was always twenty-five to thirty minutes long. That was so the concessions, which Shore owned, could get a full workout. The League got upset about this, and they wrote Shore a letter saying the Springfield organization was going to be fined if the time between the periods wasn't shortened to regulation. So the next game, the Zamboni ice-cleaning machine went out to clear the rink between the first and second periods and broke down. Ran out of gas. Shore had seen to it. By the time he got the Zamboni fueled up and functioning, it was forty-five minutes before they could get the next period going. The same thing happened between the second and *third* periods. Shore wrote the league a letter. 'How do you like my shortened between periods?' They gave up on him. They weren't going to run his place. They should have known better."

"Was there ever any relief?" I asked. "I mean, could he be funny?"

Cherry thought for a moment. "Eddie Shore could be funny, but not often."

I asked if he could think of any examples.

"No."

I was writing no on my pad when Cherry said, "Well, of course, it depends on what you mean by 'funny.' One time Shore said to me 'When I was on the ice with my hockey stick, I used it like a scientific tool; in your hands it's a blunt instrument.' That could be considered 'funny' if you happened to be overhearing it, I guess, but it wasn't so funny if you were looking into Shore's face and he was yelling it at you. No, that was not very funny. It isn't even funny thinking back on it."

"Did you learn anything from your association with him?" I asked.

"I never learned a thing. We used to drink to forget. The only thing I ever learned was that if you could put up with Eddie Shore, you could put up with anything."

I asked, "When was the last time you saw him? Has he survived?"

"Oh, nothing's ever going to drop Eddie Shore. He's a survivor. A millionaire. Investing in the Ice Capades. You know, in some ways I liked him . . . the magnetism. He's well over seventy now, but he still has the fire. Back in the June drafts he was in the Hospitality Suite up in Toronto or some place, and somebody bugged him. So Eddie Shore knocked him flat."

Apparently it was this kind of bellicosity that caused the most traumatic event in Shore's life. One night in Boston during his playing career he was rammed in a humiliating check that sent him skidding along the ice on all fours, by a Toronto player, Red Horner, blind-sided evidently, because Shore scrambled up and took off after Ace Bailey, a Toronto player who had not been responsible. Shore probably should have known it was Red Horner, who had such a thoroughly bad reputation for shenanigans of that sort that on one occasion an official scorer in Boston refused to credit him with an assist. "Give him an assist? I wouldn't give that son of a bitch the time of day!"

In any case, Shore pursued Ace Bailey and decked him from the rear, flung him down like a doll, and Bailey's head hit the ice. He recovered, but he never played hockey again. He almost died. It was a very serious business. Bailey's father brought a gun to Boston and vowed to kill Shore. Shore was suspended and eventually absolved, but his reputation for being what was called an "ice thug"—what they now called a "goon"—was thereafter established. He was known as this even by people who had never seen a hockey game, and for those who went to watch the Bruins, Shore was the one certainly the most booed, and it was not good-natured either—as it is when the mayor or governor gets up to throw out the first ball at a baseball game—but intense and solemn.

Of course, that changed eventually. In one of the moving moments in hockey history, at a ceremony at the first All Star game, which was held at the Maple Leaf Gardens in 1934, Ace Bailey came out onto the ice, moving very carefully, wearing dark glasses, to present a lineup of the all-star players with medals and sweaters. When he came to Eddie Shore, the two embraced, and down the lines the All Stars began banging their sticks on the ice in tribute to the gesture and to the reconciliation of the two. Even so, the mood about him slowly changing, it took longer than it should have for him to get into hockey's Hall of Fame. It was finally a considerable fuss by the press and the fans—those who had once held Shore in such low esteem—that did the trick.

I asked Cherry what Shore would have made of someone like me fumbling around in his Springfield empire.

"Well, you would have been a Black Ace, for sure. You would have painted some chairs and blown up some balloons."

"Yes."

Cherry paused. "I'll tell you one more interesting thing about Shore and his goalies. He made them practice in empty rinks, no one else on the ice at all, and in Springfield in that deep gloom with half the overhead lights out, they would play these imaginary games."

"Not even anyone to shoot the pucks?" I asked.

"Not even a puck," Cherry said. "Everything was imaginary. Shore would sit there in the stands and watch his goaltenders dive at imaginary pucks driven at them from nonexistent wings and making imaginary saves. These—what would you call them?—'surreal' practices went on for hours. One of the reasons for the formation of the Player's Association in 1966 was because of this sort of thing. It kind of drove people batty."

"What was its purpose?"

Cherry said, "Well, I think it was sort of like taking your waking dreams—the kind where you lie awake and make save after save in your imagination—and actually moving this mental exercise out onto the rink. At least I suppose that was the idea."

"Did the goaltenders have to sweep the imaginary pucks out of the net if the imaginary forwards scored on them?"

"I don't know if he went that far."

I said I thought the exercise was just my sort of thing. "Grapes, I could make a great move out there, just a lightning kind of jab, and hold my glove up with the imaginary puck in it. I'd say, 'Hey, coach, how'd you like that one?'"

"Yeah?" Cherry smiled. "Don't forget he always had the last word. He'd tell you the puck was behind you, sitting in the netting, and if you missed another one like that, you'd be blowing up a whole bunch of balloons. The Ice Capades always seemed to be coming to town."

After I took Marianne Moore to the World Series I wrote to ask her a few questions about the afternoon we had spent together—why she wore two watches, for example. She wrote back. She answered the questions—the one about the watches, that she wore two because she had a "security obsession about arriving on time." A correspondence ensued. We decided to do a book together about sporting events. We would go to them together. She would provide a description in her quirky, imaginative vision of things, and I would balance this with a more pedestrian view of the same event. We planned to go to a professional football game, a wrestling match, hockey, tennis at Forest Hills, and so forth. Alas, the project was never completed. We did, however manage to get to a boxing match. . . .

Marianne Moore II

Until she met Ali, her favorite boxer had been Floyd Patterson. She had met him at an autographing party to which she had been taken by a neighbor. The hostess was "Miss Negro Bookclub"—a titular choice Miss Moore found arresting—and Sugar Ray Robinson was the chairman of the event. "His competence and unsensational modesty were very pleasing," she wrote me about the occasion. "I met Floyd Patterson and Buster Watson also, his assistant trainer. Floyd was very courteous and I was very rude, interrupting Buster when he was talking to two other men. I resolved never to be so rude again. I bought books for some boys . . . and another for myself in which Floyd wrote my name and 'all the best.'"

She read the book with care—*Victory Over Myself*. She remembered phrases from it: "I never thought of boxing as a profession; it was a grind . . . but a way out for me and my family"; "boxing is supposed to be a dirty business but it has made me clean and enabled me to do some good for others." I think she was also moved by the description of Patterson's childhood: he was so intimidated and shy that he hid from the outside in a cubbyhole he found in the foundation of an elevated subway trestle in the Bronx.

I arranged for a row of seats for his fight against Chuvalo. It was not at all clear that Marianne Moore was going to enjoy the evening. She had not been to a prizefight before, and people hitting each other was an activity she could not condone. A few days before the fight she wrote me, "Marred physiognomy and an occasional death doesn't seem an ideal life objective. I do not like demolishing anything—even a paper bag. Salvaging and saving all but dominate my life."

175

I asked her in the cab on the way to the fight if violence had ever intruded; it seemed an odd suggestion to apply to such a fragile person.

"In Brooklyn I intercepted a small boy who laid down his schoolbooks to slug a classmate," she replied. "When I said, 'If you don't stop, I'll beat you up,' he said, 'He cursed my mother.' I said, 'Then it's justified, but lay off him.' "

She closed her eyes, as if in thought, and then she said, "One time I was driving in a taxi going through the Bowery; I looked out and saw a man with a knife creeping up on another. The car was going quite fast, about as fast as we're going now, and I can't tell you what the end was." She made a small snorting sound. "Violence! I didn't know what it meant. If I was wild enough to come home late at night, I didn't know enough to be timid. Once, I was amazed when my friend asked, 'Do you want me to go in with you to see if anyone's in the house?' I was astonished. 'Someone in the house?!' But now I have been trained to call out, 'Who is it?' and look out the little peephole, and when I see my good friend, or a neighbor, I feel craven."

Miss Moore was wearing her famous tricorne hat, with its pointed-prow effect; when she turned to speak, it gave a sort of thrust to what she was saying, much like talking to a miner in the beam of the light from his helmet. Her tricorne fit nicely in the cab. She had other hats that would have required some jimmying around to fit—a great cartwheel of a stiffened felt hat that if one were walking along beside her one had to get under, crouching along Groucho Marx–like, to hear what she was saying in her soft, erratic voice. She told me that she had picked the tricorne for the fight "because my other hats keep anyone behind me from seeing."

We picked up some friends to join us at the fight. Just as we were nearing the Garden, Miss Moore heard something from one of them about Chuvalo that shook her support of Patterson—namely that Chuvalo was so incredibly poor at the start of his ring career that on one occasion he drove across Canada with his wife in a car so decrepit that the accelerator pedal had come off, and a part of the accelerator arm; Mrs. Chuvalo had had to crouch under the dashboard and at a signal from her husband depress or raise what was left of the accelerator by hand. "Bring her up a touch; we're coming into a town." Miss Moore was moved by this nearly to the point of shifting her allegiance. She asked to be told the story again.

It was obviously on her mind during the fight. We had good seats in the mezzanine, far enough away so that the physical side of the fight was not too pronounced. Still, small gasps erupted from Miss Moore at a solid blow.

Once, I heard her call out, "George!" Another time, "Floyd!" She had a very small pad and pencil with her, though I never saw her write anything down. She seemed relieved when the fight was over. "Well, that's that," she said brightly, as if something especially wrenching had been completed, like a frightening circus act.

She wrote me subsequently when she had had time to consider things: "I did not enjoy the Patterson-Chuvalo fight at all until Floyd began to win and in the end suffered no major damage." But she could not rid herself of the Chuvalo accelerator story. "A moralist at heart, my notions of psychic adaptiveness and creativeness of muscular as well as mental endurance were enlarged by Mrs. Chuvalo's scars of battle with life when she held a finger in a fixed position to replace what should have been an automatic device in the car."

She wrote that she had also been taken by the referee's performance: "The assiduous precision of the referee in seizing the angle most advantageous from which to see every trifle impressed me most—and his impeccable appearance—nothing sticking out or dangling. Swift and compact, the embodiment of vigilance."

She had also noticed Muhammad Ali at the fight; he was sitting on the far side of the ring and jumped up into it to talk with Patterson at its conclusion. When I next saw her, I asked if she would like to meet him. She nodded. "I do not see any reason why I should not meet someone who assures everyone 'I am the greatest' and who is a poet nonetheless."

Some weeks later I was able to arrange our tea with Ali through Hal Conrad, the fight publicist. For reasons I have forgotten, we had it at Toots Shor's establishment, in mid-Manhattan. The place was almost empty when Miss Moore and I arrived—a slack time in the place, about four in the afternoon. Toots Shor himself was there, but knowing that Ali was expected, he did not sit with us. He did not approve of Ali then, or perhaps ever, and he sat at the opposite end of the room, studiously ignoring us. From our banquette Miss Moore looked over and was impressed by Shor. She had heard that he had started in the restaurant business as a bouncer. I think she expected, or hoped perhaps, that he would "bounce" someone. "His haunt is quite peaceful," she said to me. "It makes the offices of bouncer seem hearsay; no killer instinct has made itself evident."

"No, no," I said. "I think he has other people to do that for him these days. Besides, there's no one in here for him to bounce except the waiters and you and me."

"Fancy," she said.

Presently Muhammad Ali arrived with Hal Conrad. He slid in behind the table and arranged himself next to Miss Moore. He gazed at her hat, which was the same tricorne she had worn to the fight. Almost immediately, as if she had yet to arrive, he turned to Hal and me and asked who she was and what he was expected to do. Had a photographer arrived?

Miss Moore listened attentively to what Conrad and I had to say about her—a great sports fan, one of the most distinguished poets in the country. . . .

"Mrs. Moore," said Ali, turning and looking at her, "a grandmother going to the fights? How old is she?" he suddenly asked, turning toward me and whispering loudly. I was taken aback.

"Oh, forty," I said idiotically, producing the first number that came to mind.

"Is that so?" commented the champion. "The way you settled her down in here so careful I reckon she's got to be a grandmother, seventy-nine going on eighty, or maybe ninety-six." He inspected her. "They have these women up in Pakistan," he confided in me loudly, "who live to be one hundred and *sixty.* They haul pianos up and down these hills. They eat a lot of yogurt."

Miss Moore sat patiently through this, smiling faintly. The fighter turned to her suddenly and asked, "Mrs. Moore, what have you been doing lately?"

"I have been subduing my apartment," she said in her high, thin voice. "I have just moved in from Brooklyn to a new apartment which is strange to me and needs taming."

"Is that so?" The champion ordered a glass of water. "Yes," he said to the waiter. "We is tiptop at Toots." He turned back to Miss Moore. "Well, I am considering farming, myself," he said. "I'd like to sit and look across the fence at the biggest bull in the world—jes' sit and rock back and forth and look at him out there in the middle of the field, feeding."

"Oh yes," Miss Moore said. She was quite shy with him, ducking her head and peeking at him. "Can we come and look with you?"

"You can sit on the porch with me, Mrs. Moore," Ali said.

She made a confused, pleased gesture and then had a sip of her tea. He ordered a bowl of beef soup and a phone. He announced that if she was the greatest poetess in the country, the two of them should produce something together—"I am a poet, too," he said—a joint-effort sonnet, it was to be, with each of them doing alternate lines. Miss Moore nodded vaguely. Ali was very

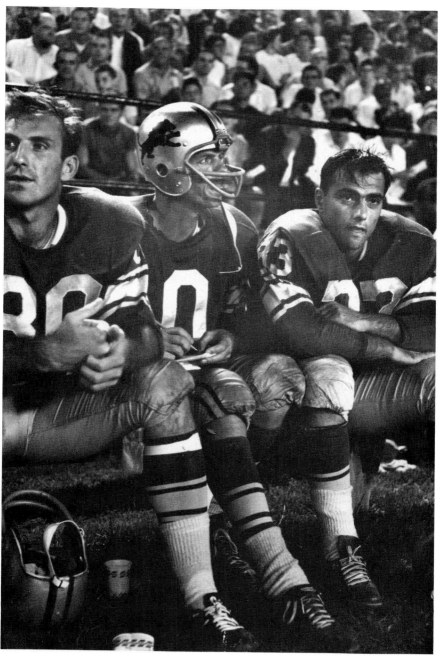

On the Detroit Lions bench, flanked by Jim Gibbons, the tight end, and Nick Pietrosante, the star running back. I wore my helmet throughout the game since I had difficulty getting in and out of it.
Walter Iooss, Jr./*Sports Illustrated*

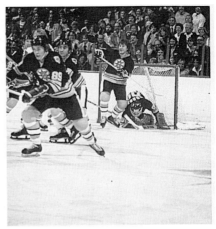

Ezra Bowen, Jr., a Sports Illustrated *editor, refereed the fight against Archie Moore and called it a draw. It is perfectly clear from the state of my nose that it was not.*

Herb Scharfman/*Sports Illustrated*

A passing attack by the Boston Bruins is foiled by my own inability to stand upright.

John Iacono/*Sports Illustrated*

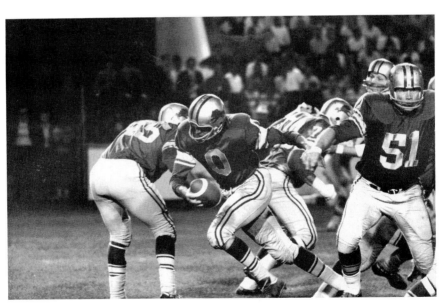

On one of the four plays I ran as quarterback of the Detroit Lions I inexplicably collapsed to the ground during a pass play—without a hand being laid on me.

Walter Iooss, Jr./*Sports Illustrated*

Playing horseshoes with President Bush at the Naval Observatory, wearing one of his cowboy hats, despite the bad fit.

David Valdez/The White House

At rehearsal as a percussionist with the New York Philharmonic. Buster Bailey, a fellow denizen of what Leonard Bernstein referred to as "the Shady Corner," is at hand to advise and supply spiritual comfort.

David Wolper

Marianne Moore and Muhammad Ali in Toots Shor's restaurant, at work on "A Poem on the Annihilation of Ernie Terrell."
AP/Wide World Photos

Interviewing Muhammad Ali in Zaire a few days after he regained the championship from George Foreman. The watermelon caused not the slightest suggestion of self-consciousness.
Lynn Goldsmith

Body English during my tour with the PGA. In the background is Abe, my elderly and diminutive caddy, affected at the time with a hacking cough.
Russ Halford/*Sports Illustrated*

With John Updike and William Styron on the occasion of Styron's receiving the MacDowell Medal in a ceremony at the MacDowell Colony in Peterborough, New Hampshire.
Harriet Gans

Safe for the moment behind a burladero *while Ernest Hemingway waits with a* capa *to play the calves at a* tienta *not far from Madrid.*

Standing with the Gruccis (the "first family of fireworks")—Felix, Jr., Jimmy, and Felix, Sr., in front of a control panel for the electrical firing of a fireworks display in New York City's Central Park.
Ken Clark

Flanked by Whitey Ford and the Yankee batboy just after my ordeal pitching in Yankee Stadium. The photograph was snapped just as I dropped in between them. They were not at all displeased that their profession had treated me as roughly as it had.

Garry Winogrand/*Sports Illustrated*

In New York, at Elaine's Restaurant with a few of its literary frequenters—from the left, Gay Talese, Jack Richardson, Jack Gelber, David Newman, Robert Brown. Elaine, the proprietress, is in the foreground.

The photographs that accompanied the Sidd Finch April Fool's Day spoof in Sports Illustrated *did a lot to convince readers that Finch—a 168 m.p.h. pitcher—was the real article.*

Lane Stewart/*Sports Illustrated*

*At the America's Cup Race (*Gretel *vs.* Weatherly*) in the early fall of 1962, aboard the destroyer* Joseph P. Kennedy, Jr. *with the Presidential party.*

Medora Ames Plimpton at the age of eight.

Francis T. P. Plimpton, lawyer, ambassador to the United Nations.

much the more decisive of the pair, picking not only the form but also the topic: "Mrs. Moore and I are going to write a sonnet about my upcoming fight in Houston with Ernie Terrell," he proclaimed to the table. "Mrs. Moore and I will show the world with this great poem who is who and what is what and who is going to win."

"We will call it 'A Poem on the Annihilation of Ernie Terrell,' " Miss Moore announced. "Let us be serious but not grim."

"She's cute," Ali commented.

A pen was produced. Ali was given a menu on which to write. He started off with half the first line—"After we defeat"—and asked Miss Moore to write in Ernie Terrell (which she misspelled "Ernie Tyrell" in her spidery script) just to get her "warmed up." He wrote most of the second line—"He will catch nothing"—handing the pen over and expecting Miss Moore to fill in the obvious rhyme, and he was quite surprised when she did not. She made some scratchy squiggles on the paper to get the ink flowing properly. The fighter peered over her shoulder.

"What's that say?" he asked.

"It doesn't say anything. You could call them 'preliminaries.' 'Terrell' should rhyme nicely with 'bell,' " Miss Moore said tentatively. I could see her lips move as she fussed with possibilities. Finally, Ali leaned over and whispered to her, " 'but hell,' Mrs. Moore."

"Oh, yes," she said. She wrote down "but hell," but then she wrestled with it some more, clucking gently, and murmuring about the rhythm of the line, and she crossed it out and substituted, "he will get nothing, nothing but hell."

Ali took over and produced his next line in no time: "Terrell was big and ugly and tall." He pushed the menu over to her. His soup arrived. He leaned low over it, spooning it in, and glancing over to see how she was coming along. While he waited, he told Conrad and me that he was going to try to get the poem out over the Associated Press wire that afternoon. Miss Moore's eyes widened, perhaps at the irony of all those years struggling with *Broom* and the other literary magazines, and now to be with a fighter who promised instant publication over a ticker machine. It did not help the flow of inspiration. She was doubtless intimidated by the presence next to her, especially at his obvious concern that she, a distinguished poet, was having such a hard time holding up her side: speed of delivery was very much a qualification of a professional poet in his mind. He finished his soup and ordered another. The phone arrived and was plugged in behind the banquette. He began dialing a series of numbers—hotels, most of them—but the room numbers he requested never seemed to respond.

Finally, seeing that she had not got anywhere at all, he took the poem from her and completed it. It was not done in a patronizing way at all but more out of consideration, presumably that every poet, however distinguished, is bound to have a bad day and should be helped through it. He tried some lines aloud which he eventually discarded: "When I hit him with my right / He'll become a colored satellite. . . .

"Now, let's see," he said as he began to write. He had moved close to her, so that she appeared to be looking down the long length of his arm to watch the poem emerge. "Yes," she said. "Why not?" as he produced a last couplet. The whole composition, once he had taken over, took about a minute. With the spelling corrected, it read as follows:

After we defeat Ernie Terrell
He will get nothing, nothing but hell,
Terrell was big and ugly and tall
But when he fights me he is sure to fall.
If he criticize this poem by me and Miss Moore
To prove he is not the champ she will stop him in four,
He is claiming to be the real heavyweight champ
But when the fight starts he will look like a tramp
He has been talking too much about me and making me sore
After I am through with him he will not be able to challenge Mrs. Moore.

The stratagem of involving her in the poem, particularly as a pugilist herself, was clever: Miss Moore nodded in delight, despite its being a truncated sonnet. She made a tiny fist. "Yes, he has been making me sore," she said.

A photographer arrived—something of a surprise. He was from one of the wire services. I suspect that Muhammad Ali, knowing that he was meeting someone of distinction, if not quite sure *whom,* had arranged for the photographer so that the event could be recorded. Miss Moore did not seem to mind. She allowed Ali, who continued to dominate the afternoon, to dictate the poses. His idea was to have the photograph show the two of them working on the poem. "We've got to show you *thinking,* Mrs. Moore," he said. "How you show you're thinking hard is to point your finger into the middle of your head." He illustrated, jabbing his forefinger at his forehead, closing his eyes to indicate concentration. She complied, pursing her lips in feigned concern as she pondered the poem. The photographer clicked away happily.

Miss Moore then expressed a wish to see the Ali shuffle—a foot maneuver Ali occasionally did in midfight, which looked like a man's trying to stay upright on a carpet being pulled out from underneath him. Ali said he would be delighted to show her the shuffle. He thought it would be best to do it out in the street where he had room to do her a really *good* shuffle. But when we walked outdoors, a crowd immediately collected—I think the word was around the neighborhood that the fighter was in Toots Shor's—so we came back through the revolving door and he did the shuffle right there in the foyer. Miss Moore was delighted. She asked him to do it again, and when he went out and did the shuffle for the people in the street, she watched him through the revolving door.

"Well," she said when he had left, "he had every excuse for avoiding a performance. But he festooned out in as enticing a bit of shuffling as you would ever wish to see."

"He 'festooned'?" I asked.

"He certainly did. He was exactly what I had hoped to meet."

Subsequently, I wrote Miss Moore to ask her what she had thought of her afternoon at Toots Shor's. What was her opinion of Ali as a poet?

She wrote, "Well, we were slightly under constraint. And the rhyme for Terrell ["Hell"] being of one syllable is hardly novel. . . . Cassius has an ear, and a liking for balance . . . comic, poetic drama, it *is* poetry . . . saved by a hair from being the flattest, peanuttiest, unwariest of boastings."

She was especially pleased that the poem (which she now thought might be titled "Much Ado about Cassius" rather than "A Poem on the Annihilation of Ernie Terrell") showed a strong sense of structure, which indeed involved herself: "He begins by mentioning a special guest and concludes with mention of the same."

Yes, that *had* entranced her—the conceit of stepping into the ring against the "ugly and tall" Terrell, wearing one of her less-encumbering hats, and taking Terrell out with a hook.

She then went on to produce a whizbang of words about Ali.

The Greatest, though a mere youth, has snuffed out more
dragons than Smokey the Bear hath. Mighty-muscled and fit, he

is confident; he is sagacious, ever so, he *trains.* A king's daughter is bestowed on him as a fiancée. He is literary, in the tradition of Sir Philip Sidney, defender of poesie. His verse is enhanced by alliteration. He is summoned by an official: "Come forth, *Cassius."* He is not even deterred by the small folks' dragons. He has a fondness for antithesis; he will not only give fighting lessons, but falling lessons. Admittedly the classiest and the brassiest. When asked, "How do you feel about being called by the British 'Gaseous Clay'?" his reply is one of the prettiest in literature. "I do not resent it." Note this: beat grime revolts him. He is neat. His brow is high. If beaten, he is still not "beat." He fights and he writes.

Is there something I have missed?
He is a smiling *pugilist.*

The name "Popper" in this account is a pseudonym, though close to the original. The "Popper" family sued the *Detroit Free Press* when this excerpt from *Mad Ducks and Bears* was published there. The deposition stated that the boy's classmates had ridiculed him after the piece had appeared and that he had become a "bed wetter." I was appalled. The boy I had most identified with on the field was "Popper"—indeed the hero of the piece. My own situation in the lawsuit was resolved by speaking at the "Poppers'" favorite charity. In Bloomfield Hills I stayed with the "Poppers" and indeed slept in "Popper's" bed. By this time the boy had been sent away to a military school. The "Secretary of Commerce" was apparently not something his parents had in mind for him.

Popper

That fall, Alex Karras, the great Detroit Lion tackle, swept by a sense of civic responsibility that somewhat startled those who knew him, became a head coach in the Bloomfield Hills Pony League, which was composed of a number of teams named after NFL franchises—the 49ers, the Rams, the Raiders, the Vikings, and so forth—and restricted to youngsters nine to ten years old. Originally, he had been offered the job of coaching even younger kids in the Bee League, where seven- and eight-year-olds played, but he felt there was probably "too much crying down there for me to take on the job."

Karras's team was the Bloomfield Hills Jets. His second son, Alex Jr., played on it, as did one of John Gordy's two sons and Joe Schmidt's son, Billy. It was an oddly frustrating experience for Karras. The Pony League teams played each other on Friday afternoons or on weekends, which meant that Karras, involved in his own turbulent football wars, was often away when his charges had their games. He did the best he could. As soon as his own game was over, he would hurry down the ramp to the locker room, lob his helmet into his cubicle, and reach for the phone to call home.

"Hey, Alex, that you? How'd the Jets do? You *lost!* To the Chargers? What happened? Six fumbles!" and he would sit and listen to his son's explanations, his face torn with despair despite the fact that around him his own teammates might be shouting and carrying on about their own victory, and that some fifteen minutes before he himself had been scuttling around in a real-life adult backfield, reaching for the quarterback with self-satisfying success.

During the autumn, I came out to Detroit to watch the Lions play a few of their home Sunday games, and on one occasion I arrived a few days early in the hope of watching Karras's Bloomfield Hills Jets in action. Alex gave me directions, and in the late afternoon I drove out to the high school grounds where the Jets were going through their last drills before playing the Bloomfield Hills Vikings the next day.

I stood on the sidelines and watched. Wearing his golf hat, Karras reared above his team like a derrick. Almost immediately I could see that there were a number of distinctive characteristics about a Karras-coached team. After a run-through of each offensive play, the Jets center was required to form the huddle by stationing himself at the proper eight- or nine-yard distance behind the line of scrimmage, raising his arm aloft so it could be seen, and shouting at the top of his lungs "Hud-*dle!*"—apparently an attempt to get the players grouped quickly around their quarterback. It was a cry one could hear across a couple of fields, as echoing and forlorn as a loon's, and it indicated to anyone in the vicinity who followed Pony League activity that Karras was at work with his team.

I took a few notes. Almost all the players looked like choirboys, an appearance that was not even belied by the accouterments of football warfare; they stared out from beneath the rims of their helmets with enormous gentle eyes, and their high voices, clear as whistles, were as unferocious as bird calls in the evening. All of them were required to wear plastic mouth guards, which were attached to their helmets, and when they set them in place they seemed en masse to have regressed to the use of pacifiers.

Some of them, of course, did not like what they were doing. After every play involving contact, an inevitable grasping at imaginary wounds would occur, usually the elbow or wrist; or a sudden limp would devastate a player, and he would come hobbling up to Karras and say, "Sir . . ."

"Popper what the hell's wrong? You're wetting in there like a little girl. No one even hit you. Go on back."

"Yes, sir."

Not only was Karras tough on his charges, but predictably he was not above keeping his team on edge with his own brand of needling. At one point his quarterback, a youngster named Reardon, complained after an unsuccessful pass that he could not see his intended receiver. "Mr. Karras, I can't see Brookmeier. He's too small."

Karras blew his whistle to stop practice. "Brookmeier," he called out. A helmet atop a small boy turned. "Brookmeier, your quarterback can't see you. *Grow!*"

On another occasion, Karras called out, "I want the pass-return team over here. Quick!"

The youngsters milled around uncertainly.

"I want the eleven people who are on the pass-return team over *here*. You all know who you are."

A group began to form around him.

"Well, it's about time," Karras said. "Our special teams must have pride. Okay, let's hear it for the pass-return team."

"Yay!" they cheered.

"What is the best of the special teams?"

"The pass-return team!"

"Are you proud to be on the pass-return team?"

"Yes, sir!"

"Well, you dummies," said Karras. "There *is* no such thing as a pass-return team." The youngsters looked at him, betrayed, eyes solemn and large in the shadows of their helmets. Karras shook his head.

"All right," he called. "Everyone gather round." The entire squad moved in around the forlorn "pass-return" team, Karras in the middle, towering above them.

"Okay, that's enough practice for today," he said. "But first I have some questions. Who are you playing tomorrow?"

"The Vikings!"

"Once again."

"The Vikings!" they all shouted in unison.

"Who are a bunch of turkeys?"

"The Vikings!"

"Who are we going to slaughter?"

"The Vikings!"

"Dismiss," said Karras.

He watched them troop off toward the sidelines. A few mothers were standing in the gathering darkness. Back in the high school parking lot other mothers waited in their cars, the headlights on, and the youngsters moved reluctantly, as if what each had been playing at—aping an adult pastime of ferocity and hitting at each other—should not properly conclude by going to one's mother, perhaps (the ultimate indignity) to be clasped briefly and asked if he was "all right" before being driven home, holding his helmet in his lap, in the family Chevrolet.

Karras, his son, Alex, and I walked to his car. "I'm wrung out from psyching my team up," he said. "There's nothing left for *me*. I'm playing Green Bay on Sunday. What kind of a game am I going to have against them! Jesus!"

"What sort of personnel do you have on the Bloomfield Jets?" I asked as we headed for home. "Certainly you've got a lot of football heritage," I pointed out, thinking of his son, and Gordy's, and Joe Schmidt's.

"They're okay, those kids," Karras said. "But the squad is very weak in reserves. Wait until you see them in action tomorrow. The rule is, they all have to play. Did you see the one called Popper? Popper is about one foot tall and he's all voice. He's very bright. If Popper could play the game he talks, no one else would walk out on the field; they'd all go home and hide in their basements. He wears number one, and he's the single worst football player I've ever seen. I don't think he's made contact with *anyone* this year."

"What position does he play?"

"I think he plays somewhere in the line," Karras said. "It's hard to tell because he sidles away from the guy carrying the ball. He doesn't want to get involved. He wears glasses. He's *very* bright. He's going to be Secretary of Commerce one day. . . . When I was playing football at his age, the kids had names like Slivovitz and McTawney and Bragodnic, really tough Polack and Irish and Eyetie names, and nicknames like Turk and Hammer and Jughead, and some of them had already lost their front teeth. Popper," he said in despair.

From the backseat Alex, Jr., said that a lot of the kids didn't really like to play. A couple of weeks before, the guy opposite him in the line of the Bloomfield Hill Raiders had said, "I'm really going to get you. I'm really going to push your face in the dirt." Alex blocked him properly on the first play and the kid had broken into tears and gone back to his bench.

"I'll tell you one thing," his father said. "Those Raiders didn't *all* break down and cry. They beat us about one-sixty-eight to nothing."

I asked, "How have the Jets been doing?"

"What's our record?" Karras asked, turning back to look at his son. "We beat somebody, didn't we?"

"Oh, Dad," Alex, Jr., said from the backseat. "We beat lots of people."

"I have all sorts of problems as a coach," Karras went on. "My best player, a kid named Robertson, came up to me before the last game and said, 'Mr. Karras, I can't play.'

" 'What?' I said.

" 'I've got a French horn lesson at four-thirty on the day of the game.'

"Well, I near fainted away. A French *horn* lesson. We finally solved it. We moved the French horn lesson up a half hour and the teacher allowed Robertson to come dressed in his football outfit, shoulder pads and all. He sat in her parlor on a straight-backed chair with the music stand in front, and when the hour was up, he took out the French horn mouthpiece, clapped in the football mouthpiece, and came running out to play. He had a *horrible* game. It's not the way to get ready for The Big Game."

I stayed for dinner at the Karras house, standing out in the kitchen having a drink with his wife, Joanie, while she occasionally turned a spoon in the stew. Drawings by the two youngest Karras children were pinned to a cork board—square-shaped houses with big windows, and chimneys with lines of smoke coming out. I asked her how much she herself could get involved in football—whether she let it permeate her life as much as it did the males in her household.

"Oh, no," she said. "The wives and mothers have to stay on an even keel. They can't get wrapped up in games the way the males do—it would drive a household crazy."

Her husband was in the living room playing with the younger children. Was he easy to live with during the season?

"There are always the sullen silences if things aren't going right," Joanie said. "It's unpleasant to live with, but it's common enough. During the season the first few days of the week are calm, but then the pressure begins to build. One night Al climbed out of his side of the bed, dragging the comforter with him. He draped it over his shoulder and looked at me sleepily and said that he was off to play the Green Bay Packers."

"What about after a loss?"

Joanie turned back to the stew. "Oh, after a loss there's usually a half hour of blowing off steam when he gets home, but he feels fine after that. Once I remember I took the family to pick him up at the Detroit airport after a big loss, and we went to have supper at a Howard Johnson's with Nick Pietrosante, Jim Gibbons and his wife, and some others, and everyone was grousing and staring into their shrimp cocktails and really *beside* themselves, until finally Alex, Jr., who was just three then, piped up and said, 'Well, back to the old drawing board.'"

After dinner I left for my hotel. With The Big Game in the Pony League coming up, the Karras household went to bed early. When I returned the next afternoon, driving through a slight rain, I found the house full of tension. Alex, Jr., stood in the hall, fully dressed in his football paraphernalia and wearing his helmet. His father was pacing through the rooms. Even Joanie seemed affected. She shook her head and told me that her days had been full enough of gossip and chatter about the NFL as it was, and now, like opening a closet door and finding someone standing there, the Pony and the Bee Leagues had suddenly made their presence known.

"The kids have their ups and downs about it," she said. "One time young Alex came to me and said, 'Mom, I have a bad shoulder. Do I have to go to practice?'

" 'Yes, Alex,' I said. 'Put on your uniform. Think of your father. He played five games with two torn cartilages . . .'

"You know what young Alex said to me? He said, 'Yes, but he had Novocaine.' "

Joanie stayed home with the smaller children. Peter Karras had gone off earlier to play in *his* league. Alex, Jr., sat in the backseat of the car. "Are you going to give us a big pep talk, Dad?"

"Why, what's wrong? Didn't you like the one I gave you last week?" Karras turned laboriously from the wheel, maneuvering his big shoulders around so he could glance briefly at his son.

Alex, Jr., did not answer. He was looking out the window at the passing scenery. "Mr. Stump usually gives the pep talk," Karras told me.

"Who's Mr. Stump?"

"He's the defensive coach. His first name's Dick, but I call him Mr. Stump. I give it a 'Mistah Stump!' He cried out the name in the car like a sea captain calling for his boatswain's mate. "Mistah *Stump!* Sometimes I think Mr. Stump is putting everybody on with his pep talks." He shook his head. "Wait till you hear him. Couple of years back *I* gave a pep talk before my old school. At Iowa. They had the worst team that year. I went back for a homecoming, and they asked me into the locker room before the game to talk to the team. So I thought, Shall I give them a real Win-It-for-the-Gipper sob talk, or a big long Vince Lombardi scream and knock over a few lockers and act like a gorilla? I gave them neither; I looked at my feet a lot and mumbled a few things. What I remember is that there was a black guy right in front of me—Levi Williams, hell of a good tight end—and while I talked he had on this big grin, like I was telling him the funniest thing in the world, some great honky joke that really grabbed his ass. I couldn't figure him. So the team went out on the field and they got beat something awful. A real horror. But this fellow Williams came up after the game and he *still* had this same tremendous grin on his face—and hell, he'd really been *laced* out there; Iowa was beat about forty to nothing. I said, 'Hey, man, you all right?' He told me that he liked what I'd said in my pep talk. I said, 'Hell, man, you got beat 40–0.' He said, 'Hell, man, you *not* give that talk and maybe we get beat 80–0.' He was one grand man, let me tell you."

When we reached the playing field it was overcast and threatening rain. Karras had left his rain gear at home; he was wearing the golf hat that read JEWISH OPEN and brightly polished cowboy boots. Alex, Jr., stood beside him and looked across the field at the Vikings. "They're all big," he said.

Karras collected the team on the high school gym steps for his pep talk. "We better hold on here a bit," he said. "No one seems to be here," he explained to me. "Just reserves. Where are my stars? I'm missing my quarterback and my best running back. No sense in panicking; they're only half my starting backfield. The quarterback is probably washing dishes . . . Mistah Stump? Do you have a few words for us?"

His assistant coach stood up. He was a big man who wore a trench coat, and he had a Coke in one hand. "Men," he said. "We're going to win this one . . . and we're going to win it big. I don't want crumbs. I'm not interested in crumbs. *You're* not interested in crumbs. I want the whole slab of bacon." He took a swig of his Coca-Cola. "I want you to hit them out there. We want blood, sweat, and tears—otherwise you can go home. This game isn't milk and cookies. No, siree, it's blood and *guts.*" He sat down.

"Thank you, Mistah Stump," said Karras. He rose for his own pep talk. "Boys, I'm tired of losing. Are you?"

"Yes!"

"Now the Vikings have lost three games this season. After we're through with them this afternoon, how many games will they have lost?"

Everyone shouted, "Four!"

"I want this one. Do you?"

"Yes!"

"Now, tomorrow's Halloween. I don't want anybody thinking about Halloween. I want you to think about winning and hitting the other guy and bringing home the bacon. Right?"

"Right!" they all yelled.

A latecomer came hurrying up wearing his helmet, his mouthpiece inserted, and a big number one on his jersey.

"It's Popper," said Karras. "Boy, are we glad to see you."

Popper removed his mouthpiece. "Did I miss anything?" He had a clear, bright voice.

"You missed Mistah Stump's pep talk. And mine," said Karras.

The boys began milling around. There were only a few minutes to go and they began aping their elders' pre-game rituals—boxing each other on the shoulder pads and running in place. Popper stood off to the side. I watched him, a small vigorous figure with a pale intelligent face and a spotless uniform. He was chattering away to himself. "Popper is here," I heard him whisper. "They'll tremble in their boots when they hear that Popper is here." He looked across the field at the Vikings. "They're not so big," he said. "Popper is going to stomp them and ring their bells." He walked over to his coach. "Mr. Karras," he said, tugging at his sleeve and looking up. "Their shirts are going to run *red with blood* when Popper gets ahold of them."

"Yes, yes, Popper," his coach replied.

"Mr. Karras, their brains are cooking with the awfullest fear."

"Popper, sit down and calm yourself."

"Mr. Karras, when I tackle them, I'm going to put their light bulbs out."

"Sure, Popper. Now just don't burn yourself up thinking about it. Save yourself."

Popper sat down on the gym steps, his hands in his lap. After a while, across the field the referees' whistles began to shrill. Popper jumped up. The team was quiet as the players trotted across to their bench. Their captain, the middle linebacker, a youngster named Simon, chugged out under his over-sized helmet to the center of the field for the coin toss. Karras had instructed him what to do. "He's a good player," he said to me as we stood in front of the bench. "He's three feet tall and he weighs thirty-three pounds, but he sticks like a burr."

Apparently the team lost the toss, for the referee signaled by extending his leg that the Jets were to kick off, and then, turning and catching an imaginary ball, indicated that the Vikings were to receive. But when Simon came trotting back to the bench, he allowed that he had actually *won* the toss.

"Wha'? Wha'? Well, then, why the hell are we kicking *off?*" cried Karras. He looked betrayed under his golfing cap.

"It's psy—psy—" Simon stuttered.

"Are you trying to tell me there was a *psychological* reason?" Karras exclaimed. "Jesus Sweet Christ!"

To avoid hearing more, Simon turned and scampered out to his team, drawn up in a line and waiting for him to kick off. At the referee's whistle he ran forward and, perhaps frantic in his anguish at having made a tactical error, sent a wobbly kick down to the ten yard line, where it bounced and eluded some potential receivers who looked forlorn and not especially anxious to fool with it until finally the least nervous of them picked up the football and ran it up to the twenty-three. Simon was one of the tacklers.

"Nothing wrong with that," Karras said, looking pleased. "Shows what a heady team leader can do."

The Vikings moved for a few first downs before kicking eighteen yards, and then the Jets' offense took over.

Karras sent in the offensive plays by shuttling quarterbacks. It would have given him the greatest sense of power if they ever turned out to be what he expected, he said sadly. He would instruct his quarterback to call "The power left on 'go,' " pat him on the back as he ran out for the next play, and stand peering forward through his big spectacles in the hope of seeing his orders translated into a recognizable physical facsimile. Instead, the play itself would convolute and heave, with perhaps a fumble for good measure, and when the quarterback arrived back on the sidelines Karras would ask, "Now, damn it, what in God's name was *that?*"

"Oh, sir," the quarterback would answer, "they're kicking us and *everything!*"

The second time the Jets got possession of the ball, they did better. They made a first down, but then stalled with fourth and six to go. Since the team was on its own thirty-five, the situation seemed to call for a kick, but Karras sent in an end-around play. "I don't believe in punting," he told me. "These people can kick the ball just about fifteen yards. Only the very suave coaches call for a punt. The Viking coach punts. The Viking coach is very suave."

His tactic worked; the end-around went for twenty yards and the Jets had a drive going, supported with high-pitched yells from the bench. Before every play the Jet center raised his loonlike yell of "Hud-*dle,*" and finally after one distant grouping down at the far end of the field, we saw the Jet players run a short plunge and then leaping up and down, barely discernible in the gloom. We had scored. All of the Jets began slapping each other's palms as they trotted back toward the bench, a massive imitation of the familiar ritual practiced by their elders involved in a score. The try for the extra point failed, but there was still general jubilation.

"Damme, Mistah Stump!" cried Karras. "Have we got ourselves some champions?"

Mr. Stump's face glistened happily in the rain.

After receiving the kickoff, however, the Vikings began marching steadily for the Jet's goal line. Seeing his defensive charges wilt before the Viking onrush, Mr. Stump was beside himself; he took off not only his trench coat but his suit coat, so that in the considerable chill and rain he was wearing no more than a sleeveless white shirt, patched against his body, and a black string tie, looped loosely to his neck from nervous tugging. "Come on! Jets! You gotta have guts to play this game," he cried. He leaned over the border of the sidelines, jackknifed, as if he were poised on the edge of a swimming pool. "Oh no! Make him go inside of you." He turned away and strode frantically in front of the bench.

"Mistah Stump!" cried Karras. "What is transpiring?"

Stump shouted at Karras. "What can you do? You ask them to move just a little bit to the outside, maybe a step or so, and they shift twelve *yards.*" He turned back to the game. "Plug up those holes. No more *flinching,* damn it!"

His cries were to no avail. The Vikings scored on an end run. Their extra point try failed as well, and the score was tied six to six.

The time it took the teams to make the two scores used up almost the entire first half, which in the Pony League consisted of two ten-minute quarters. With all the emotion and concern invested in the game, it seemed we had just barely settled down before the referee came over to Karras on the sidelines and said, "We've got one minute to go to the half."

"What are you on, Greek time?" Karras said querulously. His team had possession of the ball and was moving in Viking territory. The two men glared at each other. In the background the cry of "Hud-*dle*!" arose. "You heard what I said," the referee remarked. "One minute." He was wearing all the proper accouterments of his profession—the striped shirt and the whistle suspended from a bleached cowhide lanyard. A bead of rain wobbled on the brim of his cap. "You want me to say it again?"

There it was: they had just a few seconds in which to establish the adult prerogatives—in the case of the referee, who probably taught math in the third grade, his authority in a profession in which the man he was trying to face down was probably the most famous tackle in the country.

Karras stared at him and found nothing to say. The referee turned almost immediately and trotted swiftly toward the Jets, now breaking the huddle and moving up to the line of scrimmage. "What's with that guy?" Karras muttered. "What's wrong with Greek time? Hey?"

In the second half the teams began to slip in the mud. I was hoping to make some notes about the playing of the Detroit Lions' progeny—Bill Schmidt, the Gordy boy, and young Karras—to detect whether they reflected their famous parents on the field, whether one could tell from the boys' mannerisms—the hunching of shoulder pads under a jersey, the position of the hands on defense, the profile of their stances—that a Gordy was out there, or a Karras, or a Schmidt. It turned out to be impossible to tell, not only because of the mud and gloom but because at nine or ten the boys' frames were as thin as ropes and bore no resemblance to the quick heft their fathers carried around. As Karras said of them, "They get into positions like snakes."

The teams churned back and forth, neither scoring. Behind the Jet bench a few girls stood watching the game, shifting their weight from one long, thin leg to another. "Is that your brother?" I heard one of them ask in disgust. "He fell down. He's gross."

"It's raining. Why not?" said the other defensively. "But he *is* gross," she added reflectively. She bent and began speaking earnestly into the face of an Irish setter, cupping its head in her hands. "I'm going to petrify you tomorrow," she said. "I'm going to leap out at you with a Halloween mask. Are you prepared to be petrified?" The dog moved its tail uncertainly. His haunches lowered and he began to tug against her grip. She let go. "Stupid," she said to him. "Big stupe." She stood up. "What's going on? Who's ahead?"

"Who knows?" said the other girl. "Maybe it's a tie. Your brother fell down again."

I moved out of earshot as the team toiled on in the semidarkness. Behind us a group materialized and stood at the bottom step of the stands in back of the bench. With a start I recognized Joe Schmidt, the Lion coach, standing under a large black umbrella, his face impassive. He was there to watch his son. The rain began to pelt down harder and his wife moved in closer to share his umbrella. I wondered whether Karras was aware that Schmidt was watching. Rumors had it that recently the two were not on the best of terms.

With only a few minutes to go in the game, Karras called out, "Has anybody not played yet?"

A number of hands went up along the bench.

"Jesus Christ, Mistah Stump, we've got about ten of them," Karras said grimly. "Mistah Stump, begin sending in the reserves!"

His assistant substituted at every opportunity. The last one sent in was Popper. A small tidy figure with the big number one on his back, he ran out with quick, busy steps that carried him along quite slowly. Karras watched him go. "Okay, Popper!" he called. "Turn out their light bulbs."

"See if you can figure out where Popper plays," he said. "It's somewhere of his own choosing."

I watched. The Vikings were on the offense at midfield, and when their fullback moved forward with the ball I could see Popper receding from the play, falling back from the line into his own backfield. I was reminded of a shore bird, one of the plump plover family, retreating up the beach from a line of surf.

Still, Popper's presence on the field did not result in any change in the score. In the gloom, the game finally ended in a 6–6 tie. On the sidelines Karras asked, "Is that the end? Okay, everybody. Go over and shake hands with them."

The players began walking slowly back toward the gym, winding down, I supposed, their emotions about the game. I moved along with them, my notebook open and smudging slowly in the faint rain. I could not resist leaning down and asking the superficial questions that reporters put to players in post-game interviews. "What about the Vikings?" I asked Morton, the Jet center. "What sort of a team?"

He looked up, startled. "Well, they defense good," he said, aping the locker room banalities of his elders—his voice husky from the effort he had put into crying out "Hud-*dle*!" "They're a real good ball club. They come off the ball real good."

The boy walking along next to him said, "We proved one thing, though: the Vikings put on their legs . . . er, ah . . . at a time."

"You're saying that they put on their pants one leg at a time?"

"That's right," he said. "They can be beat. We just didn't get enough points up on the board."

"What was the problem?"

The boy shuffled along. "We couldn't get enough points up on the board," he said again, keeping to that familiar platitude, so incongruous because it was delivered in a high-pitched fluting voice. "They defense good." Then he began to have trouble. "Er, ah . . . Brookmeier . . . and then there was that time . . . well, *you* know, when . . . and what about when . . . and he *kicked* me, that big guy . . . and the rain . . ."

"But most important . . . ?"

"We just couldn't get those points up on the board"—this clear and positive.

I fell into step alongside Popper. "Popper, what is your opinion of the Jet coaching staff?"

"I think Mr. Karras is the new Chubby Checkers," he said, in reference to the somewhat stout pop star of the day. I jotted this comparison down in my book. I continued. "Popper did you put out any light bulbs?"

He did not answer. He walked with his head down. My heart sank.

"No," he said softly. "I ran away."

I had no idea what to say. "It's all right, Popper," I said finally. "One day you're going to be Secretary of Commerce."

He stopped and looked at me out of the depths of his helmet. "Isn't that funny," he said cheerfully. "That's exactly what Mr. Karras tells me."

Irving Lazar

The news along the Rialto, of course, is that Irving (Swifty) Lazar, the mega-literary agent, is writing his memoirs. He will be selling his own book to the publishers (and very likely to the networks for a miniseries and the studios for a movie), which is news because Lazar has very likely *read* what he is selling. That is not usually the case. Lazar is famous for *not* reading what his clients write. "I glanced through it" is what he often says, which most agree is an exaggeration.

He is a small man, very small, with a large head, completely bald, with elfin ears that support the frames of thick glasses with heavy black rims. A familiar sight gag among his friends is to hoist one's pant legs above the knee and settle a pair of glasses—the darker-rimmed the better—on a kneecap.

"Who's this?"

Those who haven't seen this before and recognize the similarity tend to roar with laughter. For those who don't know Swifty, or who he is, tend to think of what they see as a pair of spectacles . . . well, resting on a kneecap.

They should know. He is famous. He graces one of the verses in Cole Porter's ballad "Let's Do It" namely "Bees do it/Lazar does it." His list of clients is formidable: Ernest Hemingway, Irwin Shaw, Truman Capote, Gore Vidal, Larry McMurtry, Vladimir Nabokov. He has made a great deal of money for them. Twenty years ago he engineered a one-and-a-half-million-dollar two-book deal for Irwin Shaw. Perhaps reading their work isn't that important. Why should he? To make suggestions? Lazar's favorite author, Vladimir Nabokov ("the greatest writer in the world") once described those who tried as "avuncular brutes."

Several years ago Irving called me to say that a movie company was interested in my playing a small "cameo" role in a film adapted from a

Harold Robbins novel entitled *The Lonely Lady.* Pia Zadora was the star of the film, which was to be shot on location in Rome. Irving didn't think the project was worth my while: the movie company would pay for my transportation, a hotel room in Rome for a week, and that was about it. I couldn't expect more than three or four thousand dollars for playing the part.

"How much of a role is it?" I asked.

"Kid, it's no big deal," Irving said. He often calls me kid when he gives me advice. "It's a cameo role."

"Swifty, have you read the script?"

"I've glanced through it."

So I asked him to send it on. One of the reasons was that Pia Zadora is of that variety of blond, pouty-lipped sex kittens—exemplified by Brigitte Bardot—who have a nasty grip on my heart strings.

The script arrived. In brief, the story turned out to be a kind of adaptation of *All About Eve* except that the woman (Pia Zadora) who yearns for the top and will do anything to get there is a scriptwriter rather than an actress. My part, I discovered, was that of one Walter Thornton, the elder statesman of scriptwriters ("the most famous writer in America," according to the script). Pia considers Thornton a kind of stepping-stone; she seduces him and, as I recall, marries him briefly before casting him away and moving on. The Thornton role was much longer than Lazar had led me to believe and certainly was more challenging: one bedroom scene called for him to bring Pia Zadora to the "edge of orgasm."

All this . . . well, made me wonder if perhaps a trip to Rome might not be a bad idea. Of course, there was the problem of the small payment, and this I felt had to be readjusted radically. While aware that many people given the opportunity would rush off to do the role gratis, I had to worry about the effect of such a performance on my family. I could disguise the reason for my trip to Rome, but suppose that one day they wandered into a Saturday matinee and suddenly saw Dad up there on the big screen involved in the "bringing her to the edge of orgasm" business. Or, more to the point, if my mother, who is in her eighties and a Massachusetts woman, had decided to go to the movies with them. What an uproar!

Not only that but also there was the possibility of considerable damage to my own psychic self and confidence if it turned out I had been unable to bring Pia to the "edge of orgasm" or even close.

So after a great deal of thought I decided I would be willing to play Walter Thornton for a hundred thou.

I telephoned Lazar.

"It's about *The Lonely Lady,*" I said.

"It's not worth it. Not worth your time."

"Swifty . . ."

"Kid, I can't get you more than a couple of thousand. It's a cameo role."

"Swifty, did you read it carefully?"

"I glanced through it."

"But, Swifty, it's a costarring role. I have to bring Pia Zadora to the edge of orgasm and everything."

I went on to describe the plot to him, my part in it, the bedroom scenes, along with my doubts considering the family, the anguish it might cause them and my mother.

"Swifty," I said finally, "I was thinking of a hundred thousand."

There was a long pause at the other end. I heard Lazar clear his throat. "Kid," he said. "We'll start at *two hundred thousand.*"

I don't remember my reaction—stunned, perhaps bemused at the jump from two thousand to a hundred times that amount in the course of a minute.

Ultimately I never went to Rome. Lazar called up in a few days. "They didn't go for it," he told me. I suppose I regretted it to some degree, but I never thought very much about it except to tell the story on Irving from time to time.

I never saw the film. But one day my curiosity got the best of me. Discovering the identity of the actor picked to play Walter Thornton, I telephoned him in California. Lloyd Bochner. A veteran of many fields of acting (he spent eight years in the Stratford-on-Ontario Repertory), he told me that he had spent a splendid time in Rome: "I loved it."

I asked him if he would mind telling me how much the producers had paid him.

"Not at all. A hundred thousand."

My original asking price! Lazar had priced me out of the market!

"Well, what was it like?" I asked, referring to the bedroom scene.

"Well, there was exposure, but not of me. Pia was totally nude. I was wearing shorts. But no shoes."

"Of course not."

"According to the script, I was not able to satisfy her. I tried all sorts of tricks, but none of them worked."

"You weren't able to push her over the edge," I commented.

"Something like that," Bochner said.

I asked him if the role compared with some of the others he had done.

I could hear him laughing at the other end of the line. "You won't believe this," he said. "I'm probably best-known for playing Cecil Colby in *Dynasty*. I died while in bed with Joan Collins."

"What?"

"I had a heart attack while performing."

I whistled in awe. I marveled at his luck in getting in bed with leading ladies. I said, "I hope you got *her* to the edge of orgasm before succumbing."

"You'll have to ask Joan," he answered promptly.

I wouldn't ever presume to advise Irving Lazar about these memoirs of his. But he's welcome to what I have described. The timeworn ingredients are all there: sex, money, movie stars, a surprise ending. It's certainly worth more than a glance.

Paul Tavilla

Paul Tavilla arrived at my apartment with a suitcase full of large purple grapes. He raised the lid to show me. Among them was a hairbrush, which he removed. "These are Ribier grapes," he explained. "Black exotics from California. Perfect." He ate one. "Seedless?" I asked. "Surely they're seedless."

"Not at all. Seedless grapes are light colored, not dark enough to pick out against the sky."

Tavilla, a large, ebullient man in his fifties, had come down from Boston on an early flight of the Trump Shuttle, which was appropriate because the purpose of his visit to New York was to catch in his mouth a grape tossed from the top of Trump Tower on Fifty-seventh and Fifth.

Tavilla does this as a hobby: he catches grapes dropped from high buildings. Indeed, he is listed in *The Guinness Book of World Records* as the champion in this rather specialized field, having in 1988 caught a grape in his mouth from the top of the John Hancock Tower in Boston, a drop of seven hundred eighty-eight feet.

Tavilla had come to New York to try some of its taller structures in the hope of breaking his own record. On his behalf, I had called the managements of some of the giants. The World Trade Center. That was Tavilla's preference, because success there would have left only the Sears Tower in Chicago (the world's tallest) as the final challenge, unless he were willing to camp under a blimp at four or five thousand feet.

The World Trade Center turned us down. So did the Empire State Building. The Chrysler Building. Not worth the bother, was their consensus.

That left Trump Tower, not a record, but at sixty-three stories, quite a feat. I managed to reach Donald Trump on the phone. "I have a favor to ask," I said. I could imagine him cringing at the other end hearing this dread request, invariably related, I would guess, to projects involving large sums of money. "Well," I said, "it's to allow a man to catch a grape in his mouth from the top of your building."

I could hear Trump breathing. "A grape'd go right through the guy," he said finally.

"The guy's apparently whole," I said. "He's a champion at it. He caught a grape off the John Hancock in Boston."

Trump sighed slightly. He referred me to a vice president of operations. "He'll set it up, provided we're covered by insurance."

I thanked him. I said I hoped he would come out and watch. "Yeah," Trump said noncommittally.

On the way to the tower by taxi, Tavilla told me something about himself. A produce dealer, he had long been famous among the stalls of the New England Produce Center in Chelsea, Massachusetts, for catching in his mouth just about anything thrown at him—bits of fruit, cherries, melon balls, bananas (sliced), raisins, cherry tomatoes, even small plums arching across the aisles.

"You can wake me out of a deep sleep, throw something in the general direction of my face, and I'll catch it," he said. "I'm like a dog."

He told me about the John Hancock record. The grape was dropped by his son-in-law, Russell Hagopian, who is a dentist.

"How nice to have one in the family," I remarked. "A dentist. Has he had to . . . ah?"

"The teeth don't come into it at all," Tavilla explained. "You catch the grape in the pit of the mouth, right here . . ." He threw his head back and demonstrated, jabbing a finger into his mouth. "Right here."

"How fast is the grape going?" I asked.

"About a hundred and ten miles per hour. Just about terminal velocity," Tavilla said. "Oh, I can feel it. It hurts. A big sting. But if you catch it and you set a record, it doesn't hurt." He looked out the taxi window. "You couldn't get the World Trade Center? My son-in-law isn't coming down because a record isn't involved. Know what I mean?"

"The Trade Center said the benefits didn't outweigh the 'downside.' That's the way they talk."

Tavilla turned back from the window. "What about that big ape. Wasn't he climbing around the Trade Center?"

"King Kong."

"You'd think there'd be a lot more downside from an ape—I mean something *that* size—than from a few grapes."

The cab drew up in front of Trump Tower. We got out and craned our necks, gawking up at the obsidian slab of the tower. Tavilla's enthusiasm returned. "It looks taller than I expected," he exclaimed.

The garden terrace had been picked for Tavilla's try—a setback on the fifth floor. Inside are a terrace café and the top level of the atrium mall. Big plate-glass windows look out. We were shown there by three security men wearing black suits. The terrace is set about with garden-furniture chairs and umbrellaed tables. Tavilla felt his best chance was to stand in the shrubbery that borders the terrace, close to the side of the building, its deep-blue expanse rising up to where we could see the minuscule faces of the grape-drop contingent looking down and then, just barely visible, the extension of the grape dropper's arm.

The grapes came down one by one, at intervals of two or three seconds. They pelted around Tavilla, those that hit the terrace paving stones making a little slap sound. Others flicked through the bushes. Some, wafted by the wind currents, hit the side of the building far up and floated in little shreds. Tavilla was having difficulties. His footing in the shrubbery was uncertain. Twenty minutes went by. Curious faces peered through the plate-glass windows. Donald Trump had not appeared. The security men began joking among themselves.

My own attitude about Paul Tavilla during all this was curious. I had come to truly like him during our short acquaintance—his ebullience, his good nature, and especially that he was not in the least self-deprecatory about the lunatic thing he was doing: a large middle-aged man, head back, mouth agape, lurching through the shrubbery of the Trump terrace garden, the patter of grapes in the leaves around him, for no other reason than showing off (eventually, one hoped) this unique talent. He behaved like a man possessed—waving at the tiny faces high above, signaling them to keep the grapes coming. A grape hit him in the noşe. Another glanced off the side of his face. I saw his lips moving. *Son of a bitch.* At the twenty-third minute, a grape splashed in and out of his mouth. He stepped back out of the shrubbery and shouted that it didn't count. The grape had to emerge whole. Back into the bushes he went. At times I found myself bent nearly double, laughing at the spectacle—turning away from him so he wouldn't notice. But I also worried. Tavilla had not always been successful. In the spring of 1986, he went to Dallas to try to catch a grape from the sixty-eighth floor of the

Interfirst Plaza. Some thirty pounds of grapes were dropped one by one from the office building, which is seventy-two stories high, and Tavilla, bothered by high winds and the sun reflecting off the windows, said afterward that he'd seen only a half dozen of them. The sidewalk around him was stained purple. He gave up after two hours of staring aloft, his mouth ajar. I read a news item about this and became curious about Tavilla because it seemed he had an extraordinary passion at which he was not very good.

"They were small California grapes . . . flying all over the place," Tavilla had told me that morning.

The minutes crept by. A half hour. *Son of a bitch.* The three security men ventured into the drop area and tried it themselves. One of them kept his tongue stuck far out, as if he could flick in a grape like a chameleon. A grape exploded on his shoulder.

As he bent, I caught a glimpse of a small pistol on his belt. A crowd in the atrium stared through the plate glass at the activity. What could they have thought, seeing the three security men, heads back, openmouthed, moving crablike across the terrace, and in the bushes the gray-haired man, his mouth wide, stumbling about, looking up, waving at someone or something above? I went inside. In the café, people at the window tables picked at their salads. They hardly took notice. The passersby in the atrium paused for a while. It was impossible to see the grapes. One woman, watching the security men darting about, speculated to her companion that a modern dance was being rehearsed. I was reminded of the Charles Addams cartoon of a small crowd watching a startled businessman being pulled down into a manhole by an enormous octopus and one onlooker saying to another: "It doesn't take much to collect a crowd in New York." I went back onto the terrace. Tavilla seemed pale, and sweat glistened on his forehead. "Keep 'em coming," he called out. "We'll get it."

Finally, after forty-one minutes, he did. He turned toward us in the shrubbery and flung his arms aloft, pumping them like a triumphant fighter. He stepped out onto the terrace paving and puffed the grape out onto his lower lip. We gathered around, congratulating him. He showed us the grape. It was cracked but whole. Some four hundred had been dropped. Two Trump employees appeared with brooms and large dustpans to sweep up the myriad purple husks.

"That was a bitch," Tavilla was saying cheerfully. "There's no footing over there in the bushes. One hit me in the nose. D'ja see that? I was getting dizzy."

"Any doubts?"

"Heck, no!" he said forcefully. "I'm the champion. Hey, throw me some."

He gave a bunch of grapes to one of the security men, the one with the little pistol at his hip, who backed up and began throwing the grapes half the length of the terrace. Tavilla moved like a big frog. *Snap. Snap. Snap.* He was awfully good at it. He ate a few. His jaw moved. Others he dropped on the paving. The dustpan man pouted.

"The secret is to forget your mouth," Tavilla explained. "It's a question of eye concentration. On the Carson show I told Johnny this. Then I threw him a grape and it hit him in the eye."

I went back into the atrium. A crowd was still there. They watched Tavilla hop and snag one going over his shoulder. A young woman was asking a policeman what was going on.

"He's catching grapes, lady. He caught one from the top of the tower."

"Why is he doing it?"

He produced a line from a movie. Or a cartoon book.

"This is New York, lady," he said politely.

Warren Beatty

For some time now I have been sitting by the phone, waiting to hear from Warren Beatty. He is in New York making his film *Dick Tracy*. He knows "my work," as they say in Hollywood. I had a small role in his film *Reds*. I know exactly what he is going to say when the phone rings and he is on the other end. He is going to say, "Is this the man who has never had an olive?"

It is a kind of ritual between us. I once told him that, to my knowledge, I had never eaten an olive. Very likely I have had part of one, in a salad, perhaps, but I have never knowingly eaten one; I have never reached into an empty martini glass and popped one of the things into my mouth.

Warren has the most astonishing powers of recall. He remembers my telephone number in New York when the exchange was Lyceum. So when he telephones and I answer, he doesn't say, "Hello, it's Warren," or whatever. He asks, "Is this the man who has never had an olive?"

I always reply by asking, "Warren, is that you?" which is nonsensical, since who else would call up and start asking about olives?

I have known him for years—not well, of course, because there is something quite ephemeral about Warren: he materializes briefly, like a face at the window, and then disappears for years at a time. Nothing is more typical of this than my experience with him on *Reds*. I happened to be staying as a guest at Hugh Hefner's Playboy Mansion in Holmby Hills. Coming up from the grotto swimming pool late one night, I discovered Warren apparently asleep on the floor of the foyer just by the front door. I found out later that he had just returned from the Soviet Union, where he had been trying (unsuccessfully, it turned out) to get the Russians to let him film *Reds* on location—specifically in Leningrad, where the October Revolution took

206

place in 1917. Some extensive carpentry work was being done on his house; he had arrived at Hefner's—a face in the window—looking for a room for the night.

So there he was, lying on the marble floor, with his head on a knapsack. I looked down at him, and before his eyes snapped open and he brought up the business about the olive, I said, reversing the usual order of our ritual, "Is that you, Warren?"

He opened his eyes and immediately said, "Wiggen. Henry Wiggen." At this time I had no idea what he was talking about. It turned out that Henry Wiggen was a character in the screenplay of *Reds*—a rather obnoxious gentleman who runs a magazine called *The Cosmopolitan* and has dishonorable intentions toward Louise Bryant, played by Diane Keaton. In the mansion that night none of this was described. Warren—and I don't think he ever moved his head from the knapsack—simply said he now had me in mind for a small part (Wiggen), and could I come that summer to London, where *Reds* was to be filmed?

Of course, of course, I said. I was enormously pleased. At the very least it proved the old Hollywood adage that it was simply a question of being in the right place at the right time—Lana Turner "discovered" at the counter in Schwab's drugstore. A door had been opened on a whole new career!

But then a few months went by, and nothing happened. No contracts arrived. No script. Not a word from Warren. I began to think that he'd had second thoughts. Perhaps he had discovered that my main acting experience had been at an all-boys school in New England when I was cast as a "young widow" in a drama called *Seven Keys to Baldpate* almost entirely because of my ability to scream. There were tryouts and I had won.

Then one day early that summer I was sitting in my New York apartment and the phone rang.

"Is this the man who has never had an olive?"

"Is that you, Warren?"

It was, and he had called to say that he had Diane Keaton with him and that he wondered if he could drop around to introduce her, since we had a couple of scenes together.

Of course, of course. I went to the kitchen and mixed myself a gin and tonic. The two of them arrived. Warren had the script with him in black covers. The presence of the two seemed to diminish the size of the apartment. I noticed the windows weren't washed. A small tear in the living-room carpet suddenly seemed a foot in diameter. We chatted rather aimlessly, I thought, not about *Reds,* but about the hot weather and how Warren's house was coming along and whether Diane liked baseball, and it occurred to me during all this that they were *staring* at me. What was important was not whether I could act, but whether I *looked* like Henry Wiggen.

Sure enough. After ten minutes or so, Warren said they had to be on their way.

"Well, don't you want me to read?" I asked.

"It doesn't really matter," Warren said.

"Well, I'm so glad you dropped in," I said as I took them to the door.

The apartment seemed to reestablish its proportions after they had left. The sun shone brightly through the windows. I picked up the cat and began speaking to it. "What do you suppose," I said, "Warren meant when he said it didn't matter?"

The phone rang. It was Warren. This time he didn't say, "Is this the man . . . ," et cetera. He was calling from his limousine. He said, "Diane and I have been talking it over, and we think it's best if we heard you read."

"You want me . . . to *read.*"

"We're on our way back," Warren said.

Of course, of course. Well, there it was, I thought, as I hung up the phone. My limitations as an actor would be immediately evident. I could cancel London, I told the cat, as part of my summer plans.

The scene Warren wanted me to read involved a rendezvous in a hotel tearoom with Diane Keaton, who, as Louise Bryant, is aspiring to be a writer. She is showing Wiggen some of her work, but he, though the editor of *The Cosmopolitan,* is more interested in her: his manner is oily.

Diane Keaton sat opposite me on the sofa. It was startling to have such a famous face close at hand and to have it behave very much like any other face. One is inured to the still photographs of the famous looking out from magazines and newspapers: it was as if a storefront mannequin had come to life. Her eyes—copper green and speckled in the sunlight—blinked. Her mouth moved. "Mr. Wiggen, I brought some stories. . . ."

"How nice," I said archly.

We went over the lines a few times. Suddenly, Warren leaned forward out of his chair and took the script from me.

"All right," he said, *"now* do it."

"But, Warren, I don't know the lines. You haven't given me a chance to memorize them."

"Don't worry about the lines," he said. "You've read them enough to know what sort of character you are. Go ahead."

I repeated the lines as best I could remember them. Then I improvised. Would she be interested in going to Coney Island and riding on the Swan Boat in the Tunnel of Love? What was her favorite cocktail? Did she like to have *lots* of them? I reached for her hand. My voice took on a curious, unctuous whine.

"That's fine," Warren said. He stood up.

"Do you want me to try another approach?" I asked anxiously.

"It doesn't really matter," he said.

I am poor with dates. It may have been a few months or even a year later. Time is of small consequence in anything involving Warren. I had almost forgotten *Reds* and Henry Wiggen. I was in Monte Carlo with the Grucci fireworks family. We were there competing for the fireworks championship of the world, which indeed the Gruccis eventually won. The phone rang in my hotel room. Through the static of a long-distance call I heard a voice saying, "Is this the man who has never had an olive?"

"Is that you, Warren?" I shouted.

It was, and he was telling me the dates I would be required to be in London.

So I went and performed. I wore a high turn-of-the-century collar and a watch chain and looked very dandified. Warren, who also directed the film, took more than thirty takes of our scene in the hotel tearoom. I went to the opening night in New York. The searchlights outside the theater pointed straight up. My scene was early in the film. During the intermission Paul Newman came by and said, "Hey, not bad."

It was the way he said "hey" that was especially pleasing—slightly surprised, as if I had performed a kind of conjuring trick. It pumped me up.

Indeed, afterward it occurred to me that at the Academy Awards an Oscar should be given for the best performance by someone from another "discipline" who hasn't the slightest idea how to act. From my own field I can think of Norman Mailer, who played Stanford White in *Ragtime;* Jerzy Kosinski, who played a party intellectual in *Reds;* John Irving in *The World According to Garp;* and Kurt Vonnegut, who turns up as Rodney Dangerfield's teacher in *Back to School.*

So I continue to keep an ear out for the phone. The rumor is that a lot of the actors in *Dick Tracy* wear rubber masks to better resemble the grotesque characters from the comic strip—B. B. Eyes, Flat Top. I wouldn't mind that. Anything to keep my hand in as a member of the Screen Actors Guild. Firing a machine gun from a window. Being zapped by someone and falling backward in a heap. I'm perfectly willing to resurrect the scream from *Seven Keys to Baldpate.*

The phone rings. It is someone I don't know from Bear Stearns. Or Shearson Lehman Hutton. Or Salomon Brothers. They invariably give their names and ask, "How are you this morning?" They have extremely interesting financial proposals. Can I spare them a moment? No, I say. I am waiting for a phone call.

The MacDowell Medal is one of the most prestigious awards anyone in the arts can receive. The MacDowell Colony itself is in Peterborough on the Massachusetts–New Hampshire border. Individual "studios" are set about in the heavily wooded complex in which those who get fellowships can concentrate on their varied disciplines. In midsummer a large tent is put up in case of inclement weather for the award ceremonies. In 1988 William Styron was selected for the honor. An old friend, one of those involved in the earliest days of the *Paris Review,* he asked that I speak on his behalf. I was touched and delighted. John Updike, himself a MacDowell Medal winner, introduced me. He talked about how much the *Harvard Lampoon* had meant to the both of us. He made reference to my rather arch accent by saying that he had seen a Tom Hanks vehicle entitled *Volunteers* in which, "suppressing his natural Brooklyn accent," I had "amazingly well imitated a stuffy-voiced upper-class middle-aged Wasp." General laughter.

I was tempted to refer to this in my opening remarks—reminding the audience that when Martin Gable, the Brooklyn-born actor, was asked about his cultivated accent, he would reply, "Affected, my dear sir, affected."

I resisted this. I rose and said as follows.

William Styron

We are gathered here to judge if William Styron is deserving of the MacDowell Medal. Perhaps at the conclusion of my remarks we should have a vote. My own opinion is that Styron has been honored half to death. The Prix de Rome in 1952. The Pulitzer in 1970, along with the Howells Medal of the American Academy of Arts and Letters that same year. He won the American Book Award for *Sophie's Choice.* The Légion d'honneur, commandant no less! A chair at the American Academy. His desk drawers are full of medals, scrolls, academic hoods, ceremonial pins, commemorative cups, keys to cities, especially in the South. Dolled up, I suspect Bill could very well be taken for an Ethiopian general.

The point of all this is, of course: Does Bill really need the MacDowell Medal? If all these other honors heaped up on him over the past years haven't been enough to bolster his confidence and his self-esteem, is one more, even the prestigious MacDowell, going to *help?* Are there not others of us here who need such morale boosters as the MacDowell *more?* . . . whose desk drawers are *not* heavy with medals, scrolls, academic hoods, trophies, and so forth? After all, we're not here to honor Bill with our presence. We're here to seethe with envy. I, for example, have only one trophy at home—a small tray with the inscription on it: "To a Good Sport, George Pemberton." George Pemberton is a friend of mine. I stole it from him.

We crave such things. Recognition. Applause. I had a roommate at Harvard who relished recognition to such a degree that at a football game when the stands would erupt after a Harvard touchdown or even a touchdown by the opposition, he would rise from his seat and bow first to one side, then to the other, then raise his hands in lordly but subdued gestures borrowed from the British royal family as if the cheers were actually directed at him. He was a philosophy major and he felt he had to catch applause on the run, as it were, because he doubted there'd be very much after he left college.

Some years ago we published a story by Dallas Wiebe in the *Paris Review* based on the familiar figures of speech that a person will give up a portion of his anatomy to achieve a particular goal, especially recognition at the highest levels, as in "I'd give an arm and a leg to pitch for the Chicago White Sox." The main character in the story is an aspirant writer who by the age of sixty-six has never had one word published. He calls his agent, a somewhat typically satanic figure, and he says, "You know, I'd give my left pinkie to get into the *Paris Review.*" Somewhat to his surprise the agent replies that he thinks he might find a buyer. Apparently he has connections with Mr. Scratch. And sure enough. The writer gives up his left pinkie in an operation that costs him fifty dollars and the *Paris Review* publishes a short story for which it pays him sixty dollars, which is about right. So he makes ten dollars. These contracts and the operations continue. For his left testicle he gets a short story published in *Tri-Quarterly.* For his left hand he gets published in *Esquire,* a short story entitled "Moles' Brains and the Right to Life." For both ears his ability becomes such that the *New Yorker* accepts a short story and his reputation soars as one of the finest short-story writers in America. These stories are published (for his left arm) in a collection brought out by Doubleday, as you'll remember, in September 1981. His first novel, *Flibberty Gibbet,* published by Knopf, loses him his left leg and wins him the National Book Award. His right leg: the Pulitzer Prize for *Brachiano's Ghost,* published by Macmillan in 1983. And in 1984, as we all know, his right arm gets him not only an O. Henry Award and a chair at Columbia but the MacDowell Medal!

Mr. Wiebe's story is entitled "Night Flight to Stockholm," and at its conclusion the protagonist, minus his eyes, is on his way to receive the Nobel Prize. There's not much left of him, as you can imagine; indeed, what there is fits nicely into a little wicker basket and he is hoping, as the plane touches down, that after his acceptance speech they'll be able to get some champagne into him.

Bill Styron, at least as far as we can tell—he is wearing a suit—has not made any such sacrifices. He appears whole. It may very well be that Bill will stand up before us all and *refuse* the MacDowell Medal, fearing perhaps that some appendage wil drop away if he doesn't.

There are those, of course, who have done this, for whom honors do not mean very much. Jean-Paul Sartre turned down the Nobel Prize. William

Saroyan and Sinclair Lewis turned down the Pulitzer Prize. In 1976 Gore Vidal was elected to the Institute of Arts and Letters. He sent them back a telegram saying that the institute had done itself a great honor in electing him, but that he could not accept membership because he already belonged to the Diners Club. Some time later, in Bulgaria of all places, at a conference there John Cheever reprimanded Gore for the tone of his telegram. "The Diners Club is so tacky," he said. "Couldn't you have at least said you belonged to Carte Blanche?"

Bill is being honored here today for his lifetime achievement as a writer—in other words, for the entire corpus. One is reminded that when T. S. Eliot arrived in Stockholm for the Nobel Prize, a reporter asked him for which of his publications he was being honored. Eliot replied that he thought it was for the entire corpus. Upon which the reporter asked: "What year was that published?" Afterward Eliot observed what an excellent title *The Entire Corpus* would make for a mystery novel!

I have been on hand for a number of the occasions at which Bill has been honored, and indeed expect to go to Stockholm one day to see him honored there. Some years ago—almost twenty, actually—Styron was elected to the Institute of Arts and Letters. We had a libation-marked preceremonial luncheon at the 21 Club in Manhattan in order to prepare him and ourselves for the induction ceremonies. As you know, the inductees sit up on the stage while the audience, seething with envy, of course, watches as each in turn has his achievements intoned by a species of Town Crier into a microphone. As part of the inducement of seeing Bill through this, his wife, Rose, had organized the 21 lunch. It was during the lunch that Bill suddenly discovered in the jacket pocket of his suit coat a yo-yo. I've forgotten, frankly, how it got there. It may have been in that pocket for years—the detritus of some summer day long past when a Styron child had stored it there, or possibly Styron had purchased it that morning. There is no accounting for the impulse-buying habits of those reared in Virginia's Tidewater! In any case, there was the yo-yo on the table among the Bloody Marys, I can see it to this day . . . string, little loop for the finger, nothing too fancy, just a fine run-of-the-mill yo-yo. Bill then told us—perhaps to give us something to look forward to at the ceremonies, or at the very least to keep us awake—that during the speeches he was going to reach into his pocket, take out the yo-yo, slip the loop on a finger, and then drop it alongside the chair, "sleeping it" as we used to say, nothing fancy like Around the World or Walking the Dog, but just letting the yo-yo spin at the bottom of the string for a second or so, and then, with a little snap, spin it smartly back into his palm and that would be that—just a little insouciant gesture! All of us at the table at 21 were massively delighted to hear this. It meant that good ol' Bill didn't take these ceremonial occasions all that seriously. He was still one of us. He knew that secretly we all seethed with envy at his good fortune in being elected to the institute. So this little lovely iconoclastic act with the yo-yo meant that Bill was hardly overcome with the panoply and pomposity of the occasion-to-come, and what's more he was going to prove it to us. Good ol' Bill! He was at one with Sartre, Lewis, Vidal, and William Saroyan!

So we journeyed by taxi up to the academy on 155th and Broadway, as excited in our anticipation as if we were going to a Tennessee Williams play—quite a departure from the usual mood of that audience that files into the academy on those occasions as if facing three hours of a Japanese Noh play, which indeed the occasion resembles to some degree. Very often people in the audience make book on the number of inductees on the stage who will start to slumber as soon as their induction notice is intoned by the Town Crier personage. But on this warm spring afternoon in the audience our little group sat on the edge of our seats, staring at Bill up there on the stage as if transfixed. Indeed, I was so taken up with the excitement that I turned to the person sitting next to me, a stranger, dozing, head nodding, and I whispered to him as follows: "Any minute now, up on the stage, Bill Styron, that fellow in the blue suit, is going to reach into his suit-coat pocket and produce a yo-yo with which he will perform."

Well, I wish this story had a more interesting conclusion. On occasion during the speeches I saw Bill's hand drift toward his side pocket and I nudged the fellow next to me and whispered, "Now!" But nothing. Nothing. I cannot tell you why. Perhaps in his remarks later on Bill will elucidate. He may have gotten cold feet. Or fallen asleep. I can only tell you that on the one or two occasions I have run into the man who was seated next to me, he has shied away, moving to the other side of the cocktail party. I think he knows that I am going to accost him and whisper to him something I know is going to happen.

Actually I would not have been surprised if Bill *had* performed with his yo-yo. This type of puckish irreverence—though it may have failed him on that occasion—is an irresistible part of Bill's character. Down in South America a number of years ago, on a trip up the Amazon, Bill persuaded a group of tribal youths that the English word for *good morning* was *Norman Mailer,* intoned in a curious singsong rhythm and to be delivered with a bright smile.

215

He got them doing this in unison—fifteen or twenty of them: "Nor-man Mail-er!"

My mother, who is eighty-seven, is thinking of taking a trip up the Amazon, and I have warned her about this—so that she can take it in stride if a row of semiclad, spear-carrying tribesmen appears at the river's edge and calls across the water: "Nor-man Mail-er!"

This spring Bill was installed as a member of the academy, which means that he was awarded the right to sit in a chair alongside forty-nine other immortals—specifically the chair in which had sat before him Lillian Hellman and then Erskine Caldwell. I did not go to the ceremony, remembering, I suspect, the keen disappointment brought on by the nonappearance of the yo-yo twenty years before. I am told that this year was the Year of the Big Drowse—that a combination of a warm day, a faulty sound system, and a heavily accented and quite long speech by Señor Vargas-Llosa put a large percentage of the immortals to sleep. A friend of mine in the audience, watching the eye fluttering, said that from the collapsed-strawman attitude of many of the immortals seated, often precariously, up there on the stage, it looked as if individual gas pellets had dropped from the bottom of their chairs into basins below. Whether Bill succumbed, I don't know. One doubts it, sitting in a chair formerly occupied by Lillian Hellman!

I *did* go to the ceremony last spring in the French consulate at which Bill was awarded the Légion d'honneur—vaulting right over the lower ranks of the Légion to the highest echelon there is: commandant! . . . as if a seaman were suddenly plucked out of a rowboat and pronounced an admiral. This rather upset Leonard Bernstein (another Ethiopian general), who was there to hang the medal around Bill's neck and himself was a commandant of the Légion but who had worked up through the ranks to get there. He said as much in his speech . . . just to get it on the record . . . and then in a highly emotional moment he hung the medal around Bill's neck, kissed him first on one cheek, then the other, and then held Bill's head cupped between his hands as if considering the highest French accolade—*la grande bise.* Not since the Union charge toward Bloody Lane at Antietam has a Southern boy's face paled to such a degree as Bill's during that moment of indecision! Lenny resisted the temptation, and he beamed at Bill and like a pair of Presbyterians the two thumped each other happily on the back.

It was in France I first met Bill—back in 1953 when the *Paris Review* was founded. Indeed Bill provided the magazine's manifesto, which led off the first issue, in which he promised the readership that we would shun critical work in favor of creative and not use words like *zeitgeist*—a word, I might add, which crops up two or three times in *Sophie's Choice.*

At the time Styron was not happy in Paris. In fact he was homesick. Peter Matthiessen tells the story that at a little Breton restaurant named Pi-Jos— where we all went from time to time—Styron broke down at the end of a meal and announced that he had "no more resistance to change than a snowflake" and that he was seriously considering "going home to the James River to farm peanuts."

In any event, while contemplating peanut farming, Bill was sitting in his Paris digs writing, and one summer afternoon he asked me if I would like to collect a few mutual friends to hear what he had just completed. He would read it to us—a lengthy work of fiction, he said it was, nearly a novella. We met in Peter Matthiessen's studio in Montparnasse, a charming high-lofted room with a skylight wall covered with ivy through which the afternoon sunlight dappled a red-tile floor. Matthiessen had rented me the studio. He with his family had gone down the Basque coast for the summer. I can't remember exactly who came to the reading—Jimmy Baldwin was there, I recall; Harold L. Humes, one of the founders of the *Paris Review;* and his girlfriend, who was affectionately known by all of us by the awkward nickname Moose. There may have been three or four others. Frankly, I was not sure I was going to enjoy the evening. In Paris there tend to be more compelling ways of spending an evening than listening to a friend read from his work, especially if described as being of near-novella length. There have been incidents in literary history of considerable failures on occasions such as this: Tolstoi fell asleep within minutes when Turgenev began reading him *Fathers and Sons.* I can't remember the name of the Romantic poet who went to a fellow poet's home to read him his latest work, but I can remember his response when it was suggested that what he'd read wasn't very good. He bristled for a while and then he said: "The sherry you gave us at lunch was downright filthy!"*

Robert Southey was addicted to reading his lengthy and very often bad epics—before they were published—to such friends as Coleridge, Scott, and Wordsworth, who were his neighbors in the Lake Country. One of the problems was that Southey was extremely prolific—indeed he wrote over one hundred volumes during his life. It was about Southey that Lord Byron suggested: "A bard may chant too often and long."

---

*I have since discovered that Tennyson said this to Benjamin Jowett.

One can imagine the gloom of Coleridge or Wordsworth seeing Southey striding for their front doors with a manuscript in hand. In the winter of 1811 Shelley came to Kerwick in the Lake Country and Southey had himself a new listener. There is a vivid description of this: "Southey immediately lodged Shelley securely in a little study upstairs, carefully locking the door upon himself and his prisoner and putting the key in his waistcoat pocket. . . . 'Now you shall be delighted,' Southey said. 'Sit down.' Shelley sighed and took his seat at the table. The author seated himself opposite and, placing his manuscript on the table before him, began to read slowly and distinctly. The poem, if I mistake it not, was 'The Curse of Kehama.' Charmed with his own composition, the admiring author read on, varying his voice occasionally to point out the finer passages to invite applause. There was no commendation, no criticism; all was hushed. This was strange. Southey raised his eyes from the neatly written manuscript; Shelley had disappeared. This was still more strange. Escape was impossible. Every precaution had been taken, yet he had vanished. Shelley had glided noiselessly from his chair to the floor, and the insensible young poet lay buried in profound sleep under the table."

Not only did these thoughts cross my mind, but as a reader Bill Styron is hampered—and has been ever since I've known him—by harboring a resident frog in his throat that no amount of Department of Public Works excavation, hacking, blasting, flooding with water, and so forth seems quite to dislodge. It is a permanent fixture—rather like Gaston Lachaise's *Woman* in the garden of the Museum of Modern Art.

Nevertheless, I purchased the obligatory wine to get us through the evening, and some Brie cheese, and some long loaves of bread. Our little group met, and after watching the sun set from the little balcony that overlooked the Montparnasse railroad yards, we went and settled around Bill. After warning the frog that he was about to begin, he began.

The work is, of course, Bill's extraordinary novella, *The Long March,* about a war-weary World War II lieutenant who is called back from the reserves into active service to train for the Korean conflict. One of the most memorable antiauthoritarian figures in contemporary fiction must surely be Styron's Captain Mannix, the enormous doomed figure of the forced march.

It was long after dark when Bill finished. The lights in the Matthiessen studio were so ineffectual—or perhaps the fuse box had given up, I can't remember which—that Humes, or someone, had looked around and pro-

218

duced a candle, so that Bill, his face as luminous in the light as a moon, could finish that last page and turn it facedown beside him.

Part of the excitement of all this was that we were hearing something for the first time and exclusively—as if we were the first people into a great artist's studio to see a new work, or in a concert hall to hear a world premiere of a piano concerto.

When it was over, after quite a pause, Jimmy Baldwin leaned out of his chair in the darkness, and he said, "Well . . . Mister Styron," in such a way that you knew—by how he said it—that it was an accolade, a benediction. It must have been one of the first honors of Bill's illustrious career (the MacDowell now the most recent) and perhaps one of the most cherished. You knew after that expression of approbation that Mister Styron was not going home to the James River to farm peanuts!

PLACES

The selection that follows is an extract from a number of sketches I wrote for *Harper's Magazine* on the 1962 America's Cup races off Newport, Rhode Island, the series between *Gretel* and *Weatherly*. Before publication I felt that I should show this particular section to Jackie Kennedy, an old friend, because it depicted a private interlude that involved her children. I did not think she would object since it was such an affectionate portrait. But she did. We talked about it at a dance in Palm Beach. She said she didn't mind anything I wrote about her, or the president, but that her children were off limits, however agreeable what I had to say about them. I was disappointed. But I said, Of course. We were dancing at the time, I remember. The *Harper's* editors were upset and startled because obviously such an intimate portrait of the president was rare, and perhaps newsworthy. "It's so innocuous," they said. "I'm sorry," I said. The president himself agreed with the *Harper's* crowd. He liked his daughter's competitiveness—very much a Kennedy trait. So we had it printed privately for him and the family—a few copies. The title of the booklet was "Go Caroline!"

With the children grown, Jackie has changed her mind. "I was too protective," she told me. "What you wrote are like pictures in a photograph album. So do it."

223

Newport

Bailey's Beach, the exclusive beach club more properly known as the Spouting Rock Association, is situated on the curve of a small bay on the ocean end of Newport. Two or three hurricanes have swept in and almost demolished the low-lying clubhouse and myriad rows of cabanas, but the place has endured, and last year expanded its plant with the construction of a large, controversial, and fancy swimming pool. Up to that time the members had been content with the ocean—though its temperature rarely gets into the seventies; it is commonly choked with long strands of kelp, and often sports a rich purple color which results from some bacteriological phenomenon—a true "wine-dark" sea. The swimming pool was installed only after an acrimonious debate between the traditionalists on one hand, who felt that such a thing would change the character of the club beyond repair, and a Young Turk contingent which was done with emerging festooned with kelp from the cold, purple sea. The swimming pool, completed in July, two months before the America's Cup Race, had been a great success. Even the *grandes dames* of Newport, who with their parasols have walked the gentle curve of the promenade past the cabanas for decade on decade, now do their promenading around the pool.

President Kennedy would arrive at the beach with his children early—at eleven, a couple of hours before the promenading ritual—and the beach then, even on the most brilliant days, was usually deserted.

Of course, secret service men were on hand—inconspicuous but present. Like chameleons they take on certain characteristics of their surroundings. When Eisenhower played at the Newport Country Club they fanned out ahead of his party disguised as caddies—carrying canvas golf bags which one could see contained two or three rusty irons and a wood alongside the wooden stock of a carbine. At Bailey's Beach, guarding Kennedy, they shifted into blazers and flannel trousers in order to blend in, but you could always distinguish them because they looked chilly—their blazers buttoned from top to bottom (to keep the armaments from view, presumably)—and somewhat forlorn . . . waiting for someone, it would seem if one didn't know their function . . . waiting endlessly by the cabanas for some luncheon date to show up.

The president usually stayed at the beach for a couple of hours, using his father-in-law's cabana, playing in the sand with his children. His son, John, Jr., is at that stage where it takes very little in life to satisfy him. To be tumbled in the sand, or lifted in the air, or balanced on his father's knee is a thing of infinite pleasure. Walking, he kept his arms up to hold his balance, and he churned about rockily, usually wearing a large grin with a tooth in it.

Caroline: another matter. A spray of sand thrown up by a slide Ty Cobb would have approved of, and she suddenly materialized—wearing an orange tank suit wet from the sea. She leaned forward on her haunches. A "contest" she wanted set—and she pressed her father eagerly for instructions.

The competition was to be provided, it was apparent, by Alice Ormsby-Gore—a taller girl, six or seven years older than Caroline, who arrived at the president's side in somewhat more stately fashion, sank to the sand and stared reflectively at the sea. She is the daughter of the President's friend, David Ormsby-Gore, the British ambassador, and was visiting at Hammersmith Farm with the Kennedys for a few days. She bears her father's rather long face, with shy, expressive eyes, and an Old World beauty that during her childhood will remind people of a Tenniel drawing. She looked somewhat harassed as she sat in the sand—and at Caroline's insistence upon a "contest" a stricken look crossed her face briefly—the sort one sees on a swimmer out of control and being tumbled by extremely large surf.

As for Caroline, she is bewitching. Far more successfully than the secret service, she has the gift of epitomizing, even emphasizing her surroundings— so that watching the Bolshoi at practice she is the essence of solemnity, and on the beach, her hair full of sand, she is *its* creature—a gamine's moppet face, bright with high coloring, her eyes, large and blue, connected across the bridge of her nose by freckles brought back from the Italian sun that summer. Close to, these eyes inspect one with a sense of appraisal rather than curiosity, or the blandness that would be typical of her age, so that there is the tight feeling under her quick clinical scrutiny that one had better come up with something, and in a hurry—a rabbit, perhaps, produced from some inner pocket.

The president now found himself in this position—having to produce a "contest," yet another in an unending succession, one suspected. Well, he said, wouldn't it be fine for the girls to race down to the ocean and bring him back some seawater so he could test its temperature. First one back wins.

Instantly Caroline jumped to her feet. She dug her bare feet into the sand, poised her body for flight, staring determinedly at the sea and waiting for her father's command. Her opposition, Alice Ormsby-Gore, rose slowly and got herself set for the start rather sulkily—one sensed that her eyes had rolled slightly for the heavens, and a small sigh escaped her as the contest was set.

The president plays his favorites. It wasn't "one-two-three-GO!" that he said to get the girls started, but "one-two-three-go-CAROLINE!"—his daughter's name the trigger-pull, and grinning, he leaned forward to watch her go.

She runs like a sprinter—back straight, head steady, only the underpinnings moving, and these churn at only one speed—top. She flew down toward the water, seventy or so yards away, calm that day, and purple as usual. After her, a number of strides behind, was Ormsby-Gore, who, being taller and at the gawky stage, ran loosely, like a deer getting up, and though she had started off at the president's order she cruised along without much conviction and hardly at full speed. She hung back, dawdling, and one suspected she knew she was too old to be doing such a thing, running to carry seawater in her cupped hands. But she went through the motions, at least, heading slowly for the ocean, glancing back occasionally just to check—after all, it had been the United States President who had asked for the seawater and *that* was to be taken into consideration.

No such peregrinations of mind impeded Caroline's headlong flight. She reached the water's edge, stooped, and here she came back across the sands, her hands cupped now—the seawater within, leaking out as she ran at top speed for her father sitting in the sand waiting for her. She passed Ormsby-Gore, who turned and loped along behind, watching as Caroline reached the president, went to her knees in the sand, and held out her cupped hands. The exertion of her flight hadn't bothered her at all; she was hardly winded. The president leaned forward, put her thumbs apart, and peered in her palms. A drop fell to the sand, the last of the seawater: the small open palms were damp, no more.

"Well, where's my seawater?" the president asked. He grinned at her.

His daughter looked at him. A curious torment was evident—frustration, perhaps, annoyance at being hoodwinked into what was evidently a Sisyphean task. She strained to decide what attitude to take—and then suddenly it came: the whole business was to be dismissed *instantly.* The past was to be put from mind, and only the future considered. She came up off her haunches and shouted eagerly at her father, "Another contest! Set another contest!"

The president blinked at the urgency of the command and from the short range of its delivery. His jaw worked slightly as he pondered anew. Well, he said (and one felt he was casting about), we'll have a simple one this time. He pointed out a black rock jutting up from the sand like a half-buried suitcase fifty or so yards away. The girls were to race to it (that would be one heat), then back in a second heat—and Ormsby-Gore would be handicapped a few seconds each way because she was "older." The last provision was accepted by Ormsby-Gore phlegmatically: she inspected a kneecap solemnly and had nothing to say.

Caroline once again leapt to her feet and dug in for a racing start, eying the black rock ahead.

"Okay," said the president. He cocked a finger like a starting gun. He called out: "One-two-three-go-CAROLINE!" and watched his daughter churn for the rock like a homing bee. A few seconds later, he called to Alice, also poised for a racing start and seemingly more determined this time—"Okay, Alice! GO!"

Off Ormsby-Gore went, legs and arms flailing, puffs of sand kicking up behind. She put considerable attack into her run. The competition was evidently one she approved of—with no frills, no carting of kelp and seawater in her hands . . . simply now a test of speed and an opportunity to prove herself. Moving swiftly, she caught Caroline and passed her with twenty yards still to go to the black rock. For Caroline the handicap had simply not been sufficient. There wasn't any question of her going faster. When she runs, she only has one speed—top—and thus short of Ormsby-Gore falling down—a possible if slight chance considering the flailing characteristics of the Ormsby-Gore style—defeat seemed inevitable.

Suddenly Caroline veered off sharply to the left and headed for a rock closer at hand—an absolutely insignificant rock, barely the size of an orange, and falling to her knees she grasped it covetously and looked back somewhat nervously but hopefully at her father—for acknowledgment that *this* indeed had been the rock designated.

The president would not commit himself. He grinned enormously. Grace under pressure might not have been indicated by his daughter but certainly guile. He made a spontaneous movement with his hands, almost as if he meant to clap them together.

Ormsby-Gore went on to the original rock. She touched it, sat down, and looked back. She may have had some sort of expression to bestow on her beaten opponent, but when she turned and saw Caroline ensconced down the beach, her fingers challengingly clutched at *her* stone, she kept her face absolutely expressionless.

"Well, all right," the president called to them. "Come on back *now!*"

Ormsby-Gore leapt up from her rock like a flushed gazelle. Even at that distance the set of her jaw was evident. Handicapped as she was, and fairly this time, she meant to catch that orange-tank-suited hostess of hers, endlessly twinking in front of her, competition after competition, like a mechanical rabbit just out of reach. Her effort was even more prodigious than that offered in the first heat, so that she gained on Caroline quickly—the two of them straining towards the president, abreast now, seemingly hell-bent to extinguish him from their path, and at the last, feet from him, they hurled themselves to the sand, the race finished in a fine upflung sand spray, and the two of them looked up at him for his judgment.

"Well," said the president. He brushed away a pattern of sand that had collected on him. "Well, well. I don't see why that wasn't a dead heat . . . a tie," he said, smiling.

Ormsby-Gore, who apparently felt the last burst of speed had done it, squinted slightly, as if she'd been addressed in a foreign language to which perhaps concentration would offer a translation. But no—a solution was not forthcoming, and her preoccupation went elsewhere—to her kneecap again, to a sidelong glance at the president, then a long reflective look at the sea.

Caroline wasn't interested in the decision, either. Dead heats didn't have much value to savor. Again the past was put away, dismissed *instantly.* She put her mind to something else: she wanted to show her father some "secret caves."

Where are these caves? the president wanted to know.

Caroline pointed at a jumble of rocks at the end of the beach. She tugged at his hand.

The president looked and felt that the "caves" were pretty far for him. But he said he'd pay them a visit when she got them "cleaned up." Why didn't she and Alice see to that?

Reasonable enough that seemed, and the two girls hopped up on the cement promenade and hastened past the rows of cabanas toward the end of the beach—Caroline leading the way, marching swiftly. Ormsby-Gore kept close behind, hurrying along herself—delighted, apparently, that "contests" had been suspended for a while at least. On the walk a few of the delicate parasols were out by then, swaying as their bearers turned to watch the two.

The president sat at rest in the sand—this latter-day King of Argos, his charges off on their labors. He watched them move down the promenade. His section of beach was quiet. Then John, Jr., appeared again—thumping sturdily through the sand toward his father. His grin, the tooth shining in it, was enormous. He fell down and got up again. The grin seemed to remain fixed throughout the tumble. But as he neared his father the grin suddenly vanished, his face worked briefly, and it was evident he wanted to say something. His father leaned forward a trifle anxiously. Was there a request? A few words tumbled out past the single tooth, but they were unintelligible. Another attempt. Still unintelligible. The president seemed vaguely relieved. For a time, at least, a smile was all he had to cope with. Articulation was not yet there, though it would come, of course. The president lay back in the sand, lifted his child up on his knee, balanced him there, and looked up at him solemnly.

In 1968 the National Football Alumni Association was formed—primarily to see if the Players Association and the owners could be pressed to change an agreement that denied pension benefits to any player who had retired before 1959. In large part they had been rebuffed. The only help the Players Association had offered was to organize an exhibition basketball game to raise money so the old-timers could start their own pension plan.

As a result, the old-timers had decided to bring legal action against the NFL owners and the Players Association. Leon Hart, the great Notre Dame and Green Bay athlete, described an emotional meeting at which Rocco Cavelli, a 350-pound former middle guard who had played for the Philadelphia Eagles and the Boston Yankees, and was nicknamed "the Walking Billboard," had jumped to his feet and cried, "Let 'em have it! Sue! Throw the bomb!" and the cheering had started, and someone else had cried, "Let's go for six!" and another, "Clothesline 'em!"—a series of football exhortations erupting from men so excited that they had regressed to the phrases of the profession of their youth.

Hart, who was an official in the Alumni Association, told me that his organization was meeting in Las Vegas at the same time as the defendants in the suit. Many of the great names in football would be there—Marion Motley, Alex Wojceikowicz, Bruiser Kinard, Dante Lavelli, Eddie LeBaron, a whole bunch of them—and the confrontation with the younger stars would be dramatic.

"Will I get a chance to hear some stories out there?" I asked.

"Will you hear stories? Holy God!"

Las Vegas

The NFL alumni were meeting in Caesar's Palace. When I arrived, I noticed that the team representatives of the Players Association were across the Strip in the Flamingo and that much was being made of their stay. A floodlight sign announced their presence, and each player had his name on an individual sign set into the grass in the traffic island in front of the hotel.

About forty-five of the NFL alumni had turned up at Caesar's Palace, many with their wives. When I met them, I discovered that the topic of the moment was not the organization's legal action, but its pride in the singing voice of Rocco Cavelli, "The Walking Billboard," who had been persuaded to perform during the Frank Sinatra, Jr., supper show at one of the hotels on the Strip the night before. Someone had tipped off the management that he had a fine voice. At first there was consternation that the stairs leading up to the stage would not bear his weight, which was three hundred and fifty pounds, so he had sung from his table, in a sweet soaring voice, picking up in quality and volume after a somewhat nervous and quavering start. "D'ja hear Rocco last night?" I was asked by an old-timer on the way through the hotel to the alumni breakfast. "Well, man, you sure missed something great!"

The breakfast was held in a purple-carpeted meeting room with high ceilings, a buffet table set at one end and large round tables set for eight or ten places, on each a centerpiece of an individual long-stemmed rose in a thin glass.

Leon Hart took me over to a table and introduced me around: to Alex Wojciekowicz, the center famous for his absurdly wide stance over the ball, who had been one of the Seven Blocks of Granite from Fordham whom

232

everybody, to my relief, referred to as "Wogy"; Ray Monaco, who was an ex-Redskin; Bill Dudley, who played his famous years with the Steelers; Marion Motley, the great Cleveland running back; and two or three players' wives. Other people came and went, sitting down with their coffee cups and listening to the stories, perhaps contributing some, before moving to another table where the same sort of conversation was going on. Motley was the only black in the room, and I realized how few old-timers *would* be blacks because of the discriminatory practices of their times.

The conversation started up again after the introductions. They were talking about the hardest hitters they had faced. Motley said that Chuck Bednarik of the Eagles was a bitch, and so was Wojciekowicz (who looked across at him and grinned), but the worst was Tom Kennedy of the New York Giants. "He followed me everywhere. When Otto Graham called a trap play in the huddle, I always said 'Oh, no' because I knew that I'd find Kennedy waiting for me in the gap. What a war we had! In his house, which is in Maryland somewhere, I'm told Kennedy has a photograph hanging on the wall showing the two of us in a play in which I knocked out all of his front teeth. He's got this brass plate underneath which reads 'Marion Motley Knocking Out My Teeth,' with the date. He was a rough one."

Someone across the table said, "You had a rough one over there in Cleveland in that guy Chubby Griggs, that three-hundred-pound tackle. Why, he'd have your brains out if you *looked* at him."

"You know something?" said Motley. "You know who kicked the extra point in Philadelphia for the Cleveland Browns in the championship game?"

"Wasn't it Lou Groza?"

"Groza had hurt himself. He picked up a fumble and headed for the goal line. There were some people in front of him." Motley got out of his chair to demonstrate. "He wanted to move *this* way, and then he wanted to move *that* way . . . but what happened was he didn't go any way at all. He crumpled like a napkin was thrown down." He threw a napkin on the table. "He pulled some muscles, so he couldn't kick. The guy who came in for him was Chubby Griggs, that's who."

"Is that so? That guy who weighed three hundred pounds could *kick?*"

"That's so."

Ray Monaco said, "Big mistake for a lineman to pick up the ball like that. I remember a guy called Eddie Ulinsky, an offensive guard on the Browns, who picked up a fumble in a game against Washington, and he got hit by every Redskin there was—just *bam bam bam bam*—and after it was all over he pulled himself up and he said to this running back, 'Man, I know you get *paid* for running the ball, but Jesus *Christ!*' "

The laughter rose around the table. Motley slapped his knee and revolved the cigar between his teeth.

"What did Ulinsky weigh?"

"Oh, he'd go two hundred and thirteen pounds. Six-footer. Maybe a touch shorter. He was bald-headed the first time I ever saw him, which was when he was barely twenty-one. Big hairless bastard. Excuse me, ladies."

Wojciekowicz stirred and said that he could remember the one time he had tackled Motley. As he told the story, he spoke about it as if Motley were not sitting across the table; he referred to him by name rather than addressing him personally: "What happened was that they gave the ball to Motley and he came right up through the middle, just *pounding.* I was playing linebacker off to the flank, and I knew I was going to have to tackle the bastard from the side. That's not good for me; I like to kill a man from the front. That's the way to handle power—to whipsaw these power runners like Norm Standlee and Motley and get 'em under the neck, and backward they go. Of course, if you hit 'em in the shoulder or the knee, then *you* get killed." He wiped his mouth with a napkin. "Well, as I was coming at Motley from the flank, I kept thinking, *How'm I going to* do *this, where am I going to hit him?* So I got to where I could throw myself in front of him." He looked up. "How much did you say you weighed?" He seemed to be noticing Motley for the first time.

"Two forty."

"Well, I'll tell you something. After I made the hit on Motley, I didn't want to get up. I lay there and I thought, *Well, I've heard a lot about Motley and now I know why.*"

Motley nodded as if to thank him for the compliment, and said, "At two forty I was the oldest and biggest guy on the team. I started when I was twenty-six."

"Bigger even than the defensive tackles?"

"Well, Lou Rymkus was the biggest of the tackles and he weighed two thirty-two. I was the biggest guy until Ernie Bland came along and then Chubby Griggs."

"Ernie Bland," someone said with a sigh of recognition.

"He was what?"

"Oh, he ran about two forty-six, around in there."

"I'm told he was living around Baltimore and died recently of bladder trouble. I never seen a guy so afraid of a woman. A woman would come around training camp and the big man would hide behind a tree and peek out like a buffalo was waiting for him."

I sat enthralled. There seemed to be a number of distinctive characteristics to the ritual: each storyteller always got undivided attention from around the table; no matter how preposterous or exaggerated the tale might seem, there was never any dissent or wonderment, but rather an occasional remark of "That's right" and a nodding of heads in accord; the players described in the stories were usually identified by their weight, invariably to the last digit—such as "Well, Mayberry, who was two sixteen, maybe two seventeen on a cold day . . ." and everyone would nod because they had a clear physical picture of the player involved. The stories usually divulged that the old-timers had all played on both offense and defense, which was the custom before the platooning system, and many of them had played both ways for the full sixty minutes of a game. They were very proud of that fact. Ray Monaco told me during a pause in the storytelling that at a football players' golf tournament in Fort Lauderdale, Florida, a foursome of three old-timers and one young player, Chuck Mercein, a Yale graduate who played with the Packers and then the Giants, had got to talking about playing "both ways," and Mercein piped up and admitted that he didn't know what "both ways" meant. Gary Fincemelti, an enormous old-timer who had played defensive tackle and offensive guard for the Eagles, was so upset by this ignorance that he hit two drives into a pond, missed his third attempt completely, and left the golf course to go somewhere and sulk.

Mayhem was almost invariably an ingredient of the stories. "It took thirteen years before I lost any teeth," Wojciekowicz was saying. "It happened in an exhibition game against the Chicago Bears in the Milk Fund game in nineteen fifty. I was with the Eagles then. Chuck Bednarik, who played middle guard, came down with the flu, and Greasy Neale took me aside and said, 'Wogy, old man, it's going to be like the good old days; you've got to play sixty minutes, both offensive and defense, but remember that it's only an exhibition game and you can pace yourself.' Well, I did a damn fool thing. I told Ken Kavanaugh about it, who was playing offensive end opposite me, thinking maybe they'd go easy on me, and he went back to the Bear huddle and they ran every play at me, until finally their fullback, Osmanski, came ripping through and his elbow caught me in the mouth and out came two teeth. I still had to go the sixty minutes, but everyone had their adrenaline going by then and we beat the tar out of them. I had the best game I ever played. I tried to kill Kavanaugh and everyone else too." He slammed his fist into his palm. "I *love* to play tough against the Bears."

"That guy Ed Sprinkle of the Bears was a tough one," Motley said. "I fixed him one day. Coach Paul Brown warned us about him. 'He'll hit you anywhere and anytime.' Well, early in the game Sprinkle hit Tony Adamle a terrible blow on the Adam's apple and then ran off the field laughing."

Everybody nodded.

"That's right. He was holding his sides he thought it was so funny. Well, when we got back on offense, I told Otto Graham in the huddle to call a pass play which would put me into Sprinkle's area. It was just fine. I got to him and *tried* to get him in his Adam's apple but something went wrong and I got him far south of there, if you catch my meaning. Excuse me, ladies."

After the chuckling had died away, someone said that the guy who really got Sprinkle was Charley Trippi of the Cardinals, who got so angry that he pulled Sprinkle's helmet off with one hand, just like lifting the lid off a pot, punched him with the other, and then walked off the field.

From the other side of the table Leon Hart cleared his throat and said, "Well, you all remember who gave Charley Trippi *his*—John Henry Johnson, that's who. What a headhunter he was. He hit Trippi with a roundhouse right, his arm extended, and the plastic surgeons had to redo the whole of Trippi's face—jaw, nose . . ."

Beside me I heard a wife suck in her breath.

"You know, there's a fine line between being *nasty* and being *dirty*," Hart was saying. "I don't know whether Sprinkle was nasty or dirty, but John Henry was just plain dirty. There was a time in San Francisco when I caught a pass, and some defensive guy got me by the ankle and I was dragging against him. Out of the corner of my eye I caught sight of John Henry coming for me, getting set to clobber me with that roundhouse right, so I shifted the ball to under my left arm and as he came in I gave him a short pop with my right fist and down he went before he could get that punch of his uncorked. Really coldcocked him. The referee said, 'Okay, Hart, that'll cost you fifteen yards.' I cried out, 'But didn't you see what he was going to do to me?'

" 'Sure,' said the ref. 'And I probably would have done the same thing you did. But you did the hitting, so it will cost you fifteen.' " Hart laughed. "I'm probably the only guy who ever carried the ball on a play and got penalized fifteen yards for unnecessary roughness."

"The hell you are, man," Motley said. He was beside himself with delight. "The same thing happened to *me.* In a game against the Redskins. Can you believe it. The gun had gone off at the half and I'd run the ball out of bounds and I was turning around to give the ball to the referee." He jumped out of his chair to demonstrate. "The play was *dead,* but Eugene Pepper was coming at me, hell-bent, and he was getting ready to hit, first with his elbow, then with his fist. Like this. Well, I countered before he could do anything, and I hit the nose guard of his helmet and broke all my knuckles."

On the other side of the table Bill Dudley rocked back and forth in his chair. "That's right. You got thrown out of the game!"

Motley turned his cigar in his mouth. "Ox Emerson came in for me, and he had a big heyday."

"What did Eugene Pepper weigh in at?" someone asked.

"Oh, two thirty—right in there."

"That was like Pepper," Dudley, who had played with the Redskins for a short stint, said. "I mean, to try to smack Motley when the play was dead. His timing was always way off. He was the guy on the team who was supposed to pretend to be hurt so that they could get the clock stopped. But his act wasn't any good—it looked like he was having a convulsion—and his timing was terrible. He'd fake his injury just after the gun had gone off and the game was over."

"That's right."

"Or he'd be thrashing around on the ground and the ref would come rushing up and ask, 'Are you hurt?' and Pepper would forget and say, 'No, of course not.'"

Wojciekowicz leaned forward, the ballroom chair creaking under him, and said, "You know, sometimes you *got* to crack someone. When Hunk Anderson came to the Lions from the Bears in thirty-nine, and co-coached us with Gus Henderson—this was before I went to the Eagles—he said there was only one way to handle the Bears. He ordered us to slug them for the first three plays of the game—every lineman in front of us. We did it. You could hear the punches, *bam bam bam* all the way down the line. We got penalized three times fifteen—forty-five yards—back to our thirty-five yard line, but that's as far as the Bears ever got that day. They were supposed to be the big bad bears and we were supposed to be the meek pussycat lions, with our paws up, and they were *surprised.* Bulldog Turner, Joe Strydyhar, Musso, all those big people—they couldn't believe it. They kept ducking. We beat them 10–0, right there in Chicago!" He made a convulsive motion in his chair which jarred shivers across the water in the glasses, and the ice clinked. "Golly, I *love* to play against the Bears."

An announcement was made that the room down the corridor was ready for the meeting, and that it was time to get down to business. The players around the table rose and stretched.

It was a closed meeting, but that afternoon I was invited to the final session. Jim Castiglia, a former back who had played with the Redskins, Eagles, and Colts, spoke from the rostrum. First he mentioned and commended Rocco Cavelli's singing performance at the supper show, and Cavelli, an enormous tublike man, rose to raise an arm in acknowledgment to shouts of approbation. Next, the Wogy Award was given: a bottle of bourbon to Buck Evans, the oldest veteran in the room. The award seemed to serve no other purpose than to indicate the warmth and good will for the white-haired, slightly stoop-shouldered gentleman. He was a Harvard man, class of 1923, who had played with the Bears. He had an old Bears game program with him which he had shown me before the meeting. In it was a column of news notes from around the football league, and we had both admired the fact that the Dayton Triangles had a Chinaman playing for them who was called "Sneeze" Achui. Evans rose and addressed the group from the rostrum, speaking in a soft stutter; he said that he was going to be seventy-three in April, which was as good a time as any to start thinking about a pension. He grinned and said that he hoped that everyone would oblige and arrange one for him. He sat down to a storm of applause.

Jim Castiglia then reviewed their meetings and the progress of their struggle with the Players Association. He was confident, he told them. Four years ago the Alumni Association had twenty-one members; now they had eight hundred. Their cause was justified. There was so much money in the NFL pension fund that the opposition was thinking of lowering the retirement age to forty-five, at which point a veteran who had played ten years— subsequent to the cutoff date of 1959—would receive in the neighborhood of fifty thousand dollars annually! And yet the old-timers, who had formed professional football and played for twenty dollars a game, were left out in the cold. It was a mockery. If Vince Lombardi hadn't died, things might have been different; he had pounded his fist and told the owners that they *had* to include the older fellows. Well, now the Alumni Association had taken things into their own hands. They would prevail with their law action. "The vehicle is there," Castiglia said. "It's on the expressway."

When the meeting broke up, a few of the old-timers asked me to join them for dinner, but I said I was going to see some friends from the Players Association.

"You going over to the other place!"

"Just to visit," I said.

"We've met them. All they think we want is a handout. They don't care. All they want to do is finish up their meetings so they can go out and play some golf and get some desert sun so they'll look better for the girls they'll find in the evening."

"Aw, the kids can't concentrate right anymore," another old-timer said. "How can they? Got all these goddamn billion-dollar contracts, and they wear hats indoors and buckles on their shoes and clothes fitting for a whore. Why, I saw Dan Pastorini, that kid who plays quarterback for the Oilers, over in the lobby of the Flamingo Hotel, and he was wearing these two- or three-inch stilts on his shoes. Now why? He's a big tall boy in his bare feet. What in tarnation is he wearing that kind of shoe for—less'n he wants folks to take him for a basketball player."

"Hey, do you know who he reminds you of?"

"Who you talking about?"

"Pastorini . . ."

"He reminds *me* of someone?"

"That's right. He reminds you of Bob Waterfield in his good years quarterbacking the Rams, that's who. He'll be a great quarterback if he survives."

"Now don't you be telling me who reminds me of who! A kid who walks around on built-up shoes reminds me of *no one!*"

I went across the Strip to the Flamingo. Evidence of the presence of the Players Association was everywhere. Placards on wooden easels directed the press to different conference rooms. Some of the players were in the casino. Bill Curry of the Colts was wearing a buckskin jacket. Pastorini of the Oilers did indeed have stilts on his shoes, which raised him up to six-four or -five. He was wearing a gold chain around his neck.

I sat around for a while with a group of them. The matter of the Alumni Association grievance was not even on the Players Association agenda. "What's wrong with you guys?" I asked. "What they're asking, as I under-stand it, might cost everyone playing maybe ten dollars or so more a month."

None of them seemed to know much about the alumni demands. "They should get it from the owners," someone said.

"These people are all your old heroes," I said. I said Karras told me that he kept a picture of Bronco Nagurski on his dresser.

"Is he over there—Nagurski?"

"No, but Marion Motley is."

Bill Curry remembered that Motley had been one of the coaches in the East-West game some years before, and he had taken Ken Willard aside, a very bright undergraduate who had been an All Scholastic fullback, and said, "Young fella, you got your foots lined up all wrong."

"That was Ken Willard's introduction to professional football," Curry said, not unkindly.

Ed Podolak, the great running star of the Kansas City Chiefs, asked, "Hey, did they tell you how they played both ways and how they folded up their helmets and stuffed them in their back pockets?"

They looked out at the action around the tables.

When we left for dinner, everyone walked very slowly through the gaming room, like cowboy stars, and the young girls looked up from the keno tables. . . .

Harding Point Golf Course, California

All the golfers I talked to on the tour agreed that the most unfortunate position out on the course was to play immediately in front of Arnold Palmer and his Army. If one had to play in front of one of the superstars, Jack Nicklaus was the golfer one would hope for, because he was slow, so that however large a following he had, one could move on ahead of him and open up space between his gallery and one's own group. As for playing *behind* golfers like Nicklaus and Palmer, well, that was simply a matter of patience—waiting until their cohorts had moved their easy, elephantine meanderings beyond range.

At the San Francisco pro-am, I and two other amateurs were to be partnered by the professional Rod Funseth. I noticed in the evening papers, which published the starting times for the next day's play, that our foursome was scheduled to tee off immediately in front of Palmer's group.

It was overcast the next day, but Palmer had a big crowd with him. As I had been led to expect, golfing that day was not like playing in a tournament at all but rather like being in a migration, the Great Trek, during which, because of some odd ceremonial ritual, one was asked to carry along a golf club and strike at a golf ball from time to time. One stepped out from the multitude to knock the ball along the line of march, standing and concentrating on the shot while the oblivious crowds rolled along beside the fairway, like the slow flow of a stream around a rock in a riverbed. There was only one person they had come to see hit a golf shot, and that was Arnold Palmer.

On the fourteenth at the Harding Park Golf Course I was nearly engulfed by the Army. The hole is a long par four. On the golfer's left as he stands on the tee the fairway slopes sharply into gullies covered with heavy brush, and after a bit the hill drops off abruptly to Lake Merced, sparkling far below. When I stepped up to drive, the advance elements of Arnie's Army were streaming along the fairway, the mass of them on the right getting themselves into position for his appearance immediately behind us. I hit my drive off the heel of the club, perhaps compensating, wanting to keep my ball away from the crowds on the right, and it shot off at an angle and into one of the gullies on the left, not more than 50 yards or so from the tee. I sighed and went down there with my caddy to look for it. The rest of the foursome, Rod Funseth in the fore, continued down the fairway. I called to them that I would catch up if I could. My caddy and I both took clubs out, smacking through the underbrush in the hope of uncovering the ball.

In the meantime, Palmer and his group had finished the thirteenth and they had come up on the elevated fourteenth tee. I found my ball after a long search, and I was thinking about how to play my shot when I happened to glance back up at the tee behind me. There was Palmer looking intently down the fairway. I was so far down in the gully that I could only see the upper part of his torso. From the set of his shoulders I could tell that he was braced over his ball and that the rest of my foursome was now far enough away from him to lace into his shot. He had not noticed me; if he had, I doubt he would have taken me for a member of the team in front, since by now Funseth and the rest of them were more than three hundred yards away down the fairway. He would have taken me for a groundkeeper, perhaps, clearing out underbrush with a scythe.

"Wait!" I called.

He looked down, almost directly it seemed, off that high tee, as if he were peering over the edge of a large container. I thought afterward that he had the abrupt look of someone sitting at his desk who sees something move in the bottom of his wastepaper basket.

I raised my driver and waved it, so he could identify me as a fellow golfer.

"Down here," I called. "I'm sorry." I shouted, "I'll be right out," as if in reply to someone pounding on a washroom door.

The caddy handed me a club. I settled over my ball, my back up against a bush. I took a quick look back up at the tee. Palmer was looking on, and behind him were the other members of his foursome and their caddies and a few officials and a back line of spectators, all grim as they stared down. I hit a shot that bounced up out of the rough onto the fairway.

"Let's go," I said. We ran up after the shot, the caddy trotting hard, the clubs jangling thunderously in the bag.

I barely got my feet set before hitting the next shot—ripping up and letting it fly on down a fairway by now thickly flanked by Arnie's Army waiting for his drive.

I hurried down between those lanes. Some cardboard periscopes came up from the back ranks of the crowd and peered. I could catch the glint of glass. A couple of hundred yards ahead I could see the rest of our foursome on the green. Behind, Palmer was still waiting. We were not yet out of range.

"Lord," I said. The clubs jangled furiously. Fleetingly I thought of a *Golfer's Handbook* record I had noted the day before—a speedy round by an Olympic runner from South Africa who was able to whip around the Mowbray Course in thirty-odd minutes.

"I'm going to pick up," I called to the caddy.

I scooped up the ball on the fly like a centerfielder bending to field a hit, and we veered and headed off the fairway for the Army, stepping in among them. There were a few stares but then the heads began craning for Palmer's shot. We walked along with the crowd and I joined the others on the fifteenth tee. Funseth and my partner looked up when I climbed over the restraining ropes to join them. I apologized and said I had picked up. I was doing so badly. They said never mind; one of them had birdied the hole, and the team was all right.

I was telling a friend about the experience later that morning. "I didn't see what else I could do," I said. "Picking up, I mean." I described what had happened, playing the shots in front of that grim gallery on the fourteenth tee: Palmer and the rest of them—a tableau of generals, with their staffs, they might have been, surveying the pageantry of battle from a hill, except that immediately in front of them something had gone wrong: a soldier's drum had fallen off, rolling down a gentle slope, and he was rushing after it, his cockade askew, and the drum was beginning to bounce now and pull away from him. . . .

"You did the right thing," my friend said. "Picking up."

"I think so."

"That was not a pleasant experience."

"It certainly wasn't," I said.

He cleared his throat. He said that well, nothing could compare with an experience *he* had had with Palmer and his Army. I've forgotten what tournament he said it was, possibly the Masters or the PGA, one of the great championships, for sure. He was a spectator on the golf course at a position where the big-name players were coming through. While waiting, on the side of the fairway, he had stepped into one of those sentry-box structures called Port-O-Let, chemical toilets that are set about courses during tournament week. After a while he opened the door, which made a shrill squeal, and he stepped out into the bright sunlight. When he had stepped into the Port-O-Let there had been quite a few people trudging by, the advance guard of Arnie's Army. Now, he said, with himself and the Port-O-Let at its apex, an enormous fan of people had materialized that stretched away toward the distant green, a double line of faces—thousands, it appeared—all straining to see. And there, not ten yards away, standing over a golf ball that he had hit nearly out of bounds, and getting ready to swing, was Arnold Palmer. At the creak of the hinges Palmer looked back, and he saw my friend standing in the door of the Port-O-Let.

"What did you do?" I asked.

"Well, my gosh," my friend said. "I stepped right back inside and pulled the door shut. It was the typical reaction, I mean, stepping out and seeing all those people. It was like slipping through a door and finding oneself alone on the stage of a fully occupied opera house. What happens is that your eyes pop and you back up right through the door you came out of."

"Of course," I said.

"I really slammed that door."

"What happened then?"

"Well, after a second or two, there was this knock on the door of the Port-O-Let, and it was Palmer. 'Listen,' I heard him say, 'come on out, there's no hurry.' Well, I thought about that great mob of people out there, all looking and maybe getting ready to laugh and all if I stepped out of the Port-O-Let. So I said through the door, 'No. You go right ahead, Mr. Palmer. I'm in no hurry either. I don't want to disturb you.' Well, I heard his footsteps in the grass, moving away, and the increasing quiet of the crowd, which had been murmuring, and I knew he was standing over his ball and they were settling down for his shot. But the murmur started up again, and I was surprised, because I hadn't heard the click of his club going through the shot. Then I heard footsteps and there was this knock on the door. 'Listen,' he said. He sounded very apologetic through the door. 'I find it's hard to concentrate on my shot thinking about you shut up in that box. I'd appreciate it if you would come out.' Well, I didn't want to come out. I did, finally, of course. I pushed the door open with that big screech, those damn rusty hinges, and I stepped out. It was very bright in the sunlight after the Port-O-Let, and there was Palmer looking worried and serious, and he said he was sorry to have inconvenienced me. I said, 'Oh, no, not at all.' There was quite a lot of laughter, and I sidled off and tried to get lost in the crowd. But people kept grinning at me, heads turning, you know, 'There's the Port-O-Let guy,' so finally I hurried across the fairway and watched someone else, Kermit Zarley, I think, someone like that, where there weren't too many people around."

"That's something!" I said.

"Yes, I think so," he said.

"Some terrible things can happen out there in tournament golf," I said.

"You're right," he said. "Terrible things."

Palm Desert

Not far from Palm Desert I found a par-three eighteen-hole golf course that stayed open under the arc lights. I saw it advertised on a billboard. I played on it twice, giving up the evening festivities to do so. I was so damn ashamed of my golf. It was a long drive from my motel. I never saw anyone else on the course. There was a man wearing a French beret and cowboy boots in charge. The slight wind off the desert was chilly. The grass had an eerie silver quality under the lights, still and unnatural, like an enormous metallic expanse of carpet. The golf balls shone as bright as moths. Over the golf shack an illuminated sign turned. The g of golf was missing—*olf olf olf* it announced in its slow turns.

I played alone—trudging the course hauling a golf wagon after me. I played four balls. To keep from being too bored, I imagined each ball as having its own player. I wrote their names down in the score card. Each was a columnist. Leonard Lyons and Suzy Knickerbocker were two of the players, along with Arthur Krock of *The New York Times,* and General S. L. A. (Slam) Marshall, the military historian. Each had his (or her) own ball. For identification purposes in case I got confused I marked the brand names on the score card. I remember General Marshall started with a Titleist Eight. Leonard Lyons had a practice ball with a red stripe.

Sometimes, if I was hitting the ball badly, I would give up the imaginary game and hit my shots morosely and tag after them across the course with my mind empty. But then a good shot or two, and I would pick up the game on the next tee. The competition was lively. Curiously, each player began to take on certain characteristics that remained constant. Suzy Knickerbocker (using a Royal Two) was a deadly putter. She had a tendency to shank, but was strong on recovery shots. Lyons was strong off the tees, though he had a propensity for landing in traps, and his putting was inaccurate and often hysterical. Arthur Krock was short but accurate. General Slam Marshall's game was disgraceful. He hit two shots in a row into a pond. He began to emerge in my imagination. His problem was a war wound acting up. His playing partner was Suzy Knickerbocker. "General," she would say, "you're bleeding slightly." "Yes," he would say, "but the pain isn't bad. I can shake it off."

The second night I played the course I got quite immersed with the fortunes of my imaginary foursome.

The Lyons-Krock team were pressing for a Nassau bet of five dollars— that is to say, five dollars bet on the outcome of the first nine, five dollars on the second, and five dollars on the winner of the match—press bets, of couse, which meant that the team behind could accept a loss and renew the wager for the remaining holes. The Knickerbocker–Marshall team, not so sure of themselves by reason of General Marshall's severe hip injury (it was now vivid in my mind), felt that they would be better off at a *three*-dollar Nassau. Not only that, but they wanted a handicap of two strokes a side.

My lips moved briskly on the first tee as the terms were discussed. My voice rose somewhat sharply to identify Suzy Knickerbocker's complaints as she fought for the handicap of two strokes a side.

"I think you're unprincipled!" she shouted at Arthur Krock. "My partner's crippled!"

"Robbery!" he yelled. He emitted a fierce Bronx cheer.

I looked around. The course stretched silver and empty to the borders of the dark night. The man with the beret was out of sight, back in his fieldhouse. The moths, dazzled, circled the arc lights.

The controversy started up again. Leonard Lyons said: "I think General Marshall is fudging. Nothing wrong with his damn hip."

"Damn right," said his partner, Krock. "Absolute disgrace."

"What do you call all that *bleeding*?" Suzy Knickerbocker asked. My voice rose high and shrill. I looked around again. The *olf* sign turned eerily across the metallic lawns. "He's almost *dying*!" she said.

"A natural state with the military," Lyons said archly.

I heehawed at the Lyons pleasantry. The breeze was cool off the desert. The moths were huge around the arc lights. "Look at those moths," I said aloud. "Big as towels."

Who was speaking? I pulled myself together. The terms of the wager were finally settled. A four-dollar Nassau bet was established. The two-stroke handicap would stand for the first nine, and then there would be an adjustment depending on the nine-hole totals. No one was particularly pleased. I separated the four balls. The Marshall-Knickerbocker team won the coin toss and the honor. There was a short discussion between the two as to which one would lead off.

"All right, Susan," the General finally said wearily. "Let me take the honor and lead the way."

I drove his ball smartly into a water hazard.

The other three stepped up and I hit their balls more or less to character. Lyons had a shot that dropped six feet from the hole. The whole foursome was out of sorts, though, and there wasn't much mention of the feat.

Suddenly all around me, the ground seemed to shudder slightly, a sighing groan swept around like a wind, and I whirled, sand wedge in hand. "Wha'? Wha'?" From countless water points geysers of spray rose, and water began to spring up from the nozzles of sprinklers and work out across the grass and then sweep in great arcs covering the course. I ran for my cart, and pulling it after me I wheeled crazily through the maze of water and fountain, sprinting in front of long sweeps of spray as they came curving in their patterns. I reached the little clubhouse where the proprietor, the young man wearing a French beret, was leaning against the counter watching me come.

"That's a helluva trick," I said when I'd caught my breath. "A man could drown out there."

"Don't blame me," he said. "The whole system works automatically. The watering goes on even when it's raining. There's nothing I can do."

"There ought to be a warning device out there," I said. "A siren, perhaps. Or maybe you ought to fire off a cannon."

"It's late," he said. "You know what *time* it is? No one's *ever* been caught out there when the system went on." He was peeved. "You trying to win a bet?"

I paid him for the extra time. "There are four balls out there. They are yours to keep if they haven't floated away."

In 1983 *New York* magazine planned a feature on Elaine's restaurant on the Upper East Side. The establishment was frequented largely by writers (it was "discovered" by two editors from the *Paris Review,* Fred Seidel and Nelson Aldrich) until a more fashionable, predominately West Coast contingent began to take over. But Elaine herself—often referred to as the Large Lady, as in "Let's go up to the Large Lady's for a nightcap"—had a special fondness for the literary crowd. They were always seated at what were considered "good" tables. A number of the more frequent customers were asked to contribute to the *New York* magazine piece.

At first I thought I'd write about the time I was bitten in the ankle in Elaine's by an English gossip columnist named Nigel Dempster. Seated at the table, he was agonizing over how difficult it was to dredge up suitable material in New York for his column. Suddenly he dropped to the floor and began worrying my leg in a mild way just above the ankle. The people in the restaurant watched in astonishment. I had to suppose that what he was up to was a curious twist on the old adage that "dog bites man" isn't much of a story but that "man bites dog," or a variation thereof, is. Perhaps he would work what he was doing into a column. I never thought to ask. In sum, it seemed too

puzzling a story to interest *New York* magazine readers, indeed
one without either a denouement or a moral. So I wrote as
follows:

Elaine's Restaurant

A couple of years ago Channel 12, the Philadelphia public-television station, had a fund-raising auction with a vast number of items offered, one of which was called "A Night on the Town with George Plimpton." I told the authorities down there that they were welcome to offer such a thing, but I doubted it would fetch very much.

Some weeks later I was telephoned and told that a gentleman named Jerry Spinelli had bid and paid four hundred and some-odd dollars to the television station for the "Evening." He and his wife would be coming up to New York.

I wondered vaguely what to do with them. We have a pool table at home. Perhaps the thing to do was to invite them home for drinks; we'd play some pool, and then leisurely we'd eat at some midtown restaurant—perhaps Gallagher's Steak House—so it would be an easy matter to put the Spinellis on a sensible train back to Philadelphia. I didn't know what else to suggest. I had called Spinelli to see if he and his wife would enjoy the theater . . . was there anything in particular they would like to see?

"Oh, no," he had said in an odd, strangled voice. He seemed very shy. "How about pool?" I asked. "Would you like to shoot a bit of pool?" "Poo?!"

A couple of weeks later the Spinellis turned up at the apartment. They arrived at seven o'clock. "How about a spot of pool?" I said to Mr. Spinelli. He was a thin, young man, with a quick, furtive smile.

While Mr. Spinelli and I played a somewhat desultory game, my wife took Mrs. Spinelli, whose name was Eileen, to show her the apartment. It was on their tour that my wife discovered the circumstances of the Spinellis' presence. While the Spinellis were looking at some books in the library, she

251

pulled me out into the hall. She whispered hurriedly, "Jerry Spinelli's a writer."

"Oh, God."

"He's writing a novel." She went on to say that apparently he worked in the dawn, before he went off to his job, and also when he returned home in the evening. The writing had not been going well. That fateful night, Eileen Spinelli had been watching the Channel 12 TV auction—her husband flat out and exhausted in the bedroom—and when the "Plimpton Evening" was offered, she telephoned in her bid on impulse, feeling that the logjam in her husband's literary career might be broken by having a New York literary "connection."

"Oh, Lord!"

"To pay for this," my wife said, "Eileen Spinelli told me she took just about *everything* they had out of savings. Four hundred and twenty-five dollars. She left five dollars in there to keep the account open."

"What about the husband when he found out?"

"He was shocked."

I glanced into the library. The Spinellis were leafing through a large book on the coffee table.

I wondered aloud if we shouldn't somehow pay the couple's debts to Channel 12 and make ourselves the donors.

"We don't live in Philadelphia," my wife said practically.

"Then we'll have to turn this into a literary evening."

"Right."

"They won't enjoy Gallagher's Steak House."

"No."

"We'll have to go to Elaine's."

When I told the Spinellis that we were going to Elaine's, Jerry Spinelli brightened visibly. He had heard a lot about it. "Do you think anybody'll be there?"

On the way up by taxi, I murmured a prayer that there *would* be a good literary crowd in Elaine's . . . at the very least the Saturday Night Live crowd, who seemed to get twenty of their number around a small table and all talk at the same time; if no luck there, perhaps a couple of *Esquire* editors could be pointed out, even if they were, in fact, stockbrokers. Indeed, I was perfectly willing to stretch a point—anyone with a beard I intended to identify as Donald Barthelme, the *New Yorker* short-story writer.

At Elaine's, the desirable places are what people in the know refer to

252

as "the line"—perhaps ten tables in a row along the wall opposite the bar. When we arrived, I took a quick glance at the line: The sudden fancy crossed my mind that Madame Tussaud herself had been working for a week to get it set up for ourselves and the Spinellis. At the first table, just by the front door, Kurt Vonnegut was sitting with Jill Krementz. With them was an older man who looked vaguely like James T. Farrell. "Kurt," I said. I pushed Mr. Spinelli forward. "Kurt, this is Jerry Spinelli, from Philadelphia. Jerry, Kurt Vonnegut." I took a chance. "Jerry, may I present James T. Farrell. This is Jerry Spinelli from Philly."

"Mr. Farrell" looked somewhat bewildered.

I introduced Jill Krementz, and then we moved on to the next table. Irwin Shaw was sitting there with Willie Morris, the former editor of *Harper's,* and the novelist Winston Groom. I introduced Spinelli to the table; there were pleasant nods and handshakes all around. At the next table, we paused to introduce ourselves to Gay Talese, who had just published *Thy Neighbor's Wife,* and A. E. Hotchner, the author of *Papa Hemingway.* "Mr. Talese, Mr. Hotchner, may I present Jerry Spinelli, the writer from Philadelphia." When he heard me introducing him as the "the writer from Philadelphia," Mr. Spinelli beamed. We moved on to Bruce Jay Friedman, sitting with a large crowd. "Bruce, Mr. Spinelli, the writer from Philadelphia." Bruce rose and presented Mr. Spinelli to his friends.

We were approaching—very slowly because of all the bowing and introductions—the most famous table at Elaine's, the one just beyond the side door that leads out to the kitchens and the Siberian reaches of the restaurant out back. Often the table is empty, with a plain white RESERVED sign on it, but when the sign is removed, the table is almost invariably occupied by Woody Allen and his entourage. It is an odd table to be the most desired. Not only is it immediately adjacent to the ebb and flow of Elaine's waiters as they rush back and forth from the kitchens, but also it is just off the path of those forlorn people being herded back into the back room—what is officially referred to as the Paul Desmond Room, because the famous musician liked the quiet back there. Not only that, but the Allen table is on the route to the rest rooms; the traffic is considerable, with one of the main reasons being to get to table-hop en route to and from. Thus, the Woody Allen table, on the periphery of all this, is a place where one is jostled constantly, trays of osso buco sail alarmingly overhead like dirigibles, and when Allen is there, people stand in the doorway to the Desmond Room and stare.

At Elaine's, there is one famous house rule. At a place where table-hopping and squeezing in at a table to join even the vaguest of friends ("Mind if I join you?") is very much de rigueur, it is *not* done at Woody Allen's table. Even on the way to the Gents, nothing more than a side glance at the brooding figure of Woody Allen, mournfully glancing down at his chicken francese, which I am told is his favorite dish, is permissible. To interrupt his meal by leaning over and calling out "Hi ya, Woody, how's it going?" would be unheard of.

All of this was very much on my mind as our little band approached the Allen table, where the actor-writer was indeed in residence with a number of his friends. My first inclination was to stick to protocol and pass up his table to move on toward the far corner of the restaurant, where I spotted Peter Stone, Dan Jenkins, Herb Sargent, Michael Arlen, and others available for introductions.

But I thought of Spinelli's four hundred twenty-five dollars, and the long trip up on Amtrak, and the five dollars left in the savings account, and the half-finished manuscript in its typewriter-paper cardboard box.

"Woody," I said, "forgive me. This is Jerry Spinelli, the writer from Philadelphia."

Woody looked up slowly. It was done very dramatically, as if he were looking up from under the brim of a large hat.

"Yes," he said evenly. *"I know."*

We stood there transfixed. Allen gazed at us briefly, and then he returned to his contemplation of the chicken francese on his plate.

We moved off to our table. As I recollect, we skipped Peter Stone, Michael Arlen, and the other luminaries in the corner. Jerry Spinelli wanted to talk. He was beside himself. His face shone. He was not quite sure what had happened. "Did you hear *that?*" he asked. "Jesus *Christ!*" He ordered a bottle of Soave wine. He brandished a fork and spoke about Kafka. He asked about agents. He told us a little about his novel, which was about the life of a young boy. He wanted to know if Harper & Row was a good house. In the midst of his euphoria, his wife, Eileen, turned to me. "We've done a terrible thing," she whispered to me. "He's going to be unbearable. We've *spoiled* him!"

Three months ago, I received a letter from Jerry Spinelli. He was writing to tell me that his novel had been published by Little, Brown. It was a cheerful, chatty letter. Though he did not mention it, I knew he would want me to give his best regards to the gang up at Elaine's.

Norfolk, Nebraska

Every once in a while I wonder vaguely what I will do very late in my declining years—when just sitting in a chair may be all I *can* do. The notion has kept recurring that, being a fireworks enthusiast, I would delight in being retained (at a nominal fee, mostly for travel) by Oriental fireworks manufacturers to be assisted out to a field and settled into a chair, possibly with a headrest attached, so that looking up into the night sky would be comfortable, where my function would be to decide on names for their new aerial shells. I would be known as "The Shell-Namer."

May I hasten to explain. Aerial shells (or "bombs," as fireworks people call them) from Japan, China, Taiwan, Korea, and so forth, always were imported into this country, or listed in their catalogs, with wonderfully fancy descriptive names attached. A shell would be labeled "The Monkeys Enter the Heavenly Palace and Drive Out the Tiger." Or "Running Cur Violates Heavenly Clouds." The importers felt this was all too farfetched and imaginative (and difficult to discern in the sky, anyway), and so in the American catalogs the Oriental nomenclature would be simplified to something like "Sky Monkeys" or "Frolicking Dogs," and they would have done with it.

But one day that is what I have in mind to do—to get out there to the Orient where the new shells are being tested. I would sit out in the fields in my small bamboo chair (cushioned) with a note pad. I would watch a shell soar up, open above the rice paddies, and perform, and I would write down "The Blue Ox Comes Down the Turnpike," or perhaps "The White Parrot Escapes from the Yellow Wicker Cage," whatever, and if my imagination failed, I would call down to the pyrotechnician by the mortars and ask him

255

to send up the same kind of shell for a second viewing: sorry, but I had not been inspired.

I had always assumed that I would be very much a loner at this—a solitary figure with a small suitcase stepping slowly down to the platform of a dusty RR station in Yunnan Province. It seemed improbable that I could find anyone else who would like to tag along—it is a somewhat specialized retirement program, after all. Very recherché.

Inded, I could think of only one candidate who might be interested in coming with me—a shoe-store owner in Norfolk, Nebraska, named Orville Carlisle. First of all, he was a fireworks expert. In fact, off in a side room to his shoe store he had a fireworks museum, surely the only one of its kind in the world. Coming from a small mid-America town, he would provide a fine balance and perspective to our nomenclative choices if he agreed to come. He would keep me in check. And besides, he is a fine phrasemaker. He says things like "It's colder than a well digger's nose."

I went out to Nebraska to see him not long ago. He is an old friend, and I wanted to see his museum. It occurred to me that during my visit I'd ask him that if things got slack in years to come, would he be interested in going to Japan or China with me as a shell-namer? Equal status. He would have his little bamboo chair and I'd have mine. We'd confer. Perhaps we would not agree. We would call down to the pyrotechnician and ask for another shell of the same variety. The sky would blossom.

Norfolk is one hundred and twelve miles from Omaha and eighty from Sioux City, serviced by a commuter airline called AAA. No one at the ticket counter seemed to know what the initials stood for—if anything. Carlisle and his wife, Mary, met me at the little airport and we drove into town.

Carlisle is a thin, spare man, lively of manner, who seems slightly surprised by just about everything, so that his speech is sprinkled with mild expressions of wonder such as *jiminy cricket, heck, Criminentlies, Jiminy krautz,* et cetera, the sort of words one remembers from the balloons in comic strips. His wife is hard of hearing, but she can read lips remarkably. In the car at red lights Orville would turn on the overhead light and, speaking directly at her so she could follow his lips, would give a quick synopsis of what we had been talking about.

First, we chatted about the town. Longtime residents, I was informed, pronounced the name Nor'*fork*—because the original German settlers established a community on the north fork of the Elkhorn River that they wanted, not unsurprisingly, to call North Fork.

"The people in Washington, who are about the same now as they were then," Carlisle explained, "got it bollixed up, somehow, and the postal authorities gave us the name Norfolk, like the place in Virginia. In fact, last year a couple came through who was *looking* for Norfolk, Virginia."

"Oh, come on, Orv!" I said.

"Well, that's what they were saying around town. You've got to remember that the squirrels are not always up in the trees. The point is that the old-timers say Nor'fork."

"What's that business about the squirrels in the trees?"

"That there are a lot of nuts on the ground."

I thought for a bit. "Oh, yes, I see."

"There are other ways of saying that someone's not quite with it," Carlisle went on to explain. "You can say his elevator doesn't go clear to the top. Sometimes I say that he or she is a bit light in the konk."

"Oh, yes."

He switched on the overhead light and turned to his wife.

"I was telling George about the pronouncing of *Norfolk.*"

"Oh, yes," she said, nodding.

Carlisle wanted to show me his shoe store (Carlisle's Correct Shoes, it's called) and the fireworks museum before we turned in. As he unlocked the store, I remarked on the extremely heavy traffic on Norfolk Avenue just behind us. "Is something letting out?" I asked.

"It's Saturday night," Orv told me. "Those are the kids cruising out there—four or five of them to a car. It's the big ritual in these parts. I suppose there's some kind of communication between them—where the action is. Sometimes it's such a parade of cars the building here shakes."

Inside it was quiet. It was apparent from the long rows of shoe boxes that Carlisle's business consisted mainly of work shoes and children's shoes. "Not much high fashion in here," he said. "We stay out of it. Our slogan is 'How do they feel?' not 'How do they look?' A big seller in here is a Pecos Red Wing with a steel toe . . . so your foot will survive when behind the barn you're stepped on by a crittur. The soles on those shoes will wear like a pig's nose. After all, when the shouting's all over, that's what we are: agriculture."

Overhead was a long wire for a puppet bicycler carrying a balancing bar to run up and down to amuse the children. "Kids come into a shoe store thinking they're going to be vaccinated," Carlisle explained. He manipulated the puppet for me. It soared down the length of the store, and then back. If that did not calm the children, there was always the huge cast of

Robert Wadlow's bare foot to awe them. Wadlow was the more renowned of the world's giants. The Musebeck Shoe Company supplied its retailers with an aluminum cast of his foot to reflect its slogan, "We Fit All Sizes."

And then, of course, if the children are still distracted and broody, there is always the fireworks museum with *its* treasures. It is not large as museums go (about twenty-four by twelve feet) but it is chockful of memorabilia, all defused and harmless. Very little in Carlisle's museum is not of interest—at least to me, a fireworks buff. Most of the items on display induce pangs of nostalgia for the days before World War II when all kinds of fireworks were available to the public. My particular favorites in Carlisle's museum were the cardboard novelty devices made to resemble fire engines, or ocean liners, or animals, or various kinds of buildings, all of which after varying performances (usually the emission of smoke and a piercing whistle) would blow up in a sharp report. Perhaps the most original of those Carlisle showed me was a representation of a cardboard outhouse, which he told me performed by pouring smoke out of the half-moon ventilator and then slowly destroying itself in a series of small flatulate explosions.

Carlisle, who was sixty-eight in July has been collecting fireworks, cap pistols, and various noisemakers (including exploding canes that *bang!* when you hit the ground with one) for sixty years and has had them on display in the shoe store for twenty.

His involvement with fireworks was due largely to his father, a "traveling man"—a rather more glamorous descriptive than *salesman*—who sold Palmer Candy out of Sioux City and eventually settled in Norfolk. Norfolk was the jumping-off place for his sales territory, which extended from Rushville, Nebraska, to the west, up to Winner, South Dakota, to the north—a "wild and woolly part of the West in those times," as Orv noted. His father was a generous man, the more so because his own childhood was relatively deprived. His father was a Methodist preacher who kicked his son out into the world after the boy turned down an ultimatum to give up playing baseball on Sunday. ("Go, and never darken my doorway again!")

"So the result was," Orv said, "that our father was always very openhanded when it came to his three sons. He brought us back things from his travels—and always, on the Fourth of July, fireworks . . . piles of them, horrifying the neighbors, and on the Fourth he'd take the stuff out on the front porch to parcel it out to us. He'd sit in the swing and from time to time he'd sing out in that big voice of his, 'Spread out! Spread out!' to keep us from getting too close to each other.

"Then, of course, heck, we got the Gilbert chemistry sets at Christmas. Those sets had a lot more in them in those days—potassium nitrate, barium nitrate, strontium nitrate, with which you could make colored flares. We could make chlorine gas, and we tried it out on grasshoppers to find out if it was lethal. It was. We had the components to make nitroglycerin, but we got scared halfway through, cold feet, and we flushed the stuff down the drain."

His next association with pyrotechnics was with the Readers, an Italian fireworks family up in Yankton. He learned enough from them to help with the big fireworks affair of the summer (besides the annual Fourth of July festivities), which was the sham battle arranged by the Lyck Company out of Omaha and sponsored by the American Legionnaires. Orv would help prepare the "battlefield" with ground bombs, small sticks of dynamite, flares, and so forth, through which the old soldiers, bursting out of their uniforms, and pretty well "snookered up," as Orv described them, would caper, miming the actions of the Battle of St. Mihiel, or the Marne, or Chateau Thierry (the battles changed every year, so no one would feel slighted by having one's battle not included), while their families watched from the hill. "Roman candles would be shot back and forth," Carlisle said, "though I don't remember any Germans. No one wanted to play them. Everything was started by a large choir singing 'Just Before the Battle, Mother.' Very stirring stuff."

As the town specialist in pyrotechnical matters, Orv, or "Oz," as in *The Wizard of . . .* as many of the townsfolk know him, is on call for many more occasions than simply the Fourth of July. When the high school orchestra plays Tchaikovsky's *1812* Overture in the City Auditorium, Carlisle stands backstage and, on the conductor's cue for the cannon barrage called for in the score, fires a pistol through a hole into a fifty-five gallon drum. One year a thunderstorm happened by, and right on the button, following a terrific lightning bolt, a thunderclap lifted everybody in the auditorium out of their seats. Carlisle laughed. He said, "You haven't heard a thunderclap until you've heard one that comes out of a Nebraska thunderstorm. A lot of folks there thought I was responsible and that it was my finest hour."

Almost any loud noise in Norfolk is attributed to Orv. Back in the 1950s when sonic booms from military planes were more common, Carlisle would hear a particularly loud clap, the phone would ring almost instantly, and whoever was at the other end would inquire anxiously, "Orv, you all right?"

Carlisle's reputation in the fireworks field extends far beyond Norfolk.

He is a consultant to the National Fire Protection Association. Five years ago the Smithsonian Institution reached him to find out if their windows were going to stand up to the concussions of the massive fireworks display organized on the mall (which the Smithsonian fronts) on the occasion of Ronald Reagan's inauguration. "I told them there were two very reputable fireworks companies involved and they had nothing to fear."

Not long ago Orv got into a phone exchange with a striped-bass fisherman from Atlantic City, New Jersey, who wondered how a rocket could be best utilized to carry his lure out beyond the surf line. Did he need a permit from the authorities to do such a thing? "We worked on it," Carlisle told me. "He didn't need a permit, but an awful lot of rockets. He was going to lose one every time he got the lure out there in the ocean. The notion didn't seem to bother him. Fishermen are crazier than duck hunters."

"Lighter in the konk," I suggested.

"Yes, lighter in the konk. Exactly." He turned to his wife. "I was saying that fishermen are light in the konk."

"Oh, yes," she said.

Of course, the Fourth is Orv's big day. One time, he actually fired three shows on the Fourth, the first one at the country club in the early evening, the aerial shells against a sky still tinted with the sunset, so the members would have plenty of time for dancing later; a display just on the edge of town; and finally another a few blocks away at Memorial Field, where just about everybody, according to Orv, had gotten "sloshed" from waiting around.

More recently, Carlisle shoots his show—fireworks provided by Rich Brothers from Sioux Falls, which he carefully choreographs—at Skyview Lake, where between fifteen and twenty thousand spectators turn up to watch. He has been doing that show since 1976, "knocking their socks off" each time. Last year, though, the Jaycees, who raise the money for the event, got offered a big deal by a discount store for putting on the show under its sponsorship. They asked him to be involved, but Carlisle didn't want to be part of a commercial venture. "Lots of love and trouble goes into my fireworks show. I can't dance, or sing, but I can shoot fireworks."

His wife interjected: "The thing is Orv was born only two days after the Fourth. He asked his mother why he wasn't born on the Fourth, and she said, 'Well, son, you were a firecracker with a slow fuse.'"

"That's right," Carlisle said, laughing. "That's absolutely right."

* * *

The next morning Orv Carlisle gave me a tour of Norfolk. We went by the steel mill, which stands on what Orv says was the best coyote and jackrabbit hunting area in the country. We drove by Skyview Lake, where he does the fireworks shows, and down by the plant where they make disposable hypodermic needles. We went past Mary's Café, which is the truckers' favorite spot in town, and out into the countryside. Rolling fields. Tree lines of oak and maple. Orv said that these had all been planted by the early settlers. "Gee whiz, there weren't any trees here at all except the cottonwoods and willows down in the creek beds. Just the roll of the Great Plains, horizon to horizon. They planted the trees to keep the farmland from blowing away. The wind whistles down from Canada in the winter—colder than a well digger's tool."

"I thought it was 'nose'—'colder than a well digger's nose.'"

"Either one," Carlisle said. "They're interchangeable."

It occurred to me I had yet to ask him about coming to China and Japan as a shell-namer. I was going to, but it did not seem appropriate while he was showing me through his hometown.

We were driving by a swimming hole called Silver Hole. "It's a good name," Orv told me. "The cottonwoods give off this silver fuzz, which layers the surface of the water so thick that when a kid dives in, he makes a hole right through the stuff."

We went over to Highway 81, which runs from Canada down to Mexico and in its brief passage through Norfolk turns into Thirteenth Street. We passed by the house in which Johnny Carson, the talk show host, lived as a teenager. The house, an upright white clapboard structure with a rather scruffy lawn in front and a lone rocking chair on the front porch, was up for sale.

"Oh, I remember him," Carlisle said. "There was a young man's club in town which was organized to keep us from getting mixed up in dens of iniquity. Local older men showed home movies. Carson, who was in junior high school at the time, turned up every once with his ventriloquist's dummy. Edgar Bergen and Charlie McCarthy were very big then, and every kid starting off in show business had his dummy to help him. Carson did magic tricks. He had that old one where you put a cigarette in your ear and it looks like it goes right through your head and comes out your mouth. You could tell he was on his way."

At one point, Carlisle told me, some people in town wanted to change the name of Thirteenth Street to Carson Boulevard, an idea he did not warm up to. "After all," Carlisle said, "we have some other Norfolk people who have gone out and made a name for themselves."

"And who are they?"

"Well, there's Don Stewart, who was the surgeon on the soap opera *The Guiding Light.* He's a Norfolk boy. And then we have Thurl Ravenscroft, or at least we have his *voice.* It's his real deep voice that comes out of Tony the Tiger and says 'Gree-e-e-a-a-a-t!' in the Kellogg's Frosted Flakes ads."

"Oh, yes," I said. "Of course."

Carlisle himself had one great chance for renown and fortune. In 1954, he invented a solid-propellant motor for lightweight rockets, and a parachute recovery system so the rocket could be reflown—thus pioneering the industry of modern model rocketry. Carlisle's first two models, the Mark I and the Mark II, sit on display in the Smithsonian Institution in Washington.

The returns from his invention could have been considerable had things gone as planned. Officials in the industry estimate that a million hobbyists in this country, most of them teenagers, have bought various kits to fashion rockets that soar up and float down in parachutes from heights that vary from several hundred to a thousand feet. Some of the more complex kits contain two- or three-stage models; some, rather than use parachutes, turn into gliders at the apex of their rise and sail back to the ground. One company actually sells a miniature rocket-camera that snaps a single picture of the earth below when it reaches the top of its climb.

All of these are propelled by what Carlisle contributed: a round tube of slow-burning propellant that fits into the bottom of the rocket and is disposable after use, meaning that a single rocket can be used indefinitely.

For complicated legal reasons (he spent three years in court) Orv lost his exclusivity of patent rights ("a patent is simply a license to fight," he complained to me), specifically for failing to give a completely adequate notice of infringement to a competitor.

"What if it had all worked out?" I asked him. "What would you have done differently with your life. Would you have left Norfolk?"

"Oh, I don't think so," Orv said. "My friends are here. I grew up in Norfolk and it's a good place. I don't think much would have changed. I might have done some more duck hunting and goofed off more."

I had once seen Orv off his home turf. He came to New York to help me celebrate the publication of a book I had written about fireworks. The city, as he put it, "boggled his mind," and one morning he stayed all to himself in his hotel room.

"Did you go out to see the Statue of Liberty?"

"Well, I saw it from the airplane. Trouble was I felt hemmed in. No place to run to. More people were on the street than there are in all of Norfolk, all going everywhere but straight. Guess what? I came to the conclusion that it's a great place to visit. It's no big deal for most people, but it was for this old dog. I'm a country jake at heart. Going home, I felt I was on my way to be decompressed."

Hearing all this made it seem unlikely I was going to get Orv to China for our retirements. But I asked. I told him about naming fireworks. We would go to the Orient with our little chairs and sit in the testing fields. He brightened visibly. He knew a lot about the Oriental fireworks nomenclature. "Ogatsu," he said (naming a famous Japanese fireworks firm), "had a catalog with almost two thousand items listed in it. Some of those names threw me clear out of the wagon: 'Dragon Skipping a Ball with a Report.'"

"That's a good one," I said.

"'Spring Wind Makes the Willow Grow.'"

"Excellent!"

"How about 'Five Dragons with Flashlight Parasol'?"

"I would travel many miles to see such a thing in the sky."

"Or 'Celestial Maiden Welcomes Heroes with Encircling Dews.'"

"We can hardly do better," I said. "So you're with me. You'd go?"

"Of course," he said. "Taiwan. Macao. I'll be there." He seemed a little wistful. "We'd have to come back from time to time. Wouldn't we? To get refreshed and do some duck hunting?"

I thought for a bit. Then I told him I had a better idea. We'd establish *such* reputations as shell-namers that the Orient would have to come to us. They'd come to Norfolk.

"Now there's an idea," Carlisle said warmly. "We'll cut those shells loose from Skyview Lake. I'd like that just fine. Just *fine*!"

Soldier's Field, Cambridge

Last fall, thinking of it as a kind of Christmas present given in advance, I offered to take my nine-year-old daughter, Medora, to her first Harvard–Yale football game. Actually, it was a selfish idea—an excuse to see my alma mater play against the Yales—and, as I expected, her enthusiasm was guarded. She has other ideas about Christmas. She has seen *The Black Stallion* six or seven times, and a horse, steaming in the winter air out on the lawn, is what she hopes to see through her window when she awakens on Christmas morning. It was easy to tell the Harvard–Yale game wasn't even on her "list." She looked at me gravely through the gray-green eyes she has inherited from her mother and asked, "What is it?"

"It's a football game," I explained, "so important that it's called The Game. There is no other The Game. A Yale coach named Ted Coy once told his players before The Game that they would never do anything quite as important in their lives as what they would be doing that afternoon." I went on to say that Percy Haughton, the Harvard coach from 1908 to 1916, had tried to get his players pepped up before The Game by hauling a bulldog, the Yale symbol, into the locker room and actually strangling the animal.

"He did *what?* Killed a dog?" Medora's eyes blazed. I had made a bad error.

I explained that it was just a legend. "He never actually *did* that," I said. "He couldn't. A bulldog hasn't got a neck." I went on to say that what Haughton had done was ride around Cambridge dragging a papier-mâché bulldog from the rear bumper of his car. That was how the legend had started.

Medora wasn't placated in the least. "That's even grosser," she said, "pulling a dog around from the back of a car!"

264

"More gross," I corrected her, and tried hurriedly to explain that papier-mâché—a word she had apparently not heard in her young life—wasn't the name of a bulldog breed, as she suspected, but meant that the dog was fake.

I assumed that was the end of things. The Harvard–Yale game as a Christmas present was out. But the night before the Game, just after her supper, Medora appeared at my study door and announced, "I'm ready. I've packed."

I was delighted. I retrieved the two tickets I was planning to give away, and early next morning we took the shuttle to Boston. The plane was crowded—many aboard, judging from the heavy coats and the predominance of blue and red in their attire, on their way to the Game. Medora and I sat together. She was wearing a yellow jumpsuit, but the rest of her outfit, somewhat to my dismay, was blue—the Yale color. Her woolen hat was blue, and so were her parka, scarf, socks, shoulder bag, and sneakers. "My favorite color is blue," she said simply.

It worried me. I had ulterior motives (besides the chance to see The Game) in taking Medora to Cambridge. My vague hope was that she would become impressed enough with Harvard to think about working hard at her studies so she might go there one day. I knew it wasn't important *where* she went as long as she approved of the choice herself. But I hoped it wasn't going to be Yale. After all, it would be one thing to sit in the stands and root for her as she performed for the Smith College field hockey team, or the Rutgers gymnastic squad, or whatever, but to think of her across the football field joyfully waving a blue pennant and yelling "Bowwow-wow!" with the Yale team poised on the Harvard goal line, while I raised a feeble "Hold 'em!" across the way, is a possibility too intolerable to consider.

"I should tell you something," Medora was saying beside me in the plane. She pointed to a tall blue feather a man a few seats in front of us sported from his hatband. It had a white *Y* on it. "There's my favorite letter." When I asked her why, she said it was because the yacht club where she is learning to sail has a blue pennant with a *Y* in the center and she likes to see it snapping in the wind from the bow of the club launch.

"What's wrong with an *H?*" I asked.

"Well, it looks like a house with two chimneys that are too tall," she said as she produced a note pad from her shoulder bag and with her brown hair brushing the paper as she bent to her work fashioned an *H.* She finished it with some squiggles of smoke emerging from both chimneys.

"See?"

"Yes," I said.

Her interest in yachting is another vague worry. Medora spends her summers on the water. Her lips are pale from the salt. Her yellow slicker lies discarded on the lawn when she comes home exhausted; retrieved, it is flung over a shoulder as she heads for Gardiners Bay the next morning. I keep hoping she'll spend more time on the tennis court. She can hit a tennis ball with authority, although she seems slightly hesitant about how the game is scored. Surely that will come. I see myself, like John McEnroe's father, peering out from under a white tennis hat, arms folded on the balustrade overlooking some exotic court, in Monte Carlo, say, and watching Medora move to the net under a high, kicking serve to Pam Shriver's backhand.

Medora was looking out the plane window. I interrupted her reverie. "When we get to Cambridge, would you mind if I bought you a Harvard hat?" I asked her. "We're going to be sitting among a lot of Harvards and there'll be confusion with all this blue you're wearing."

She nodded vaguely. She had some things she wanted to show me from her shoulder bag. She produced a four-page handwritten "newspaper." "Sherman Reddy and I are the editors," she told me. The front page dealt with the November election. CARTER IS DEFEETED the headline read in my daughter's recognizable penmanship. The subhead announced RAGEN WON THE ELECTION BY FAR. The news story was brief. It read: "Carter worked very hard but he was defeated. In 1981 Ragen will be Presedent. Let us hope he is good." Underneath this story was a poll on whether Ragen would be good. He got one yes and one no—the two editors apparently being not only the pollsters but also the sole respondents as well. I asked Medora, who was the only girl in her class to "vote" for Carter, what was wrong with President Reagan. "He laughs too much. He thinks everything is funny," she said. The rest of the paper was made up of "advertisements," most of them for restaurants *(Dining out tonight? Have a fish . . .)*. There was one recently added story.

MEDORA TO SEE THE GAM.

"It has an *e* on the end of it," I said.

She brought out her pencil to make the correction.

"Perhaps you could do an extra on the Harvard–Yale game," I suggested as Medora returned the newspaper to the bag. She said she would discuss it with her coeditor.

She had brought along some good-luck tokens she showed me—a stuffed koala bear in a miniature straw basket suspended by a ribbon from her neck. The bear was nestled on crumpled-up pieces of tissues—"to make him comfortable," Medora said. She took him out to show him to me, revolving him solemnly between thumb and forefinger before returning him to the basket. "I hope he's the right one," she said. "I have another one, which looks exactly the same, who is bad luck."

"How do you tell them apart?" I asked.

"If I have really bad luck," she explained, "I know I've got the wrong one with me."

"Perhaps you could throw that one away," I suggested.

"It's better not to," she replied. "In case the other is *really* bad luck."

She then showed me an ivory whistle made of two intertwined fish. She said if the Yale players heard it they would, as she put it, "shrivel."

The day in Boston was brilliant and cold; the wind ruffled the surface of the Charles as we drove beside it in a taxi from the airport. I said that in the spring the crews came out on the river—"Eight men in a line, one rowing behind the other. The boats they row in are as thin as pencils," I said, trying to be graphic. "They're called shells." Medora tried to look suave at this explanation. What an enormous amount of odd pursuits there were in the world, I thought, and how difficult it was to make sense of them to a nine-year-old. We saw a number of sights that required my saying something about them—the scrum of a rugby game on the lawn of the Harvard Business School, the tailgaters along the banks of the river—"drinking cocktails out of the back of their cars," was how I tried to describe it—the gay activist contingents chanting at the gates of Soldier's Field, the first raccoon coats she had ever seen.

We got out at Harvard Square. I had time before the game to show her part of the college. We wandered along the walks. I tried to think what would give her a sense of the history and the character of the university and yet would be interesting to someone infatuated with horses and sailboats. As we walked through the gates into Harvard Yard I said that I remembered that the Boylston Professor of Rhetoric was by tradition allowed to graze a cow in the Yard, though no holder of that position had been known to avail himself of the privilege. Professors rarely came with cows. Medora seemed especially interested. Was it possible to graze a *horse* in the Yard? she wished to know. "And what about birds?" she asked. "If I go to Harvard will I be able to bring Tiffany?" Tiffany is her parakeet. My heart jumped at her mention of the college. I said I was sure it could be arranged.

We started for Harvard Stadium. I bought her a wool Harvard cap and a large red Beat Yale button. She exchanged the red hat for the blue one she had been wearing, but she dropped the button into her shoulder bag. I shrugged. Perhaps it was too big for her tastes. Outside the stadium I bought a Harvard banner and a game program.

We found our seats and Medora almost immediately came down with an acute case of the hiccups. "Am I going to hiccup for the entire game?" she asked me.

"I don't know," I replied. "What do you think?"

She said she wasn't sure.

As the teams came out onto the field I opened up the program to see who was who and discovered I had been gulled by a vendor into buying a *Harvard Lampoon* parody of the official program. The lead story was about a headless Yale player—Aemon Bonderchuk: "the horrible freak who hopes to lead the Elis to victory"—and, sure enough, there were some photographs doctored so that it indeed looked as if Yale had a headless player. According to the story, Carmen Cozza, the Yale coach, had been asked about him: "Aemon? Sure. Nice boy. Good hands. Big heart. No head."

I showed a picture of Bonderchuk to Medora. "Look at this. Yale has somebody out there with no head."

"How awful," she said. "Was it a Harvard person who did that to him?"

After a while she said that she thought seeing the headless player in the program had startled away her hiccups. "I'm cured," she said. She gave a sigh of relief and looked out on the field.

"Does Yale have its bulldog over there?" she asked, squinting toward the opposite sideline. When I said I thought so, she asked what the Harvard mascot was.

"A Puritan."

"What's a Puritan?" Medora asked.

"He's a man with knee britches and a tall conical hat with a buckle on it. People like him founded Harvard."

As I brooded in the stands it occurred to me that there seemed to be so much more that Yale had to offer an impressionable young girl. Their songs were better. The bulldog, while hardly a comfy sort of animal, was infinitely more pleasant to have around than a Puritan, and he enabled the Yale songs to have catchy lines like "Bow-wow-wow." Why couldn't Cole Porter (Yale '13), who had written so many of those gems while an undergraduate, have gone to Harvard? Why had Leonard Bernstein (Harvard '39) waited until *West Side Story* before doing his best? The Yale band was playing one of Cole Porter's most memorable tunes, "March on Down the

Field," and I realized with a start that I was singing along, my lips moving involuntarily.

It didn't turn out to be much of a day for Harvard. The wind, which remained brisk and into which yellow biplanes towing advertising messages above the stadium barely made headway, played havoc with the football—especially, it seemed to me, when Brian Buckley, the lefthanded Harvard quarterback, tried to pass or when the Crimson's kicker, Steve Flach, went back to punt. On the whole, the brand of football was spotty, as symbolized by a play midway in the game when Flach, back to punt, took a snap that skittered along the ground like a dog running for him, leaping at the last second for his chest and bouncing off. By the time Flach had the ball under control, the Yale line was on him. He took a feeble swipe at the ball—the kind an elderly aunt might aim at a terrier nipping at her feet—and missed it. The Yale middle guard, Kevin Czinger, picked up the ball and started for the goal line. There wasn't a Harvard man within yards. A number of Yale men raced up to join Czinger, and it was while this pack of players was running unencumbered by anything more serious than a scrap of windblown paper scuttling across the field that Czinger suddenly went down as if he had run into a trip wire, apparently having stumbled over the heels of one of his teammates. A gasp went up in the stadium—not really of dismay from Yale fans or relief from Harvard rooters, but at the realization, I think, that because the game was being telecast throughout the East, this dreadful pratfall was being beamed into any number of places—bars in Hoboken, New Jersey, or Erie, Pennsylvania, perhaps—where people were quite likely scornful of Ivy league football to begin with and where now, peering up at the TV screen at the end of the bar, they saw a Yale player, racing for the Harvard goal line with a football under his arm, surrounded by his fellows, suddenly stumble and collapse as if poleaxed. And they would never know that after the game it would be discovered that Czinger, far from having been tripped, had torn a back muscle.

The enormity of this, of course, was lost on Medora. I kept an eye on her. Every once in a while I caught her staring at the field in deep thought, lost in some internal consideration. Sometimes her lips moved slightly—a recitation of some sort—and when she caught me looking at her, she would start and smile quickly, her eyes sparkling. Once she said, "Gee, Dad, that's great!" though I hadn't said anything to elicit such a remark. She had her mind on something.

"What do you think of it?" I asked.

"I think my hiccups are coming back," she said, but she seemed to offer it as an afterthought, rather than what was really on her mind.

I had spent much of the first half attempting to explain the meaning of third down and ten. My father has always said that there are two things that women, however brilliant, fail with great charm to understand: one is the International Date Line, the other is third and ten. "Ask Lillian Hellman about third and ten," he once said abruptly at lunch. "See what you get." I never did that, but Medora certainly did nothing to suggest my father's theory was in error. "I like it better when they kick," she said. "Why can't they kick all the time? My friend at school told me that they have sixty footballs for each game. They keep them in sacks."

Could she have been thinking of baseballs? I said, "That seems like an awful lot of footballs."

"Oh, no," she said positively. "You wait and see."

In the middle of the second quarter Medora said that she really liked the blue *Y*s on the Yale helmets. She announced it with a faint sigh, as if she had been making comparisons and had come to a decision. As I brooded over this disaffection, I was reminded that Alex Karras, the great Detroit Lion defensive tackle, had once told me that at the end of his illustrious career he had discovered his children were all Los Angeles Rams fans. They liked the way the horns curled up the side of the Rams' helmets. "To think," Alex said sorrowfully, "that I went out and slaved in the trenches all those Sundays to send my kids through school, getting my thumbs bent back so that I went like this in pain—'AIEEE!'—while all the time the kids were rooting for these guys across the line because they had nice-looking logos on their helmets designed by some interior decorator in Pasadena."

The wind didn't let up. Before the half, Yale scored, and then again just after the third quarter began. Medora and I didn't see the second score. We spent the third quarter standing in line for a hot dog. The facilities at Harvard Stadium are notorious. The rest rooms were described in the game program parody as being "located under sections 6, 7 and 31 of the Loeb Drama Center on Brattle Street." It went on to call the stadium itself: "The oldest standing concrete structure in the United States since the collapse of a similar arena sixteen years ago. In its present condition, the Stadium is capable of supporting virtually two thousand people."

When we got back to our seats Medora discovered that she had lost her good-luck koala bear. Apparently it had tumbled out of its tiny wicker basket. She didn't seem especially put out by its loss. "It was probably the bad-luck bear anyway," she said. She reached in her bag and produced the backup charm—the intertwined ivory fish—and in the hubbub around us I heard the faint whistle that was supposed to make the Yale players shrivel.

Medora's mittens had disappeared, too. I felt her shivering. She curled up against the sheepskin coat I was wearing. I took her bare hands and rubbed them. On one of her thumbs I noticed a face she had drawn with a ballpoint pen; the back of her hand was decorated with a button with the word PUSH above it.

"What's this?"

She was embarrassed. "A push button," she said.

"What happens when you push it?"

She shrugged. "It starts engines and things," she said. She was still trembling.

I suggested, "Start up the heaters. Your mother will think I'm trying to kill you out here. Jiggle your feet. Then push the button for Harvard. They're not doing very well."

"Are they losing?" she asked.

"I'm afraid so."

"How much longer will it take them to lose?"

"About ten minutes," I said. "When you see the white handkerchiefs come out on the Yale side—then you'll know."

I tried to entertain her. We watched individual players to see what happened to them when the ball was snapped. I took another crack at third and ten. I told her about the pigeon that had caught the attention of the huge crowd one year—a pigeon that had settled down a yard or so from the goal line. A number of people in the stands noticed that in pecking here and there in the grass, the pigeon seemed to go right to the brink of the goal line and then back away, as if forced to do so by some psychic power. The stands took sides. Megaphones were raised. Cries began to go up, "Go, bird, go!" erupting from the far side and "Hold that pigeon!" from the Harvard supporters. At the opposite end of the stadium the football players toiled on in what must have seemed a bewildering maelstrom of sound—standing in the huddle as a crescendo of pleading would give way to shouts of triumph as the pigeon, unbeknownst to the players, had turned toward or away from the goal line. Medora wanted to know if the pigeon had crossed the goal line. I said I couldn't remember.

Medora began making a paper airplane from a page torn from the *Lampoon* parody. "I'm going to fly this down to the field with a message on it," she said. With her hands trembling from the cold she laboriously wrote a sentence across the inner folds of the airplane; after creasing it and preparing it for flight, she wrote "Open, open" along its length to indicate it should be read by whoever picked it up.

"What did you say in it?" I asked.

She spread the airplane apart. The message read: "Yale stinks. Right?"

How odd, I thought, as she showed it to me, that she should add that demure *right?*

She refolded it and asked me to throw it for her. She wanted it to reach the Yale huddle. So I tried to do it for her, half standing and attempting to sail it into the wind. The airplane stalled and crashed into the hat brim of a man two rows down from us and fell off into his lap. He turned and could see from my expression, and the fact that my arm was still extended, that I was the one who had thrown the paper airplane. He looked, from the glimpse I had of him, like a professor or perhaps a Harvard overseer. He opened the airplane and read the message. He didn't look at me again. From the heavy set of his shoulders, I sensed that he was gloomily reflecting on an educational system that had produced a grown man capable of setting down such an infantile thought and in such execrable handwriting. I kept hoping he would turn around again and catch sight of Medora, who was giggling into the folds of my sheepskin coat.

From our side of the field the Harvard undergraduates began a melancholy chant of "We're Number Two! We're Number Two!" Across the way the handkerchiefs began to flutter in the Yale stands. Medora said she felt sorry for the Harvard team. I wondered vaguely if it was healthy to decide to go to a college because you "felt sorry" for its football team.

The game ended. The spectators in the Yale stands counted down the last seconds and the gun went off. I took Medora down to the field so we could hear the Harvard band and see what the field was like after it had been kicked up by the players' cleats, and I eased her up to a Harvard player standing with his parents so she could see how large he was. A faint odor of liniment and grass drifted off him. She peered at the eyeblack above his cheekbones as if she were inspecting a painting. He must have felt embarrassed under her scrutiny. He turned away. I heard him say to one of his group, "Thank God, Priscilla didn't come here. You say she's up at Dartmouth? What's she doing up *there?*"

Medora asked about his eyes. I told her that athletes often wore eyeblack to cut down the sun's glare. She said it made them look neat, like Indians.

Did the Yale players wear the stuff, too? Oh yes, I said. She announced that she thought she might wear it out on her Sunfish—the glare was just terrific off the water.

We slowly headed out of the stadium, Medora holding my hand. I commented to her that at times during the game she had seemed distracted. Was something on her mind? Had she had a good time?

"Oh, Dad, it was great," she said. "I liked the story about the pigeon. I wish you could remember if he went across the goal line."

We crossed the Anderson Bridge and walked up Boylston Street past the Houses. I pointed out the windows of the Elliot House room where I had lived. Someone had hung a hastily lettered sheet out of the row of windows below. SO WHAT IF YOU WON, the message read. YOU STILL GO TO YALE.

"Six U.S. presidents went to Harvard," I found myself saying to Medora as we strolled along. "William Howard Taft was the only one to come out of Yale, if you don't count Gerald Ford, who went to the law school there, and Taft was such an enormously fat man that they had to enlarge the doors of the White House to get his bathtub inside. Did I tell you that Harvard was founded a hundred and forty years before the Declaration of Independence?"

"Yes, Dad, you did."

I took her to some postgame parties. We went to the *Lampoon* building where in the crowded Gothic hall I pointed to a suit of Japanese armor hanging on the wall and told her I had worn it in a curious baseball game against the *Harvard Crimson,* the undergraduate newspaper. The *Lampoon* was famous for its high jinks. A couple of years after I'd left, the editors had plotted to steal a battleship out of Boston Harbor. "They only had men on the board then," I told Medora. "Now they accept women. You could be the editor. You could plot to steal a battleship." I twirled the ice in my drink. It was my third. She stood, a diminutive form beside me, in the crush of the cocktail party. An undergraduate editor of the *Lampoon* turned up. I told him that I had admired the game-program parody; I had been reminded that we had done one like it when I was an undergraduate. In fact, I could remember editing an article entitled, *Why Harvard Will Not Go to the Rose Bowl This Year,* one of the reasons being, as I recalled, that California was "in some kind of time zone."

The undergraduate looked at me gravely over his plastic glass. "Funny," he said without a smile.

It was dark when we left. We walked past Lowell House. I pointed up to the belfry. I told her the bells would be pealing if Harvard had won. They made a wonderful racket. In fact, the bells were something of a neighborhood nuisance because they were so loud; the person playing them sometimes got mixed up so that it sounded as if the bells were tumbling down a rock slide. The Cambridge citizens complained. In fact, they threatened to shut down the bells. I told Medora that in revenge the great Lowell House legend was that all the people who lived there synchronized their watches and simultaneously flushed every toilet in the place.

"Why did they do that?" Medora asked.

"It apparently puts a terrific strain on the plumbing system," I said. "Floods things all over town. So it was a kind of weapon. It was to tell the Cambridge citizens and the college administration not to fool around with their bells."

"I would like to have heard them," Medora suddenly said.

I thought she was referring to the Lowell House plumbing, but it turned out to be the bells. "I wish Harvard had won," she said wistfully, "so that you could stand here and listen to them."

Impossible to tell about Medora. Didn't she want to listen to them too?

Not long after our trip I wandered into her room when she wasn't there. Tiffany, her parakeet, was scrabbling around in its cage. Her room has always been an irresistible place to visit from time to time to see what is new in there—to check on the detritus of her complicated schoolgirl life. A "secret" note from a school chum pinned up on the cork bulletin board. What she has dropped into her fish tank lately. The newest of the mice figurines she has added to a fearsome array on a shelf.

On her desk was a draft of a newspaper that she was apparently putting together as a Christmas present. Green holly leaves were pasted at each corner. The headline read YALE BEATS HARVARD BY FAR, the subhead, SCORE IS 14–0 YALE ON FREEZING DAY. Involuntarily, I glanced back over my shoulder, to make certain I wouldn't be caught prying in her room, and then turned back to read: "Harvard fans had little to cheer about yesterday as Yale handkerchiefs fluttered in the air. There was lots of cheering coming from the Yale stands. Harvard players slipped too much on the grass. At the end of the game the two gold posts were torn down by Yale fans. The Harvard fans went off to partys to drown their sorrows."

A pile of photographs from newspaper sports sections were waiting to be pasted in. I recognized Earl Campbell of the Houston Oilers in one of the pictures, vaulting into a dense pile of tacklers, the distinction of what team Campbell actually played on being of little significance to the young editor. I couldn't resist browsing through the paper. On the second page was a large advertisement for cats illustrated with a dozen silhouette studies of cats with their tails hanging down, as though the cats were sitting on an imaginary shelf. Medora does a great many of these studies.

What caught my eye was a story on the same page under the large headline (with a line through the second word, the spelling of which had apparently stumped her): BLACK ~~STAL~~ HORSE BUYED. The text, again with a number of words crossed out, read as follows: "The black horse arrived in a truck shortly after nightfall. It was dark outside. His name was ~~Abraham Lincoln Tom, Blueboy~~ Prince!" I suspected I knew then what those thoughtful silences I had detected on that chilly November afternoon were all about—not about whether she was going to hiccup or whether a pigeon had crossed a goal line, or even whether she preferred Harvard, or Yale, or even Princeton. Names were under consideration but not the names of colleges.

A small story caught my eye on the last page of the paper. The headline read, HARVARD NOT DISCORAGED.

The story underneath, in its entirety, read: "Harvard is not discoraged."

This mysterious piece turned up in manuscript form in the files, surely written in answer to the kind of request asked by junior editors at *Vogue* or *Mademoiselle*—"Who is your favorite person?" "Who would you like to have as a father if you didn't already have one?" etc. Here the editors, I think from *Harper's*, asked for my impression of an Arcadia.

Arcadia

An island. Something along the lines of the Seychelles—a coastline of granite rocks, like Henry Moore sculptures, rising out of a warm tropical sea.

A few incidentals—a large and perfectly balanced boomerang, for example; some bright-colored bathtub toys with small propellers and keys to wind them up, the ingredients and tools for making and firing large aerial fireworks (along with an instruction booklet), athletic equipment, and a substantial amount of fishing gear including a number of small red-and-white bobs.

The island compound would feature a dining pavilion among the palm trees, or a hall, rather, a somewhat baronial edifice with excellent acoustics within, so that the conversations, even very whispery ones, would not drift up into the rafters among the ceremonial flags and get lost. On hand would be an excellent butler, quite deaf but faithful and agreeable to helping with the fireworks.

The compound would contain a number of guest houses, small, mushroomlike structures set apart from each other with views of the sea, as I see them, very well appointed inside, a white fan turning slowly in the ceiling and a large porcelain washbasin with a fluffed-up towel alongside, neatly folded. Into these accommodations every afternoon I would hear the guests being installed—the houseboys chattering excitedly among themselves as they carried the baggage down the quay.

Inevitably my practice would be not to see the guests before dinner—my own day being quite somnambulant. Oh, a little boomerang tossing perhaps, the construction of an aerial bomb or two, some bait casting in the mangrove swamps, and surely a bit of a tub before dinner.

It's not that I feel unfriendly toward my guests, or unfeeling, but simply that my personal pursuits are not especially conducive to their companionship, especially sitting in a tub winding up a small blue tugboat.

Also, the guest list is composed of people I have never met. Not only that, they are dead. Ludwig II, the mad king of Bavaria, dined alone with busts of various dignitaries—Louis XIV and Marie Antoinette among them—set on chairs down the length of the banquet hall at Linderhoff, carrying on an animated if slightly one-sided conversation with them. *My* guests (if one is truly able to indulge in one's fantasy) would be the real shades. No marble busts in *my* Arcadia! Since this is a self-indulgent exercise all the people relaxing in their mushroomlike guest houses waiting for dinner are simply on hand to satisfy my own curiosity.

Many of them seem to be seagoing people—the captain of the *Mary Celeste,* of course, to find out what happened to him and to the crew of that deserted brigantine; Joshua Slocum, who also disappeared at sea; and Richard Haliburton, who may have fallen off the stern of a Chinese junk, though it would be best to get it from him firsthand; and the captain of the *Iron Mountain,* the paddle-wheeler whose barges came floating down the Mississippi but never the *Iron Mountain* herself. Amelia Earhart, of course, and Judge Crater. What an interesting guest *he* would be. Ambrose Bierce, who disappeared into Mexico on a reportorial assignment, his last recorded sentiment being prophetic: "To be a gringo in Mexico, ah, that is euthanasia." Or speaking of Mexico, what about the mysterious being Ben Traven. He'd be worth at least one night. And Captain Kidd, for his vanished treasure. Jimmy Hoffa, to ask if he really was shredded. Shubert, to inquire about the Lost Symphony, and perhaps to persuade him to play a bit on a standup Yamaha in the corner. What about al Hikim, whom the Druse believed to be the reincarnation of God and was believed to have disappeared from his palace in 1014? And while one couldn't get *all* the Lost Tribes of Israel into the mushroom guest houses, at least a few lieutenants might be invited to find out what happened in *that* case.

Some of my choices of dinner partners would be more quixotic. I'd like to hear personally from George Stjernhjelm, the great Swedish poet, why he was so convinced that Adam and Eve spoke Swedish. I've always wanted to know why Thomas Cromwell, Oliver's great uncle, was so anxious to get Henry VIII to marry Anne, the daughter of the duke of Cleves. The king took one look and hated her. The marriage took place but was never consummated, and Cromwell lost his head. Frightful error of judgment. So he could have a brandy or two at dinner and reminisce about that, and perhaps he could give an odd little talk on matchmaking. And what about General James Longstreet's fateful decision not to roll up Cemetery Ridge when he had the chance. Finally, I've always wondered what it would be like to wear heavy armor and joust in a tournament—to look through a small slit in a helmet and see an opponent across a quarter of a mile of tilting green and to feel the great horse beginning to move. The Black Prince might describe that. Henry II of France was killed in one of those tournaments, so he might not be as enthusiastic as the Black Prince, who died in his bed, but a lively discussion—pros and cons—might ensue at the banquet table.

From time to time the athletes turn up—Babe Ruth to tell the table about his "called shot" home run in Chicago, and maybe before dinner he'll hit fungoes to us out in the cleared field behind the main house with the frigate birds from the sea wheeling far above.

The island is large enough to require a morning's hike to get to the sea on the other side with the surf out beyond the reefs. On the way, small ponds, and a thick copse on a high ridge where the "confusing fall warblers" flutter in, exhausted from the long flight across the water. Binoculars, a bird guide, and time to figure the warblers out. No tsetse flies. No taxes. Quick sudden squalls with warm rains and the bright sun afterward. The tropical wind is steady until the evening, when it dies and it is time for the fireworks.

The lovers spend a week in June. Madame Récamier, Madame de Pompadour, Diane de Poitiers, Nell Gwyn, Cleopatra, Heloise, Cyrano, Lord Byron, Valentino, Errol Flynn—and Catherine the Great would say if it were so about the horse in the harness. They would try on the new bathing suits. The women swim in the pool at night or walk down to the beach, the sand cool underfoot. The butler gets huffy and threatens to leave and go back to work for the Whitneys if the guests don't behave. "Decorum! Decorum!" Mark Twain arrives in a white suit and after dinner and brandy he gives a little speech and perhaps he reads a story—"My Grandfather's Ram." Sidney Bechet plays his soprano saxophone out beyond the palms.

Homer's crowd turns up—Paris, Achilles, Helen, Menelaus, Priam, the whole lot. Cassandra tells everyone's fortune, which is easy because all down the length of the table the guests have finished out their lives . . . everyone but me. I pull away my palm. "Next time, please." Down the line Paris clears his throat and reminisces about the mountain and how, when Athene began describing Helen of Troy, he began to forget about tending his herd of oxen.

I don't know how much of this would be possible to take. It would tend to be numbing if Paris, for example, had not since his death taken the time to learn to speak English and one had to hear everything through a translator. Or if the captain of the *Mary Celeste* turned out to be defensive and stuffy.

So an important implementation to this Arcadian paradise would be a swift means of escape—preferably a drug runner's cigarette boat, the deep rumble of a motor in it. I leave the dinner wearing a deerstalker cap and an evening cape. I go on board *The Blue Mist.* She cuts through a quiet sea like a knife, and then it gets rough, the seas piling up, and the cigarette boat slaps out great sheets of water from under her prow. A skyline turns up on the horizon—Miami, Tampa, Galveston, perhaps Mobile. We tie up at the city pier. I walk around downtown. I feel hungry. I step into a diner. I take off my deerstalker hat. The counterman looks up. He waits for my order. After a pause I say, "Would you like to know what General Longstreet had to say about not rolling up the Union forces on Cemetery Ridge?"

He looks startled.

I come to my senses.

"I'll have a fried egg sandwich, please, on white bread."

INDULGENCES

Fireworks

"What are fireworks like?" she had asked.
"They are like the Aurora Borealis," said the King, *"only much more natural. I
prefer them to stars myself, as you always know when they are going to appear . . ."*

OSCAR WILDE
The Remarkable Rocket

The great thing was to do it yourself—
just the nudge of a lighted punk to a fuse, a small commitment that seemed
such an insignificant act, and yet the result was so decisive and visible . . .
the sudden puff of a colored ball emerging from the long tube of a Roman
candle, the quick rush and fading hiss of a rocket, the popping busyness of
lawn fountains that smoked and sputtered and sent the family cat scurrying
under the upstairs bed. Anyone could do it. Even "the snake in the grass,"
that curious pellet that elongated and convoluted into a length of gray-black
ash, had its quality of mystery. Whoever lit it suddenly had the extraordinary
alchemist's gift of turning an inert object into something else. And fireworks
provided a sort of equalizer, especially for those kids who were not good at
sports, and were taken last on the pickup teams, and knew they were doomed
to spend most of the long summer afternoons in the far reaches of right field
when they were not stepping up to the plate and striking out. They, too, on
the Fourth of July had the capacity to create something just as satisfactory as
a ball caught up against the fence—or a base hit—and make a big racket about
it besides . . . with only the requirement of nerve enough to reach forward
with the punk to the brightly papered device on the lawn and touch it to the
fuse to set the thing off.

I always thought it was the best day of the year. It was in the middle of the summer, to begin with, and when you got up in the morning someone would almost surely say, as they did in those times, that it was going to be a "true Fourth of July scorcher." School had been out long enough so that one was conditioned for the great day. One's feet were already leather-hard, so that striding barefoot across a gravel driveway could be done without wincing, and yet not so insensitive as to be unable to feel against one's soles the luxurious wet wash of a dew-soaked lawn in the early morning. Of course, the best thing about the day was the anticipation of the fireworks—both from the paper bag of one's own assortment, carefully picked from the catalogs, and then, after a day's worth of the excitement of setting them off, there was always the tradition of getting in the car with the family and going off to the municipal show, or perhaps a Beach Club's display . . . the barge out in the harbor, a dark hulk as evening fell, and the heart-pounding excitement of seeing the first glow of a flare out there across the water and knowing that the first shell was about to soar up into the sky.

Christmas was all right, but it was over too quickly, and was almost inevitably fraught with dashed hopes. Rather than the Savage .475 Special rifle (complete with barrel scope) that one had specifically asked for, the "big present" turned out (the heart sank as one noticed the conformation of the package under the Christmas tree) to be a dartboard. Grandmother—one had counted on her—inevitably turned up at the house with a Norwegian sweater she had bought "especially" on a cruise that summer through the fjords.

The Fourth of July had none of these disappointments, unless it rained, which I do not ever remember happening until fireworks were banned and when it did not make any difference. The day was always bright.

A big part of it when I was growing up were what rightfully became the bane of the fireworks industry—the cherry bombs and silver salutes. They were the first objects, after a scout knife, matches, and one's first BB gun, that a youngster was truly lectured about—vociferously, the admonishing tone, the dire warnings about what the cherry bomb could do to fingers or eyes. I can remember the helter-skelter flight after nervously lighting my first cherry bomb off a stick of punk, peering around the corner of the tree at the steamlike smoke in the grass, and starting at the violent report.

There were various accessories that could be used with a cherry bomb. I remember an iron device like a football kicking-tee on which one balanced a tennis ball; when the cherry bomb went off underneath, it knocked the ball straight up, far above the elm trees and the rooftops, finally just a speck in the sky; the great thing was to circle under the ball with a baseball glove as it began to rematerialize; there was time enough to construct an entire mental scenario—the last out of the World Series, a "loud" foul as they used to say, and a lot depended on its being caught because the bases were loaded, and there was the business of waving everyone off that responsibility, shouting out to one's five-year-old sister, standing by on the lawn, wide-eyed, with a lollipop in her mouth, "I've got it! I've got it!"

There were other uses for the cherry bomb that I heard about among school chums but never had the nerve to try: with its lacquered and thus waterproof fuse, the cherry bomb was a favorite for lighting and flushing down a toilet at school to see what would happen; the inevitable was a pipe bursting a floor or two below with devastating effect, particularly if a class happened to be in session. Fortunately, the bulk of those devices were around in midsummer when schools were not in session. It was obviously not an experiment one wanted to try in one's own house.

On the Fourth, there were other, more refined items that also utilized a sharp bang. One of my favorites was the SOS Ship—a squat, cardboard ocean liner, about five inches long, with people painted standing along the rail; belowdecks their faces peered out of round portholes; it was a craft quite suitable for launching in a pond or a swimming pool; it had a single funnel with a fuse sticking out of the top which, when lit, caused (according to the catalog) "A Shrill Siren Whistle Followed by Several Loud Reports Ending in Complete Destruction of Ship." For a young boy there was something agreeably satanic to hold the destiny of these painted people in his hand and to launch them on their last journey—one could see their immobile passive faces staring imperturbably out of the portholes as the liner bobbed out into the pool while above them the ship's funnel began to send out its last despairing shriek.

A companion piece was a cardboard fire engine that did more or less the same thing, including an equally cataclysmic finale which was described in the catalog as "A Whistle Followed by a Brilliant Flash of Flame, Ending in Complete Conflagration of Fire Engine." Only in the fertile minds of fireworks designers could the notion exist of a fire engine exploding and burning up!

There was a whole series of self-destruct items—a "Gothic Castle," among them, and perhaps the most bizarre—"A Wild Elephant . . . A Ferocious Beast That Belches Fire, Goes Mad and Destroys Itself!"

The prices were within a youngster's fiduciary parameters. For example, for five dollars in 1935, from the American Fireworks Distributing Co. in Franklin's Park, a suburb of Chicago, one could order a "Children's Assortment," which included four boxes of sparklers, twelve Python Black Snakes, twelve pounds of various-sized firecrackers, a Catherine wheel, firepots, and Roman candles—a total of fifty-six listed items!

What one chose was carefully culled from brightly colored pamphlets printed on cheap straw-colored paper with illustrations that could hold the attention of a boy for the better part of a day. Once again, they were at least as exciting as those that arrived in the weeks before Christmas. The Christmas catalogs were geared for adults and they seemed to emphasize kitchen appliances and chinaware, all at enormous expense, whereas the items in the Fourth of July catalogs were not only mostly within one's own means but they were absolutely consistent and to the point: Everything in there was calculated to terrify mothers.

The catalogs had a hyperbolic style (an "Octopus shell" had twenty-four tentacles) that kept one lingering on a page—the imagination ignited by the bright illustrations and the carny prose. "Tom, Dick, and Harry," the description might read, "a red-hot trio! Tom—a powerful No. 2 Flash Bomb; Dick—a beautiful No. 3 Star Shell; Harry—a big No. 3 whistling aerial bomb. Touch a match to it and away goes Tom with a big noise, sailing high in the air before he bursts with a loud report. Dick follows with a terrific shower of beautiful stars. Then away goes Harry with a screaming whistle before he bursts in the air with a big bang. New. Different. Sensational. Order plenty!"

While the copy was always flamboyant and hypnotizing, perhaps the first suspicions in a youngster's mind that one should not believe everything one read came from these catalogs. Even if "Tom, Dick, and Harry" did everything one hoped of them out there on the lawn, there were other items that did not live up to expectations. "Extra-Large Python Snakes," the description would proclaim. "Just light one of the pellets, and out comes a black *snake*, little by little, until it reaches a length of three to four feet!"

I lit perhaps thirty of them—all when I was about ten years old—perhaps the first firework item to which I was ever allowed to touch a piece of lighted punk; and even though I watched their performance prudently, as usual from behind a tree, I never saw one of the "snakes" produce more than half a foot of length until—in a quite touching final convulsion that looked more like a death than a birth—the thin piping of gray-black ash would shrivel up and collapse upon itself.

So one learned to be careful about catalog copy. The choices were made with great care. A couple of weeks before the Fourth, the fireworks themselves arrived. Parents inevitably took the packages and hid them away somewhere, but usually they could be ferreted out and the devices within lined up to be gloated over.

They were inevitably, in their flamboyant colors, pretty, but there was always that fine fringe of danger one was aware of. Indeed, if one learned to suspect the sales pitch in a fireworks catalog, perhaps the first English sentences that one truly absorbed were those on the items themselves: *Do Not Hold in Hand After Lighting,* or (even more awe-inspiring) *Lay on Ground— Light Fuse—Get Away . . .* these were among the first positive indications to a youngster that the written language was of use in imparting extremely important information.

The Fourth itself always seemed to be the longest day of the year. So much went on: when one's own allotment of daytime fireworks was done— the cherry bombs, the smoke bombs, the parachute shells, and so forth— there were friends with theirs to join down the block. Twilight was awaited eagerly, since the bulk of one's "best" fireworks were for use in the darkness. The colored stars rose from the lawns up above the trees.

And then, of course, there was the professional show. Not only did these soft summer evenings have perfect weather, but perhaps they were the first community gatherings one experienced in childhood—the first instance of communal activity. The crowd had gathered for a common purpose. There was the occasional pop of a firecracker at its perimeter, or perhaps a sparkler or two fizzing and spitting a shower of sparks amid the scampering of children; then at the end of the dock or across the baseball diamond where the scaffolding with the lances outlining the American flag was discernible in the gathering darkness, a red flare suddenly glowed. Expectant murmurs sifted through the crowd, the flare dipped, and then there was the thump of the first canister of the evening going up, the faint flutter of its passage, and the faces turning to the sky in expectation of what was going to happen up there.

One of the first truly romantic figures to my mind was the man who was responsible for that, the pyrotechnist or, as he was known, the "fireworks man." He was only seen once a year—unlike a soldier or a fireman, or a baseball player, who were ubiquitous enough so that after a while they tended to be run-of-the-mill. The fireworks man, on the other hand, was not only seen once a year, but it was at night, and just for an instant . . . coming ashore from the fireworks barge and striding down the dock, or appearing across the country-club lawn from the distant firing line. Somehow I remember the fireworks man as solitary, aloof, coveralled, perhaps sooty, staring straight ahead as he came, perhaps reflecting back on the trench-war violence he had just been a part of, indeed responsible for, and he seemed oblivious to us as we sucked back, wide-eyed, to let him pass: "The fireworks man! The fireworks man!"

The first pyrotechnician I actually came to know—long after those childhood years—was a man named John Serpico. He was the proprietor of a small manufacturing plant—the International Fireworks Co.—in North Bergen, New Jersey. I had found his firm's name in the telephone directory and phoned to ask if I could come out to his plant and buy fireworks from him to set off a minuscule display at a friend's country home where I was spending the weekend—thinking of what I was bringing as a rather unique house present. Serpico was hesitant. After all, the entire fireworks situation has changed. Shortly after the war the anti-fireworks laws in many states, including my own, New York, had become extremely stringent; all commercial fireworks, even Roman candles and sparklers, were banned. The crack of fireworks heard during the Fourth, the occasional whiz of a bottle rocket, were illegal fireworks, either smuggled into the state or purchased off the back of a bootlegger's station wagon. Thus Serpico had no commercial fireworks for sale, and it was improper both for him to give professional fireworks to an amateur and for me to set them off without a license and permission from the local authorities. But I think Serpico appreciated my passion for fireworks; he must have sensed it in my voice over the phone. He also learned that I had been a demolition specialist in the Army, which meant that I would be careful and concerned with safety factors. He agreed to provide me with a small allotment and a mortar from which to fire them.

His compound was a forlorn stretch of land, flat and heat-blasted, fronting on the cattail marshes of the New Jersey swamps—a collection of small buildings and trailers in which aerial shells were either being made or in storage. There were two animals on the premises which served to symbolize the wasteland quality of that melancholy place: a large police dog with three legs and an almost apoplectic temper—he crashed endlessly against a length of chain trying to get at strangers—and the other a crippled goat. It, too, had a missing leg, as if to be thus handicapped was the conditional trademark of the International Fireworks Co. The goat was far more placid than its canine companion. It browsed among the frames of the American flag set pieces out in the sun, hopping oddly from one dusty clump of grass to the next.

Serpico himself had a large purple splotch on one cheek that one might have supposed was firework-related but was, in fact, a birthmark. He took me on a tour of the sheds. He showed me an aerial shell—a round canister, in dimensions not unlike a biscuit tin, wrapped in brown kraft paper and utterly functional-looking compared to the brightly designed fireworks prepared for the public. It had a black fuse at one end encased in a length of brown tubing and at the other—he turned the shell over to show me—the base that contained the propellant charge to eject the firework from the mortar and up into the air. What then happened, Serpico went on to tell me, was that the shell, tumbling end over end as it went up into the night, had a time fuse inside that burned until its fire reached the bursting charge that broke open the canister at the top of its climb and ignited small cubes of a mixture of oxidizers and fuels called "stars." These would spray into the air and burn in the familiar patterns of the aerial display.

The containers Serpico made at his plant ranged from three to twelve inches in diameter—the twelve-inch shell being a projectile that weighed up to a hundred pounds and was shot out of a huge mortar a small boy could hide in, with iron handles on the side so that two men could lurch it into position. The half dozen shells that Serpico gave me were four inches across the top, one of them—which he told me was a "three break and report"—was two feet in length; it seemed mammoth and forbidding. He gave me a railroad flare to light the shells and a single mortar to fire them from. Although I knew that there was not the slightest danger, no matter how hard the box of shells was jostled, I remember wincing as I drove away and bounced across the railroad tracks at the far end of Serpico's compound.

When I arrived at his country place my host was somewhat surprised. "Ahem," he said, looking at the small carton of shells. "What do I do with these things?"

His wife said, "This doesn't mean jail, does it, or anything like that?"

"There are only about four or five in there," I said. "When it's dark, I'll go out in the field and set them off for you."

I dug the mortar in. Their little house party came out to watch from the patio. I could see the glow of their cigarettes. I lit the railroad flare and touched off the first shell—a break and report—scampering from it, a bit panicked, through the meadow grass; first there was the thump of the propellant charge driving the shell out of the mortar, and then above I heard the pop of the canister opening; I looked up to see the curved spray of red and blue, and quickly, the flash of the report, the boom echoing in the hills . . . feeling then, for the first time, the extraordinary exhilaration and sense of self-fulfillment that comes with setting off a large professional shell.

I thought about the pleasure of it afterward as I stalked around the kitchen. There is a kind of delicious trepidation involved. First, after lighting the fuse, there is sometimes a wait before the shell—with a kind of *harrumphing* sound—leaves the mortar whose iron clangs with the sudden blow of the propellant charge. Until this happens, the mind races with the worry that the shell may refuse to budge. It will have to be removed. So the relief when the shell goes up is considerable. Even then it takes so long for a large shell to reach its apogee—up to four or five seconds—that an additional worry takes over. One waits, looking up into the darkness, until the possibility occurs that the shell is coming back down, this awful projectile, invisible in the night, what pyrotechnicians refer to as a "black shell" . . . and then just as one thinks about scurrying desperately for cover, far up the shell snaps open in its huge enveloping umbrella of stars, so intensely beautiful that it invariably produces a cry of delight, partly in appreciation of the shell's aesthetics but also in relief that the thing has gone off properly.

It is an infectious practice. After a while, friends would step out of the shelter of the patio, or come out onto the beach, wherever, and ask if they could set one off. I would give them firm and rudimentary instructions: "Just keep the body away from the top of the mortar . . . above all, don't look down in there to see if anything's going on!"

Some were nervous. The first sight of the mortar-pipe with the fuse drooped over the edge of its mouth, just barely visible in the twilight, the hissing of the railroad flare, sparks dripping molten to the ground, and the uncertainty of what the ignition would do to this somnolent device waiting out of sight, like a beast in its lair, was extremely unsettling to them; they tended to approach the fuse in a low, tense crouch, poised for flight, as if offering a morsel to a leopard. Sometimes, safely behind them, I called out, "Remember Ralph Waldo Emerson: 'As soon as there is life, there is danger!' "

Of my friends, the writers seemed to be the ones who most enjoyed the sensation of setting off a shell, especially those who were having difficulty with their own work, and suffering the so-called "writer's block." I understood why, I thought: it was the frustration of not being able to put on paper what was so vivid in one's mind—the agony of confronting Mallarmé's blank page—compared to the simple act of igniting a fuse and immediately producing a great chrysanthemum of color and beauty high above, punctuated with a splendid concussion, while below, people would gape in wonderment and call out "Wow!" It was the kind of reaction that writers always hoped for with their own work but never received in such visible and adulatory form. The best one could expect from a reader was a low *hmmm,* whereas fireworks could produce loud "Ohhs!" and "Ahhs!" Often, having sent up a shell and seeing it perform, an author would run up in the darkness and ask to try another—a bigger one, this time, a "huge Jap shell, please!"

I remember Norman Mailer at one of our July fireworks parties in the Hamptons. He wanted to fire a shell. He had his bourbon drink in a blue glass, really more a *vase,* the sort of receptacle one usually finds in the back of a kitchen cabinet when everything else in the house, even the plastic cups, has been commandeered. He held the drink in one hand, safe out behind him, and he approached the fuse with the railroad flare in the other. The mortar held a six-inch Japanese shell. I watched him—struck again by the grotesque attitudes that people get into when faced with igniting a shell. In his case, he seemed not unlike a scientist intent on catching a lizard by the back of the neck. The shell came out almost instantaneously. His surprise at the shock of its emergence—a six-inch shell of that type weighs about eight pounds—toppled Norman into a complete backward somersault through the sawgrass. Astonishingly the blue vase remained upright as he pinwheeled around it; not a drop of bourbon splashed out. He got up and took a sip and asked if he could do another. "Do you have anything slightly larger?"

Of course, there were the occasional traumas. Fireworks were, after all, dangerous enough if ill-used, and even, on occasion, unpredictable if used properly. On one occasion at our house in the Hamptons, which is on the sea, a large eight-inch shell fired at our annual summer fireworks party sailed back from the beach in a fog-laden wind and burst lower than it should have. One of its stars, still burning, dropped in among the spectators, landing on the upper arm of a Chicago broadcasting executive. It burned through his sweater, giving him a nasty singe indeed . . .

After being treated at the Southampton Hospital, he went home to Chicago with a large Band-Aid on his wound and then—a man I had never met before (he had come as the guest of a friend)—he sued me for eleven million dollars!

The process-server himself was rather embarrassed by the enormous sum. After he had served me the paper, he hung around my office at the *Paris Review,* a rather rumpled older man, I remember, who said that in his many years of this nasty business he had never served a paper of such mammoth proportions. "Did a building blow up?" he asked.

The incident got into the press. I told a newspaper reporter that anyone who had an arm valued at eleven million dollars should be pitching for the Chicago White Sox. The executive was not amused. He let it be known that he had been "burned from head to foot"—somewhat of a jump from his original complaint that he had a scar "three and a half inches long and two inches wide."

Not long afterward I met a famous litigation lawyer at La Costa, the Teamster resort north of San Diego; he had read about the lawsuit in the newspapers. He asked me to dinner. We drove to the restaurant in his Rolls-Royce. His clients included some of the great names in the entertainment world, though his early years in the law had been—he made me understand—in the lower echelons of the legal society. He had done a lot of work in Chicago.

"Who is representing you?" he asked.

"My father's firm."

He knew the name, but he was not in the least agreement that a corporation law firm—which my father's is—was right for the job. "No, no, wrong. You should get a good tough Court Street lawyer to do the job."

I did not know what the term meant.

". . . somebody who'd really want to mix it up with this guy. Put him on notice. Countersue. Your father's firm is too gentlemanly to do that sort of thing."

My friend tapped the steering wheel of his Rolls-Royce. "And if none of that works," he said, *"I'll put in a call to some people in Chicago!"*

I have wondered what that extreme measure might have entailed. I imagined the scenario as being something out of the film *The Godfather*—along the lines of the famous scene of the horse head in the bed—except that, in this case, the intimidation would have been done far more subtly. And presumably with fireworks. The television executive would arrive back from his day's work to find a brightly colored fountain fizzing mysteriously on his lawn; or late at night, the colored ball of a Roman candle would soar up past his bedroom window, or an SOS Ship would start screaming in his bathtub. Investigating a strange hissing sound, he would open up the cellar door and look down the steps to discover a long length of fuse slowly burning off toward something behind a pile of empty suitcases in the corner. . . .

None of this happened, of course. The matter was settled out of court, the man being paid a small pittance by the insurance company.

Despite the unpleasantness of this incident, my obsession with fireworks continued. During the Lindsay Administration in New York City, I kept pestering the mayor and other officials to allow more fireworks shows, especially in great barrages out of Central Park, to such a degree that the mayor finally made me his fireworks commissioner, a completely bogus designation which is not on the city rolls but one which I have perpetuated through succeeding administrations and a title to which I answer at the drop of a hat.

I got to know a number of fireworks people in the metropolitan area—in particular, the Grucci family from Bellport, Long Island. They allowed me to help choreograph shows for them—an international exhibition fired from Central Park, Venetian Night in Chicago, shows at Shea Stadium on Fireworks Night, Ronald Reagan's Inauguration and the Brooklyn Bridge Centennial among others. It was a great stroking of the ego to choreograph a large fireworks show. It allowed the chance—since the shells were sent up by electrical impulse—to put extraordinary effects in the sky, which were witnessed not just by folks sitting around on the lawn but by literally over a million people roaring in excitement at what they were seeing.

And yet, curiously, the small, more intimate shows are the ones I remember most vividly. I remember one in particular that John Serpico, my first mentor, and I did in the mountains of Vermont—an occasion to mark the graduation of the class of 1975 from Bennington College. I had been asked by one of the members of that class, a tall, lovely girl named Pamela Morgan, if there was any point in trying to persuade her senior tutor to let her do her senior thesis on the history of fireworks. I had said, "Of course! What a remarkable framework on which to put so much! And what a novel and clever way to present history! Think of the great personages who had been obsessed by fireworks—Queen Elizabeth, Peter the Great, Louis XIV, Queen Victoria, John Adams, ever so many."

Alas, her tutor did not share my enthusiasm. She ended up doing her thesis on the poems of Paul Éluard.

But perhaps imbued by my enthusiasm for fireworks, she was able to convince her senior committee that her class should choose some kind of pyrotechnic event for its graduation rather than the perfunctory rock-'n'-roll band.

I obliged. John Serpico and I drove up into those lovely mountains with a van of shells. On the slope just down from a long expanse of lawn that stretched back to the college buildings, we dug in the mortars. The commencement was in the evening. Where we waited, we could hear the speeches drifting across the lawn. When they were done, I stepped forward and through a megaphone I read off a list of the graduating seniors as, behind me, John Serpico lit a shell for each one. Sometimes, to speed things along, I would read off ten names in a row and when I had done howling their names through my megaphone, Serpico would light a quick-match fuse to send a whole flight of shells up simultaneously, bouquets bursting in great profusion over the lawns.

There was a vague attempt in some cases to match a firework with the character of the student graduating: the harum-scarum performance of a Korean hummingbird shell for the class cutup, the lovely comet shells for the class lovelorn, a huge chrysanthemum for Pamela Morgan herself. The college dean—a brassy disciplinarian, apparently—got herself a sharp single report (what some fireworks people call a maroon) and nothing else, and from the lawn, after the echoes of that shell had drifted away, booming in the hills, I could hear the thin sound of laughter.

The long echoing of the reports coming off those dark blue hills must have resembled the sounds made when General John Burgoyne came through with his Loyalists and Hessians in the fall of 1777 and ran into the Green Mountain Boys. The hills collected the reports and hid them in their folds and ravines, and then suddenly released them, quite a time after, so that it seemed that what had produced the sound was some agency other than ours. When the display, and its final echoes, finally died away, it was replaced by the faint high calls of the students celebrating, flower bouquets tossed in the air in picayune imitation of the great fireworks' burgeonings just moments before, and I could see many couples standing in embrace on the expanse of that vast lawn—slender forms just barely visible now in the gathering darkness.

Golf

My woes in golf, I have felt, have been largely psychological. When I am playing well, in the low nineties (my handicap is eighteen), I am still plagued with small quirks—a suspicion that, for example, just as I begin my downswing, my eyes straining with concentration, a bug or a beetle is going to suddenly materialize on the golf ball.

When I am playing badly, far more massive speculation occurs: I often sense as I commit myself to a golf swing that my body changes its corporeal status completely and becomes a *mechanical* entity, built of tubes and conduits, and boiler rooms here and there, with big dials and gauges to check, a Brobdingnagian structure put together by a team of brilliant engineers but manned largely by a dispirited, eccentric group of dissolutes—men with drinking problems who do not see very well and who are plagued by liver complaints.

The structure they work in is enormous. I see myself as a monstrous, manned colossus poised high over the golf ball, a spheroid that is barely discernible fourteen stories down on its tee. From above, staring through the windows of the eyes, which bulge like great bay porches, is an unsteady group (as I see them) of Japanese navy men—admirals, most of them. In their hands they hold ancient and useless voice tubes into which they yell the familiar orders: "Eye on the ball! Chin steady! Left arm stiff! Flex the knees! Swing from the inside out! Follow through! Keep head down!" Since the voice tubes are useless, the cries drift down the long corridors and shaftways between the iron tendons and muscles, and echo into vacant chambers and out, until finally, as a burble of sound, they reach the control centers. These posts are situated at the joints, and in charge are the dissolutes I mentioned—typical of them a cantankerous elder perched on a metal stool, half a bottle

of rye on the floor beside him, his ear cocked for the orders that he acknowl-
edges with ancient epithets, yelling back up the corridors, "Ah, your father's
mustache!" and such things, and if he's of a mind, he'll reach for the controls
(like the banks of tall levers one remembers from a railroad-yard switch
house) and perhaps he'll pull the proper lever and perhaps not. So that, in
sum, the whole apparatus, bent on hitting a golf ball smartly, tips and convo-
lutes and lunges, the Japanese admirals clutching each other for support in
the main control center up in the head as the structure rocks and creaks. And
when the golf shot is on its way the navy men get to their feet and peer out
through the eyes and report: "A shank! A shank! My God, we've hit another
shank!" They stir about in the control center drinking paper-thin cups of rice
wine, consoling themselves, and every once in a while one of them will reach
for a voice tube and shout, "Smarten up down there!"

Down below, in the dark reaches of the structure, the dissolutes reach
for their rye, tittering, and they've got their feet up on the levers and perhaps
soon it will be time to read the evening newspaper.

It was a discouraging image to carry around in one's mind; but I had an
interesting notion: a month on the professional golf tour (I had been invited
to three tournaments), competing steadily and under tournament conditions
before crowds and under the scrutiny of the pros with whom I would be
playing, might result in five, perhaps even six, strokes being pruned from my
eighteen handicap. An overhaul would result. My Japanese admirals would
be politely asked to leave, and they would, bowing and smiling. The dissolutes would be removed from the control centers, grumbling, clutching their
bottles of rye, many of them evicted bodily, being carried out in their chairs.

The replacements would appear—a squad of scientific blokes dressed in
white smocks. Not too many of them. But a great tonnage of equipment
would arrive with them—automatic equipment in gray-green boxes and
computer devices that would be placed about and plugged in and set to
clicking and whirring. The great structure would become almost entirely
automatized. Life in the control center would change—boring, really, with
the scientists looking out on the golf course at the ball and then twiddling
with dials and working out estimations, wind resistance, and such things, and
finally locking everything into the big computers; and with yawns working
at the corners of their mouths because it was all so simple, they would push
the "activate" buttons to generate the smooth motion in the great structure
that would whip the golf ball out toward the distant green far and true. Very
dull and predictable. The scientists would scarcely find very much to say to

each other after a shot. Perhaps "Y—e—s," very drawn out. "Y—e—s. Very nice." Occasionally someone down in the innards of the structure would appear down the long glistening corridors with an oil can, or perhaps with some brass polish to sparkle up the pipes.

That was the vision I had. I began the overhaul myself. I obviously would have to look the part. A month before I left on the tour, I outfitted myself completely and expensively with new golf equipment. I had played golf since I began, which was when I was twelve or so, with a white cloth golf bag that bore the trade name Canvasback for some reason; if the clubs were removed, it collapsed on itself like an accordion or like a pair of trousers being stepped out of. It was light as a feather, and caddies always looked jaunty and supercilious under its weight. I often carried it myself. It had a small pocket with room for three balls and some tees. It had eight clubs in it, perhaps nine—two woods and a putter and the rest, of course, irons with two or three missing—an outfit hardly suitable for tournament play.

So I bought the works. Clubs and a new bag. Sweaters. Argyle socks. A small plastic bag of gold golf tees. I bought some golf shoes with flaps that came down over the laces—my first pair; I had always used sneakers. The golf bag was enormous. It seemed a dull conservative color when I saw it in the late afternoon gloom of a Florida golf shop. But when I took it out on a practice round the next day, it glowed a rich oxblood color, like a vast sausage. It was very heavy with a metal bottom with brass studs around it, and when I first went out, I felt guilty seeing in on a caddy's back. But the clubs let off a fine chinking sound as the bag was carried, as expensive and exclusive as the sound of a Cadillac door shutting to, and the fact that porters, caddies, and I myself, whoever carried it, were bent nearly double by its weight only seemed to add to its stature.

It was proper to have such an enormous bag. I thought of the caddies coming up the long hills of the Congressional on television, wearing the white coveralls with the numbers, and those huge bags—MacGregors, Haigs or Wilsons, with the pros' names stamped down the front—with the wiping towels dangling, and the bags nearly slantwise across their shoulders, with one hand back to steady it so the weight would be more properly distributed.

Still, I never really got accustomed to my great golf bag. The woods had brown woolen covers on them. In my early practice rounds in the East I used to follow the clubs at quite a distance, and off to one side, as they were carried down the fairway, as one might circle at a distance workmen moving a harpsichord into one's home—self-conscious and a little embarrassed.

I was particularly aware of the big bag on trips—particularly lugging it around in a railroad station or an air terminal, where intense men with briefcases hurry past, and there are tearful farewells going on, and melancholy groups of military people stand around with plastic name tags on their tunics to tell us who they are. A golf bag is such an immense symbol of frivolity in these parlous times, so much bigger than a tennis racket. When I arrived in Los Angeles by plane to head upstate for the Crosby tournament, the terminal seemed filled with soldiers. There had been many on my plane. At the baggage claim counter the gray-green military duffel bags began coming down the conveyor belt, one after another, and the soldiers would heft them off and set them to one side in a great mound. My golf bag appeared among them with its rich oxblood glow, obscene, jingling slightly as it came toward me on the conveyor.

A porter gave me a hand with it. We got it outside to the traffic ramp with the rest of my luggage and he waited while I arranged to rent a car for the long ride up to Monterey.

"You must be going up to the tournament," the porter said.

"Why, yes," I said gratefully. "The Crosby."

"George Knudson just came through a while ago," he said. "And George Archer. Always tell him 'cause he's, man, *tall.*"

"That's right," I said. "He's as tall as they come."

He hefted the bag into the trunk of the car.

"They set you up with a new bag, I see."

The bag was so new that a strong odor drifted from it—a tang of furniture polish.

"A great big one," I said. "They're getting bigger, it seems."

I fished in my pocket for a tip.

"Well, good luck up there," he said. He wanted me to tell him my name, some name he would recognize from the tour so he could announce to them back in the terminal, "Well, you know, So-and-so just came through . . . on his way up to the Crosby."

"I guess I just head *north,*" I said. I waved an arm, and stepped into the car.

"Yes, that's where it is. Up the coast." He smiled. "Well, good luck," he said. "I play to a five myself."

"No kidding?" I said.

"Well, that's nothing compared to you guys. I play out on the municipal course. And at Ramble Beach."

"A five handicap is nothing to be sneezed at," I said.

"I wish it were a four," he said.

"Sure," I said. "Well . . ." I tried hard to think of an appropriate golf term.

"Well, *pop it,*" I said.

He looked startled.

"I mean really *pop* it out there."

A tentative smile of appreciation began to work at his features. I put the car in gear and started off. As I looked in the rearview mirror I could see him staring after the car.

Birdwatching

I should admit at the outset that my credentials as a birdwatcher are slightly sketchy. True, birdwatching *is* a hobby, and if pressed I tell people that I truly enjoy it: on picnics I pack along a pair of binoculars and the Peterson field guide. But I am not very good at it. Identification of even a mildly rare bird or a confusing fall warbler is a heavy, painstaking business, with considerable riffling through the Peterson, and then a numbing of spirit since I am never really *sure.* As a birder, I have often thought of myself as rather like a tone-deaf person with just a lesson or two in his background who enjoys playing the flute—it's probably mildly pleasurable, but the results are uncertain.

Pressure to better myself as a birder has been consistently exacted on me by my younger brother and sister, who are both good birdwatchers and can hardly wait for fall and the possibility of being confused by warblers during the migration.

Sometimes, when we are all going somewhere in a car, they involve me in a birding quiz that utilizes the Peterson guide. My sister will say, opening the book at random, "All right, the two of you, see if you can guess this one."

She summarizes: "Four and three-quarters to five and one-quarter inches in length. The bird is short-tailed and flat-headed with a big pale bill; finely streaked below. The head is olive-colored and striped, and the wings are reddish. Its flight is low and jerky with a twisting motion of the tail—"

"Got it," snaps my brother. "A cinch."

My sister looks at me.

"Well, it's not a brant goose," I say.

"That's very perceptive," she says.

"What's its call?" I ask, indulging in a holding action since I've never been able to remember or indeed hear in my inner ear the dreamy *tseeeee-tsaaays* or the syrupy *zzzchuwunks* that pepper Peterson's descriptions.

My sister reads directly from the book. "This bird 'perches atop a weed, from which it utters one of the poorest vocal efforts of any bird; throwing back its head, it ejects a hiccoughing *tsi-lick*. As if to practice this "song" so that it might not always remain at the bottom of the list, it often hiccoughs all night long.' "

"You're making that up," I say in astonishment. "That doesn't sound like Peterson at all."

"An absolute cinch," says my brother. "You *must* know."

I decide to take a guess. "A red-eyed vireo."

Both of them groan.

"What is it, Oakes?" my sister asks.

"Henslow's sparrow."

"Of course," she says smugly.

Despite such shortcomings, I was invited last winter to participate in the National Audubon Society's seventy-third annual Christmas Bird Count. I accepted with alacrity, if only in the hope of improving my birdwatching ability, and perhaps, at the least, so I could learn enough to do better in the Peterson contest with my brother and sister.

For the uninitiated, the Christmas Bird Count was originated in 1900 by the editor of *Bird-Lore* magazine, Frank M. Chapman, who wished to organize a substitute for a traditional Christmastime wildlife slaughter known as the "side hunt," in which the gentry would "choose sides" and spend a day in the woods and fields blazing at everything that moved to increase their team's total toward the grand accounting at the end of the day.

Chapman's first Christmas count involved twenty-seven people and twenty-five localities. The largest list of birds spotted came from Pacific Grove, California (36 species), and Chapman himself reported the second largest (18 species) from Englewood, New Jersey. Those pioneer bird counters could not have been particularly proficient since the 1972 count near Pacific Grove was 179, and the New Jersey count nearest to Englewood was 72.

From its modest beginnings, the Audubon Christmas Bird Count has mushroomed over seven decades—until last year, during the two-week Christmas period, some 20,000 observers were involved. The participating teams (each has one day of search time allowed and is confined to an area with a fifteen-mile diameter) numbered over 1,000.

Over the past few years the competition for the highest count has been between three areas in California (San Diego, Santa Barbara, and Point Reyes, where in 1971 a huge army of 193 observers was mustered); Cocoa Beach, Florida, where the redoubtable Allan Cruickshank is the field marshal; and Freeport, Texas, a relatively new count organized sixteen years ago by ornithologist Victor Emanuel, who worked at the job until, in 1971, Freeport set the Christmas Bird Count record of 226 species, an astounding total considering the limitations of the fifteen-mile circle of land and water.

The Freeport count was the one I decided to join. Emanuel was described to me as being young, eager, and perhaps best known in birdwatching circles for his observations of the Eskimo curlew on Galveston Island in 1959. I told him nothing of my birding inadequacies. A week before Christmas I flew to Houston and drove down to the Freeport area, arriving in the late evening at an A-frame beach house on the Gulf of Mexico (appropriately called "The Royal Tern") just in time to hear Emanuel give a pep talk to his team. His group was young—many of them in their twenties, quite a few beards among them—and an overall mood of intense dedication prevailed, as if a guerrilla operation were afoot.

Emanuel's pep rally essentially sounded as follows: "All right, let's try to get *both* cormorants, the double-crested and the olivaceous. Get close. Compare. It's the only way. The green heron is a problem bird, and so is the yellow-crowned night heron. And the least bittern, a tremendous problem! We've only had it once. Flush him out. He lurks in the cattail areas. Leap up and down. Clap your hands. That sort of behavior will get him up. Ross's goose? I'm concerned. We only had four last year. Look in the sky every once in a while for the ibis soaring. Search among the green-winged teal for the cinnamon." He ran his finger down the list through the ducks. "An oldsquaw would be very nice. The hooded merganser is a problem. Hawks! Cooper's and sharp-shinned—not easy at *all*. You people in the woods, make a special effort. Look at all the buteos for the Harlan's. The caracara is a big problem, especially if they're held down by the rain; but they might be flying around. Rails? We're relying on you people in the marsh buggy for the rails, and the purple gallinule as well. As for shorebirds, last year we did not do well at all."

"We did our best," someone called out from the shadows.

"Emanuel's right. We only missed the marbled godwit," a bearded man said from the corner.

Emanuel continued as if he hadn't heard: "We have a barn owl staked out. Keep an eye out for the screech owl. We have often missed him. There ought to be some groove-billed anis around. Can't miss *them.* They have weird, comical calls and they look, when they move around, like they're going to fall apart. Check every flicker for the red-shafted. Say's phoebe might be around. Check the ditches. Bewick's wren, a *big* problem bird." He tapped his list. "Now," he said. "I'm very worried about the warblers. Last year we were lucky with vireos; we got five different species, and we got seventeen out of the possible twenty warblers. The cold weather is going to drive the insect eaters like warblers farther south. So I am not at all sanguine about the vireos and warblers. I'd be surprised if we get more than ten. Check every myrtle warbler for the bright yellow throat that's going to mean Audubon's." He paused. "Now, meadowlarks," he said. "Keep your ears open for the western meadowlark's song. It's quite different from the eastern's, and it's the only way to distinguish between the two species."

Someone interrupted from the back of the room. "Do you realize that the eastern has learned to *imitate* the western?"

Shouts and cries of "Shut up, Ben!" The man next to me whispered that it was Ben Feltner, a great birding rival of Emanuel's, the first man to spot the famous Galveston Island Eskimo curlew, then thought to be extinct.

Emanuel continued unperturbed. "The sparrow that'll give us the most problem is probably the lark. Search the edges of the brush. It's been missed, and it's very upsetting to miss. Henslow's is another." My heart jumped. My sister's voice, reading from Peterson, sang in my head. "It's better than a groove-billed ani to find a Henslow's," Emanuel was saying—"a *devil* of a bird. Watch for those reddish wings."

What a moment, I thought, to make an impression—to call out to that roomful of experts, "And don't forget that twisting tail in flight, and that soft hiccough, the *tsi-lick* that marks the Henslow's." I stirred, but said nothing.

"Longspurs," Emanuel was continuing. "This might be a year for longspurs with the cold snap bringing them in." He folded the list. "Well, that's the end. Good luck to all of you. Don't forget to look behind you. Too many birdwatchers forget to do that—to see what it is that they've stirred up while walking through. My own prognosis is that if we bird well and hard, we'll beat two hundred tomorrow, and possibly even get up to two-twenty, but it will take some doing."

A few hands clapped sharply in the back of the room, and someone offered up an exhortatory cry: "Down with Cocoa Beach!"

"I've got them psyched up," Emanuel said to me as people got up from the floor and began to stir around. "They have to be. It's not only Cocoa Beach I'm worried about, but San Diego. It's all very nerve-racking."

"I can sense that," I said truthfully. "I feel as though I've been spying on a professional football team's locker room before the Big Game."

"No one's going to get much sleep," Emanuel said.

"Absolutely not."

The next day, on the run, I kept notes. Victor Emanuel kept me with him as a partner. (Most teams covering the twelve areas of the Freeport count worked as pairs or trios.) Emanuel's personal plan was to hit as many areas as he could to see how his teams were working. My notes, somewhat helter-skelter, read as follows:

Eight cars crowded with birdwatchers are moving slowly down a cart track, bouncing in the ruts, and then the line turns into a field bordering a large pond. It is barely light. Rhode Island Reds are crowing from a nearby barn. From the farmer's bedroom window the cars moving slowly in a row through the dawn half-light must suggest a sinister procession of some sort—a Mafia burial ceremony.

The horizon toward the Gulf sparkles with the constellation of lights that mark the superstructures of the oil refineries, illuminating the tall streamlike plumes of smoke. Electric pylons are everywhere. Quite incongruous to think that this highly visible industrial tangle can contain such a rich variety of birdlife. I mention it to Emanuel. He has just whispered to me that the year before a least grebe had turned up in this area. At my comment I could see his face wince in the dim light and he snorted. He tells me that only a fraction of the wildlife John James Audubon observed when he visited the Texas coast remains. But, still it is a birder's paradise. Why is that so?

"Trees," he says, "large and thick enough to contain and hold the eastern birds; and yet the area is far enough south to get southern and western birds. The cover is so good that the area gets more warblers in its count than Corpus Christi does, which is much farther to the south. Furthermore, there is great diversity—cattle-grazing land, the beaches, swampland, ditches, and the Gulf. Since the count started in 1957, the same basic hundred thirty-six species have turned up every year—which gives you some idea of the huge diversity of the regular bird population."

*　*　*

I am tagging along having a good time. I am in awe of Emanuel. Just a flash of wing, or the mildest of sounds, and he has himself an identification. He is so intense that I rarely ask questions. But he shows me things. I have gazed upon the groove-billed ani. True, the bird does fly as if it were about to come apart at the seams. A black wing fluttering down here, a claw there. I have done nothing on my own. Early in the dawn I saw a woodcock flutter across the road, but I was too intimidated to say anything about it. I know the woodcock from New England. Then, at the pond where we were peering at the barely discernible shapes of the ducks beginning to stir out on the slate-black water, the experts rattling them off (gadwall, canvasback, pintail, et al.), someone said, "Oh, did anyone spot the woodcocks coming across the road from the pasture?" And I said, "Yes!" like an explosion. "Absolutely!"

Emanuel caught the despairing eagerness in my voice. He has a nice gift for hyperbole. "That's a terrific bird," he said to me. "Well done!"

We got in Emanuel's car and headed for another area he wanted to bird. I asked him about the Eskimo curlew. He said he hadn't been the first to see the one that had caused all the excitement. On March 22, 1959, two Houston birders—Dudley Deaver and Ben Feltner, the fellow I saw at the pep talk the evening before, wearing the blue jay insignia on his field jacket—had been birding on Galveston Island looking for their first whimbrel, or Hudsonian curlew. In a flock of long-billed curlews they noticed a smallish curlew that they assumed was the whimbrel. But there was something odd about it. It had a very buffy look, and most noticeable was a bill much thinner and shorter than the whimbrel's. With considerable excitement they realized they might be looking at a bird that had last been collected in the United States near Norfolk, Nebraska, on April 17, 1915, and that had been categorized as "probably extinct." The only uncertainty lay in Ludlow Griscom's description in Peterson's field guide that the leg color of the Eskimo curlew was dark green. The legs of the curlew they were looking at on Galveston Island were slaty gray.

Two weeks later they took Emanuel out to see what *he* thought. They discovered the little curlew several miles from where Deaver and Feltner had made the original sighting. "You can imagine how exciting that was," Emanuel told me. "Damn, it was like seeing a dinosaur."

Emanuel was also bothered by the leg color, but some research disclosed that not all reports described the Eskimo curlew's legs as dark green. A number of authorities put them down as a "dull slate color" or "grayish blue."

The curlew returned to Galveston for four years in a row. A number of Texas birders got a chance to look at it—on one occasion from about one hundred feet away through a thirty-power telescope, powerful enough to fill the eyepiece with the bird. All of the experts were convinced. It was a time, Emanuel told me, that he thinks back on a lot.

We met a birder named Dave Smith, who had come in from Wheeling, West Virginia, because he felt his home turf was so limited. Emanuel said, "Hell, I thought you'd come out here for the glory of the Freeport count."

"No," Smith said. "There's not enough swamps in Wheeling."

I asked Emanuel what he considers the qualities of a great birder, and he began talking about Jim Tucker. "He is a superb birder. He found us the red-necked grebe at the Texas City dike. He is a vegetarian. He never sleeps. He's got terrific, keen hearing, and since hearing a a bird counts just as much as seeing one, that's a grand asset. He eats a cracker and keeps going. He stays out on a bird count day until eleven P.M. and he's critical of people who aren't out at midnight at the start, so they can spot, say, a sanderling in the moonlight on the beach, or catch the calls of a migrant bird overhead. One of his most extraordinary feats was to lead a party that spotted two hundred twenty-nine species in a single day in Texas, a new national record.

"Now his partner is Roland Wauer. He has the great gift of being able to pick up birds through his binoculars rather than scanning with his eyes. You can imagine what an advantage that is, being able to scan for birds through the binoculars. He'll look down a ravine with his glasses and he'll say, 'Oh, wow, there ought to be a gray vireo in here somewhere,' and he'll *find* it. That's quite a team, those two."

At lunch, which we were having in a restaurant near the beach (not as much roughing it as I expected), a balding gentleman assigned to count on the beaches came rushing up behind Victor Emanuel, who was bending over a cup of soup at the counter, and cried out: "Oregon junco!"

Emanuel started at the sharp explosion of sound behind him. Then, when he had spun around on his stool, he seemed skeptical.

"But it had pinkish sides," the gentleman said proudly. "It didn't look at *all* like the slate-colored junco. There were a lot of *those* around, maybe fifty or sixty, but this fellow was a single junco playing around in the ruts of the road just off the beach."

Emanuel said, "Sometimes the slate-coloreds have pinkish sides."

"Oh," said the balding man. He looked crestfallen.

"No harm in reporting it at the tabulation dinner tonight. The jury will decide."

"I'll think about it," said the man. "I wouldn't want to be taken for a fool."

Emanuel has just given me a lesson on how to tell the difference between Sprague's pipit and the water pipit. Both have the habit of rising vertically out of the gorselike shrubbery of the hummocky country hereabouts, fluttering quite high, as if to look to the horizon to see if anything's of interest, then dropping back quite abruptly to the place where they started from. It's the method of descent that is different. The Sprague's closes its wings at the apogee of its climb and falls like a stone until it is just above the ground, where it brakes abruptly and banks into a bush. The water pipit, on the other hand, drops from the top of its flight in bouncy stages, like a ball tumbling down steep stairs.

"That's a great thing to know," I said. "I'm not sure it's a piece of knowledge I can do very much with. I mean it's not a distinction of daily usage."

Just then, a pipit sprang up in front of us, fluttering up, and then dropped sharply back to earth.

"Sprague's," I said.

"Absolutely brilliant," said Emanuel. "You see, you never know."

Emanuel had to take an hour out of birdwatching to be honored at a chamber of commerce meeting. A punch was served and chocolate-chip cookies. A number of birders were there, looking uncomfortable, minds on their lists and anxious to move on.

An official of the chamber rapped for silence. He had an American flag in his lapel. He said in a clear, sincere, municipal voice that the community was proud to have the great Freeport bird count in its area. Texas was number one, as everyone was aware, but the nearest municipality, Houston, had been letting everybody down with the Houston Oilers, and the Houston Astros, and the Houston Rockets, who were not displaying the Texas winning spirit worth a damn. It was refreshing to know that at least the bird count team was number one. He called out, "We've got to be number one in something!"

He looked (rather desperately, I thought) at Emanuel, who nodded vaguely and said they had a very good chance to be.

"Well, go and *bust* them," the official said, with a gesture that slopped some of the fruit punch out of his glass. "What we might do," he went on, "is put some sort of statue around here to show that this area is number one in birds. A big, tall stone, or maybe a *brass* bird." The muscles of his face subsided in reflection. The buzz of conversation rose around the room.

With the official greeting over, a number of the townspeople came up to offer suggestions to help us with our lists. I heard one person saying to a member of the count team, "I just promise you—there was a falcon, a big tall falcon, sitting on a branch behind the bank. Sure'n shootin' you rush over and he's there to be spotted. Big tall fellah." The birdwatchers listened politely. Emanuel nudged me and said that it was often worthwhile. The Freeport count, he said, had always relied on the "hummingbird lady," who had a feeding station to which three kinds of hummingbirds had come the previous year. She didn't know enough to distinguish one from another, but the birds came to her, and they'd had a count team in her garden that came back with the ruby-throated, the buff-bellied, and the rufous. Of course, that had been a warm Christmas. Still, a team was assigned the "hummingbird lady," and they'd be making their report at the tabulation dinner.

A somewhat brassy female reporter came up to David Marrack, a British-born birdwatcher, and asked: "I am hearing that the warblers—is that the right word?—are off. Is that bad news for your bird-hunters . . . I mean *watchers?*"

Marrack replied: "The cold has destroyed the insects. *Quod*—no warblers."

"I beg your pardon."

He inspected her. "It's too bloody *cold,*" he announced clearly.

We are running through cottonwood thickets looking for Harris's sparrow—the biggest of the sparrows, which summers in the subarctic forests (Emanuel tells me) and winters in the central plains, west to north Texas. With the cold weather, a specimen should be in the vicinity, most likely in amongst the white-crowned sparrows. Every once in a while in our search we step around the whitened bones of a cow skeleton—drowned by the flooding of the creek that flows by just beyond the trees.

In midafternoon Emanuel spots a bird in the top of a tree. He begins swaying back and forth in his excitement. "Oh my." Without taking his eyes from his binoculars, he motions me forward.

"A Harris's sparrow?" I ask.

"It's better," he whispers. "Much better. It's a rose-breasted grosbeak. No one else will get this. Oh, terrific. It's only been seen once before on the count." We stare at the bird. I can see the wash of pink at its throat. When it flies, the sun makes it blaze, and then oddly, a barn owl floats out of the trees behind it.

An hour later something happened that eclipsed the excitement of the rose-breasted grosbeak. The two of us had not been seeing much, winding down after the long day, and I was trailing along behind Emanuel, idly speculating about what sort of a bird he most closely resembled. It is not an uncommon speculation. William Faulkner once said he would like to be a buzzard because nothing hates him or envies him or wants him and he could eat anything. I myself have always opted for hadadah ibis, a large African wading bird that when flushed from a riverbed springs into the air with a haunting loud bellow, which gives it its name, and defecates wildly into the water below. It is not so much the latter habit that I envy as the *habitat* of the bird, to be able to perch on the smooth bark of the acacia and overlook the swift water of the river and see what comes down to it, that great variety of life, and what happens.

I had no intention of pressing Emanuel on such a fancy, but my own speculation, watching him peer this way and that through the shrubbery, furtive and yet sleek, is that he might pass . . . well, as a brown thrasher.

Just then, he froze in front of me, staring at a spot twenty or thirty feet in front of him. His bird glasses came up. "Oh my," I heard him whisper. "Wait until I tell Ben."

"Is it Harris's sparrow?" I asked.

"My God, no, look. . . . It's the magnolia warbler. Oh, Ben is going to die, absolutely die! Don't you see? It's a first for the count." He was almost breathless with excitement.

I spotted the warbler through my glasses. Beside me Emanuel kept up a running whispering commentary. "My first thought was that it was a myrtle warbler. Then I saw yellow underneath, and I knew we had something good.

White eye-ring, very delicate yellow pip over the beak. No doubt. Oh, wow! It will *kill* Ben. Green back. Two wing bars, one short, one long. White in tail. Very prominent. Very beautiful."

He took out a pad of paper and began writing down a description of the warbler, which was now fluttering about in a bush in front of us.

"He's feeding well. The magnolia is very common in migration, but it's never lingered like this. It's such a joy to find a warbler in winter."

Just then the bird flew. "Ah!" cried Emanuel happily. "The white flash in the tail. That's the absolute clincher." He turned, his eyes shining with excitement.

"Oh, yes," I said. I struggled for something else to say. "That's the damnedest thing I ever saw," I said.

The tabulation dinner was held at a roadside café called Jack's Restaurant in the town of Angleton, which is about halfway between Freeport and Houston. Almost all of the bird count teams (fifty-five people altogether) were there. We sat at long tables arranged in rows along three sides of a brightly lighted banquet room with red-and-green Christmas crepe pinned up between the light fixtures. The place was taut with expectation. Some of the birders gossiped about what they had seen; others affected a smug air of superiority and mystery, containing themselves until the tabulation. I overheard Emanuel saying to Ben Feltner, "I got a bird's never been on the Freeport list."

"You're kidding," said Ben.

Emanuel grinned enormously. "You'll jump out of your seat."

"What is it?"

"I won't tell you. It's a warbler."

Ben stared at him. "Come on."

"You'll have to wait," Emanuel said.

After the dinner Emanuel began the proceedings with a short speech. He announced that the panel that would rule on questionable sightings would consist of himself, Ben Feltner, and Jim Tucker. He said that it was important to maintain the integrity of the Freeport count, and that the panel would strive for a high degree of accuracy. It was important that the judgments be made right away, that very evening, so that those birdwatchers who had accidentals or rare sightings to offer should be prepared to substantiate them. He hoped no one would be *defensive* about his birds; it was a necessary procedure.

Emanuel's master list was divided into three categories—the regular species (birds seen on practically every Freeport count); the essential species (birds seen on most counts but that were present in low numbers and required hard work to locate, and are the keys to a successful high count); and finally the bonus birds, which are rare and not to be expected at all.

Emanuel rattled his list, looked down at it, and began—calling out the name of a bird and looking around the room for someone to raise a hand in acknowledgment that the bird had been seen. Some of the acknowledgments produced cries of delight—and often the team responsible, sitting together at the table, slapped each other's hands like delighted ballplayers running back to the bench after a touchdown.

Sometimes, though, a missed bird, especially if it was an "essential" species, brought cries of woe.

"Horned grebe?" Emanuel looked around. No hands were up. Dismay.

"Ross's goose? Black duck? Goldeneye?" Gloom.

But then Dennis Shepler heightened spirits considerably by putting his hand up for the cinnamon teal. "Three males, two females," he said. Shouts of approbation.

"Bald eagle?"

A hand went up. Pandemonium! The birder described it as a single adult, soaring over the lake. Emanuel cried out, "Wonderful, marvelous." Spirits were lifted; some good-natured badinage began—the eagle team being joshed for sighting "a crated bird." "They brought it with them!" someone shouted happily.

The tabulation went on. No hummingbirds had been seen at the "hummingbird lady's" feeder. Horrified cries. Emanuel shook his head. He paused before going on, as if someone would surely recollect that small buzz of color and announce it. He waited, then disconsolately went on. A caracara had been seen. Abruptly the mood shifted again. Shouts of delight. One of the team responsible said they had watched the caracara catch a shrike and eat it. More shouts of glee. I wondered moodily if the shrike would be remembered in the count.

"Peregrine falcon?" Two had been seen, but no pigeon hawks were acknowledged. Groans. The marsh buggy team got a solid round of hand-clapping for having flushed up a yellow rail.

The climax of emotion came with the approach of the count to the plateau of 200. When a few hands went up for the parula warbler, the 200th bird identified, the entire room rose amidst a storm of clapping and cheering.

At 203 the master list was done, and it was time for the birdwatchers to stand up and offer bonus species. The room quieted down. The 204th species was a pyrrhuloxia, a bird I had never even heard of. The birder, who was an expert from New Jersey, stood and described the specimen in a soft and very difficult stutter, everyone at the tables leaning forward in sympathy with his effort to get his description out. He talked about the bird's yellow bill and its loose crest and how he'd seen it in the salt cedars. One heavily bearded birder astounded everyone by announcing *four* bonus birds—my old pal the Henslow's sparrow, a fish crow, an eastern wood pewee, and the Philadelphia vireo. Each was described; he said he had flushed the sparrow out of dry grass. He didn't mention the hiccoughing song. A Swainson's hawk was 209. Then Emanuel himself rose and announced his two prizes, the rose-breasted grosbeak and the magnolia warbler, grinning in triumph at Ben Feltner as he described the latter. Feltner's eyebrows went up. He pulled at his beard. It was difficult to tell how he was taking it. Emanuel said that I had been along with him and was there for verification; I gave a slight nod at Feltner and looked very arch. There was a tumult of applause when Emanuel sat down.

The 215th, and last, bird offered was a Harlan's hawk. The birdwatcher was quizzed quite sharply by the panel. The hawk was in the light phase, he said, and the sun shone through the tail, which was completely pale except for a black marking toward the end. No, he hadn't seen the back of the bird. It was paler than a red-tailed. The panel looked skeptical; Emanuel tapped a spoon against his front teeth.

Emanuel's panel then disappeared to discuss not only the bonus birds but questionable sightings from the master list. They came back and Emanuel announced that seven birds had not been allowed. He did not say which seven—that might have embarrassed some people who may simply have been overzealous.

The balding man from the beach had his Oregon junco accepted. I grinned at him, and he came over. "Good news, eh?" he said. "Well, *I* was confident. I know the Oregon junco very well; I've trapped them, and banded them, and maybe the jury took that into consideration. There're not many people around who know the Oregon junco like I do, *nosir!*"

Afterward Emanuel told me the sort of process the panel had gone through. "Well, we knocked out the olivaceous cormorant from the master list; we'll have to assume it was a double-crested. The spotter didn't mention the white border along the pouch, which is an essential field mark, and besides, it's very difficult to distinguish the olivaceous unless you get a size comparison with the double-crested. So we let it go. We dropped the gray-cheeked thrush because the observer who saw it hasn't had that much experience and his description wasn't right. It's *not* uniform brown with a grayish tail. And it's extremely rare in winter. We also dropped the yellow-throated vireo because the observer didn't emphasize the vireo's slower and skulkier movements. He probably saw a pine warbler. Then from the bonus birds we voted out the Philadelphia vireo, and also the sighting of the wood pewee because it's easily confused with the eastern phoebe. As for that fish crow, well, heavens, his voice is unmistakable, that nasal *cah,* and that essential was never mentioned. The Harlan's hawk just didn't sound right either; it could have been a red-tailed.

He went through the list, ticking off the disallowed birds with obvious sorrow. Some of the votes of the panel had not been unanimous, and every rejection lowered the chances of winning the bird count championship. "Let's see," he said. "That's two hundred and eight birds. I'm scared," he said. "We'll have to keep our fingers crossed."

A few days later, Emanuel called me in New York to tell me how Freeport had fared in competition with other high-count areas. He recapitulated that the areas that bothered him competitively were the three major California counts. To his delight he had found that the cold weather had hurt these California counts as much as it had Freeport's and that San Diego and Santa Barbara were tied with only 195 species.

That left Cocoa Beach, Florida, to be worried about. Two years before, Cocoa Beach had beaten out Freeport by just one species, 205 to 204. Emanuel decided he was going to wait until after the count period ended (January 1) before calling Allan Cruickshank, his counterpart, to find out what their total was. In the meantime he was going off to Mexico to take his mind off the competition by doing some birding down there. His special loves are hawks, and there are two hawks in Mexico he would just about fall down and die to see—the orange-breasted falcon, which hangs around ruins (he told me), and the blackcollared, or chestnut, hawk.

In mid-January he wrote me a letter in which he said that the Mexico trip had been an astounding success. He had not seen his two hawks, but his letter was lively with accounts of sightings of flocks of military macaws, "a veritable din of squawking as a magnificent flock came pouring over the side of the mountain."

He wrote that on his return he had gone back down to Freeport on December 31 with a friend from Tennessee "to show him some birds." While there he decided to drop in on the "hummingbird lady" to find out what had happened on count day. She was sitting with her mother in the parlor watching the Dallas Cowboys on television. "Well," she said, *"certainly* two kinds of hummingbirds had turned up that day." Emanuel's eyes widened. The hummingbirds came to the feeder every morning at 8:00 A.M. ("You could almost set your clock by them"), and that day was no exception. She had seen them a number of times. The trouble was that the ladies from the count team hadn't arrived until midafternoon, when the birds had left the feeder for the last time. Emanuel gave a whoop at this, making the mother, who was idly watching the Cowboys standing around during a timeout, start in her seat, and he forthwith boosted the Freeport count to 209.

It turned out to be a fortuitous visit—since a January 7 call to Cruickshank produced the information that the Cocoa Beach count was also 209. Thus the two leading bird count areas in the country were matched in an unprecedented tie.

I wrote Emanuel a short letter of congratulations. I told him that I was proud to have been on a championship team, even if their triumph had to be shared. I didn't tell him that I myself had had a birdwatcher's triumph of sorts recently. I had found myself seated next to a lady at dinner who had begun talking about birds quite without my prompting (the dining room had framed Audubon prints on the wall, perhaps that was why), and she said that the trouble with people who enjoyed birdwatching was that so many of them were unbearably *pretentious.* "Now take those disgusting people who take so much stock in that ritual of the Christmas Bird Count . . ."

"What a coincidence," I said. "I was on the Freeport count."

She was very arch.

"Oh?"

Something stirred in my memory. "I'll bet you can't *guess* what we turned up," I said. "Perched on a weed, its head thrown back, and uttering the feeblest of hiccoughing noises, a sort of *tsi-lick.* Are those enough hints for you?" She looked at me with a gaze of distaste. "Flattish head, as I recall," I went on, "with a tail that twists in flight. Why that's *Henslow's sparrow,"* I said quickly, in case she knew enough to interrupt me.

I hitched my chair forward. "How are you on pipits?" I asked. "Would you care to hear a rather nice field characteristic that'll straighten them out for you? Let's start with Sprague's," I said in a strong voice that turned heads at the table. . . .

Christopher Cerf and Tony Hendra were the architects of a famous parody of the *New York Times,* which was called *Not the New York Times,* edited out of my New York apartment. Both went on to a new concept—publishing in book form a prognostic look-back at a decade yet to come. Contributors were asked to imagine themselves in the nineties writing about what had happened in the eighties. My effort was inspired by a rumor (well-founded, it turned out) that Truman Capote was having difficulty finishing his Proustian epic *Answered Prayers.* The concept in what follows is that Capote has resorted to trying another's style—in this case Ernest Hemingway's—to break his writer's block . . . much as a stutterer can speak clearly and without hesitations by using a different accent. Thus, the unlikely combination of Capote's sensibility melded into Hemingway's style, using as a model the latter's famous story "The Snows of Kilimanjaro."

Truman Capote did not like this at all. Upon reflection I cannot blame him. I wrote a letter of apology. Truman told acquaintances that I had come and "scratched at his door for forgiveness." We never spoke again. I avoided him at parties for fear of his voice cutting across the room. It is with mixed feelings that the following is included. . . .

Parody: Truman Capote
as Hemingway

Studiofiftyfour, a converted movie theater fifty-seven feet above sea level, was said to have been the liveliest discotheque in New York City. Close to the top seats in the balcony was discovered a matchbook cover[1] bearing the White House seal. No one knows what the White House aide was seeking at that altitude.

It was morning and had been morning for some time, and he was waiting for the plane. It was difficult to speak.

"Can you see all right?" the attendant from the fat farm asked as they approached the ticket counter.

"It's okay unless the bandages slip," he said. "Then it's all fuzzy."

"How do you feel?"

"A little wobbly."

"Does it hurt?"

"Only when I sit down."

He thought about the railway station at Karabük and the headlight of the Simplon–Orient cutting the dark now, and he thought about his enemies and how he wished he had them laid out across the tracks. They would make a long row. Perhaps a mile. Too many, maybe. But he had fought often, and they had always picked the finest places to have the fights. The tea place in the Plaza Hotel with the palms. The El Morocco with the zebra stripes. The Bistro in Beverly Hills. That was where Jerry

---

[1]"Snows," in this case, apparently refers not to the material that falls on mountains but to a white powder that is arranged in a thin line by such a pusher as a matchbook cover and is then ingested up a straw into either nostril—a practice referred to as "snorting."

Zipkin[2] came out of the dark restaurant gloom that time, blinking his eyes, and he had hit him right along the chops, twice, hard, and when the Social Moth—that was what Johnny Fairchild called him, wasn't it, old cock?—didn't go down he knew he was in a fight.

He wished it had been at El Morocco, which was a good place to fight, with the palm trees and the high ground off the dance floor where the band played.

"Do you have any bags to check?"

He came to with a start. The gauze head-bandages from the face-lift had slipped down on one side.

"I'm sorry about the one eye," he said. "But I have two bags. I will carry the smaller on board."

"All right," the flight clerk said. He was a fine desk clerk with high cheekbones and a plastic identification badge. He had good hands, too, and it was with pleasure that through the one good eyehole he watched the clerk tie the baggage check to the handle of the big Vuitton with one hand, as it was supposed to be done if the bag was to be dominated properly, with the good brusque motion of the *recorte* and the baggage check truly fixed. He thought about the baggage itself, jiggling down the conveyor belt, and how it would disappear through the leather straps that hung down like a portcullis and maybe he would see the bag again at the LaGuardia. The LaGuardia was not the same since they had built the rust-colored parking building that obscured the view from the Grand Central Parkway, but then we were not the same either. He would miss the bag if it did not turn up at the LaGuardia, and went instead to the Logan, which was in Massachusetts and had the fogs. He would sorely be troubled if the bag went to the Logan. He had always packed a neat bag. It was a fine experience to open the bag up in the hotel room and see everything laid out just the way he had packed it, with the knuckle-dusters next to the big Christmas stocking he liked to hang at the foot of the bed.

"Smoking or nonsmoking?" the flight clerk asked him. He answered through the bandages. He asked for a window seat. Just then it occurred to him that when the stewardess came by with the tray of steamed towels and

---

[2]A familiar social figure of the times, in later years referred to as the "Social Moth" for criticizing a party to which he had not been invited in front of a man who turned out to be the host and who threw Zipkin down a staircase, at the foot of which he was caught by Nan Kempner, one of the great beauties and Zipkin-catchers of the day.

the tongs to grip them, which was what he truly liked about first class, he could not use the fine hot face towels because of the bandages on his face. It came with a rush; not as a rush of water or of wind but of a sudden evil-smelling emptiness.

He thought about being alone in the motel room in Akron with the big table lamps, having quarreled in Memphis, and he had started his enemies list, and how long it was, and he had used the Dewey decimal system to arrange it in the green calfskin notebooks. Under K there was Stanley Kauffmann, who had written forty unproduced plays and ten unpublished novels, which had wrecked him just about as much as any other thing had wrecked him, but it did not stop him from trying to wreck people who were writing true stories about Christmas in Alabama and how they hung the mule from the rafters. And Tynan, under T, Kenneth Tynan,[3] who had worn the same seersucker overcoat since the year the dwarfs came out on the Manzanares along the Prado road, and who wrote snide about his party in the Plaza where John Kenneth Galbraith[4] had danced the Turkey Trot. Under A, he had Dick Avedon, who had hung snide two portraits of him in the exhibition that had him young in the first and like an old goat in the other. He thought how good the notebooks felt to the touch, and how he could buy fill-ins at Cartier when the lists became too long, and how he could look in them when the time came. Vengeance went in pairs, on roller skates, and moved absolutely silently on the pavements.

He looked through the eyehole of his bandages at the standbys. They would begin to call them soon enough, and some of them would sit in coach. He had sat in coach once. But that was when he was beginning as a writer, and now that he was successful he liked the face towels and the tongs to grip them, and the crêpes with shrimp within and the tall green bottles of California Pinot and the seats that went back when you pushed the button. They had the buttons in coach but they did not have the hot towels and the other things. So when the time came and he had to work the fat off his soul and body, the way a fighter went into the mountains to work and train and burn it out, he didn't go into coach. He went to the fat farm, where they took his face and lifted it, and took a tuck in his behind as well, and they put the

---

[3]A drama critic and essayist whose work often appeared in the *New Yorker*.

[4]A tall cranelike economist of the times who espoused the curious Keynesian theory that it is better to set high prices than to pay them.

bandages on afterward. The sprinklers washed the grass early in the morning and the doctors had taken his vodka martinis away from him, and later on, up in the room, they took the cheese away from him too.

He thought about the people in the notebooks he wished were not there. He wrote things simply and truly that he had heard at the dinner tables when he sat with the very social and listened with the total recall that was either 94.6 or 96.8 percent, he never could remember which. They did not understand him when he wrote about this and wrote about what they talked about at the Côte Basque. So they cut him: Slim Keith, Mariella Agnelli, Pamela Harriman, Gloria Vanderbilt, Gloria Guinness, and so did Babe Paley, whom he loved and who called him "daughter." He knew he would never be invited to dine with Mr. Paley under the great tiger painting at the polished table which reflected the underside of the silverware. He tried not to think about that. You had to be equipped with good insides so that you did not go to pieces over such things. It was better to remember that the difference about the very social was that they were all very treacherous. Almost as treacherous as the very gauche were boring. They played too much backgammon. Lee Radziwill! The Princess, who looked fine in jodhpurs, although she never wore them that he could remember at the backgammon table, had a fine nose and a whispery way of talking. She had told him how Arthur Schlesinger had thrown Gore Vidal out of the White House onto Pennsylvania Avenue, which was the length of two football fields away from the front steps, a long toss for anyone, but which was logical enough if you knew what a great arm Schlesinger had and how he had gripped Vidal by the laces and spiraled him. He had remembered because it was a good story, and it told about Arthur Schlesinger's great arm and the proper way to grip Vidal if you had to throw him a long distance. So he had told the story in an interview in Playgirl *which was not as good a publication as* Der Querschnitt *or the* Frankfurter Zeitung, *but had a substantial number of readers anyway, and so Vidal sued him. The Princess did not support him. She said she could not remember telling him such a thing, which meant that she was treacherous, either that, or that she had a recall of .05 or 1.6, he couldn't decide which, which was not a great talent. He decided he would not take her to Schruns that Christmas where the snow, which he had never skied, was so bright it hurt your eyes when you looked out from the* Weinstube.

He hoped there would not be three nuns on the plane. That had been a superstition he had held to for as long as he could remember. It was involuntary, but then he was not a complete man. It was an inconvenience also. You could not dictate to the airlines not to seat three nuns. Once on his way by air to the chalet in Gstaad he had looked through the curtain into coach and three nuns were sitting in a row and he had called out, "Nuns! Nuns! Three nuns in coach!" It spoiled everything about that trip, but he knew he could not brawl with three nuns and ask them to defenestrate, even though they were over the Kaiser-Jägers at the time which had the sawmill and the valley above where it was a good place to walk the bulldog. Brawling with nuns was not part of the code by which he lived. Besides, if the nuns fought, the odds were three to one, and maybe more if the bishops sitting behind the nuns involved themselves.

He thought about the very rich, who were just the same as him, and how his talent started to erode. Perhaps it was because of the negrinos, and the cherry-pit taste of the good kirsch, and the margaritas with the salt around the rims, and the cool glasses of Tab the color of the Dese River above Noghera where the sails of the sailing barges moved through the countryside for Venice where off the Lido Beach he had sat on the bicycle paddle-boat with C. Z. Guest[5] and told wicked stories to her about C. Z. Guest. He could no longer write these wicked tales because he had the block, the writer's block, which with a wide snout like a hyena's, like death, had come and rested its head on his nice little Olivetti, and he could smell its breath. He had tried to send it away. He thought he would write about the great fights if the breath no longer dominated the Olivetti. About the Hemingway fight with Max Eastman over the chest hair in the office of Max Perkins, who always wore his hat indoors and had the sweet smile. Or maybe he could write about the time F. Scott Fitzgerald fought the six Argentinians. He would write about the zebra cushions of El Morocco where Humphrey Bogart had fought over the big stuffed panda that they had tried to take away from him, coming for the panda steadily and lumpily past the linen-clothed tables with the single roses in their thin vases, and the hatcheck girl had cried like a girl. He had once arm-wrestled with Bogart on the set of **Beat the Devil** *and he had won that one although Bogart had said, "Sweetheart, you wouldn't do this to an old character actor." He was very strong in the upper chest then, and still was, and he could pick up the front end of a Hillman Minx off a child with the best of them. He wanted to write about the night that Norman Mailer had hit Gore Vidal in the eye at Lally Weymouth's salon—the evening that Vidal had called "the night of the tiny fist." There had been the good remarks. Was it not Christopher Morley who said that a literary movement is two authors in town who hate each other? Was it not Robert Browning who had*

---

[5]One of the famous Cochrane sisters of Boston who among other things danced in the chorus of the Ziegfeld Follies before becoming a successful syndicated gardening columnist.

described Swinburne as a monkey creature "who sat in a sewer and added to it"? Ayee, that was fine. He himself had called Jack Kerouac a "typist," which was clever but he was not sure it compared and maybe it would not get into Bartlett's Quotations.

The writer's block moved a little closer. It crouched now, heavier, so that he could hardly breathe.

"You've got a hell of a breath," he told it.

It had no shape. It simply occupied space.

"Get off my Olivetti," he said.

And then the flight attendant said, "Will all those holding blue boarding passes board the plane," and the weight went from his chest, and suddenly it was all right.

It was difficult to get him into the plane because of what they had done to him in the fat farm operating room, but once in he lay back in the seat and they eased a cushion under him. He winced when the plane swung around and with one last bump rose and he saw the staff, some of them, waving, and the fat farm beside the hill, flattening out as they rose. He tried not to think about the hot towels and the tongs. He remembered that he was a new man again, his face lifted and perky as a jackal's under the bandages and his rear end tucked up and river-smooth. They had drawn him true and taut, so that his skin was as drumhead tight as the tuna's he had caught at Key West and eaten with long-tipped asparagus and a glass of Sancerre with Tennessee Williams sitting opposite. *Qué tal?* Tennessee, and he wished he had been named after a state, too, perhaps South Dakota, or Utah even, and not with a name shared with that peppery man who sold suits in Kansas City.

The plane began to climb and they were going to the East it seemed. They were in a storm, the rain as thick as if they were flying through a waterfall, and then they were out, and through the plane window he suddenly saw the great, high, shadow-pocked cathedral of Studiofiftyfour with the mothlike forms dancing, the hands clapping overhead, and the bare-chested sweepers, who built up their crotches with handkerchiefs, sweeping up the old poppers with long-handled brooms. And then he knew that this was where he was going. He thought about the smooth leather of the banquettes under his rear end and how he would look out and think about his enemies. *We will have some good destruction,* he thought.

In midwinter 1983 the editors of *Sports Illustrated* called me in for a conference on an issue coming up that was dated April 1. Perhaps they thought my background as a onetime editor of the *Harvard Lampoon* might be appropriate. The first idea was for me to do a straightforward report on practical jokes in sport. I indeed suggested this because the year before I had been fooled by an April Fool's joke that appeared in one of the major London newspapers. In that country it is a tradition to pay considerable attention to April first, especially in the media. Years ago the BBC did a famous, and very convincing, documentary about spaghetti farming. It showed farmers raking spaghetti out of trees, and the festivals afterward. It fooled a lot of people. What had fooled me was a news story that described a Japanese marathon runner who had turned up to run in the London marathon. Unable to speak the language, he had got things wrong—thinking he was supposed to run not for twenty-six miles but for twenty-six *days!* He had disappeared into the English countryside; he had been spotted running by a petrol station in East Anglia. His wife had called from Osaka, worried about him because he was such a determined sort of man. This account was sent me by my roommate at Cambridge. I fell for it. I called up Jerry Tax, an editor at *Sports Illustrated*.

"Jerry! There's a crazy Japanese marathon runner . . ." I

went on to explain. "I've got the article right here. He's been spotted in East Anglia. A great story. Jerry, don't you want me to go?"

"What's the date on the article?" Tax said after a pause.

"Uh-oh."

So I suggested writing about this sort of thing, but after a few conferences it turned out that despite research by stringers around the world, the pickings for an essay on practical jokes appropriate to April first were fairly slim. So finally Mark Mulvoy, the editor of *Sports Illustrated,* looked at me across the table and said: "George, why don't you do your own spoof for us?"

Pretty heady business! He was giving me license to try to hoodwink six million readers of the magazine. I remember leaving the conference bareheaded, without a coat, and walking out of the Time-Life Building into a rainstorm. Though a somewhat exalted comparison, the thought crossed my mind that Orson Welles must have felt the same kind of exhilaration when a network agreed to do his famous broadcast adaptation of H. G. Wells's *The War of the Worlds.*

When the story (about a pitcher named Sidd Finch who in the Himalayas had learned, mind over matter, to throw a ball at astonishing speeds) appeared, its verisimilitude was helped by the photographs. The *Sports Illustrated* photographer took a friend of his (a high-school teacher) to the training camp in St. Petersburg, Florida, to be the model for Finch. Incredibly, he was the embodiment of what Sidd Finch looked like in my mind's eye—lanky, long necked, small headed. The Mets cooperated as well, so the spoof was helped along with photos of Mel Stottlemyre, the pitching coach, conferring with Finch; or Ronn Reynolds, Finch's catcher, holding his catching hand and grimacing in pain from trying to handle the pitch thrown at that extraordinary speed.

The reaction to the article was extraordinary. Over a thousand letters were received. Many readers described how badly they had been duped. Others were furious that a magazine so devoted to accuracy should stoop to such a trick. My favorite complaint was from a subscriber who not only canceled his subscription to *Sports Illustrated* but also to *Fortune, Time, Life, Money, People,* all the Time-Life publications he had been receiving—just swept the table clear of them. "How you like them berries?" he had taunted at the end of his letter.

I continued to be interested in what would happen if somehow an athlete like Sidd Finch got into the major leagues equipped with that incredible arm. So I expanded the story into a full-length book with the same title as the *Sports Illustrated* article—*The Curious Case of Sidd Finch.*

People continue to think of Finch as a real person. "Hey, how's Sidd?" they call out. "The Mets could use him."

I grin, and if they stick around to talk about him I say that he's got a telephone number in London that I sometimes call. It never answers. But the other day I called and it was busy.

Fantasy: Sidd Finch

The secret cannot be kept much longer. Questions are being asked, and sooner rather than later the New York Mets management will have to produce a statement. It may have started unraveling in St. Petersburg, Florida, two weeks ago, on March 14, to be exact, when Mel Stottlemyre, the Met pitching coach, walked over to the forty-odd Met players doing their morning calisthenics at the Payson Field Complex not far from the Gulf of Mexico, a solitary figure among the pulsation of jumping jacks, and motioned three Mets to step out of the exercise. The three, all good prospects, were John Christensen, a twenty-four-year-old outfielder; Dave Cochrane, a spare but muscular switch-hitting third baseman; and Lenny Dykstra, a swift centerfielder who may be the Mets' leadoff man of the future.

Ordering the three to collect their bats and batting helmets, Stottlemyre led the players to the north end of the complex where a large canvas enclosure had been constructed two weeks before. The rumor was that some irrigation machinery was being installed in an underground pit.

Standing outside the enclosure, Stottlemyre explained what he wanted. "First of all," the coach said, "the club's got kind of a delicate situation here, and it would help if you kept reasonably quiet about it. Okay?" The three nodded. Stottlemyre said, "We've got a young pitcher we're looking at. We want to see what he'll do with a batter standing in the box. We'll do this alphabetically. John, go on in there, stand at the plate and give the pitcher a target. That's all you have to do."

"Do you want me to take a cut?" Christensen asked.

Stottlemyre produced a dry chuckle. "You can do anything you want."

Christensen pulled aside a canvas flap and found himself inside a rectangular area about ninety feet long and thirty feet wide, open to the sky, with a home plate set in the ground just in front of him, and down at the far end a pitcher's mound, with a small group of Met front-office personnel standing behind it, facing home plate. Christensen recognized Nelson Doubleday, the owner of the Mets, and Frank Cashen, wearing a long-billed fishing cap. He had never seen Doubleday at the training facility before.

Christensen bats righthanded. As he stepped around the plate he nodded to Ronn Reynolds, the stocky reserve catcher who has been with the Met organization since 1980. Reynolds whispered up to him from his crouch, "Kid, you won't believe what you're about to see."

A second flap down by the pitcher's end was drawn open, and a tall, gawky player walked in and stepped up onto the pitcher's mound. He was wearing a small, black fielder's glove on his left hand and was holding a baseball in his right. Christensen had never seen him before. He had blue eyes, Christensen remembers, and a pale, youthful face, with facial muscles that were motionless, like a mask. "You notice it," Christensen explained later, "when a pitcher's jaw *isn't* working on a chaw or a piece of gum." Then to Christensen's astonishment he saw that the pitcher, pawing at the dirt of the mound to get it smoothed out properly and to his liking, was wearing a heavy hiking boot on his right foot.

Christensen has since been persuaded to describe that first confrontation.

"I'm standing in there to give this guy a target, just waving the bat once or twice out over the plate. He starts his windup. He sways way back, like Juan Marichal, this hiking boot on the rubber—I thought maybe he was wearing it for balance or something—and he suddenly rears upright like a catapult. The ball is launched from an arm completely straight up and *stiff*. Before you can blink, the ball is in the catcher's mitt. You hear it *crack*, and then there's this little bleat from Reynolds."

Christensen said the motion reminded him of the extraordinary contortions that he remembered of Goofy's pitching in one of Walt Disney's cartoon classics.

"I never dreamed a baseball could be thrown that fast. The wrist must have a lot to do with it, and all that leverage. You can hardly see the blur of it as it goes by. As for hitting the thing, frankly, I just don't think it's humanly possible. You could send a blind man up there, and maybe he'd do better hitting at the *sound* of the thing."

Christensen's opinion was echoed by both Cochrane and Dykstra, who followed him into the enclosure. When each had done his stint, he emerged startled and awestruck.

Especially Dykstra. Offering a comparison for SI, he reported that out of curiosity he had once turned up the dials that control the motors of the pitching machine to maximum velocity, thus producing a pitch that went approximately one hundred and six miles per hour. "What I looked at in there," he said, motioning toward the enclosure, "was whistling by another third as fast, I swear."

The phenomenon the three young batters faced, and about whom only Reynolds, Stottlemyre and a few members of the Mets' front office know, is a twenty-eight-year-old, somewhat eccentric mystic named Hayden (Sidd) Finch. He may well change the course of baseball history. On St. Patrick's Day, to make sure they were not all victims of a crazy hallucination, the Mets brought in a radar gun to measure the speed of Finch's fastball. The model used was a JUGS Supergun II. It looks like a black space gun with a big snout, weighs about five pounds and is usually pointed at the pitcher from behind the catcher. A glass plate in the back of the gun shows the pitch's velocity—accurate, so the manufacturer claims, to within plus or minus one m.p.h. The figure at the top of the gauge is two hundred m.p.h. The fastest projectile ever measured by the JUGS (which is named after the oldtimer's descriptive—the "jug-handled" curveball) was a Roscoe Tanner serve that registered one hundred fifty-three m.p.h. The highest number that the JUGS had ever turned for a baseball was one hundred and three m.p.h., which it did, curiously, twice on one day, July 11, at the 1978 All-Star game when both Goose Gossage and Nolan Ryan threw the ball at that speed. On March 17, the gun was handled by Stottlemyre. He heard the pop of the ball in Reynolds's mitt and the little squeak of pain from the catcher. Then the astonishing figure 168 appeared on the glass plate. Stottlemyre remembers whistling in amazement, and then he heard Reynolds say, "Don't tell me, Mel, I don't want to know. . . ."

The Met front office is reluctant to talk about Finch. The fact is, they know very little about him. He has had no baseball career. Most of his life has been spent abroad, except for a short period at Harvard University.

The registrar's office at Harvard will release no information about Finch except that in the spring of 1976 he withdrew from the college in midterm. The alumni records in Harvard's Holyoke Center indicate slightly more. Finch spent his early childhood in an orphanage in Leicester, England and was adopted by a foster parent, the eminent archaeologist Francis Whyte-

Finch, who was killed in an airplane crash while on an expedition in the Dhaulagiri mountain area of Nepal. At the time of the tragedy, Finch was in his last year at the Stowe School in Buckingham, England, from which he had been accepted into Harvard. Apparently, though, the boy decided to spend a year in the general area of the plane crash in the Himalayas (the plane was never actually found) before he returned to the West and entered Harvard in 1975, dropping for unknown reasons the "Whyte" from his name. Hayden Finch's picture is not in the freshman yearbook. Nor, of course, did he play baseball at Harvard, having departed before the start of the spring season.

His assigned roommate was Henry W. Peterson, class of 1979, now a stockbroker in New York with Dean Witter, who saw very little of Finch. "He was almost never there," Peterson told SI. "I'd wake up morning after morning and look across at his bed, which had a woven native carpet of some sort on it—I have an idea he told me it was made of yak fur—and never had the sense it had been slept in. Maybe he slept on the floor. Actually, my assumption was that he had a girl in Somerville or something, and stayed out there. He had almost no belongings. A knapsack. A bowl he kept in the corner on the floor. A couple of wool shirts, always very clean, and maybe a pair or so of blue jeans. One pair of hiking boots. I always had the feeling that he was very bright. He had a French horn in an old case. I don't know much about French-horn music but he played beautifully. Sometimes he'd play it in the bath. He knew any number of languages. He was so adept at them that he'd be talking in English, which he spoke in this distinctive singsong way, quite Oriental, and he'd use a phrase like *pied-à-terre* and without knowing it he'd sail along in French for a while until he'd drop in a German word like *angst* and he'd shift to that language. For any kind of sustained conversation you had to hope he wasn't going to use a foreign buzz word—especially out of the Eastern languages he knew, like Sanskrit—because that was the end of it as far as I was concerned."

When Peterson was asked why he felt Finch had left Harvard, he shrugged his shoulders. "I came back one afternoon, and everything was gone—the little rug, the horn, the staff. . . . Did I tell you that he had this long kind of shepherd's crook standing in the corner? Actually, there was so little stuff to begin with that it was hard to tell he wasn't there anymore. He left a curious note on the floor. It turned out to be a Zen koan, which is one of those puzzles which cannot be solved by the intellect. It's the famous one about the live goose in the bottle. How do you get the goose out of the bottle without hurting it or breaking the glass? The answer is 'There, it's out!' I heard from him once, from Egypt. He sent pictures. He was on his way to Tibet to study."

Finch's entry into the world of baseball occurred last July in Old Orchard Beach, Maine, where the Mets' AAA farm club, the Tidewater Tides, was in town playing the Guides. After the first game of the series, Bob Schaefer, the Tides' manager, was strolling back to the hotel. He has very distinct memories of his first meeting with Finch: "I was walking by a park when suddenly this guy—nice-looking kid, clean-shaven, blue jeans, big boots— appears alongside. At first I think maybe he wants an autograph or to chat about the game, but no, he scrabbles around in a kind of knapsack, gets out a scuffed-up baseball and a small, black leather fielder's mitt that looks like it came out of the back of some Little League kid's closet. This guy says to me, 'I have learned the art of the pitch. . . .' Some odd phrase like that, delivered in a singsong voice, like a chant, kind of what you hear in a Chinese restaurant if there are some Chinese in there.

"I am about to hurry on to the hotel when this kid points out a soda bottle on top of a fence post about the same distance home plate is from the pitcher's rubber. He rears way back, comes around and pops the ball at it. Out there on that fence post the soda bottle *explodes*. It disintegrates like a rifle bullet hit it—just little specks of vaporized glass in a *puff*. Beyond the post I could see the ball bouncing across the grass of the park until it stopped about as far away as I can hit a three-wood on a good day.

"I said, very calm, 'Son, would you mind showing me that again?'

"And he did. He disappeared across the park to find the ball—it had gone so far, he was after it for what seemed fifteen minutes. In the meantime I found a tin can from a trash container and set it up for him. He did it again—just kicked that can off the fence like it was hit with a baseball bat. It wasn't the accuracy of the pitch so much that got to me but the *speed*. It was like the tin can got belted as soon as the ball left the guy's fingertips. Instantaneous. I thought to myself, 'My God, that kid's thrown the ball about a hundred and fifty m.p.h. Nolan Ryan's fastball is a change-up compared to what this kid just threw.'

"Well, what happens next is that we sit and talk, this kid and I, out there on the grass of the park. He sits with the big boots tucked under his legs, like one of those yoga guys, and he tells me he's not sure he wants to play big league baseball, but he'd like to give it a try. He's never played before, but he knows the rules, even the infield-fly rule, he tells me with a smile, and he knows he can throw a ball with complete accuracy and enormous velocity. He won't tell me how he's done this except that he 'learned it in the mountains, in a place called Po, in Tibet.' That is where he said he had learned to pitch . . . up in the mountains, flinging rocks and meditating. He told me his name was Hayden Finch, but he wanted to be called Sidd Finch. I said that most of the Sids we had in baseball came from Brooklyn. Or the Bronx. He said his Sidd came from Siddhartha, which means Aim Attained or The Perfect Pitch. That's what he had learned, how to throw the perfect pitch. Okay by me, I told him, and that's what I put on the scouting report, Sidd Finch. And I mailed it in to the front office."

The reaction in New York once the report arrived was one of complete disbelief. The assumption was that Schaefer was either playing a joke on his superiors or was sending in the figment of a very powerful wish-fulfillment dream. But Schaefer is one of the most respected men in the Met organization. Over the past seven years the clubs he has managed have won six championships. Dave Johnson, the Met manager, phoned him. Schaefer verified what he had seen in Old Orchard Beach. He told Johnson that sometimes he, too, thought he'd had a dream, but he hoped the Mets would send Finch an invitation so that, at the very least, his *own* mind would be put at rest.

When a rookie is invited to training camp, he gets a packet of instructions in late January. The Mets sent off the usual literature to Finch at the address Schaefer had supplied them. To their surprise, Finch wrote back with a number of stipulations. He insisted he would report to the Mets camp in St. Petersburg only with the understanding that: 1) there were no contractual commitments; 2) during off hours he be allowed to keep completely to himself; 3) he did not wish to be involved in any of the team drills or activities; 4) he would show the Mets his pitching prowess in privacy; 5) the whole operation in St. Petersburg was to be kept as secret as possible, with no press or photographs.

The reason for these requirements, he stated in a letter written (according to a source in the Met front office) in slightly stilted, formal, and very polite terminology—was that he had not decided whether he actually wanted to play baseball. He wrote apologetically that there were mental adjustments to be made. He did not want to raise the Mets' expectations, much less those of the fans, and then dash them. Therefore it was best if everything were carried on in secret or, as he put it in his letter, "in camera."

331

At first, the inclination of the Met front office was to disregard this nonsense out of hand and tell Finch either to apply himself through normal procedures or forget it. But the extraordinary statistics in the scouting report and Schaefer's verification of them were too intriguing to ignore. On February 2, Finch's terms were agreed to by letter. Mick McFadyen, the Mets' grounds keeper in St. Petersburg, was ordered to build the canvas enclosure in a far corner of the Payson complex, complete with a pitcher's mound and plate. Reynolds's ordeal was about to start.

Reynolds is a sturdy, hardworking catcher (he has been described as looking like a high-school football tackle). He has tried to be close-lipped about Finch, but his experiences inside the canvas enclosure have made it difficult for him to resist answering a few questions. He first heard about Finch from the Mets' general manager. "Mr. Cashen called me into his office one day in early March," Reynolds disclosed. "I was nervous because I thought I'd been traded. He was wearing a blue bow tie. He leaned across the desk and whispered to me that it was very likely I was going to be a part of baseball history. Big doings! The Mets had this rookie coming to camp and I was going to be his special catcher. All very hush-hush.

"Well, I hope nothing like that guy ever comes down the pike again. The first time I see him is inside the canvas coop, out there on the pitcher's mound, a thin kid getting ready to throw, and I'm thinking he'll want to toss a couple of warm-up pitches. So I'm standing behind the plate without a mask, chest protector, pads or anything, holding my glove up, sort of half-assed, to give him a target to throw at . . . and suddenly I see this windup like a pretzel gone loony, and the next thing, I've been blown two or three feet back, and I'm sitting on the ground with the ball in my glove. My catching hand feels like it's been hit with a sledgehammer."

He was asked: "Does he throw a curveball? A slider? Or a sinker?"

Reynolds grinned and shook his head. "Good questions! Don't ask me."

"Does it make a sound?"

"Yeah, a little *pft* . . . , *pft-BOOM!*"

Stottlemyre has been in direct charge of Finch's pitching regimen. His own playing career ended in the spring of 1975 with a rotator-cuff injury, which makes him especially sensitive to the strain that a pitching motion can put on the arm. Although as close-lipped as the rest of the staff, Stottlemyre does admit that Finch has developed a completely revolutionary pitching style. He told SI: "I don't understand the mechanics of it. Anyone who tries to throw the ball that way should fall flat on his back. But I've seen it. I've seen it a hundred times. It's the most awesome thing that has ever happened in baseball."

Asked what influences might have contributed to Finch's style and speed, Stottlemyre said, "Well, *cricket* may have something to do with it. Finch has taken the power and speed of the running throw of the cricket bowler and has somehow harnessed all that energy to the pitching rubber. The wrist snap off that stiff arm is incredible. I haven't talked to him but once or twice. I asked him if he ever thought of snapping the *arm,* like baseball pitchers, rather than the wrist: It would increase the velocity.

"He replied, very polite, you know, with a little bob of the head: 'I undertake as a rule of training to refrain from injury to living things.'

"He's right, of course. It's Ronn Reynolds I feel sorry for. Every time that ball comes in, first you hear this smack sound of the ball driving into the pocket of the mitt, and then you hear this little gasp, this *ai yee!—* the catcher, poor guy, his whole body shakin' like an angina's hit it. It's the most piteous thing I've ever heard, short of a trapped rabbit."

Hayden (Sidd) Finch arrived in St. Petersburg on February 7. Most of the rookies and minor-leaguers stay at the Edgewater Beach Inn. Assuming that Finch would check in with the rest of the early arrivals, the Mets were surprised when he telephoned and announced that he had leased a room in a small boardinghouse just off Florida Avenue near a body of water on the bay side called Big Bayou. Because his private pitching compound had been constructed across the city and Finch does not drive, the Mets assigned him a driver, a young Tampa Bay resident, Eliot Posner, who picks him up in the morning and returns him to Florida Avenue or, more often, to a beach on the Gulf where, Posner reports, Finch, still in his baseball outfit and carrying his decrepit glove, walks down to the water's edge and, motionless, stares out at the windsurfers. Inevitably, he dismisses Posner and gets back to his boardinghouse on his own.

The Met management has found out very little about his life in St. Petersburg. Mrs. Roy Butterfield, his landlady, reports (as one might expect) that "he lives very simply. Sometimes he comes in the front door, sometimes the back. Sometimes I'm not even sure he spends the night. I think he sleeps on the floor—his bed is always neat as a pin. He has his own rug, a small little thing. I never have had a boarder who brought his own rug. He has a soup bowl. Not *much,* is what I say. Of course, he plays the French horn. He plays it very beautifully and, thank goodness, softly. The notes fill the house. Sometimes I think the notes are coming out of my television set."

Probably the member of the Met staff who has gotten the closest to Finch is Posner. When Posner returns to the Payson complex, inevitably someone rushes out from the Mets' offices asking, "Did he say anything? What did he say?"

Posner takes out a notebook.

"Today he said, 'When your mind is empty like a canyon you will know the power of the Way.' "

"Anything else?"

"No."

While somewhat taxed by Finch's obvious eccentricities, and with the exception of the obvious burden on the catchers, the Mets, it seems, have an extraordinary property in their camp. But the problem is that no one is sure if Finch really wants to play. He has yet to make up his mind; his only appearances are in the canvas enclosure. Reynolds moans in despair when he is told Finch has arrived. Sometimes his ordeal is short-lived. After Finch nods politely at Reynolds and calls down *"Namas-te!"* (which means "greetings" in Sanskrit), he throws only four or five of the terrifying pitches before, with a gentle smile, he announces *"Namas-te!"* (it also means "farewell") and gets into the car to be driven away.

One curious manifestation of Finch's reluctance to commit himself entirely to baseball has been his refusal to wear a complete baseball uniform. Because he changes in his rooming house, no one is quite sure what he will be wearing when he steps through the canvas flap into the enclosure. One afternoon he turned up sporting a tie hanging down over the logo on his jersey, and occasionally—as Christensen noticed—he wears a hiking boot on his right foot. Always, he wears his baseball cap back to front—the conjecture among the Met officials is that this sartorial behavior is an indication of his ambivalence about baseball.

In hopes of understanding more about him, in early March the Mets called in a specialist in Eastern religions, Dr. Timothy Burns, the author of, among other treatises, *Satori, or Four Years in a Tibetan Lamasery.* Not allowed to speak personally with Finch for fear of "spooking him," Burns was able only to speculate about the Mets' newest player.

According to sources from within the Met organization, Burns told a meeting of the club's top brass that the strange ballplayer in their midst was very likely a *trapas,* or aspirant monk.

A groan is said to have gone up from Nelson Doubleday. Burns said that Finch was almost surely a disciple of Tibet's great poet-saint Lama Milaraspa, who was born in the eleventh century and died in the shadow of Mount Everest. Burns told them that Milaraspa was a great yogi who could manifest an astonishing phenomenon: He could produce "internal heat," which allowed him to survive snowstorms and intense cold, wearing only a thin robe of white cotton. Finch does something similar—an apparent deflection of the huge forces of the universe into throwing a baseball with bewildering accuracy and speed through the process of *siddhi,* namely the yogic mystery of mind-body. He mentioned that *The Book of Changes,* the *I Ching,* suggests that all acts (even throwing a baseball) are connected with the highest spiritual yearnings. Utilizing the Tantric principle of body and mind, Finch has decided to pitch baseballs—at least for a while.

The Mets pressed Burns. Was there any chance that Finch would come to his senses and *commit* himself to baseball?

"There's a chance," Burns told them. "You will remember that the Buddha himself, after what is called the Great Renunciation, finally realized that even in the most severe austerities—though he conquered lust and fear and acquired a great deal of self-knowledge—truth itself could not necessarily be found. So after fasting for six years he decided to eat again."

Reached by SI at the University of Maryland, where he was lecturing last week, Burns was less sanguine. "The biggest problem Finch has with baseball," he said over the phone, "is that Nirvana, which is the state all Buddhists wish to reach, means literally 'the blowing out'—specifically the purifying of oneself of greed, hatred and delusion. Baseball," Burns went on, "is symbolized to a remarkable degree by those very three aspects: greed (huge money contracts, stealing second base, robbing a guy of a base hit, charging for a seat behind an iron pillar, etc.), hatred (players despising management, pitchers hating hitters, the Cubs detesting the Mets, etc.) and delusion (the slider, the pitchout, the hidden-ball trick and so forth). So you can see why it is not easy for Finch to give himself up to a way of life so opposite to what he has been led to cherish."

Burns is more puzzled by Finch's absorption with the French horn. He suspects that in Tibet Finch may have learned to play the *krang-gling,* a Tibetan horn made of human thighbones, or perhaps even the Tibetan long trumpet, the *dung-chen,* whose sonorous bellowing in those vast Himalayan defiles is somewhat echoed in the lower registers of the French horn.

The Mets' inner circle believes that Finch's problem may be that he cannot decide between baseball and a career as a horn player. In early March the club contacted Bob Johnson, who plays the horn and is the artistic director of the distinguished New York Philomusica ensemble, and asked him to come to St. Petersburg. Johnson was asked to make a clandestine assessment of Finch's ability as a horn player and, even more important, to make contact with him. The idea was that, while praising him for the quality of his horn playing, Johnson should try to persuade him that the lot of a French-horn player (even a very fine one) was not an especially gainful one. Perhaps *that* would tip the scales in favor of baseball.

Johnson came down to St. Petersburg and hung around Florida Avenue for a week. He reported later to SI: "I was being paid for it, so it wasn't bad. I spent a lot of time looking up, so I'd get a nice suntan. Every once in a while I saw Finch coming in and out of the rooming house, dressed to play baseball and carrying a funny-looking black glove. Then one night I heard the French horn. He was playing it in his room. I have heard many great horn players in my career—Bruno Jaenicke, who played for Toscanini; Dennis Brain, the great British virtuoso; Anton Horner of the Philadelphia Orchestra—and I would say Finch was on a par with them. He was playing Benjamin Britten's "Serenade," for tenor horn and strings—a haunting, tender piece that provides great space for the player—when suddenly he produced a big, evocative *bwong* sound that seemed to shiver the leaves of the trees. Then he shifted to the rondo theme from the trio for violin, piano and horn by Brahms—just sensational. It may have had something to do with the Florida evening and a mild wind coming in over Big Bayou and tree frogs, but it was *remarkable.* I told this to the Mets, and they immediately sent me home—presuming, I guess, that I was going to hire the guy. That's not so farfetched. He can play for the Philomusica anytime."

Meanwhile, the Mets are trying other ways to get Finch into a more positive frame of mind about baseball. Inquiries among American lamaseries (there are more than one hundred Buddhist societies in the U.S.) have been quietly initiated in the hope of finding monks or priests who are serious baseball fans and who might persuade Finch that the two religions (Buddhism and baseball) are compatible. One plan is to get him into a movie theater to see *The Natural,* the mystical film about baseball, starring Robert Redford. Another film suggested is the baseball classic *It Happens Every Spring,* starring Ray Milland as a chemist who, by chance, discovers a compound that avoids wood; when applied to a baseball in the film, it makes Milland as effective a pitcher as Finch is in real life.

Conversations with Finch himself have apparently been exercises in futility. All conventional inducements—huge contracts, advertising tie-ins, the banquet circuit, ticker-tape parades, having his picture on a Topps bubble-gum card, chatting on *Kiner's Korner* (the Mets' postgame TV show) and so forth—mean little to him. As do the perks ("You are very kind to offer me a Suzuki motorcycle, but I cannot drive"). He has very politely declined whatever overtures the Mets have offered. The struggle is an absolutely internal one. He will resolve it. Last week he announced that he would let the management know what he was going to do on or around April 1.

Met manager Davey Johnson has seen Finch throw about half a dozen pitches. He was impressed ("If he didn't have this great control, he'd be like the Terminator out there. Hell, that fastball, if off-target on the inside, would carry a batter's kneecap back into the catcher's mitt"), but he is leaving the situation to the front office. "I can handle the pitching rotation; let them handle the monk." He has had one meeting with Finch. "I was going to ask him if we could at least give him a decent fielder's mitt. I asked him why he was so attached to the piece of rag he was using. 'It is,' the guy told me, 'the only one I have.' Actually, I don't see why he needs a better one. All he will ever need it for is to catch the ball for the next pitch. So then I said to him, 'There's only one thing I can offer you, Finch, and that's a fair shake.' "

According to Jay Horwitz, the Mets' public-relations man, Finch smiled at the offer of the fair shake and nodded his head politely—perhaps because it was the only nonmaterial offer made. It did not encroach on Finch's ideas about the renunciation of worldly goods. It was an ingenious, if perhaps unintentional, move on the manager's part.

Nelson Doubleday is especially hopeful about Finch's ultimate decision. "I think we'll bring him around," he said a few days ago. "After all, the guy's not a nut, he's a Harvard man."

In the meantime the Mets can only wait. Finch periodically turns up at the enclosure. Reynolds is summoned. There are no drills. Sometimes Finch throws for five minutes, instantly at top speed, often for half an hour. Then he leaves. Security around the enclosure has been tight. Since Finch has not signed with the Mets, he is technically a free agent and a potential find for another club. The curious, even Met players, are politely shooed away from the Payson Field enclosure. So far Finch's only association with Met players (other than Reynolds) has been the brief confrontation with Christensen, Cochrane and Dykstra when the front office nervously decided to test his control with a batter standing in the box. If he decides to play baseball, he will leave his private world of the canvas enclosure and join manager Johnson and the rest of the squad. For the first time Gary Carter, the Mets' regular catcher, will face the smoke of the Finch pitch, and the other pitchers will stand around and gawk. The press will have a field day ("How do you spell Siddhartha? How do you grip the ball? How do you keep your balance on the mound?"). The Mets will try to protect him from the glare and help him through the most traumatic of culture shocks, praying that in the process he will not revert and one day disappear.

Actually, the presence of Hayden (Sidd) Finch in the Mets' training camp raises a number of interesting questions. Suppose the Mets (and Finch himself) can assuage and resolve his mental reservations about playing baseball; suppose he is signed to a contract (one wonders what an ascetic whose major possessions are a bowl, a small rug, a long stick and a French horn might demand); and suppose he comes to New York's Shea Stadium to open the season against the St. Louis Cardinals on April 9. It does not matter that he has never taken a fielding drill with his teammates. Presumably he will mow down the opposition in a perfect game. Perhaps Willie McGee will get a foul tip. Suppose Johnson discovers that the extraordinary symbiotic relationship of mind and matter is indefatigable—that Finch can pitch day after day at this blinding, unhittable speed. What will happen to Dwight Gooden? Will Carter and the backup catchers last the season? What will it do to major league baseball as it is known today?

Peter Ueberroth, baseball's new commissioner, was contacted by SI in his New York office. He was asked if he had heard anything about the Mets' new phenomenon.

No, he had not. He had heard some *rumors* about the Mets' camp this spring, but nothing specific.

Did the name Hayden (Sidd) Finch mean anything to him?

Nope.

The commissioner was told that the Mets had a kid who could throw the ball over one hundred and fifty m.p.h. Unhittable.

Ueberroth took a minute before he asked, "Roll that by me again?"

He was told in as much detail as could be provided about what was going on within the canvas enclosure of the Payson compound. It was possible that an absolute superpitcher was coming into baseball—so remarkable that the delicate balance between pitcher and batter could be turned into disarray. What was baseball going to do about it?

"Well, before any decisions, I'll tell you something," the commissioner finally said, echoing what may very well be a nationwide sentiment this coming season. "I'll have to see it to believe it!"

Humor

Q: *I understand you have some things to say about humor.*

A: Absolutely not. Wasn't it the lemur, the true Madagascan lemur, we were supposed to be discussing?

Q: *No, I'm afraid not.*

A: Oh. Well, that *is* a shame, because I've really been boning up on the lemurs.

Q: *In that case we'll start off with some rather simple questions about humor. What strikes you as humorous?*

A: Kurt Vonnegut once described what he thought—actually it was what his *sister* thought—was the funniest sight ever seen . . . namely someone who has caught her heel somehow, and as the streetcar door opens, she emerges *horizontally*—as straight as a board, facedown, and about two feet off the ground. Kurt said his sister laughed for two weeks after that.

Q: *Do you find that especially funny . . . that horizontal woman?*

A: Yes . . . the visual, slapstick part of it—that woman absolutely horizontal out over the pavement. Of course, a millisecond later the whole scenario changes to possible tragedy; that is, unless the woman drops completely out of sight into a pothole and a little while later you hear a distant splash and a fountain of water appears up from below. That would keep the comic aspect going for a bit longer. It's a very fragile sort of thing. You never know what is going to ignite one's fancy. Just about the hardest *I* have ever laughed was during the Olympics Opening Day ceremonies produced by David Wolper when eighty-eight grand pianos, one for each key, were wheeled out onto the great balustrade of the Coliseum and a vast array of gentlemen in white tie and tails sat down to play Gershwin's *Rhapsody in Blue.*

Q: Why is that funny?

A: Well, I'm not sure that it is. No one else in my section was laughing. The person I was with pretended she wasn't with me. I think it was the thought of one of those pianists getting a phone call from his agent, telling him he had arranged to have him play *Rhapsody in Blue* at the Opening Day ceremonies. An audience of a hundred thousand in the Coliseum! The pianist would exclaim, "Oh, my God!", after which the agent would have to explain, "Well, Mel, you're not doing it all alone. . . ."

"Twin pianos? Who's the other guy?"

"No, there're eighty-eight of you all together."

"Eighty . . . !"

It may be that musical instruments make me laugh more than they should—for example, a middle-aged man straining at an English horn. Actually it's not all that uncommon a reaction. Do you remember the Cary Grant–Ingrid Bergman film *Indiscreet?* In it is a scene in which Cary Grant is explaining how at his first recital—he's learning how to play the violin—the audience starts to laugh.

Bergman asks him why.

Cary Grant says as follows: "All left-handed violinists make people laugh."

Bergman asks him if he'd ever thought of playing the violin *right*-handed. Grant produces the funniest line in the whole episode, come to think of it. He says, "I tried, but I kept moving the violin instead of the bow."

Q: What's the funniest thing you've ever seen on television?

A: On the Johnny Carson show one evening I saw Carson being attacked by a large, long-necked emu-like bird that a man—a British puppeteer, I believe—wore on his arm like a sleeve. He manipulated this bird wondrously. The one movable part was a large yellow beak. I don't believe the bird ever said anything. He simply reacted and *interacted* with what the two men were saying, looking from one to the other out of this pair of baleful eyes over that alarming beak. At one point the bird was ignited by something—perhaps a cream pie was involved, I've forgotten—and he shot forward, and behaving something like a boa constrictor, he toppled Carson to the floor so that with the other man in there trying to wrest the bird away, the television screen was suddenly filled with this spirited and comic clutter. I rose from the edge of the bed where I'd been sitting and went sailing around the room guffawing . . . I mean, truly. I'm not sure I didn't sit back down on the edge of the bed and *slap my knee.*

Q: Why that?

A: That's supposed to be the ultimate in laughter response. That and to laugh from the belly, which I've never seen, either. I believe the knee slapper is a kind of sweeping action, a glancing blow, like this . . . ow!

Q: Are you all right?

A: It's a bit more glancing than what I just showed you.

Q: To get back to that bird . . .

A: Well, once again it indicates what an exquisitely thin margin exists between high comedy and something really quite ugly—not unlike the scene that Kurt Vonnegut's sister found so amusing. When the bird suddenly went berserk and bore Carson kicking to the floor, you could see Carson giggling away throughout his problems with this monster bird, which made it all the funnier. But you knew that if Carson suddenly got uppity about what he was going through—after all, he was being *humiliated* on the floor, *pecked* at—and turned grim and *fought back* at that bird, throwing a couple of big hooks, then, of course, the whole mood of the evening would have changed. I am also very taken with the amateur pet contest that David Letterman occasionally has on his late-night show. Highly captivating! It should be announced in *The New York Times* when he is going to have one of them on the air. The animals are usually dogs who with their owners come trotting on stage *utterly* in command, full of curiosity about where they are, oozing confidence. They very rarely do what they're called upon to do, but it doesn't make any difference. Their performances, or lack of them, are highly engaging. Letterman replays them in slow motion. Brilliant concept. Sometimes the animals actually do what they're supposed to. I remember a fluffy cutie-pie kind of dog with grave black eyes leaping into a succession of boxes, each smaller than the one preceding it, until finally the dog hunkered down into a box like someone squeezing into a small bathing suit. Then a replay. The dog was exactly right for this sort of stunt. It wore one of those beguiling, sheepish looks, as if knowing it had done something quite astounding without quite knowing what or why. It occurred to me that to face a firing squad of these dogs would be as soothing a way as any to slide into the Great Beyond.

Q: I beg your pardon.
A: A very slight passing fancy, I assure you.

Q: Is nudity ever funny?
A: No. True, the behind has a kind of comic virtue—after all, the behind seen face-to-face offers a sort of vertical and quite charming smile . . . hence mooning. It would not work with the other side of the body. So by and large, nudity won't do as a comedic ploy. Why do you ask?

Q: Well, I was thinking of comic props and trademarks.
A: You mean like George Burns's cigars, Joe Frisco's stutter, and Joe E. Lewis saying things like "Post time"—signatures?

Q: Exactly.
A: Well, I doubt nudity will serve—

Q: What is the funniest prop you've come across recently?
A: Not long ago I heard about a professional wrestler called the Alaskan Ax. His stock-in-trade was that he had a kind of collapsible foldup ax he secreted in his jockstrap, which, when he would find himself *in extremis,* he would reach for and extract. He'd step back from his opponent and snap this thing open, section after section, until it elongated into an *ax!* Double-edged blade and all. And the funny thing, of course, was to see the *other* guy, whose gimmick was something quite simple, a Viking's beard, for instance, or a midget manager, and he would look over, his eyes bulging at this guy sashaying around the ring whipping an *ax* around as if it were a twig! I never saw this—never having been to a professional wrestling match—but it amuses me enormously to consider. I may have dreamed it. I hope not. If I may make a sudden interjection . . . ?

Q: I don't see why not.
A: I've often thought that a good name for a professional wrestler would be

the Grecian Urn. The Grecian Urn wouldn't be an especially potent force
. . . in fact, his stock-in-trade would be that when lifted aloft by the Brute,
or whoever, he would let loose this tiny high scream and the Brute would
put him carefully back down. The Grecian Urn would hardly be a main-
liner. He'd fight in the prelims. You'd never see him in there against the
Alaskan Ax.

Q: How are you as a joke teller yourself?
A: I very rarely attempt one. I tend to forget the essential point. For instance,
if the joke is: "My father-in-law saw a sign: DRINK CANADA DRY. So he
went up there," I tend, in the retelling of it, to leave out the operational
word *drink.* So when asked to tell the latest "good" one I've heard, I clear
my throat and say, "Well, okay, here's one: 'My father-in-law saw a sign.
CANADA DRY. So he went up there.' " I think you'll agree it loses something in my telling of it.

Q: But weren't you a stand-up comic at Caesars Palace?
A: Yes. It was a television special for DuPont called "Did You Hear the One
About?" It was produced by David Wolper, the same fellow who was
responsible for all those pianos in the Coliseum. The idea was that I would
be trained as a stand-up comic by a number of splendid helping hands—
let's see: Steve Allen, Woody Allen, Milton Berle, Jack Carter, Dick
Cavett, Phyllis Diller, David Frye, Buddy Hackett, Bob Hope, Phil Silvers, and Jonathan Winters. This extraordinary lineup of coaches were
supposed to get me ready to go onstage with a comic act in a regular show
at Caesars Palace in Las Vegas. Big-time stuff. *Very* big-time stuff.

Q: Were you provided with a routine?
A: I was. By the two head writers of the show *Laugh-In,* which was one of
the triumphs of those distant times. I don't remember much about *Laugh-
In.* Stars would put their heads through holes in the set and say funny
things.

Q: What sort of routine did they produce for you?
A: I always thought they were trying to snakebite me. In fact, years later,
David Wolper told me he had asked them for rank mediocrity in the
routine because he thought it would be more interesting to a television
audience if I *struggled* rather than breezed through an act.

Q: What sort of a routine was it?

A: Rank and mediocre . . . full of topical jokes about Howard Hughes and John Wayne. I can remember one of them. "Howard Hughes. Now *there's* a man with a lot on his mind. When he heard I was going to be performing here on the great stage of Caesars Palace, he went out and tried to sell the hotel. And let me tell you something. He doesn't even *own* the place."

Q: Mmm.

A: The upshot of this was that I went around to see the writers and I said to them as follows: "I don't think, somehow, you've captured my style." They said, "Plimpton, if we could capture your style, we'd put it in a cage and club it to death." Which was a fine line and indeed of a caliber they had not produced for *my* act.

Q: Did they change the routine for you?

A: No, they didn't. They tried to encourage me by saying I had an infectious smile. They admitted it wasn't infectious enough to pull me through the whole act but that I should certainly utilize it as often as possible. There were other critiques. Listening to me rehearse those dreadful lines ("Howard Hughes. Now *there's* a man with a lot on his mind. . . .") Steve Allen said I sounded too much like Cordell Hull, who was one of the more solemn statesmen of the time. He kept saying, "Try to sound less like Cordell Hull." There were other pieces of advice. Most had to do with confidence. Milton Berle said, "Hold the whip over the audience. You're the boss; let them be the employee." Jack Carter warned me, "There's nothing worse than an insecure audience that senses that you're in trouble because they come in right away for the kill." Phyllis Diller remarked that just before going out onto the stage she whispered, literally, to the audience "I love you," I suppose in the hope they'd respond accordingly. Steve Allen echoed all of this by urging, "Even if you don't have confidence in every joke, pretend that you do, okay?"

On the other hand, Bob Hope told me, "You know, they like a sneaky fellow that tells funny lines and doesn't *think* they're funny himself." It was all very puzzling. Perhaps the most straightforward comment came from Woody Allen. He told me, not long before I went out, "it could be fun . . . but I doubt it." The most bizarre suggestion was Jonathan Winters's, which was that I should make my entrance by pulling the curtain back just a bit, sticking my head out like a man peeking out from behind a shower curtain, and I should say, "Hi!"

Q: Did you practice your routine in front of Woody Allen?
A: I didn't dare. I told him I was not very confident about my writers.

Q: Did they give you any advice before you walked out on the stage?
A: Steve Allen told me not to worry when my tie dropped off. It was not *if* but *when!*

Q: What about more practical advice?
A: Well, that's enormously practical advice.

Q: What was it like out there on the big stage of Caesars Palace? Did you remember to flash the infectious smile at them?
A: Well, it wasn't the infectious smile that was getting them; it was Steve Allen's infectious *laugh.* Fortunately he was in the audience. Come to think of it, that's an enormously important adjunct to a comedy act—the infectious laugh. There have been some famous examples: William O. Harbach. He was the producer of Steve Allen's television show and had a very distinctive bellow from the back of the theater. And, of course, Ed McMahon's, whose chuckling is so often the saving of Johnny Carson's opening monologue. In any case, Steve Allen's laugh rose out of the darkness of Caesars Palace, carrying with it, thank God, a great variety of chuckles, hums, giggles, ah-ahs, snickers, et cetera, nothing really *weighty* from the audience, not a knee slapper in the lot but enough to make me realize as I went through that appalling routine that there were people out there taking it in with mild pleasure. A very curious analogy came to me afterward . . . that it was like fishing at night—casting a plug (the joke) out into the darkness, hearing it splash in the distance, and then, if the joke worked, feeling the weight of the audience's response on the line; it was a heady business if the laughter rose. Then, of course, one had to cast again and sometimes there was *nothing,* as if the plug had sprung loose from the line and sailed off on its own, and all that one was retrieving was the line itself, snaking through the lily pads, not a smidgen of drag. That was when the perspiration began to prickle on the forehead; it was what comedians called flop sweat.

Q: Were you relieved when it was all over?
A: Very much so. The greatest relief was knowing I didn't have to go out there and make a living at it. That is one of the charms of participatory journalism—you're only dabbling in other people's professions.

Q: Did you take away any particularly vivid impressions of the comedians?
A: I have fleeting memories of all of them. Phil Silvers told me what it was like to live in a houseful of daughters: The toilet seats were always down. Phyllis Diller lives in a house of bright reds so that to walk around in it was like being caught in a kaleidoscope of parasol pinks. Jack Carter was always testing the material of my clothes between his fingers and talking about suits. Bob Hope told me an interesting story. He had become so conditioned to fame, to the adulatory stares, the quick smiles in the street, the "Hi, Bobs" to such a degree that when he went to the Soviet Union where people walk around with downcast eyes and no one knew him anyway, he became quite paranoid and had to hurry back to the United States to make sure that his world was still in good order. He rushed down the street to the "Hi Bobs" and the big smiles, and the nightmare was over.

Q: Are they fun to be with?
A: Well, I am literally feebleminded in the company of famous people who are comedians. I tend to assume everything they say is funny. One of these exalted folks can lean forward out of a chair in a living room, look at a watch, and ask, "Would you like some tea?" and I go very nearly to pieces. I lift a hand to bring it down upon a knee.

Q: But aren't they funnier than the rest of us? Aren't they always on, as they say?
A: Some are, I guess. To have lunch with Milton Berle is not to eat. The most original one I met was Jonathan Winters. We went to the zoo together. He kept breaking out into little skits, ignited by what he saw around him. That was what Robert Frost said about writing poetry, wasn't it?—association—*this* reminding him of *that.* In front of the bear cage Winters in rapid succession became *all* the members of a suburban family on an outing, the youngest of whom, a child, has gotten into the cage with the bears. I've forgotten the intricacies of the drama, except that the bears rather took to the child, and he to them, and the family attitude after a while became sort of ho-hum. In fact, they started taking Polaroids.

Q: *Are comedians intelligent?*

A: They are alarmingly intelligent. After all, they have to construct a view of life to put on display, and then play off it, which is not something that the rest of us are compelled to do. Except politicians, who are much less proficient at it than comedians, wouldn't you agree?

Q: *I am not here to respond.*

A: Well, considering the embarrassment you've caused by not addressing yourself to the question of lemurs rather than humor, I was hoping you'd offer a helpful . . . opinion.

Q: *What emerged from all of this? Was there anything to be deduced?*

A: My adventure reinforced that curious thing about humor, which is that it is so prevalent and yet so rare. What I mean is that everyone laughs ten or twelve times a day, just as a matter of course, unless something awful has happened—an aunt found murdered in the tool house. Perhaps a fur trapper in the woods of Maine would be low on the laugh meter because nothing much happens during his day in the woods that would dredge up even a *smile.* A funny woodpecker? I don't know. But in the cosmopolitan areas, laughter is very general because it is an essential by-product of communication. Of course, some people are better than others at producing laughter, but the fact is there are vast numbers of us who laugh. And yet the *professional* laugh-getter is an unbelievably rare commodity. In a nation of two hundred million people, the huge majority of whom laugh constantly, there are only . . . well, how many? . . . I'd be hard-pressed to name more than ten or twelve top-ranked comedians.

Q: *Why does such a distinction exist?*

A: It's because there's such an enormous gulf between the amateur, everyone's favorite in the family, the uncle from Schenectady who tells the one about the moose and the professional who performs before an audience he doesn't know in a lounge in Las Vegas.

Q: *What is the secret?*

A: I came out of it with a sense that it is very important for anyone trying comedy—at least visual comedy—to cultivate a persona, to develop an instantly recognizable character for an audience. That's why the comic in the living room, that uncle who does the terrific imitation of the moose in rut, with accompanying sounds and everything, wouldn't succeed if he tried the same act in a Las Vegas lounge. What convulses everyone ("Do the moose bit, Charlie!") at the Smiths' Saturday night party doesn't work because he has no "recognizable business," as they used to call it. He hasn't established a character. Sometimes it doesn't take much. A cigar. A cane. A stutter. Dean Martin sashays out there on to the stage with a shot glass and everybody roars with laughter and is instantly comfortable. Jack Benny used to raise a laugh simply by rubbing his hands and saying, "We . . . ll" in that inimitable way of his. We can't do that. We haven't established a persona. If we went out there and rubbed our hands together, nothing at all would happen. Nothing. It's too bad, isn't it? But then it means, of course, we can buy tickets and marvel at those rare few.

Q: *What would you suggest for someone who has no sense of humor?*
A: In a place like Caesars Palace you can take your cue from the musicians in the band, that is if you can see them back there in the shadows. They have heard the comedian's routine night after night. If you see them chuckling away, their teeth shining, you can assume either that it's a first night and they're hearing the routine for the first time or that you're listening to a comedian of considerable talent who continues to make them laugh. Watch them. Then you can let loose a laugh or two. The timing is important. You'll want to laugh when everyone else is laughing.

Q: *And the knee slap?*
A: The principle is the same. You don't want to slap your knee when the comedian is leading up to the punch line.

Q: *That's probably the most important piece of information you've divested yourself of tonight.*
A: Very likely.

Q: *What's the largest of the lemurs?*
A: Ah! Now we're on familiar ground. . . .

Managing to Wrestle

It mostly happens at cocktail parties. Somebody comes up and asks, "What's next?" It is assumed that my career as a participatory journalist continues unabated and that surely I must be getting ready to do *something*—a tightrope walk across the gorge at Niagara, a hang glide off K2, being a nightclub bouncer, playing elephant polo in Jaipur. . . . I usually murmur that I have a number of things in mind—singing grand opera, perhaps, or thumping a tambourine in a rock group, or something in big-time wrestling. . . .

"Wrestling? You mean you're going to get in there with the Sheik or Hulk Hogan?"

"No, no," I hasten to say. "I've been thinking of *managing* a wrestler." "Oh." Do I sense a flicker of disappointment?

The fact is, I *have* been giving some thought to big-time wrestling. I catch glimpses of it on television from time to time—highly theatrical, peopled by splendidly flamboyant characters. I have even come up with the name of a wrestler I might manage—the Grecian Urn. My protégé. He emerges in my mind's eye: very large, of course, up in the three-hundred- to four-hundred-pound class. Around his belly is tattooed the kind of frieze described in Keats's poem—satyrs chasing maidens, and so forth. The rest of his body sports a number of lines ("Beauty is truth, truth beauty . . . all ye need to know") that the spectators can read as the Urn is revolved slowly above the head of Hulk Hogan or whomever before being hurled to the canvas in a body slam.

I see myself leading him down the aisle to the ring. He is wearing a laurel wreath, and I suspect he minces a bit or at least is very arty once he gets through the ropes, a characteristic that would be expected by the wrestling crowd of anyone identified with the Muse. He angers and puzzles the spectators in the front rows by spouting annoying little snippets of verse at them ("Ye elves of hills, brooks, standing lakes, and groves"; "Divine I am inside and out"; "The salt is on the briar rose, the fog is in the fir trees"). Once the fight is on, the Urn directs his lines at his opponent, perhaps quoting from the "Ode" itself ("Bold Lover, never, never canst thou kiss") as he circles warily away, taunting him, mocking him for not being a member of the Institute of Arts and Letters, for not being able to identify either Molly or Harold Bloom, for not being able to spell *syzygy* or whatever. The first time his opponent gets a grip around him, he cries out, "Hold off! Unhand me, gray-beard loon!" I see him trying to bribe the referee in midfight ("Thou fair-haired angel of the evening"). On the few occasions he has his opponent under him, close to a pin, he announces with a weird grin, "I am the grass; I cover all." Then, when the tables are turned and the Urn is thrashing around in the coils of some monstrous grip, he calls out, "With rue my heart is laden." And at the last, with his shoulders an inch off the canvas, the referee belly-down, about to count him out, the Urn bellows like an expiring buffalo, "I am dying, Egypt, dying!" and it is over. I see myself helping him through the ropes and supporting him up the aisle to the dressing room. His laurel wreath is awry, and the crowd hisses and beats at him with rolled-up programs.

As for my own duties as the Grecian Urn's manager, I imagine myself getting him ready for his fights, supplying him with verses for postcontest interviews ("I took by the throat the circumcised dog and smote him thus"). Since our financial position is frail, on occasion I will apply to the National Endowment for the Arts for a grant so that we can continue. It occurs to me that these kinds of efforts on behalf of a versifying wrestler are quite analogous to running a literary magazine, which is what I do when I am not making a fool of myself as a participatory journalist.

At a cocktail party not long ago, a gentleman came up and introduced himself. "Name's Paul Carroll." He had the look in his eye of someone who was going to ask, "Well, what are you up to next?" I was wrong. He informed me that he was a fellow participatory journalist. "I write about the computer industry for *The Wall Street Journal*," he said, "but I've also done two participatory pieces for them—one was racing across the Atlantic, never having been on a yacht before, and the other was wrestling. The yacht—"

My eyes widened. "You mean, you got in against the Hulk?" I interrupted. I felt a twinge of jealousy. Why couldn't computer specialists . . . well, stick to their knitting, as my mother used to say?

"No, no," Carroll said. "The Hulk weighs over three hundred pounds. I trained for two weeks and wrestled a guy named Tricky Nikki Kasternakis. He weighs one fifty, which is close to my weight. I wanted to call myself Hulk Hoboken, since I live across the Hudson from Wall Street, but everyone thought that was obscure, so I wrestled under the name the Wall Street Warrior. I wore ankle-length pin-striped tights and came into the ring wearing a sport coat."

I could not resist hearing more about Carroll's adventures. The next day I phoned and asked him to lunch. He sat across from me in the restaurant, dark haired, slightly balding, and looking . . . well, like a *Wall Street Journal* reporter. He said he'd written a proposal letter to his superiors, egged on by the managing editor's assistant, who, something of an adventurer himself, had been to mercenary school but felt that he was "too old and too bright" to try professional wrestling.

Carroll's proposal, slightly to his dismay, was accepted. He trained at a facility in Paulsboro, New Jersey, named, appropriately enough, the Monster Factory. A full course at the Monster Factory costs three thousand dollars, and a graduate is guaranteed to be able to toss and be tossed with reckless impunity and to be proficient with such maneuvers as the splash, the front face lock, the camel clutch, the Irish whip, and the Boston crab. Carroll signed up for a two-week "sampler course" in which he learned enough moves and countermoves to get through a four-minute "match."

"The first week I spent learning how to fall," Carroll told me. "It's done solo to begin with, and then you get tossed. I was tossed by two construction workers and a guy named Frankie Angel, a 240-pound weight lifter. It's painful. I thought two ribs had cracked, and I had all the symptoms of a severe case of whiplash. I considered giving it up."

"Going back to the computer industry."

"Right."

I asked him how the match with Tricky Nikki had come out.

"We wrestled near Glassboro, New Jersey, which is where Khrushchev and President Johnson had their famous meeting. Nikki and I were on a card with Larry (Pretty Boy) Sharpe, who runs the Monster Factory, and a wrestler named Boy Gone Bad. Nikki and I spent an evening talking our match over. He wears a gold earring. Very agile. He delivers mail during the day for Johnson & Johnson. We were supposed to wrestle for four minutes. But then the concession stands ran out, and the referee told us we had to fight for five minutes more while someone went out and brought in some more soda."

I asked how many people were in the audience.

"About eight hundred," Carroll said. "There were some chants of 'bullshit.' Also, 'Wall Street sucks.' "

"Did the *Journal* let you put that in?"

"It's not in the story," Carroll said wryly. "Actually, the match turned out much better than I thought it would. After Nikki pinned me with a move called a small package, I stood up. His back was to me. That's when professional wrestlers, inevitably, if they've lost, clobber the other guy. But I tapped Nikki on the shoulder, and when he turned around I shook hands with him. Unheard of. An old-timer there said it was the nicest gesture in pro wrestling he'd ever seen." He stirred his coffee.

"I envy you," I said. "Truly."

He smiled. "There were some things to remember," he said. "One is that you always hit left shoulder to left shoulder. You stick the other guy's head under your *left* armpit. Think *left!* That's so you don't get confused and bump heads."

"Very helpful," I said. I told him I was thinking of managing a wrestler. "I can shout that at him from time to time. 'Think *left.*' "

"Has he got a name?" Carroll asked.

"He's going to be the Grecian Urn."

Carroll grinned. "What sort of a guy is he?"

"He does a lot of shouting and quoting," I said. " 'O! What a rogue and peasant slave . . .'—that kind of thing."

Carroll nodded. "You know what wrestlers actually *do* say to each other? Very often it's the move they're about to execute, just to remind the other in case he's forgotten the sequence order you've decided on. 'Clothesline, body slam, pile driver.' "

"Not my guy," I said. "Not the Grecian Urn."

Since my lunch with Carroll, I have been doing some research on pro-wrestling managers that has been giving me pause. I am not sure that I can bring myself up to their level of extravagant behavior. I can see myself shouting verses to the Urn through a megaphone, but not bashing his opponents with it, which is what a manager named Jimmy Hart does with the huge megaphone *he* carries around. Almost all managers seem to have implements that double as weapons: Jim Cornette, who manages Midnight Express, has a covered tennis racket with which he whacks his wrestlers' opponents. It makes an enormous noise. Paul E. Dangerously, the manager of the Samoan Swat Team, has an arsenal of portable telephones that he uses as clubs. I have been trying to think what would be appropriate for the manager of the Grecian Urn. A lyre, perhaps. I doubt I would use it as a weapon. Pluck it from time to time, I suppose.

At a recent social function, someone I know came up and asked, "Well, what's next?"

I paused and said, "I'm thinking of managing a pro wrestler—the Grecian Urn."

He laughed and said, "Oh, I know that one. Old as the hills." He looked at me with the faintly supercilious look of someone who knows the other fellow isn't going to get the joke. "What's a Grecian urn?"

I thought for a while. "I give up."

"About three dollars a day."

It took me about half a minute to figure it out. He helped me. "What's a Grecian *e-a-r-n?*"

"Oh, yes," I said. "Very clever."

"You can work it into your routine."

"Absolutely," I said. "I don't see why not."

CODA

Jimmy Grucci's Funeral

I knew something was wrong as soon as I walked into the house. It was Saturday of the Thanksgiving weekend, 1983. I had driven out from New York. It was early in the afternoon, the sun bright but low over the Long Island potato fields. My son, Taylor, wanted to play football out on the lawn, but my wife took me aside. "There have been phone calls," she said. "Something terrible has happened down in Bellport. The Gruccis' plant has blown up." She could hardly tell me. "The radio reports say six people are dead. Jimmy Grucci is missing."

I tried phoning the Grucci number at the factory. A busy signal came on.

"I don't think there's anyone, or even any *thing,* at the other end," she said. "They say the place is flat."

Our home is an hour farther out on Long Island than Bellport. Eventually, I reached a member of the family and later that day I drove down to see what I could do. Over the car radio the reports kept coming in. Debris from the blast was reported to be drifting down in townships ten miles away. The shock had been felt for twenty miles. There had been panic along Maple Avenue, which runs parallel to the Grucci compound. The radio said babies had been tossed out of windows by people who thought their houses were collapsing around their ears. One report described an area near the Grucci compound where trees were festooned with hundreds of little American flags, presumably from crates of novelty shells that had gone off in the explosions.

Inevitably, the radio reports described the huge cloud that had boiled up from the compound. It crossed my mind that the cloud was actually composed of a multitude of aerial shells beautiful to see individually, and

357

graced with such flowery names: Red Silk, Flower-Scattering Maiden, Gardens on a Mountain, Silvery Fish, Monkey Child, Red Peony . . . the thin tracery of the gold of the split comets, the small balls of blue, orange ring shells—as if an agency were working busily but fruitlessly to suggest a sense of order in all that chaos.

Suddenly a voice came on the radio and verified two deaths. Jimmy Grucci and his cousin Donna Gruber, nineteen years old, had been killed. I remembered Donna from the shop—a pretty, dark-haired girl who was Jimmy's special assistant and worked with him on the big shells he loved to make. She had been on board the charter boat we had taken out to watch the Brooklyn Bridge Centennial fireworks show, which the Gruccis had fired just six months before. I had watched her sitting up on top of the pilothouse with two of her co-workers—three young girls in a row—and on occasion one of them would exclaim happily as the shells went up, "Look, there goes one of mine!"

The family had gathered at Felix Grucci senior's house on Station Road. I had to talk my way past a number of police barricades to get there. The houses along the street were dark. Cars were parked out in front of the Grucci house. It was small and unpretentious, with a glass-screened porch in front and a couple of steps that led up to it. The door squeaked when pulled open.

Inside, family members were sitting quietly, some standing for lack of chairs, many of them staring at the framed tinted photographs of the Grucci children and grandchildren hanging on the wall. The screen door squeaked and Felix Grucci, Sr., was led in. His hair, usually sleek, was disheveled and stood up like a cockatoo's. He had been in the compound, I was told, just walking away from feeding the guard dog, Big Boy, when the blasts had started going off. He had been pummeled around by the explosives wrecking his plant and was lucky indeed to be alive; they had given him a checkup at the hospital. He spotted me across the room as he was being led up the stairs. He asked weakly, "You hear about Jimmy?"

The conversations were low and desultory. Occasionally, someone would describe the instant of the explosion. One of the Gruccis said she had been making a tomato sauce for the lunchtime coming up, pouring the thick paste from one pan to another; the shock wave had simply taken it out of the window.

A Grucci cousin named Bill Klein told me he was one of the first on the scene. He had just finished raking leaves at Felix junior's—Butch's—house

358

and was coming down Beislin Road in his truck, less than a mile from the compound, when the ground began to shake under his tires. Immediately he knew it was the fireworks plant. He saw the cloud rise above the trees. "A lot of stuff was going off in the cloud—titanium salutes. I could recognize them. But it was nothing that made you think of fireworks—just a black, ugly cloud rising quickly."

When he drove down Maple Avenue, residents were running out of their front doors.

"Did you see any babies being thrown out of windows?" I asked. "That's what they were saying on the radio."

"I didn't see anything like that," Bill said. "Of course, I had my head down, trying to get to the compound as quickly as I could."

The first thing Bill Klein saw when he got there was Felix senior, standing in the center of the compound, stock-still in the debris of the first blasts, and behind him, dwarfing him, a great curtain of fire and black smoke.

"We knew we had to get him out. As you know, the compound is surrounded by a tall chain-link fence. The front gate, where I parked the truck, was fastened shut with a big loop of padlocked chain. So I had to scale the fence with a friend of mine, Kurt DeCarlo. Tore the hell out of my arm getting over the wire. It was a miracle Felix was alive. He was standing there dazed with big eight-inch mortars whizzing around like pieces of shrapnel. Jimmy and Donna had died not more than thirty yards from him."

The two reached him and were hurrying Felix toward the compound fence, the old man crying, "What happened? Ruined! Where's Jimmy?" when the loaded vans, in rows behind them, went up in a final titanic blast, hurling them to the ground. Crawling, feeling the great heat behind them, they supported Felix to the locked front gate, where a fireman, staring wide-eyed over their heads at the flaming compound, was clipping away at the chain with a pair of shears to get them out.

"Could you hear the blasts out where you live?" Bill asked me.

"I'm surprised we didn't," I replied.

I did not see much of Butch, Jimmy's brother, at that first gathering. He was busy on the phone in the kitchen, or coming out to talk to officials and police, who came up the steps and stood awkwardly in the small parlor.

I had a chance to see him a few days after the tragedy. He told me he still couldn't bring himself to believe what had happened. He admitted, about making fireworks, that an accident was always vaguely in the back of the mind. "You live with it every day," he told me, "sort of like knowing that nuclear weapons are pointed at you. Except with fireworks you're literally involved. Because in the sheds you *see* the canisters packed in neat rows on the shelves. You see the stars drying on the table. Then you hear a sharp noise, like a window shade rattling up, or the slam of a door, or a car backfiring, and you think it's starting—it is beginning."

"What is?"

"That the shop is beginning to go up. You even prepare yourself mentally, imagining what it's going to be like. But when it really happens, it's nothing like what you thought. I had an idea the sound would be deep and kind of awesome, like being inside a wave, but it was different. It was a ripping and tearing sound, high and piercing, almost a kind of shriek, and much more frightening than I ever thought it would be."

He told me that on that Saturday he was just about to leave home to pay a short visit to the "shop" to do some paperwork. Then he was going to a jeweler's. His wife had given him an identification bracelet on his birthday, the day before, and he wanted to have it fitted properly. The first detonation went off as he was standing in the kitchen saying good-bye to his wife. The floor began to rumble under his feet; the house shook. Butch knew immediately what had happened; so did his wife, who stared at him wild-eyed and then began to sob. Butch dialed 911 for emergency, and then ran out into the street in time to see the mushroomlike cloud rise above the trees.

One fact Butch seemed sure of—that neither Jimmy nor his cousin was responsible for what had happened. That morning at 9 A.M. Jimmy had gone with Donna to load and finish twenty big eight-inch color shells in the assembly shed. Just before 11 A.M. Donna had called her mother to say that the two were cleaning up what they were doing and that she would soon be on her way home for lunch. Both Jimmy and Donna were outside the assembly shed when the shock wave, followed by the fire ball, destroyed them. They could not have been *in* the assembly shed—which would have been the case if either of them had made a mistake—because nothing was left of the shed except the stone steps leading up to the door. The coroner's observations were that Jimmy had turned, startled, to face the explosion and that Donna was beyond him, running, when the holocaust caught her.

"What have you heard?" Butch asked me. "I mean, about the cause."

"Lots of rumors. Arson. Saturday, when it happened, is an arsonist's day. No one is supposed to be working. Then," I said, "I heard from a friend of mine in the Pyrotechnics Guild who thought it might have been spontaneous combustion from a shell that had got wet, left out in the rain, perhaps in Korea, and then got packed away in a crate and slowly, in there, became volatile."

All week that image had been in my mind—a firework behaving like the antagonistic symbiosity of a cancerous cell. It was awful to consider—a single shell, packed in amid its fellows, slowly, in the darkness of the warehouse, changing its internal composition until now, a deadly instrument, it awaited some delicate shift of atmospheric pressure, or a certain degree of humidity, to be triggered into that first puff of smoke.

"Well, that's the point," Butch said. "A chemist will tell you that it's a million-to-one shot. And the kind of humidity you'd need to cause that type of reaction would happen only on a hot, muggy August day, not a cool November morning."

Butch could not get the behavior of the guard dog, Big Boy, out of his mind. A "mutt police dog," as Butch referred to him, he lived in a large fenced-in pen in the center of the compound. On the morning of the twenty-sixth Big Boy had somehow clambered out of the pen, which had happened only once before in the ten years the Gruccis had owned him. Jimmy was scared of the dog, and when he arrived with his cousin at 9 A.M., he telephoned his father, who was the only one in the family able to get close without the dog baring his teeth.

His father arrived and, soothing Big Boy, was able to get him back into the pen. After he had done some work in the office shed and had gone down to check on Big Boy, or perhaps to feed him, abruptly his little empire went up around him.

I asked how the town was reacting. Butch said that some townspeople, especially those who had lived in Bellport for a generation or so, had said, despite everything, how proud they had always been to have the Gruccis' fireworks factory in their midst. After all, Grucci was such a familiar name in the community—the barbershop was run by a cousin, James Grucci; the radio and television store by an uncle, Pete; the liquor store had been Grucci owned. On the Fourth of July all these Gruccis closed up shop to fire displays. No one in the Gruccis, Butch told me, had ever bolted, whatever their actual feelings, from the family responsibility, which was to fireworks. He was sure it would stay that way.

Others in the town, of course, were bitter. They made crude signs and came and picketed the ruined plant. There was one woman—the report was that she had lost a glass cabinet full of figurines—who shouted through the fence at Felix Grucci, Sr., looking halfheartedly in the rubble for his dog, who had been missing since the explosion: "Y'bum, how can you go and sleep at night?"

"Frightful."

"It's going to be hard to find a place to start up again," Butch said. "And we're going to miss Jimmy so much. You know, he loved making real big shells, an eighteen-inch shell with ten or fifteen salutes in it, but after it was done he'd become a little afraid. It's odd. He'd break out into little sores around the mouth. Do you remember the Fat Man on the Indian River? Jimmy had some big fever blisters *that* time. It's inherited. Our mother often breaks out before a big show."

"I didn't know that."

Butch thought for a moment. He said, "The thing you love kills you, doesn't it? Isn't that how the saying goes?"

I remembered and said that the famous phrase—it was Oscar Wilde's—was that "each man kills the thing he loves."

"He got it wrong," Butch said.

"It would seem so. It's the other way around, isn't it?"

I had not seen the compound until my wife and I drove to Bellport for the funeral services on November 30. We drove over and stared through the chain-link fence. The landscape had simply been tortured by the blasts into a rubble that appeared to belong to photographs one remembered of the trench warfare of World War I. Indeed, at first I saw nothing in the debris that gave evidence of human involvement. Finally I could make out the chassis of a blackened storage trailer, the steps that led up to a building no longer in existence, the yellowish hulks of the burned-out Grucci family cars in the center of the compound, iron mortars lying askew, and at my feet I could distinguish parts of aerial fireworks—the round disks used to make shell bases, the burned-out husks of paper fuses. There was a brisk wind blowing, so there was just the faintest whiff of burnt powder.

About a third of the town—Bellport's population is just above three thousand—seemed to be at the service. Many fireworks people came from around the country—the Semenzas from Ideal Fireworks in Pennsylvania, Fred Iannini, an old-timer just a year or two junior to Felix senior, the Girones from New Jersey, the Rozzi family from Tri-State in Loveland, Ohio, and one remembered that Joe Rozzi, the father, had lost *his* brother in an explosion. They all wore black suits that seemed a bit too snug around the shoulders as they settled themselves heavily into the camp chairs set up in rows.

The casket stood in front of the congregation and had been borne in by seven Grucci employees wearing dark blue T-shirts emblazoned with a spray of fireworks and the legend FIREWORKS BY GRUCCI. It was what they wore when they fired displays. The family sat in the first two rows, swaying toward each other in grief. Butch Grucci had asked me to deliver a tribute to Jimmy. I worked on one for a couple of days. I could not imagine that Jimmy would have wanted its tone to be solemn. Among other things, I said:

"Jimmy Grucci was an honored member of a remarkable profession—craftsmen whose artistic function is momentarily to change the face of the heavens themselves, to make the night sky more beautiful than it is, and in the process give delight and wonder to countless hundreds of thousands. It surely can be said that Jimmy Grucci designed, and prepared, and fired fireworks shows that were witnessed by more people in his lifetime than any contemporary artist I can think of—including the great concert virtuosi, even the most fashionable of the pop stars. Over a million people watch the annual Venetian Night show along the Chicago waterfront; over two million watched the Brooklyn Bridge Centennial this past May; Fireworks Night at Shea Stadium has invariably filled every seat. Countless millions watched this last Inauguration's fireworks on television. And Jimmy Grucci, of course, has been an integral part in making Fireworks by Grucci responsible for these beautiful and mammoth displays. One of them, designed by him, won his family the championship of the world in Monte Carlo.

"But I don't think these honors and renown—the fact that Grucci has become a household word—mattered to him as much as the simple and wonderful art of fireworks themselves. Of his family, Jimmy was the one involved to the point truly of passion. He worked in the fireworks assembly area for as many as ten hours a day, six days a week. He loved making shells. He turned and admired a fireworks shell in his hand as a collector might relish a statue of jade. His favorite was the split comet—perhaps the most famous American shell ever made: in the sky tendrils of gold split at their ends, and then once again, until the entire night sky seems like latticework. He also liked noise, of course. Big reports. He would be letting the tradition down, certainly the Italian tradition, if there weren't a loud report or two, preferably nine or ten, to accompany things. He understood that curious aesthetic balance that comes with the combination of beauty and harsh concussion.

"In the evening, after work, after all those hours of making fireworks, Jimmy would reach home and immediately telephone his brother just down the street to talk—fireworks. His recreation after dinner was to relax and sit and watch tapes of his favorite Grucci fireworks shows on the great curved extra-sized television screen at the foot of his bed. What woke him in the morning—and I might add everyone else in the Grucci household—was an alarm-clock system rigged to that same TV screen. At the wakeup hour it burst on and showed the climactic moment of the Tchaikovsky *1812* Overture as played outdoors by Arthur Fiedler and the Boston Pops—the fireworks booming and echoing over the Esplanade. There was no yawning and stretching in the Grucci household, his brother, Felix, once told me, no wiping the sleep from one's eyes. At the first sound of that alarm system, everyone was up!

"What joy fireworks gave him, and what joy he gave us with them! Perhaps Jimmy's most remarkable characteristic, I think, was not only his enthusiastic nature but his attitude about fireworks and the public—his abhorrence of even the thought of not giving the public its money's worth. In a profession where it is easy to shortchange the populace, how often I have seen him put an extra four or five shells in a show to give an audience just a bit more than what was necessary. It was as if he were saying, "Perhaps these extra shells will ignite something in you that will make you understand what the sheer wonder of it is—to take an inanimate object, a canister, a thing of chemicals and minerals, and, like a magician, an alchemist at his astonishing best, illuminate the skies with its performance.'

"There is a famous early nineteenth-century essay by William Hazlitt about the death of a great athlete of his time, John Cavanagh, in which Hazlitt says that when a person dies who does any one thing better than anyone else in the world, it leaves a gap in society. But fireworks is an ongoing and perpetuating art that will continue to have its great craftsmen. Jimmy is one of a great tradition. He is one with Claude Ruggieri, Martin Beckman, Peter the Great, Vigarini, Brock—artists all. His family will continue in that tradition. They will not allow a gap to be left in our society.

"Artists are perhaps fortunate in that they leave evidence after they have gone—books, concertos, paintings, ballets—and who here in this church will not remember Jimmy Grucci and what he brought to this art when they see an especially lovely shell blossom in the night sky?

"In the ancient Greek scheme of things, mortals were penalized by the gods when they went beyond the bounds and became godlike themselves.

In those times, the people would have said about the terrible tragedy of last week that the gods were taking exception, vengeance, because Jimmy Grucci was doing better with the heavens than they could ever dream of."

Memorial Service
for My Father

First of all, may I say on behalf of Mother, and the family, how honored we are, and what honor you pay the memory of Father, by your presence, and in such numbers. I am here to speak on behalf of the family.

There are those who must wonder—considering how much time Father gave to the public family of man—how he could ever have managed a private family of his own. But he did, as you know. He was never able to turn any of his four children to an abiding interest in the law—perhaps, I have always thought, because he tended to give his lecture on the beauty of the mortgage indenture, and indeed its position as the very cornerstone of the legal culture, at breakfast.

So he gave up on that. But in everything else he encouraged us. He cajoled us to be better, to be disciplined. He taught us the Continental backhand, perhaps the last youths in the East to learn such a thing. He wrote us wonderful letters when we went away to school—about the machinery of the mind, and what delight there was in the results of its functioning at its best.

And best of all, he made us see the pleasure of the challenge.

He loved challenges of all kinds—especially those which engaged the mind. You have heard many instances in the tributes which have preceded. I remember when he received the Légion d'honneur—a tribute he was tremendously proud of and wore the red ribbon on his seersucker coat, as many of you know, at summer lunches at West Hills. He chose to give his acceptance speech at the French consulate in French, in which he was a little bit rusty. What made it a particular challenge was that in his speech he told a funny story. That is truly a challenge—to tell a funny story in rusty French

366

to a room full of French dignitaries. I will tell you the story but not in French. I did not learn that much courage from my father. It was a story about the difficulty of communication—a United Nations kind of story. Father described how he had gone to a movie theater off the Champs-Elysées where an American Western was being shown in English with the subtitles in French. At one point a gunslinger, a very rough sort, had shot up a bar, his guns blazing, and afterward had swaggered up to the bar where he said, "Gimme a shot of red-eye!" The subtitle to translate this read as follows: *"Donnez-moi un Dubonnet, s'il vous plaît."*

Coupled with this love of challenge was a tremendous sense of tradition, that there were certain verities worth cultivating and preserving. In his seventies, I suggested that he shift tennis racquets—giving up his small-headed model which he had used for decades, always returning it properly to its wooden press, for one of the big Prince racquets that were coming into vogue then. In fact, I gave him one for Christmas. He was very polite about receiving it, but he never used it. Possibly he thought that it would give him an unfair advantage, but I think more probably it meant giving up an old and faithful ally that along with Mother's forehand had carried him to a steady succession of championships at the Cold Spring Harbor Beach Club. So he kept to his old racquet, which was called a Power Bat. Rarely has the English language, he once told me, with the possible exception of that of the mortgage indenture, been used so succinctly to describe what he wished of it. I remember telling him once that Althea Gibson used a Power Bat. He nodded and said, "A woman of exceptional judgment."

I remember father once saying to me that life was especially worth living for the surprises that come along from time to time. I know of my own generation, and those succeeding, that in their letters of condolence so many have mentioned meeting Father for the first time—and of the pleasure and surprise of running into such an inquiring, attentive, humorous, and courtly mind, and coming away with the warm and abiding pleasure of being so much the better for the experience of having met him. And the breadth of his capacities! So many of the wives, not only of his own generation, have so often remarked on what a dancer my father was—now *there* was an experience!

My son Taylor, who was six at the time, brought a large handkerchief to Walpole, tucked enormously in the breast pocket of his school blazer, to the funeral services there because he thought it was appropriate to weep on such occasions. But here, today, of course, we find ourselves at a kind of celebration—to sit here in the pews of this church and to recall how fortunate all of us here have been—family, friends, dancing partners, statesmen, civic leaders, clubmates, politicians, educators, students, lawyers, justices, citizens—to have been touched by the presence of this remarkable person, husband and parent.

One is reminded of what Callimachus said of the death of Heraclitus: "Oh, Heraclitus, they tell me you are dead, but I know you are not gone. Thy nightingales live on. I hear them sing. . . ."